Introduction to AmiBroker

Introduction to AmiBroker

Advanced Technical Analysis Software for Charting and Trading System Development

Howard B. Bandy

Blue Owl Press

ISBN-10: 0979183812
ISBN-13: 9780979183812
LCCN: 2008905105

Published by
Blue Owl Press
3700 S. Westport Avenue, #1876
Sioux Falls, SD 57106

Published 2008
Printed in the United States
12 11 10 09 08 10 9 8 7 6 5 4 3 2 1

Disclaimer

This book is an educational document. Nothing in this book is intended as, nor should it be construed to be, investment advice.

The views expressed herein are the personal views of Dr. Howard B. Bandy. Neither the author nor the publisher, Blue Owl Press, have any commercial interest in any of the products mentioned. All of the products described were purchased by the author at regular retail prices.

Investing and trading is risky and can result in loss of principal. Neither this book in its entirety, nor any portion thereof, nor any follow-on discussion or correspondence related to this book, is intended to be a recommendation to invest or trade mutual funds, stocks, commodities, options, or any other financial instrument. Neither the author nor the publisher will accept any responsibility for losses which might result from applications of the ideas expressed in the book or from techniques or trading systems described in the book.

The programs used as examples have been tested and are believed to be correct. Even so, this book may contain typographical errors and other inaccuracies. Past performance, whether hypothetical, simulated, back-tested, or actual, is no guarantee of future results. Results will depend on the specific data series used. Please verify the accuracy and correctness of all programs before using them to trade.

Acknowledgements

Tomasz Janeczko, author of AmiBroker. Thank you for creating an outstanding program, and for graciously allowing use of materials published in the AmiBroker user documentation.

Bruce Robinson and William Barack. Thank you for the many stimulating discussions, encouraging comments, and conference presentations, all of which helped motivate and shape this book.

Robert Grigg. Thank you for the many stimulating discussions and exchange of ideas, and for raising awareness of AmiBroker in Australia. Particular thanks for permission to use the schematic of AmiBroker that you developed.

Contents

Preface and Introduction

This book is intended to be a tutorial. Topics included and detail covered involved compromises between elementary and advanced, narrow and broad, superficial and in-depth. Those chosen are practical examples of tasks that you will be performing regularly. For additional tutorials, watch the on-line tutorial videos, available at *http://www.amibroker.com/tutorials*. For a more complete reference, see the AmiBroker User's Guide and the AmiBroker Reference, both available at *http://www.amibroker.com.*

This book is task oriented, rather than software oriented. Many operations can be performed in more than one way. When making a choice, clarity was chosen over efficiency. This book is not intended to be read cover-to-cover, as a novel would be read. It is intended to be a series of tutorials and reminders covering operation of AmiBroker.

The examples use a lot of screen capture images, annotated with numbered steps, highlights, and arrows. The book includes reference to all the functions, indicators, and tools documented in the User's Guide and in the Help system.

Intended Audience

People wanting:

- Description of AmiBroker.
- Description of the capabilities of AmiBroker.
- Tutorial on installing and setting up AmiBroker.
- Tutorial on setting up databases with free data.

- Tutorial on setting up subscription end-of-day databases.
- Tutorial on setting up real-time data feeds.
- Tutorial on the basic charting.
- Tutorial and reference on the Graphical User Interface - GUI.
- Tutorial on applying formulas and indicators to charts.
- Tutorial on the AmiBroker Formula Language - AFL.
- Introduction to technical analysis.
- Introduction to design of trading systems.
- Tutorial on backtesting trading systems.
- Tutorial on optimizing trading systems.
- Tutorial on validating trading systems.
- Examples of trading systems.
- Printed reference for AmiBroker structure, menus, tools.

Assumptions

While this book is intended to be a tutorial on AmiBroker, the reader is expected to be reasonably familiar with:

- Computer operations.
- Basic techniques used with the Windows operating system, such as the menu system, drag-and-drop, navigating through the file system.
- A basic text editor, such as Windows Notepad.
- A spreadsheet, such as Excel.
- Basic trading methods and terminology.

What you will find in this book

Section I – Getting Started. An overview of AmiBroker - its features and capabilities. Tutorials describing the installation of AmiBroker, setting up databases using free end-of-day and intraday data, setting up databases using subscription end-of-day data (for US and Australian markets), and setting up databases using subscription real-time data.

There are ten examples of useful things you can do with AmiBroker in just a few minutes, even if you are using the trial version. These range from manipulating the charts to applying on-screen indicators to testing and optimizing trading systems. Everything is laid out, click-by-click, with screen captures to illustrate each step.

Section II – Charting. Each of the menus and toolbars that work with charting is expanded and explained.

Topics include:

- Displaying charts.
- Adding visual studies, such as trendlines, to a chart.
- Adding formulas and technical indicators to a chart.
- Using parameters with indicators.

Section III — Analysis. The Analysis section begins with a short introduction to technical analysis and trading system development.

That is followed by an introduction to AFL - AmiBroker Formula Language, including its structure and syntax. AFL is used to write code to create your own custom charts and trading systems. This section is part tutorial, part programming manual, part reference manual.

The use of the Automatic Analysis tools, including backtest, optimization, and walk forward validation, are explained.

Several ready-to-use programs you can use as starting points for your own system development are included.

The Appendixes. Provide reference material.

Index. Menus, commands, tools, and techniques are extensively indexed.

What you will not find in the this book

AmiBroker has so much to offer that this book could easily have been expanded by several hundred pages. Readers looking for coverage of topics such as the Custom Backtester, Dynamic Data Exchange, low-level graphics, scripting, and the Automated Trading Interface will have to wait for another book. Readers looking for coverage of topics such as different types of trading systems, trading system testing, trading system validation, and the creation of C++ routines and Dynamic Link Libraries are referred to the author's companion book, *Quantitative Trading Systems* (see Appendix C, Resources).

Some conventions

AmiBroker can be used with any tradable, including stocks, mutual funds, closed end funds, exchange traded funds, commodities, futures, and Forex. For ease of writing and reading, the terms stock, symbol, issue, or ticker are often used to mean any tradable issue. When it is important to distinguish between different tradables, specific details are given.

AmiBroker is distributed and used world-wide. With the exception of setting up the database to reflect the local tradables and exchanges, most of the operations of AmiBroker are independent of location. The author resides in the United States and most of his experience is with trading in the US, which may shape some of the perspective of this book. Apologies in advance for any inadvertent mistakes or misleading statements due to his limited background – no discrimination of any kind is intended.

Versions used

AmiBroker 5.10.0 and later.

AmiQuote 2.00.

AmiBroker is regularly expanded and improved. During the life of this edition of this book, the features, capabilities, screens, and commands, will undoubtedly change somewhat. Every attempt was made to write in such a way that the book will be useful for a long time and will not soon become obsolete as new versions of the program are released. But there will be changes in the program that are not reflected in the book. For the latest and official documentation, please refer to the latest editions of the AmiBroker User's Guide, the on-line help files, and the tutorials, all of which can be found on the AmiBroker web site: *http://www.amibroker.com.*

The Author

Dr. Howard Bandy:

- Has university degrees in mathematics, physics, engineering, and computer science.
- Has specialized in artificial intelligence, applied mathematics, modeling and simulation.
- Was professor of computer science and mathematics, and a university dean.
- Designed and programmed a well-known program for stock selection and timing.
- Was a senior research analyst for a CTA trading firm.

Section I

Getting Started

http://www.amibroker.com

Chapter 1

Overview of AmiBroker

AmiBroker is a powerful, comprehensive trading system development platform. It has cutting edge charting and graphics, and fast, flexible and powerful portfolio-level backtesting, optimization, and automated walk forward validation. Its purpose is to help investors and traders identify profitable opportunities to buy and sell. It includes an extensive library of technical indicators that can be plotted along with the price chart as well as tested for profitability in a trading system. It has all the tools needed to chart, test, and trade stocks, mutual funds, commodities, and Forex.

AmiBroker has two primary modes of operation – charting and formula evaluation. The data it works with are the price and volume records of buy and sell transactions for stocks, mutual funds, and other tradable issues.

In its charting mode, historical price and volume data are displayed on the computer monitor along with technical indicators. The analyst looks for promising patterns and conditions.

In its formula evaluation mode, patterns, conditions, and rules are described using a programming language and written into a computer program. The program analyzes the price and volume data and reports on the profitability of the rules. When profitable trading systems have been found, it scans the group of stocks that are of interest to the trader and lists the current buy and sell signals. If desired, AmiBroker can send orders based on these signals directly to a broker for execution.

AmiBroker is unique among trading system development platforms in that the same code displays the indicators, tests the profitability, issues the buy and sell signals and sends the orders. It is an easy transition from chart to analysis to execution.

AmiBroker runs under Windows, including versions 95, 98, Millennium, 2000, NT, XP, and Vista. Both 32 bit and 64 bit operating systems are supported.

Any system that runs Windows efficiently will run AmiBroker efficiently.

Professional and Standard Editions

- Both support intraday as well as end-of-day data
- Standard meets most needs
- Professional is required for
    - Tick charts
    - MAE / MFE charts
    - 64 bit
    - Unlimited real-time quotes

Data Feeds

- Accepts data from any exchange in the world
- Close integration with major subscription data vendors
    - Quotes Plus
    - TC 2000
    - FastTrack
    - eSignal
    - myTrack
    - IQFeed
    - Interactive Brokers
    - Any DDE-enabled data feed

- AmiQuote downloader provides access to free end-of-day quotes from major world exchanges
- Built-in importer for MetaStock format data
- ASCII import wizard reads any data format

Databases

- End-of-day data
- Intraday data
- Any number of databases
- Any number of symbols
- Add or remove issues
- Split and distribution adjustment
- Unlimited history of price quotes
- Quotation editor
- Company information
- Fundamental information

Performance

- Fast execution of AFL code
- Fast chart drawing
- Robust and stable

Charting

- Multiple chart panes
- Multiple time frames
- Live updating
- Intraday, daily, weekly, monthly
- Line, bar, candlestick
- Fast zooming and scrolling
- Custom or automatic scaling
- Built-in indicators
    - Simple moving average
    - Exponential moving average
    - Adaptive moving average
    - Rate of change (ROC)
    - Wilder's Relative Strength Indicator (RSI)

    - Moving Average Convergence-Divergence Oscillator (MACD)
    - On Balance Volume (OBV)
    - Commodity Channel Index (CCI)
    - Money Flow Index (MFI)
    - Bollinger Bands
    - Stochastics
    - Parabolic Stop and Reverse (SAR)
    - Relative strength
- Overlay indicators over price charts
- Overlay indicators over other indicators
- Configurable indicators
- Drag and drop tools
- Chart study tools
    - Trend lines
    - Regression channels
    - Text on chart
    - Fibonacci retracements
    - Gann squares
- Chart studies are saved with the chart
- Charts independently scalable

AFL (AmiBroker Formula Language)

- Designed for charting and trading
- Over 200 built-in building-block functions
    - Pattern-detection
    - Averages
    - Statistical
    - Pre-defined indicators
    - Data manipulation
    - Trade management
- Extensive library of pre-written code
- Create your own indicators, trading systems, and commentaries
- Single code base for indicators, systems, commentaries
- User-defined functions
- Unlimited variables

- Unlimited nesting of function calls
- Local and global variables
- Multiple time frames
- Indicator builder
  - Create and plot indicators
  - Control axes, scales, color, line style
- Show Buy and Sell signals on charts
- Code stored in clear-text
- Built-in formula editor
- Any editor can be used
- Debugging, tracing, and profiling tools
- Extendable through Dynamic Link Libraries (DLL)

Alerts

- Formula-based alerts
- Display to screen
- Play sound
- Send e-mail
- Send order to automated trade execution

Scanning

- Review your database for your buy and sell signals
- Time window can be specified

Exploring

- Search your database for conditions you specify
- Report results
- Multiple-key sorting

Backtesting

- Test profitability of trading system
- Single issue or group of issues you define
- Long, short, or both
- Buy and sell arrows on charts
- Built-in trailing exits and stops
- Realistic slippage and commission

- Portfolio level fully supported
- Position sizing
- Optimization
    - Full search of parameter space
    - Non-exhaustive search
        Particle Swarm Optimization (PSO)
        Covariance Matrix Adaptation Evolutionary Strategy (CMAE)
    - Single issue or portfolio
- 3-D presentation of results
- Multiple time frame
- Equity curve creation
- Equity curve input to trading system
- Walk forward testing
- Over 20 built-in metrics
- User-definable metrics
- Fast execution
- Detailed reporting
- Report explorer
- Export results for further analysis

Automated Trading

- Interfaces to on-line brokers

Scripting

- Jscript (JavaScript)
- VBScript (Visual Basic Scripting)
- Scripts embeddable in AFL programs
- OLE (Object Linking and Embedding) Automation
- Call COM (Component Object Model) objects from AFL
- Create and automate database management tools

Configurability

- Almost everything is configurable and customizable
- Charts can be arranged as you wish them to be
- Not tied to a specific exchange or data provider
- Indicators are parameter driven

Account Manager

- Track your investments
- Calculate commissions, dividends, deposits, withdrawals

Internet Integration

- Built-in web browser for company research
- Configurable settings

Performance

- Very fast redrawing of charts
- Fast execution of AFL code

Pricing (as of August 2008)

- Fully functional, no cost 30 day trial
- New one-time license:
  - Standard Edition: $199
  - Professional Edition: $279
- Free upgrades for one year from purchase
- Renewal license (to continue upgrades): half price

Ordering

- Visit *http://www.amibroker.com/order.html*. This secure site accepts your payment using any major credit card, check, or bank transfer.

Delivery

- After paying the registration fee, you will receive a personalized keyfile by e-mail. Installing the keyfile converts your trialware version to a registered version. No other downloads are required. No other delivery method is supported.

Support

- Unlimited support for installation issues via e-mail
- Unlimited support for basic usage issues via e-mail
- Interactive help anywhere in AmiBroker (F1 key)
- AmiBroker website support page *http://www.amibroker.com/support.html*

- On-line video tutorials (the URL is for one example - there are many)
http://www.amibroker.com/video/uicustomize.html
- On-line Users Guide
http://www.amibroker.com/guide/
- Knowledge base – provided by AmiBroker
http://www.amibroker.com/kb/
- Users Knowledge Base – provided by user community
http://www.amibroker.org/userkb/
- Yahoo discussion forum – over 7700 members – over 1000 messages a month
http://finance.groups.yahoo.com/group/amibroker/

Chapter 2

Installation

AmiBroker runs under Windows, including versions 95, 98, Millennium, 2000, NT, XP, and Vista. Both 32 bit and 64 bit operating systems are supported.

All versions of AmiBroker – trial and registered, standard and professional, end-of-day and real-time – begin with a visit to the AmiBroker web site and downloading the installation file. Using your Internet browser, visit *http://www.amibroker.com*, then select the download tab. Select either the file for a New and complete installation or an Upgrade installation. If this is your first installation of AmiBroker, choose the New installation. Download the file to your computer – the New installation is about 7 MB. When the download is complete, double-click the installation file (AmiBroker510.exe, or the latest version) to run the AmiBroker Setup Wizard. Follow the directions and answer the prompts.

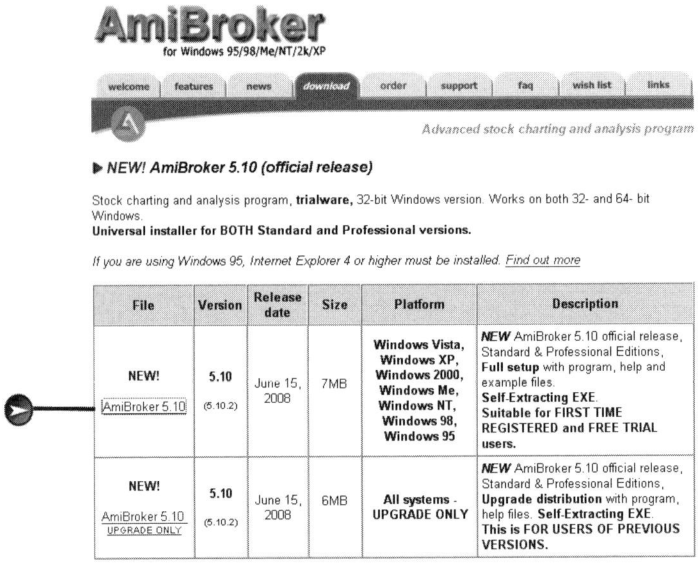

AmiBroker
for Windows 95/98/Me/NT/2k/XP

welcome | features | news | download | order | support | faq | wish list | links

Advanced stock charting and analysis program

▶ *NEW! AmiBroker 5.10 (official release)*

Stock charting and analysis program, **trialware,** 32-bit Windows version. Works on both 32- and 64- bit Windows.
Universal installer for BOTH Standard and Professional versions.

If you are using Windows 95, Internet Explorer 4 or higher must be installed. Find out more

File	Version	Release date	Size	Platform	Description
NEW! AmiBroker 5.10	5.10 (5.10.2)	June 15, 2008	7MB	Windows Vista, Windows XP, Windows 2000, Windows Me, Windows NT, Windows 98, Windows 95	***NEW*** AmiBroker 5.10 official release, Standard & Professional Editions, **Full setup** with program, help and example files. **Self-Extracting EXE. Suitable for FIRST TIME REGISTERED and FREE TRIAL users.**
NEW! AmiBroker 5.10 UPGRADE ONLY	5.10 (5.10.2)	June 15, 2008	6MB	All systems - UPGRADE ONLY	***NEW*** AmiBroker 5.10 official release, Standard & Professional Editions, **Upgrade distribution** with program, help files. **Self-Extracting EXE. This is FOR USERS OF PREVIOUS VERSIONS.**

Both AmiBroker and this author recommend accepting the default options and file locations during installation.

When the installation is complete, launch AmiBroker. The installation will have created an AmiBroker icon on your desktop. Just double-click that. When AmiBroker starts, it displays a message that it is Standard Edition and Unregistered. This is the trial version, but will be instantly converted to Registered (and Professional Edition, if you requested that) when your AmiBroker Registration file is processed.

In the mean time, AmiBroker is ready for your use in Trial mode.

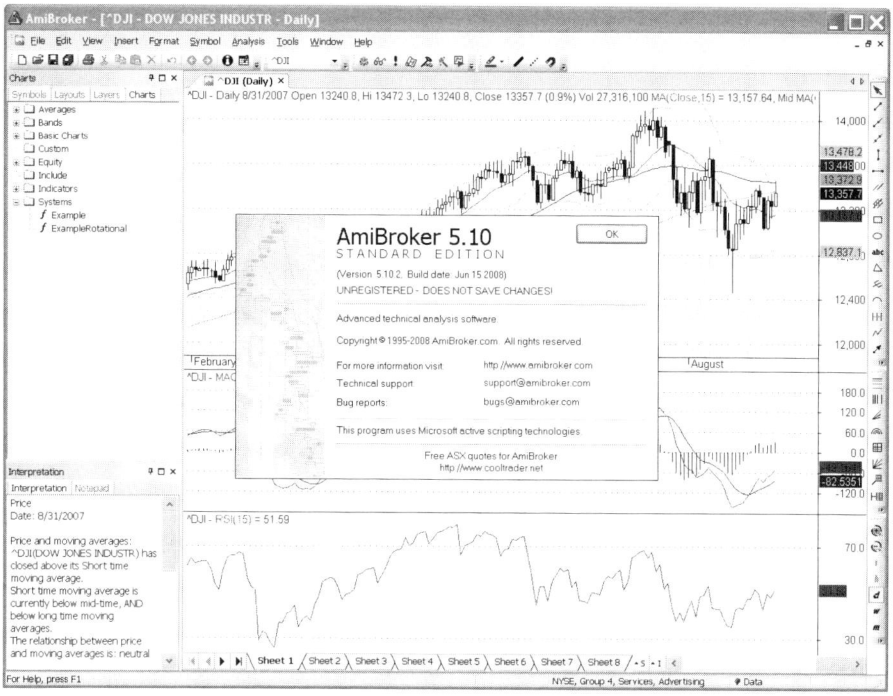

AmiBroker in Trial Mode

AmiBroker in trial mode is fully functional with a few exceptions.

- The trial version will run only 30 days. To run longer than that, it must be registered.
- When processing multiple symbols, the maximum in the trial version is five; the registered version handles an unlimited number.
- Changes, particularly to the database, will not be saved. Also, if you modify one of the chart panes, the changes you made will not be saved when AmiBroker closes.

Default Database

When you install AmiBroker, a small database is also installed. Its name is DATA and it contains end-of-day price history for the stocks in the Dow Jones Industrial Average and for the average itself. The date range is short and the quotes are not up-to-date. But it is useful for verifying that the installation was successful and for investigating AmiBroker.

You can use AmiBroker and the default database while in trial mode.

Chapter 3 - 30 Minutes to Useful Results, has some suggestions.

You will probably want a longer history and more issues. You can have as many databases as you wish. DATA is one. You can expand it or add other databases.

Block Diagram of Database

As the block diagram shows, AmiBroker has two levels of database files. The *native database* is maintained by AmiBroker and AmiQuote, and can be modified by you using the Quote Editor within AmiBroker. The DATA database is an AmiBroker native database.

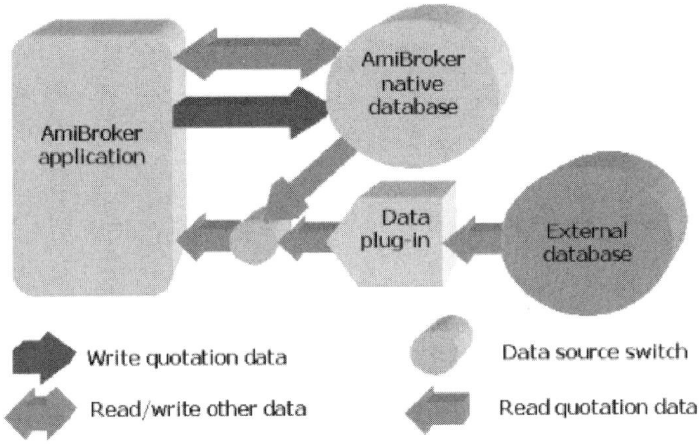

When you subscribe to a data provider, that provider will set up an *external database* that they exclusively maintain. As AmiBroker needs quotes to place on a chart or process in a backtest, the Data Plug-in reads the external database and passes the data to AmiBroker.

Database Setup - End-of-Day

Setting up a database is a two step operation. Step one is establishing the database within AmiBroker and specifying which tickers will be stored in it. Step two is filling the database with historical price quotations. Depending on the processes being used, you may be aware of the two separate steps, or they may be combined and appear to you as a single step.

If you will be subscribing to a data service, such as Quotes Plus, the installation procedure for that service will set up a database specifically for quotes from that service and will be maintained by that service. We will discuss setting up a Quotes Plus database in a few pages.

If you want to use one of the free data providers, such as Yahoo, you can either expand DATA or create a new database. The following pages describe how to do that.

Free Database Using AmiQuote

AmiQuote is a companion program to AmiBroker that manages downloading of price quotes, from either Yahoo or msn, and storing those quotes in the AmiBroker database.

Return to *http://www.amibroker.com* and download the setup file for AmiQuote. The current version is 2.00. Double-click aq2000.exe and follow the installation instructions, accepting the defaults.

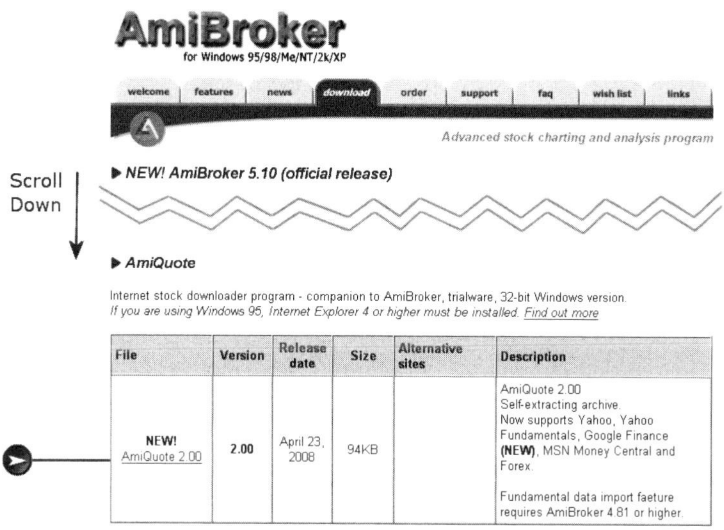

If the only information about the stocks that you want is their ticker symbol, then continue with the method described in the next few paragraphs. If you want to have the ticker and full name, and perhaps the industry sector identification, read the next section, Ticker Only; then read the section, Ticker and Full Name, that follows. It is a good idea to decide this before the database is filled with historical quotes.

Ticker Only

Begin by deciding which issues you want in your database. Find or create a list of their tickers. This does not need to be the final list – you will be able to add additional tickers and historical data at any time in the future. For example, you might want all the stocks in the Russell 1000 index – the 1000 largest capitalization stocks listed on US exchanges. (According to the Russell Investments website, *http://www.russell.com,* the Russell 1000 represents approximately 92% of the US equities market. That website also has a list of the current components of all the Russell indices.) Visit *http://www.IntroductionToAmibroker.com/resources* for links to up-to-date lists of members of various categories.

If you want to keep a copy of the original DATA database as it was distributed, here is how to make a copy of it.

1. Using **Windows Explorer**, navigate to the AmiBroker directory. If you accepted all the defaults during installation, it is C:\Program Files\AmiBroker.
2. With **Explorer**, using the **File** menu, click **New**, then **Folder**. A folder named New Folder will be created.
3. Using **Explorer**, rename that to the name you want for the original database, for example **DataAsDistributed**.
4. Using **AmiBroker** and its **File** menu, click **SaveDataBaseAs**, select the folder you just created, **DataAsDistributed**, click **OK**. AmiBroker will make a copy of the DATA database in the folder DataAsDistributed.

Continuing on to update the database named DATA with the tickers in the Russell 1000.

1. Using a simple text editor, such as NotePad, or a spreadsheet, create a file with one ticker per line. The tickers should be in all capital letters. Each ticker must be spelled the same as your data provider spells it. Save that file in the AmiQuote directory with a meaningful file name, such as RUSSELL1000.tls. If you accepted all the defaults during installation, that directory is C:\Program Files\AmiBroker\AmiQuote. Tls files are ordinary text files that are recognized by AmiBroker and AmiQuote as containing lists of ticker symbols.
2. Open AmiBroker.
3. Using the AmiBroker **File** menu, click **Open Database**, select the DATA database, click **OK**.

4. Leave AmiBroker open as the next steps are performed.
5. Decide the date you want the historical data to begin. If you plan to do extensive trading system development, I suggest having at least ten years of data available. The characteristics of the markets changed after the October 1987 crash, so data before that date has limited value in developing systems for current conditions. A starting date (From Date) of 1/1/1995 might be reasonable. Use today's date for the end date (the To Date).
6. Using the **Windows Start** menu, select the **AmiQuote** program and run it. You will find it under All Programs > AmiBroker > AmiQuote > AmiQuote.
7. Using **AmiQuote's File** menu, select **Open**. Then select the file with the tickers you want to get historical data for, RUSSELL1000.tls, and click **Open**.

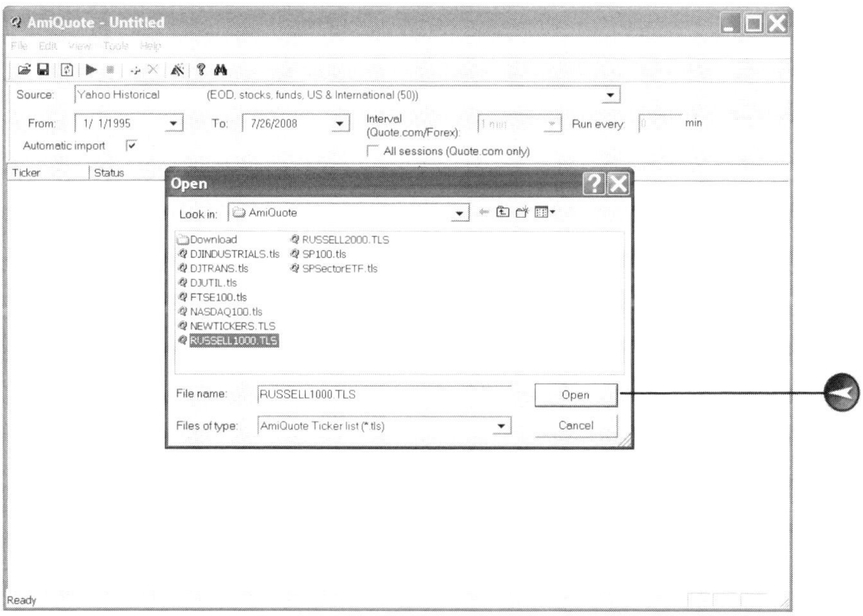

Be sure that AmiBroker is running and that the database you want updated is the current database. The name of the database in current use is displayed in the status bar in the bottom right-hand corner of the AmiBroker window. If necessary, use the AmiBroker File menu and open the desired database.

8. Be sure that AmiQuote's Automatic Import box is Checked.
9. Click the **Green Triangle** to begin the download.

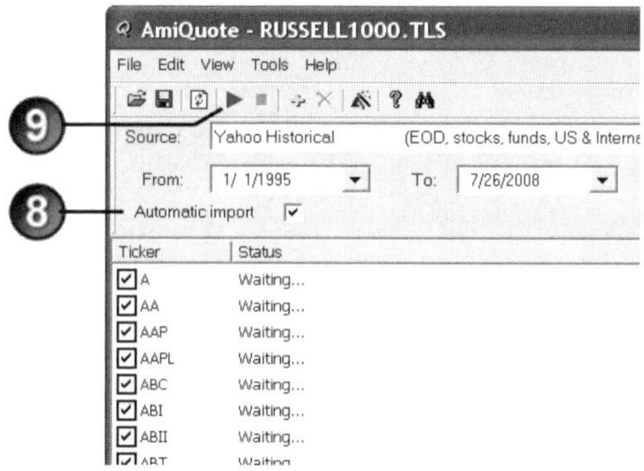

You have asked for over 10,000 years of data, each with 252 sets of Open, High, Low, Close, and Volume. Depending on the speed of your Internet connection, it will take a few minutes to a few hours for the download to complete.

10. AmiQuote will inform you of the progress of the download. If the amount of data stretches the capacity of your communications or your patience, divide the Russell1000.tls file into several smaller files and work with each part in turn. As soon as the data for any individual stock has been downloaded, it is immediately available for use within AmiBroker. You may continue to work with AmiBroker while downloading proceeds.

    When the download is complete, scroll through the Ticker List in AmiQuote. If there were problems with any of the tickers, there will be messages displayed. A common problem is that the spelling of the ticker in the tls file is not the same as the spelling the data provider uses. In this case, note that Russell Corporation used a period when specifying the Class A stock. Yahoo uses a dash character. Make a list of all the tickers that did not download properly and create a file named NewTickers.tls. Add the tickers of any other stocks you want. Using the same procedure, have AmiQuote download the new tickers.

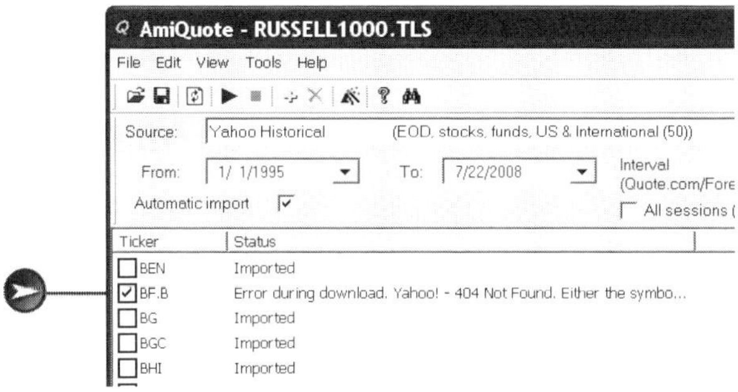

A good source for researching companies and verifying tickers that will be downloaded from Yahoo is the Yahoo financial site. *http://finance.yahoo.com/*

11. Close AmiQuote.
12. In AmiBroker, using the **File** menu, click **Save Database**.

Ticker and Full Name

If you want AmiBroker to know the full name of each issue in addition to its ticker symbol, the names must be loaded into the database. One way to do that starts with a text file, similar to the Russell1000.tls file described above, but including the full name of the issue along with the ticker symbol. Optionally, the industry group number can also be included and will be used to place each ticker in its correct category. Each line of this file has the ticker, full name, and industry group number, all separated by commas, and saved in a file with a name such as R1000FullName.txt (txt, not tls, as you will see in a minute).

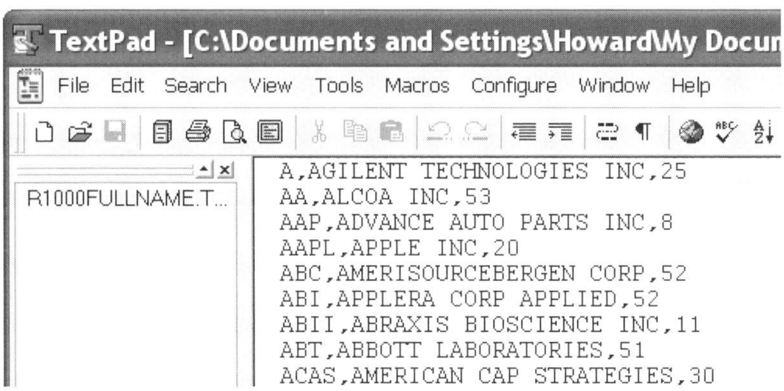

Appendix B, Industries and Sectors, has a list of the industries and their respective group numbers. There is no simple way to assign an industry, and its associated industry number, to each ticker. At times, a database of a large number of stocks (such as all US stocks), sometimes including a program to set up a database that is complete with industry number assignments, will appear on one of the AmiBroker discussion forums (see the links in the Appendix C, Resources). These quickly become obsolete with the addition of new stocks and changes to existing ones.

If you are very interested in assigning industry numbers to stocks, here are two alternative ways.

One. Download the lists of components of each of the Standard & Poor's sector exchange traded funds. One sector at a time, form a watchlist of the members. (See Watchlists, page 179.) Using AmiBroker's Symbol menu, select Organize Assignments and assign all the members of the watchlist the same Sector Number.

Two. Subscribe to one of the commercial data providers (see the links in the Appendix C, Resources). In the process of setting up their database, they will assign each stock to its proper market, industry, and group. Most of the services will store additional information, such as number of shares outstanding, dividend, and so forth, that you would have difficulty finding yourself.

With R1000FullName.txt, the file containing the ticker symbol, full name, and optionally the industry number ready, you are ready to establish the database. This must be done before symbols are entered in any other way and before quotes are downloaded. A simple jscript program, Industries.js (courtesy of Tomasz Janeczko), can be used to read the txt file and establish the database. (The program listing of Industries.js is in Appendix C, Resources, and is in the download materials associated with this book.)

Warning: If your database is already established and has historical price data, Do Not run this script – it will result in a badly confused database. Use this script only to establish a new database before loading historical quotes into it.

In order to run the script:

1. Using **Windows Explorer**, create a new folder under the AmiBroker directory to hold the new database. Assume it is NewR1000.
2. Run AmiBroker, use the **File** menu, Open **Database**, select NewR1000, click **OK**.

3. Copy or move R1000FullName.txt to your Windows Desktop.
4. Copy or move Industries.js to your desktop.
5. Double click Industries.js.
6. The script tells you that the script is started. Click **OK**.
7. After a short time, less than one minute, the script tells you it is finished. Click **OK**.

Verify that the script worked by using AmiBroker **Symbols** menu. Expand the **All** category and note that there are 1000 tickers listed. If you supplied industry codes, expand the **Sectors** category and note that the tickers have been assigned to sectors. There are no quotes yet.

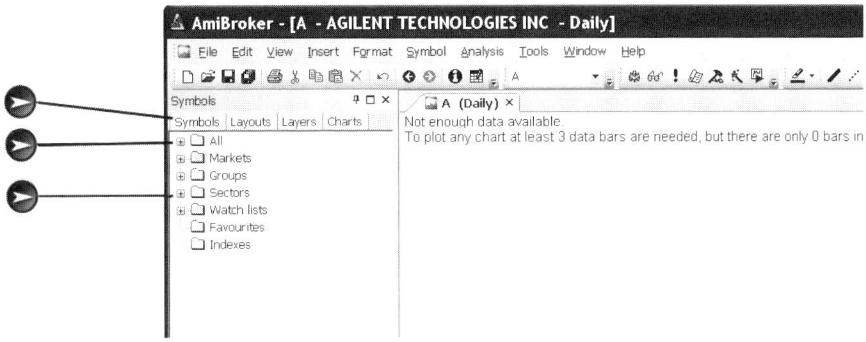

To fill the database with historical quotes:

1. Create a .tls file containing the tickers from the first column of R1000FullName.txt. Name it Russell1000.tls.
2. Follow the directions given in the section above, Ticker Only, to have AmiQuote retrieve historical data from Yahoo.
3. In AmiBroker, using the **File** menu, click **Save Database**.
4. Exit AmiBroker.

Additional Symbols

Whenever you want to add issues to your database, use this procedure:

1. Enter their ticker symbols, one per line, in the file NewTickers.tls. (It is convenient to keep all tls files in the AmiQuote directory.)
2. With AmiBroker running, open the database you want to add to.
3. Run AmiQuote.
4. Using AmiQuote's **File** menu, open NewTickers.tls.

5. Set the From Date and To Date.
6. Check the **Automatic Import box**.
7. Click the **Green Arrow** to begin the download.
8. When the download is finished, close AmiQuote.
9. In AmiBroker, **Save database**.

If you want to record the full name of the issue:

1. In AmiBroker, using the **Symbol** menu, select **Information**. The information window for this stock will open.
2. Edit the **Full Name field**.

If you want to assign categories:

In AmiBroker either:

1. Using the **Symbol** menu, select **Information**.
2. In the Categories section, make whatever assignments you wish for the one ticker you are working with.

Or:

1. Using the **Symbol** menu, select **Organize Assignments**.
2. Make whatever assignments you wish for the list of tickers you select.

Data Updates

Once the database has been established and the historical data loaded, maintaining the data by adding the latest quotes is very easy. In AmiBroker, using the **Tools** menu, select **AutoUpdateQuotes**. AmiBroker will examine the database that is open, determine the date range needed to bring the quotes for all the issues in this database up to current date, and call AmiQuote to do the download. Since only a few days data is needed for each ticker, the process takes only a short time.

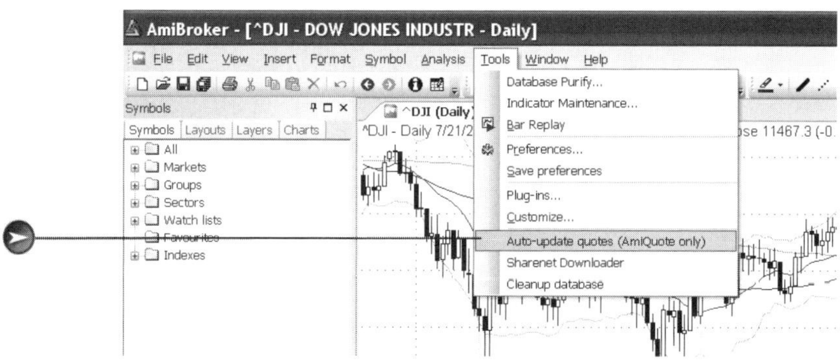

Sources of Free Data

The examples above illustrate using Yahoo as the source of historical data. There are other sources. For US markets, msn also provides free end-of-day historical data. If you wish to use that source, use the pull down menu in AmiQuote to select msn instead of Yahoo. Keep in mind that consistency is important. Different data suppliers will have different ways of preparing and presenting the data. For example, the volume multiplier may be different, or the ticker spelling may be different. After you load your database with quotes from one supplier, keep the database up-to-date using that same supplier.

ASCII Import

There are two methods of importing ASCII data: the ASCII Import Wizard (file menu, Import Wizard), and the full ASCII Importer (file menu, Import ASCII). The wizard is good for one-off imports. Its features are a subset of the full importer. If you will be importing the same files regularly, set up the full importer. (Note: the ASCII Import Wizard can create a format definition file for later use with the ASCII Importer.)

Before you start, decide which database you want the imported data to go into. If you are just practicing, create a test database and open it. Do not import into your high quality database until you are confident the import procedure is working correctly.

Download the data files and, if necessary, unzip or expand them. Open the files using a text editor such as Notepad. There should be one quote per line, fields separated by space, semicolon, or comma.

There may be a header line describing the fields. If not, identify the fields yourself. If necessary, go to the site from which the data was obtained and read their documentation.

The date field is the trickiest. The wizard understands many formats. If your data is in one of them, all you need to do is identify the order of month, day, and year. The codes are DMY, MDY, YMD. If your data does not follow one of the recognized date formats, you will need to reformat the date (for example, by using a spreadsheet) and rewrite the data file before proceeding.

The year can be either four digits or two (the final two of the year). The month can be either two digits or three characters (such as Dec or Jan).

The day is two digits. The separator can be / (slash), \ (backslash), - (minus), or not separated at all.

Assume the date for one quote is December 31, 2000. YMD formats that are recognized include:

20001231

2000-12-31

2000/12/31

2000-Dec-31

001231

00-12-31

00/12/31

00\12\31

If your data has a ticker symbol as a field in each line, the data will be stored under that symbol. If there is not an explicit ticker, the file name will be used. If your data file is downloaded as, for example, IBM.csv, the data will be stored as IBM. If your data file is downloaded with a generic name, such as TABLE.csv (Yahoo uses this file name for all its individual downloads), rename it before proceeding.

Yahoo Historical Data Download

The Yahoo site is a good place to get stock and index historical data. *http://finance.yahoo.com*

Using the investing tab, select stocks. Under research tools, click historical quotes to get this page.

Follow these steps to download the historical data for a stock or index:

1. Enter the ticker (say it is XOM)
2. Click **GO**
3. The screen will display the most recent data
4. Click **Download to Spreadsheet**
   On your desktop, or wherever your default directory to receive downloads is, you will find a file named TABLE.csv.
5. Rename TABLE.csv to XOM.csv. Use capital letters if you want your symbol to be in capitals.
6. Proceed to import XOM.csv into AmiBroker using either the ASCII Import Wizard or Import ASCII

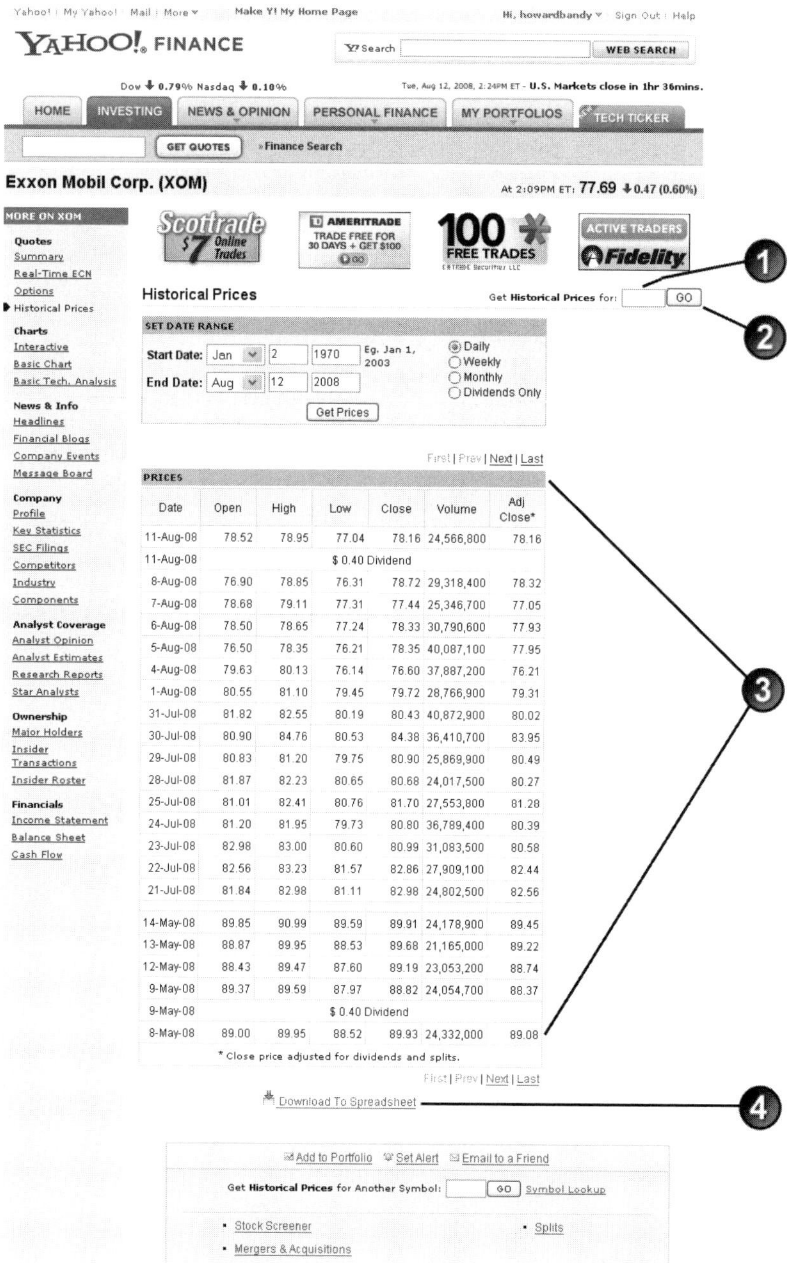

ASCII Import Wizard

The following steps illustrate how to use the ASCII Import Wizard. Before beginning, a database named TEST has been created and opened. It already has a few symbols and data for them. Data has been downloaded from Yahoo for two stocks, GE and XOM, but not yet imported. Since Yahoo downloads all data using the file name TABLE.csv, the downloaded file was renamed between downloads, so the files are GE.csv and XOM.csv.

1. Using the **File** menu, select **Import Wizard**.
2. When the dialog box opens, click **Pick Files**.
3. Navigate to the directory holding the files you have downloaded.

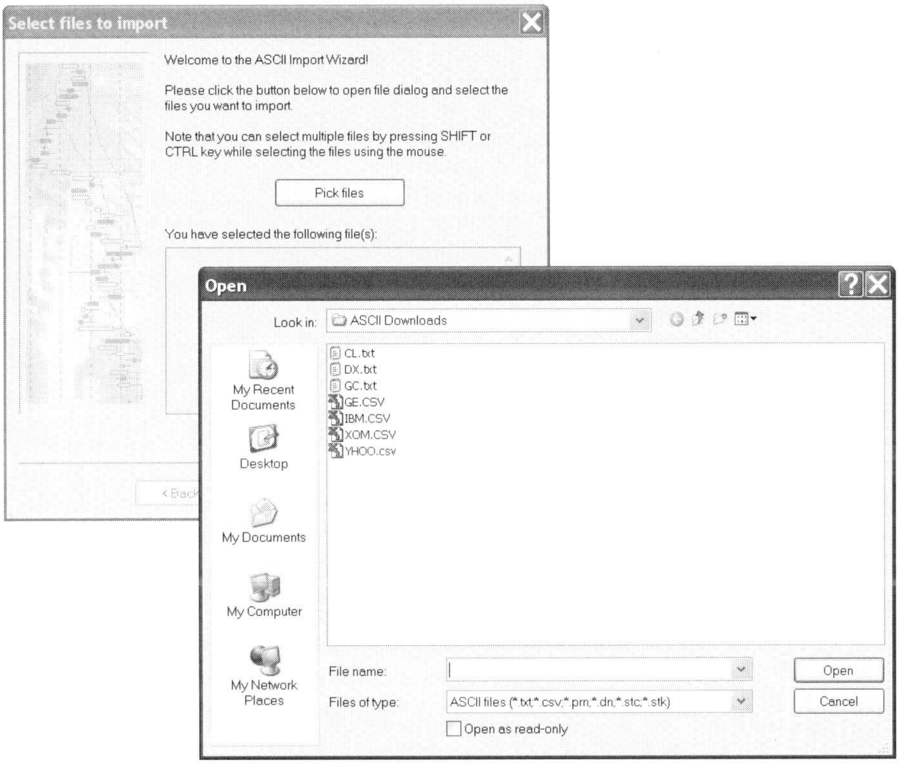

4. Since the files have identical formats, you can process multiple files in one pass, so select both GE.csv and XOM.csv. (Click one file, press the Control key and click the other.)
5. Click **Open**.

The Define Fields dialog box will open.

1. Note the format of the data in the .csv files.
2. Using the pull-down menus, define the fields for each element of data. Each element in the entire row of data must be defined.

Select **SKIP** to ignore data in the csv file that you do not want in your AmiBroker database.

3. Select **comma** as the separator.
4. Skip **1** line - the header.
5. Check **Automatically add new symbols**.
6. Click **Next**.

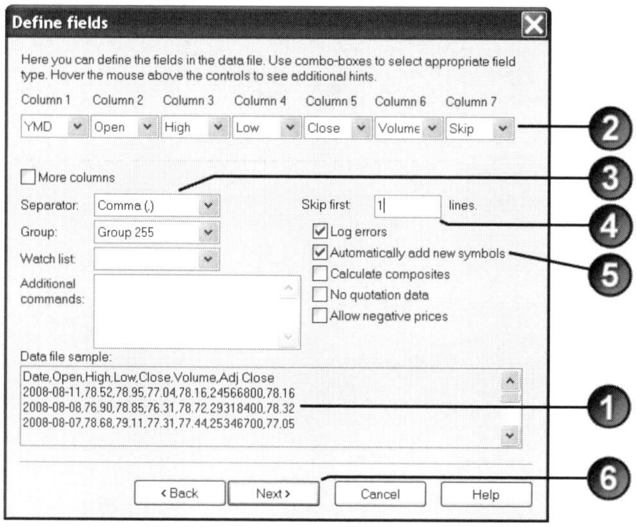

The Additional Settings screen will come up. It is on this screen that you can save the format settings that you just used. They will not help for future uses of the ASCII Import Wizard, but they will be available in the full ASCII importer. To do this, Check **Add current settings to ASCII importer definitions**, and give meaningful Description and File Name. You will see your format as we look at the full ASCII Importer in the next section.

7. Click **Finish**.

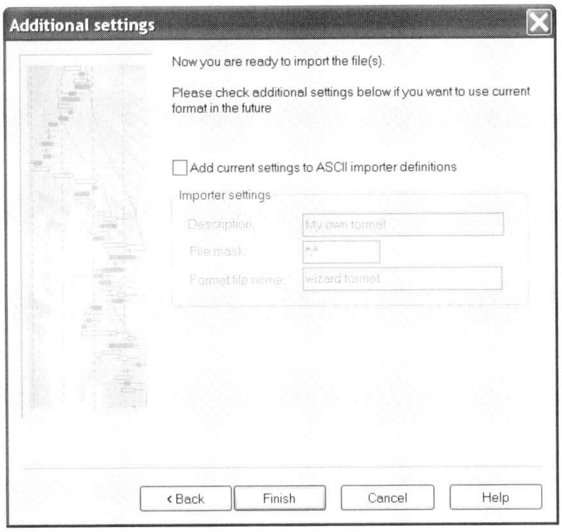

The data will be converted from ASCII, imported into the open database, and be immediately ready for use in AmiBroker.

ASCII Importer

The full ASCII Importer is much more efficient, has more capabilities, and is more complex. Rather than having to fill in a form each time you want to import an ASCII file, you can set up a format definition file, or use one of the pre-defined files. The file that was created for the import done manually using the wizard in the previous section is:

```
# Format definition file generated automatically
# by AmiBroker's ASCII Import Wizard
$FORMAT Date_YMD, Open, High, Low, Close, Volume, Skip
$SKIPLINES 1
$SEPARATOR ,
$CONT 1
$GROUP 255
$AUTOADD 1
$DEBUG 1
```

The definition files are stored in the C:\Program Files\AmiBroker\Formats directory. By copying the format file that you will be using regularly to be DEFAULT.FORMAT, all that is necessary to import ASCII files is:

1. Using the **File** Menu, select **Import ASCII.**

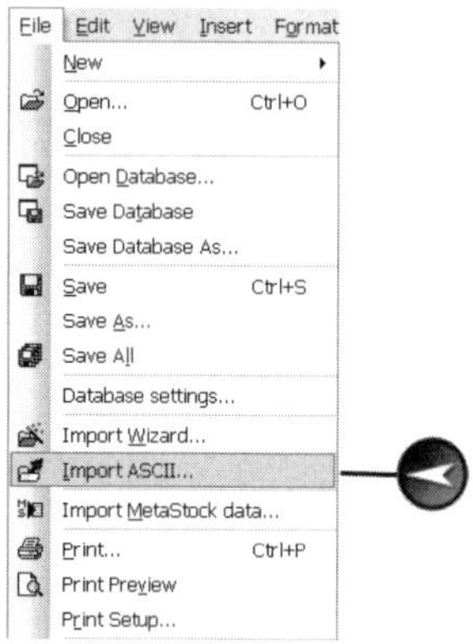

2. On the Open screen, select the file you want to import.
3. Click **Open**.

The file will be converted, imported, and made available within AmiBroker for immediate use.

The options available for controlling the processing of ASCII data are extensive. Read about them all in the AmiBroker User's Guide.

Subscription Data Providers

Free data has a cost to you – the cost of checking the data for missing quotes, bad values, unadjusted splits, and so forth, and correcting those problems. Subscription data services, such as Quotes Plus, Premium Data, CSI, and others, provide that maintenance for you and deliver cleaner, more consistent data with less effort on your part. End-of-day stock data costs about $40 per month – more for some services, less for others. Some end-of-day vendors include mutual funds at no charge; others charge extra. Commodities and futures data is an additional cost, depending in part on the fees the exchanges that clear those trades and report that data charge. Some subscription vendors provide custom indices, custom indicators, and have a wider selection of issues – and often charge an extra amount for those. Some services charge a one-time fee for loading the historical data, others do not.

If you plan to use a subscription service, be aware that each service has its own database format. Once you begin with one subscription service, they will be the only service that can keep your data up-to-date.

The installation procedure for each service will be unique to that service, but it is generally simple and well documented. Typically, the installation does three things for you:

1. Establishes the external database and the communications between the database and AmiBroker.
2. Loads the definitions of the tickers, including the ticker symbol, the full name, and the industry assignment.
3. Loads the historical price data.

After the close of trading each day, you initiate communication with the data vendor. The database is brought up-to-date, and errors and inconsistencies are corrected and re-downloaded, all automatically. Some vendors provide intraday updating – treating the latest price as though it is the closing price. At subsequent updatings, the earlier prices are replaced by the more recent ones.

Quotes Plus End-of-Day Data

Here is the procedure to set up a Quotes Plus subscription end-of-day database.

Each data provider will have their own specific details and methods, but the end result is the same – an end-of-day database that is established and loaded with historical data by the data vendor. Tickers, full names, industry associations, and other information related to that stock are all provided by the vendor, stored in the external database for that subscription, and made available to AmiBroker through an interface that is transparent to you as a user.

1. Begin with a visit to Quotes Plus' website: *http://www.qp2.com/joomla/index.php*.
2. Pull down the **Products** menu, select QP3, and click **Free Trial**.

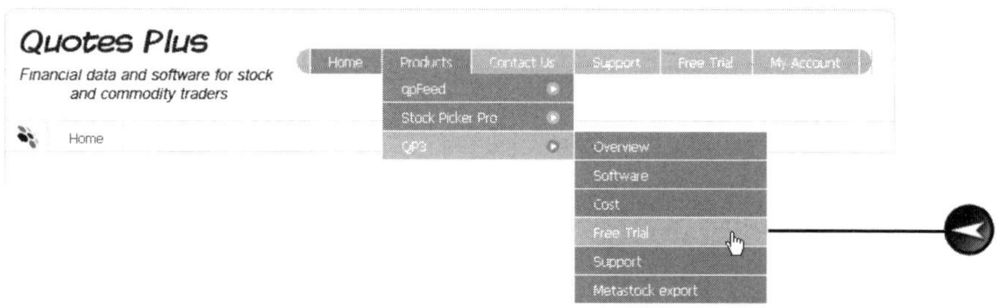

3. Fill in the contact information. You will receive an email from Quotes Plus containing a User ID, Password, and the URL link to a download utility.
4. Follow the link to the download utility and download the Qp3Setup.exe file.
5. Execute that file to start the installation of the database and download of the historical quotation data. This is the first screen you will see.

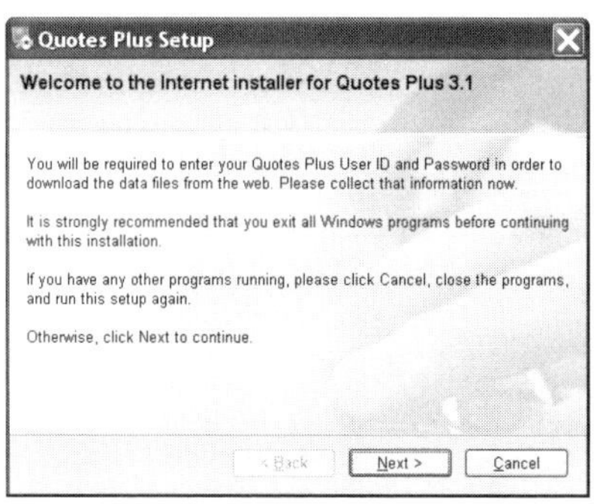

As you follow the instructions, you will be asked for your User ID and Password.

6. Select the data files you want.

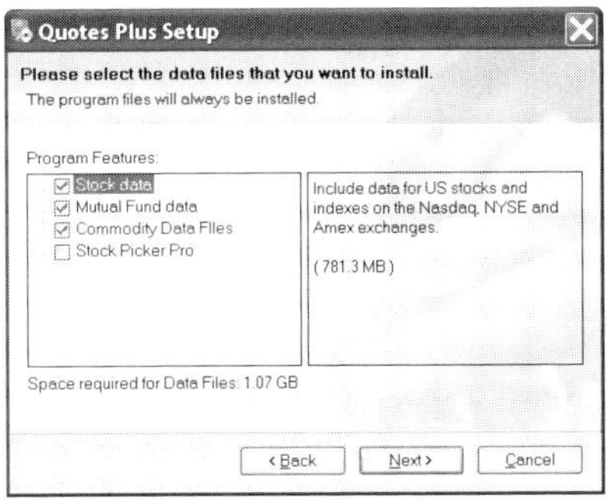

7. Accept the defaults for the location of the program (which you will use to keep the data up-to-date) and the data files. The path to the program will be C:\Program Files\Quotes Plus, and to the data files will be C:\Quotes Plus Data.
8. When the download is complete, click **Finish**.

If you selected the stock data, mutual fund data, and commodities data, the total data transmitted will be about 260MB. If that will strain your communications capabilities, Quotes Plus will mail you a CD.

Connect the database to AmiBroker.

In AmiBroker, from the **File** menu, select **New**, and **Database**. Working in the top half of the Database settings window:

1. In the **Database Folder** box, enter the name you want for your new database.
2. Check **Load this database at startup**.
3. Click **Create**.

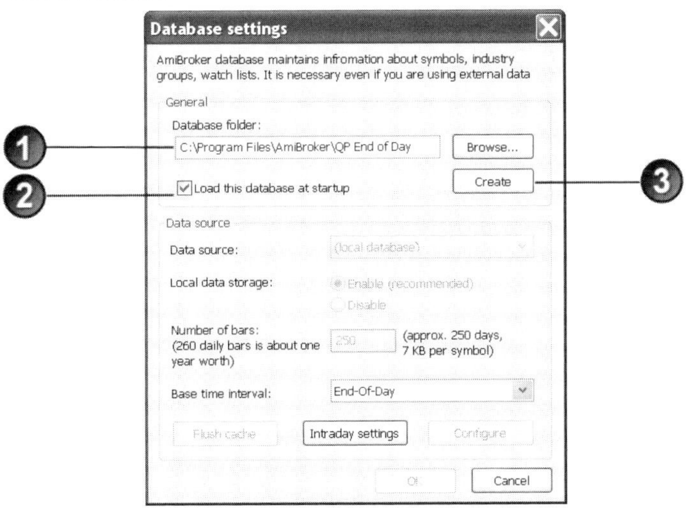

Now working in the bottom half of the Database settings window:

1. Pull down the **Data Source** menu and select **Quotes Plus data Plug-in**.
2. Click **Enable Local data storage.**
3. Enter **1000** for the Number of bars.
4. Click **Configure**.

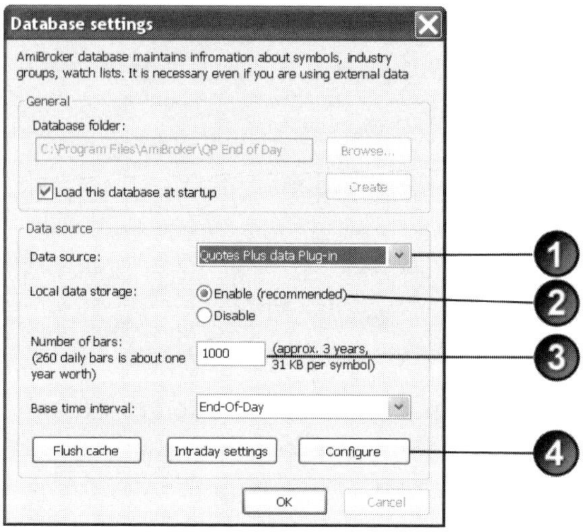

On Configuration:

1. Select the categories you want in the database.
2. Click **Retrieve**. Wait while the data is retrieved.
3. Click **Close**.

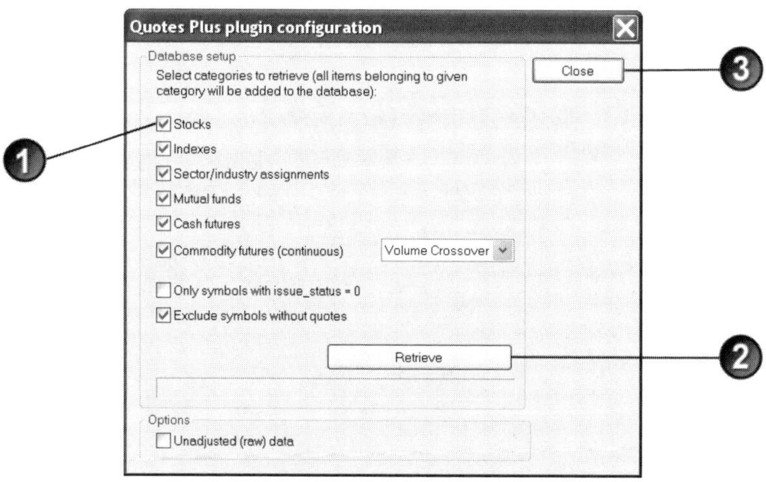

Back on Database settings, Click **OK**.

Your Quotes Plus database is now established, loaded with historical quotes, installed in AmiBroker, and ready for use.

To load a chart:

1. In AmiBroker, using the **Symbols** menu, expand the **All** category (click the + sign).
2. Click on any of the ticker symbols. The data for that ticker will load into the main chart window.
3. In AmiBroker, **Save database**.

Norgate Premium Data - End-of-Day

Norgate Investor Service provides quality end-of-day data for stock markets in Australia (ASX), Asia (SGX), and the United States (NYSE, NASDAQ, AMEX, OTC-BB, PinkSheets). Extensive historical data is available, including data for delisted stocks (an important feature for those interested in studying survivorship bias).

The data integrates very well with the symbol lists, and includes over 900 pre-built and automatically maintained watchlists for the Australian and US databases. Hourly snapshot data is available for the ASX and SGX.

Data is provided in MetaStock data format. (If you are installing Premium Data as an AmiBroker database, you will not be aware of the format of the external database.)

Norgate also provides end-of-day data for 86 liquid futures markets. Futures data is available in individual, spliced continuous, and back-adjusted continuous contract forms. All the fields required for serious backtesting (margin, point value, tick size, etc.) are populated. Data is provided in ASCII and MetaStock data formats.

Norgate is in the process of improving their integration with AmiBroker. A new native AmiBroker data plugin that will provide additional speed and features is under development. Visit *http://www.premiumdata.net/support/amibroker.php* for the latest details.

Free trials are available.

The next pages discuss setting up Norgate end-of-day data for the Australian stock market.

1. Sign up for a subscription or free trial at their web site: *http://www.premiumdata.net.*

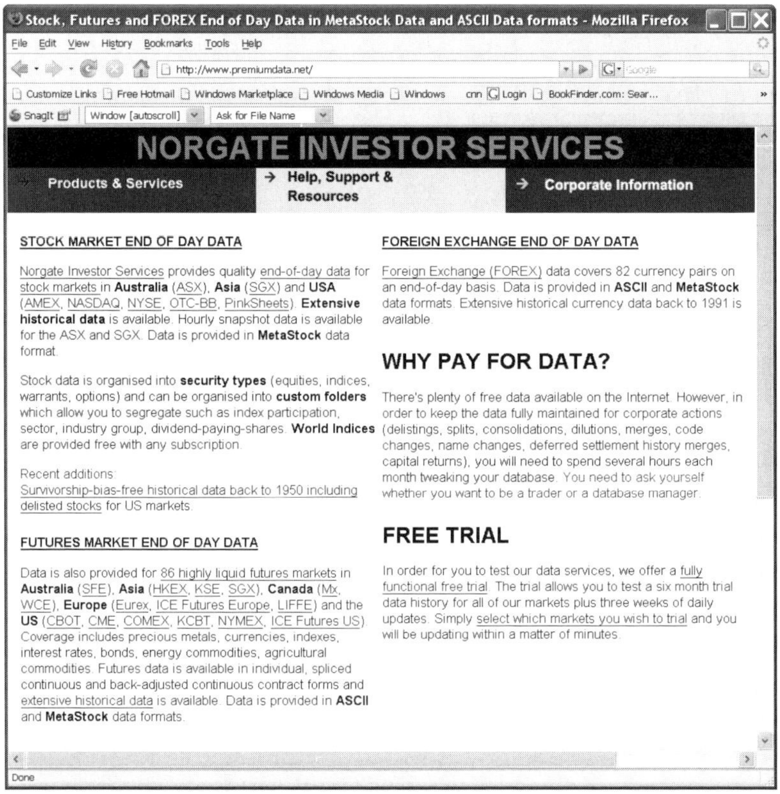

2. You will receive an e-mail with your user name and password, and a link to the download page.
3. Go to that web page and login.
4. The services you have subscribed to will be noted in the download screen. You will need to download at least three files:
   A. Program Installer
   B. History Installer
   C. AmiBroker Setup.

Premium Data / DataTools / Premium Forex Downloads

File Type	Description/FileName	Size	Approx Download Time for 56K Modem/1.5Mbps Broadband	Click below to **DOWNLOAD from**
Stocks				
Program Installer	Premium Data & Premium Charts setup.premiumdata.exe	3.1 MB	14 mins/1 mins	East Coast USA Server West Coast USA Server Australian Server European Server
History Installer	Australian Securities Exchange (Stocks) Database - Limited 12 month history for all currently listed stocks, except for listed codes starting with 'A' which have full history. InstallHistory.ASX.trial.20080808.exe	7.9 MB	34 mins/1 mins	East Coast USA Server West Coast USA Server Australian Server European Server
AmiBroker Files				
The following files are applicable for users of the **AmiBroker charting software ONLY**. Only download them if you have AmiBroker installed on your PC. More information about these files can be found at AmiBroker FAQ				
AmiBroker Setup	AmiBroker ASX Workspace Setup with GICS classifications, groups and extensive watchlists AmiBroker-ASX-PremiumData-v1.41.exe	0.8 MB	4 mins/1 mins	East Coast USA Server West Coast USA Server Australian Server European Server
Market Analyst Files				
The following files are applicable for users of the **Market Analyst charting software ONLY**. Only download them if you have Market Analyst installed on your PC.				
Market Analyst	All versions of Market Analyst have a bug related to dates prior to January 1900. This historical installer replaces just the World Indices with data that extends after this date. This file is only required if you have Market Analyst installed on your computer. This file is NOT applicable the HomeTrader version of Market Analyst as it has no MetaStock reading capabilities. InstallHistory.WorldIndices.MarketAnalyst.20070810.exe	2.3 MB	10 mins/1 mins	East Coast USA Server West Coast USA Server Australian Server European Server

To download a program or history installer, click on the corresponding server closest to you (Australia, Europe or USA).

Choose to **Save** the file to your Windows Desktop, or to some other location where you can find it readily.

Click on the server nearest to you (Australia, Europe or USA).

5. Save the files and accept all the defaults for file locations.
6. The Program Installer and History Installer must be in the same subdirectory on your computer.
7. Insure that AmiBroker is not running.
8. Locate the program installer, run it and follow the prompts. The program installer will recognise the history installer and offer to install the history for you as part of the process. If the files are too large for your communications, you may prefer to order a data history CD which will be sent out to you by ordinary mail.

9. Execute the files in this order:
   1) Program Installer.
   2) Historical Data Installer.
   3) AmiBroker Setup.

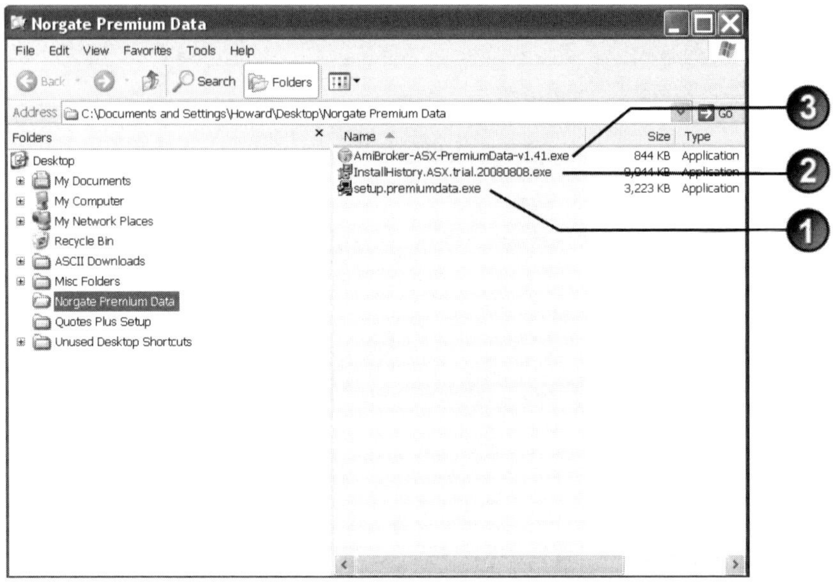

When the AmiBroker Setup runs, it will open a browser-based FAQ page explaining how to install the interface necessary for AmiBroker to use the Premium Data files.

AmiBroker Setup will establish a database in the AmiBroker directory, but it will not be usable yet. Here is how to connect the two:

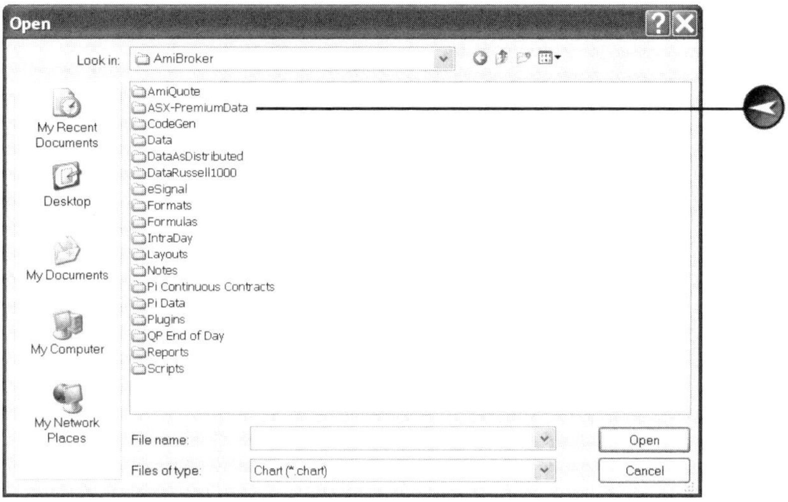

10. Start AmiBroker.
11. Using the **Tools** menu, click **ASX-Premium Data**. This will run a script with seven stages that takes several minutes.

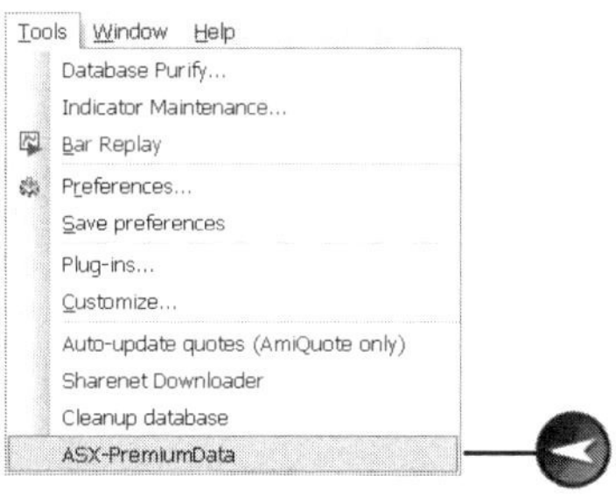

12. Using the **File** menu, select **Open Database**, select **ASX-PremiumData**, click **OK**.

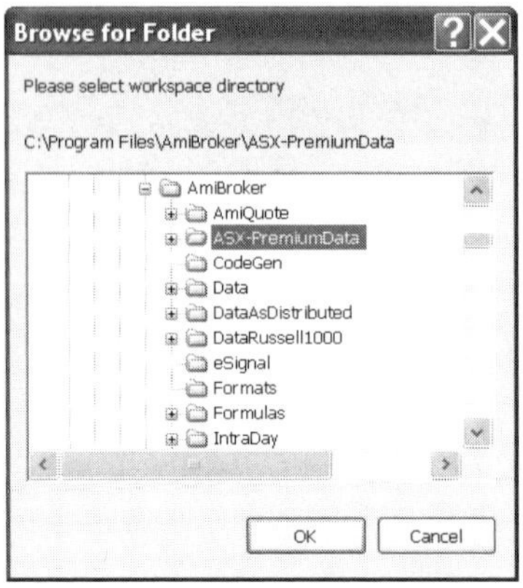

13. Here is AmiBroker with BHP in the chart window.

Database Setup - Intraday and Real-Time Data

Intraday data is data with bars shorter than a full trading day. Taking great care and using a data vendor that supports it, it is possible to combine intraday and end-of-day data in the same database. But most AmiBroker users who use intraday data maintain a separate intraday database. The next few pages describe setting up intraday and real-time data.

Free Intraday Historical Data

If you are interested in developing systems with intraday data, but are not ready to commit to a real-time data subscription, you can download intraday bars into an AmiBroker database and work with them. If your systems test out to be profitable, you will eventually need real-time data to execute them.

There are several sources of free intraday historical data. Visit *http://www.IntroductionToAmiBroker.com/resources* and scroll down to the data area for links to some of them. AN Futures sells intraday data for the e-mini S&P 500, e-mini NASDAQ 100, e-mini Russell 2000, Euro, and Yen in 1 minute bar and tick resolution. Visit them at: *http://www.anfutures.com/*. They have a demo file, ES0206MG.csv with 1 minute bars for the e-mini S&P June 2002 contract – 3/6/2002 through 6/12/2002. The third column is the date, with 20306 meant to be 2002, March, 6.

```
ES01MIG,I,20306,15:50,1165.5,1165.5,1165.5,1165.5,8,1159.5
ES01MIG,I,20306,15:51,1165.5,1165.5,1165.5,1165.5,3,1159.5
ES01MIG,I,20306,15:52,1165.5,1165.5,1165.5,1165.5,9,1159.5
ES01MIG,I,20306,15:53,1164.25,1164.25,1164.25,1164.25,6,1158.25
ES01MIG,I,20306,15:54,1162.25,1162.25,1162.25,1162.25,1,1156.25
ES01MIG,I,20306,15:55,1164.5,1164.5,1164.5,1164.5,3,1158.5
ES01MIG,I,20306,16:20,1164.25,1164.25,1164.25,1164.25,1,1158.25
ES01MIG,I,20306,16:21,1164,1164,1164,1164,1,1158
ES01MIG,I,20306,16:24,1164.25,1164.25,1164.25,1164.25,1,1158.25
```

AmiBroker can accept many date formats, but not that one, so a spreadsheet is used to transform the date into one of the acceptable formats and 20306 becomes 2002-03-06. The Excel formula to do this is: ="200"&LEFT(C1,1)&"-"&MID(C1,2,2)&"-"&MID(C1,4,2), where the 20306 is in cell C1. Make a copy of the original data file, replace the date, and save it with a new name, for example ES0206Mod.csv.

The following procedure will set up a database into which we will load the e-mini S&P intraday data. This is the same procedure used to set up the Quotes Plus end-of-day database, so the illustrations will be omitted.

1. In AmiBroker, from the **File** menu, select **New**, then **Database**.

Working first in the top half of the window:

2. In Destination Folder, choose a meaningful name for the database – such as IntraDay.
3. Uncheck **Load this database at startup**.
4. Click **Create**.

Now working in the bottom half of the window:

1. Data Source: (local database)
2. Local data storage: Enable
3. Number of bars: 100000
4. Base time interval: 1 minute
5. Accept the defaults for Intraday settings
6. Click **OK**

The database is established, but has no data in it. The ASCII importer will load the data from the csv file using the ASCII Import Wizard in the following procedure:

1. In AmiBroker, from the **File** menu, select **Import Wizard**.
2. Click **Pick Files**.
3. Navigate to the location of your modified file and select it.
4. Click **Open**.
5. Click **Next.**
6. Fill in the fields.

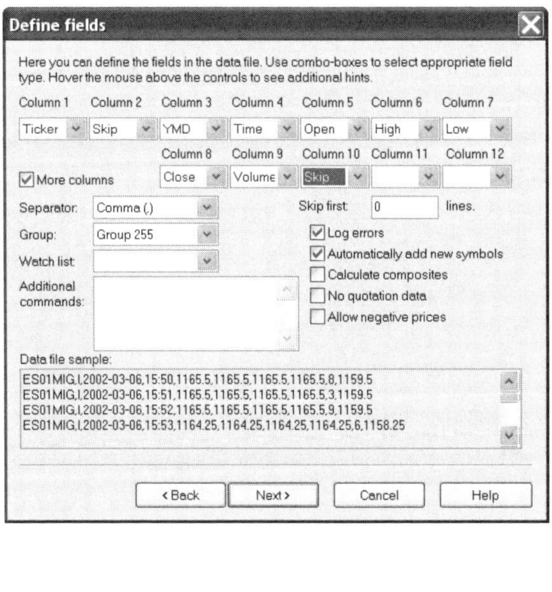

7. Click **Next**.
8. Click **Finish**. The data will be imported and the active chart will display the intraday data you just loaded.

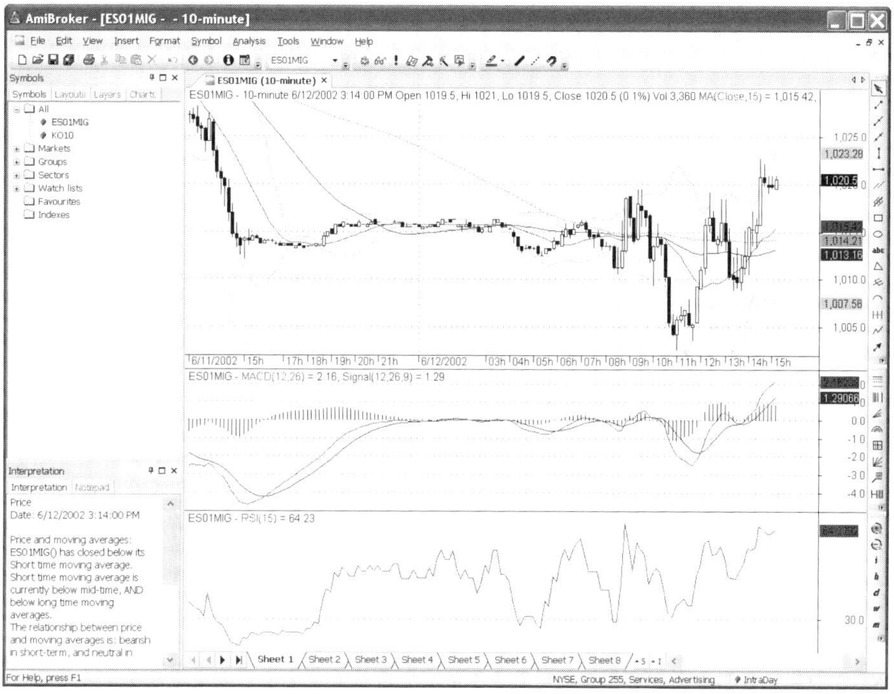

9. In AmiBroker, **Save Database.**

If you were going to import data from this vendor regularly, you could set up a macro in the spreadsheet to convert the date field, and set up a custom ASCII format in AmiBroker specifically for that file format.

But, eventually, you will need a real-time data feed to create 1 minute bars throughout the trading day.

Delayed Real-Time Data

Some data vendors offer real-time data that has been delayed 15, 20, or 30 minutes. It is priced lower than non-delayed real-time data, and often is free. From the perspective of a developer of trading systems, about the only reasons to use delayed real-time data are to try out a data service or to build up a tick-based database. And, since most of the high quality data services have a trial period, you can try the real thing for the same amount of effort. Trying to place trades using delayed real-time data is dangerous to your wealth — a lot can happen in 15 minutes.

Real-Time Data

Real-time data can be expensive. Prices range from about $50 to several hundred per month for the basic service which includes a limited number of tickers. There are additional charges for extra services, such as charting packages, Level II quotes, or getting data for a larger number of issues. Exchange fees, which are set by the exchange that clears trades for the tickers listed by them, are also added. There are different levels of exchange fees for professional and non-professional traders. Exchange fees can add up to several hundred dollars a month. Most real-time data vendors have trial periods, but the exchange fees charged during the trial are usually not refundable.

Also, check your Internet communications capacity and your communication vendor's fair use policy. Monitoring about ten symbols in the real-time quote window causes traffic of about 50 MB per hour. Done every trading day of the month, this will exceed the fair use limits of some vendors.

As mentioned earlier, some vendors support combining end-of-day and intraday data in the same database. But that can be tricky. These steps describe separate intraday databases.

Quotes Plus Real-Time Data

The procedure to set up a real-time data feed using Quotes Plus is:

1. Begin with a visit to Quotes Plus' website: *http://www.qp2.com/joomla/index.php.*
2. Pull down the **Products** menu, select **QPFeed**, and click **Free Trial.**

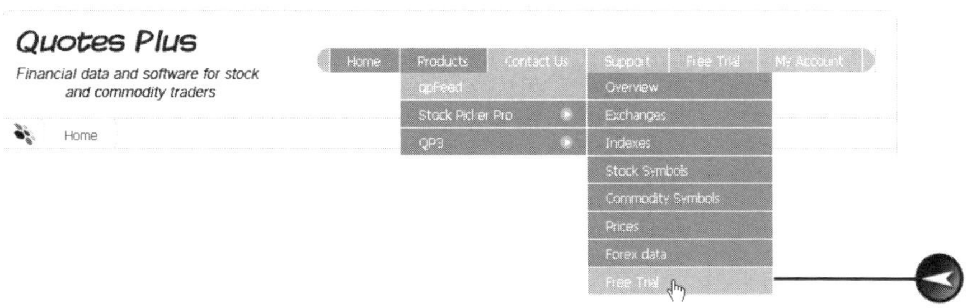

3. Fill in the contact information. You will receive an email from Quotes Plus containing a User ID, Password, and the URL link to a download utility.

4. Follow the link to the download utility and download the qpfeed_setup.exe file.
5. Execute that file to start the installation.
6. Enter your User ID and Password when requested.
7. Accept all the defaults.
8. Click **Finish** to the final dialog and the program will close.

The procedure to connect AmiBroker to the QPFeed is:

1. Start AmiBroker.
2. You will see a message saying that there is a new plug-in from qpfeed. Click **OK**.

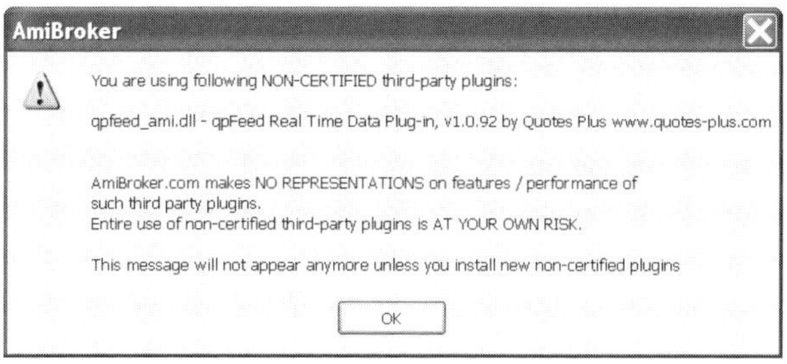

3. Using the **File** menu, select **New**, then **Database**.

Working in the top half of the box:

1. In the **Database folder** box, enter the name you want for your new real-time database.
2. Check or uncheck, as you wish, **Load this database at startup**.
3. Click **Create.**

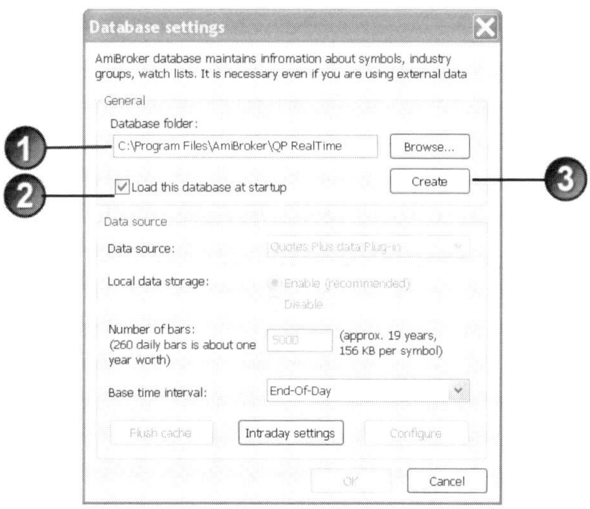

Now working in the bottom half of the Database settings box:

1. Pull down the **Data Source** menu and select **QPfeed Real Time Data Plugin.**
2. Click **Enable local data storage.**
3. Enter **25000** for number of bars.
4. Pull down the **Base Time Interval** menu and select **1 minute**.
5. Click **Configure**.
   The configuration menu will appear.
6. Select the categories you want to receive.
7. Check **Exclude symbols without quotes.**
8. Click **Retrieve**.
9. Click **Close**.
   Return to the Database settings screen.
10. Click **OK.**

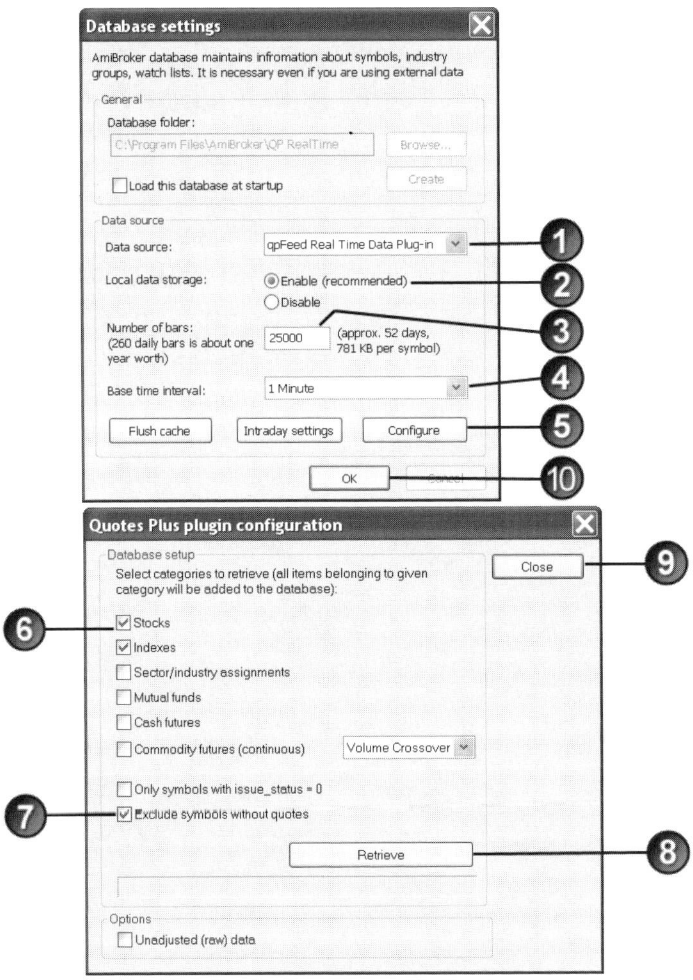

At this point, you have a database established to store 1 minute bars and the QPFeed ready to supply data. To bring up a chart:

1. Using theAmiBroker **Symbol** menu, select **New**.
2. Type in a symbol, say SPY.
   In a few seconds the chart will appear.

DTN IQ Real-Time Data

The procedure to set up a real-time data feed using DTN IQ Feed is:

1. Visit the DTN IQ Feed web site at: *http://www.iqfeed.net*

2. Click **Get Free Trial Now**. Complete the application forms. The trial is exactly the same as the subscription version. The trial turns into a subscription at the end of the trial period, unless you call to cancel it. DTN will send an e-mail with your User ID and PIN.
3. Return to that web site and Click **Download Client**. The current version is a file named iqfeed_client_4_4.exe, and is about 3 MB.

4. Run iqfeed_client_4_4.exe.
   Accept all the defaults. When you click finish on the final screen, the iqfeed program will be installed on your computer.

To set up an AmiBroker real-time database using DTN IQFeed:

1. In AmiBroker, using the **File** menu, select **New**, then **Database**.

Working in the top half of the box:

1. In the **Database folder** box, enter the name you want for your new real-time database.
2. Check or uncheck, as you wish, **Load this database at startup**.
3. Click **Create**.

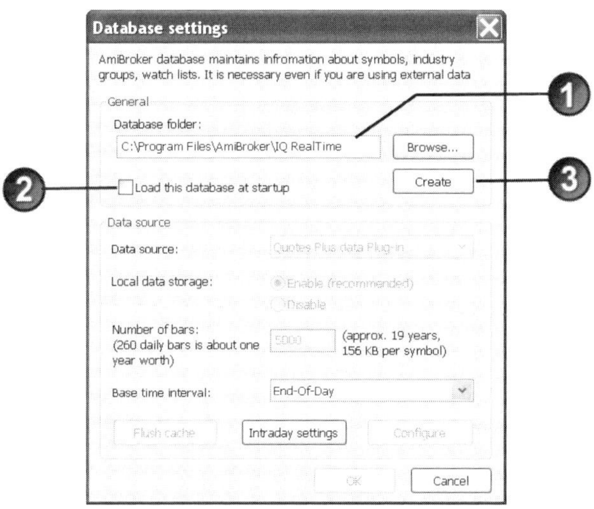

Now working in the bottom half of the Database settings box:

1. Pull down the **Data Source** menu and select **DTN IQfeed data Plugin.**
2. Click **Enable local data storage**.
3. Enter **25000** for number of bars.
4. Pull down the **Base Time Interval** menu and select **1 minute**.
5. Click **Configure**.
   The configuration menu will appear.
6. Note that DTN IQ has a bad tick filter. Accept the defaults.
   Click **OK**
   Return to the Database settings screen.
7. Click **OK.**

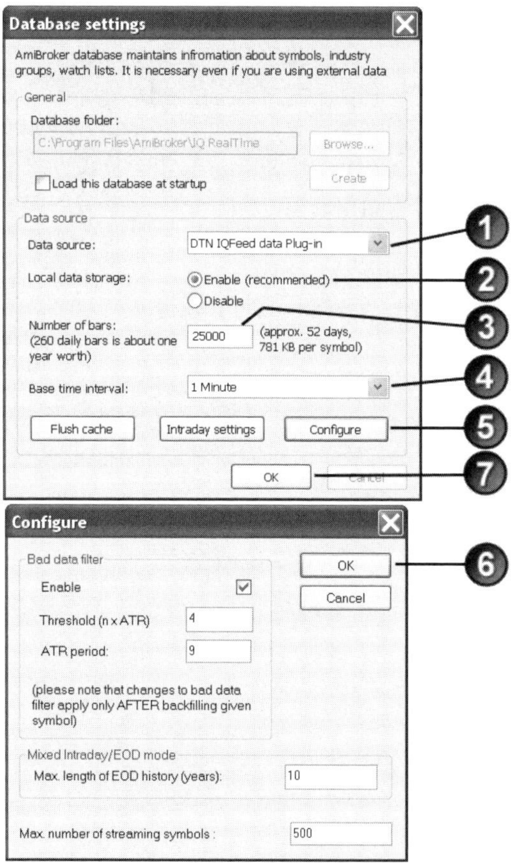

The IQ Connect Login will appear.

8. Enter your **Login**.
9. Enter your **Password** or **PIN**.
10. Click **Connect**. Your computer will communicate with the DTN IQ server.

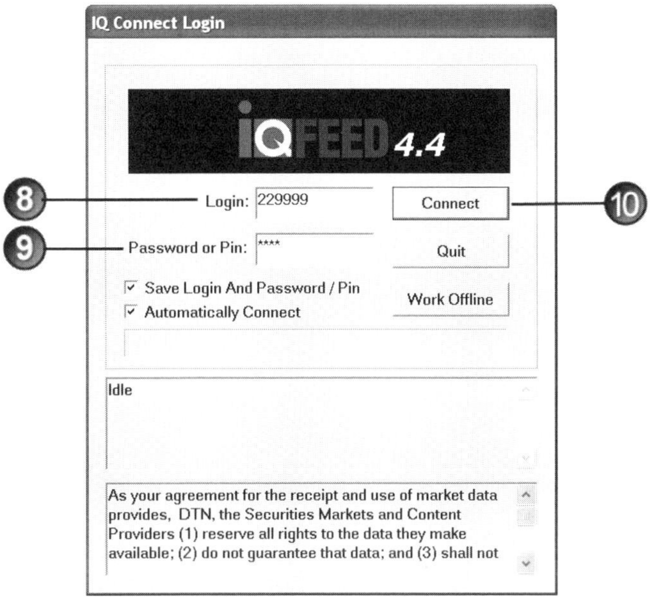

To bring up a chart:

1. Using theAmiBroker **Symbol** menu, select **New**.
2. Type in a symbol, say SPY.

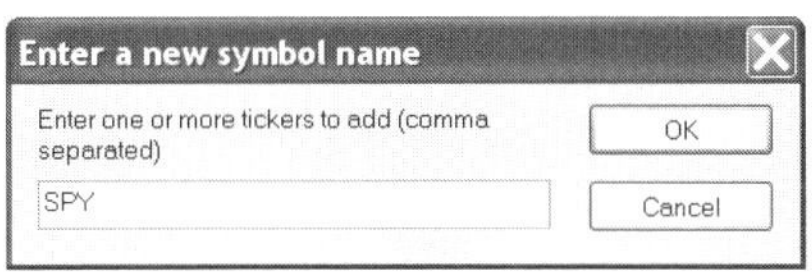

In a few seconds the chart will appear. Add other symbols, open the Realtime Quote Window, and continue.

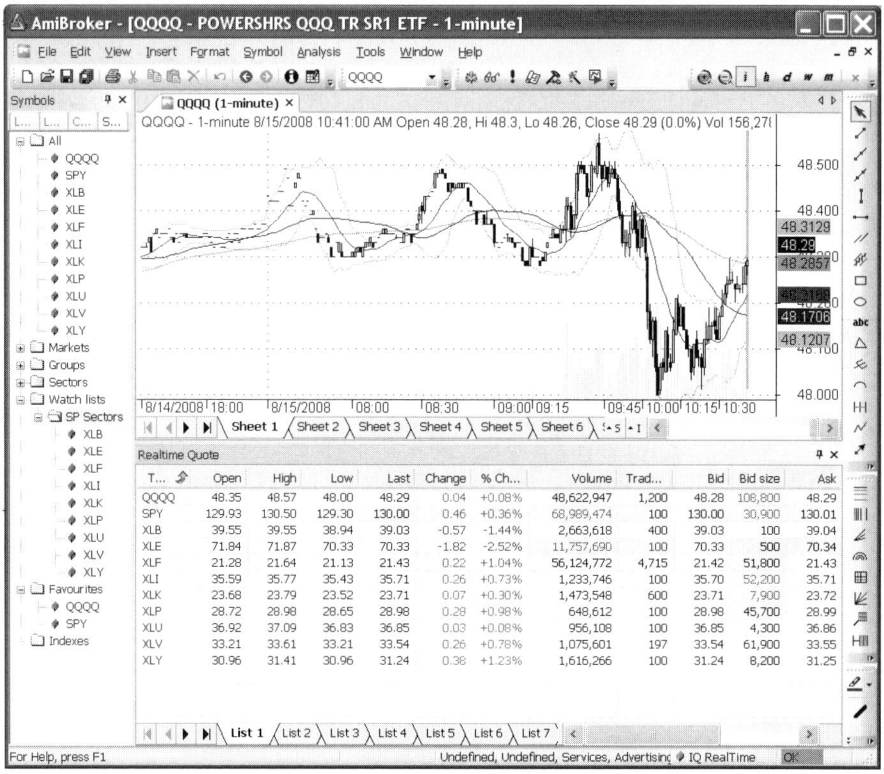

TICK DATA

Tick data refers to market data that represents the time and transaction price, and perhaps the volume, of every trade. Depending on the exchange and the data vendor, the tick data stream may also include other information, such as changes in the bid price, the asked price, the volume on each side. Just as it is possible to make display bars that represent a given amount of time, say 1 minute, it is possible to display bars that represent a given number of ticks, say 15 ticks.

In the opinion of this author, tick data is not appropriate for use by individuals and small trading companies. The highest quality tick data includes an information packet for every transaction. Some of the difficulties with tick data include: high cost; very high volume of transactions; erroneous transactions (called bad ticks - see example below); dropping of transactions when exchange activity increases (fast market conditions) or when communications capacity is reached.

Tick data is best used by larger organizations that have high capacity equipment, redundant data feeds, and staff devoted to monitoring and correcting the data.

To use tick data in AmiBroker, the Professional version is required.

If you want to experiment with very frequent data, try working with 1 minute bars instead of tick data.

This book will not discuss tick data further.

Chapter 3

30 Minutes to Useful Results

You have installed AmiBroker and the Data database. This chapter describes ten things you can do with AmiBroker - even while it is in Trial Mode - each in only a few minutes.

- Example 1 - Chart a Stock
- Example 2 - Apply a Trendline
- Example 3 - Plot a Moving Average
- Example 4 - Make a Watchlist
- Example 5 - Run an Exploration
- Example 6 - Run a Single Stock Backtest
- Example 7 - Run a Portfolio Backtest
- Example 8 - Optimize a Trading System
- Example 9 - Perform Walk Forward Validation
- Example 10 - Scan for Buy and Sell Signals

None of these is intended to be a complete description of the features used in the example. But working through them should give you a better feeling for the capabilities and ease of use of AmiBroker, and provide some experience as you read about other features.

Examples build. Later examples assume you can perform tasks described in earlier examples.

Example 1 - Chart a Stock

In this example, you will chart a stock, change its periodicity, chart a new stock, scroll, and zoom.

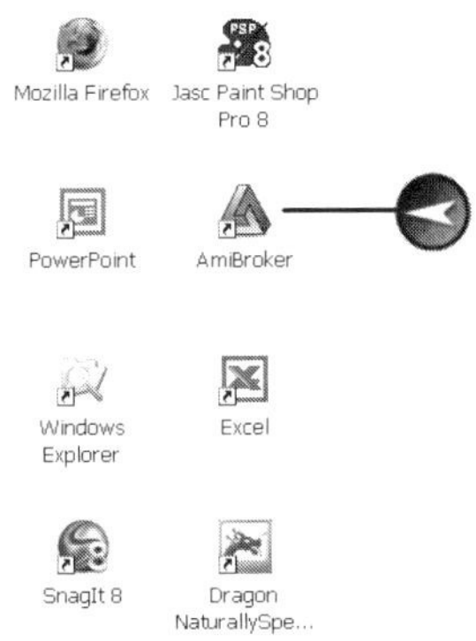

To start AmiBroker, either:

- Double-click the **AmiBroker** icon that was placed on your desktop during installation.
- Using the **Windows Start** menu, select **AmiBroker**, then **AmiBroker**.

AmiBroker will display the default chart window.

The chart window has three panes. The top pane has the price of the Dow Jones Industrial Average in candlestick format. Applied to those prices are several indicators - some moving averages and a set of Bollinger Bands. The middle pane has an MACD indicator. The bottom pane has an RSI indicator.

The prices are from the data that is installed in the default database named DATA. The chart is displaying Daily data, one bar for each trading day.

To display the data in weekly format, click the **Weekly** view icon in the View toolbar.

To choose a new symbol to plot:

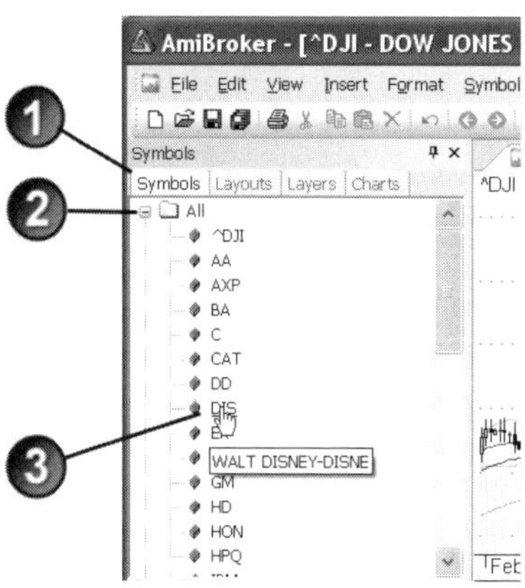

1. Click the **Symbols** tabbed menu.
2. Expand the **All** category by clicking on the + sign. The list will expand to show all of the ticker symbols in the database.
3. Click one of the entries, say DIS.

Since the charts were last displayed using weekly bars, they remain in weekly bars when the new symbol is plotted.

Return the chart to daily bars by clicking on the **Daily view** icon in the View toolbar.

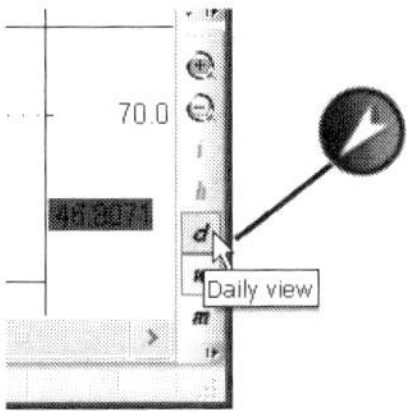

Using the **Scroll Bar** in the lower right corner of the window, scroll back in time (to the left) to display earlier data.

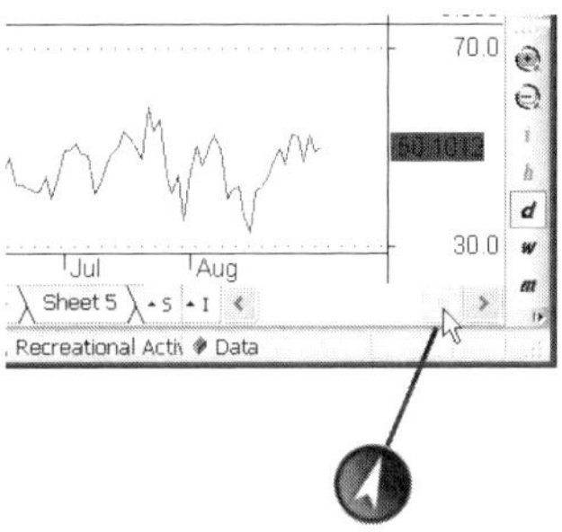

Using the **Zoom In** icon on the View toolbar, zoom in to see fewer data bars, but in more detail.

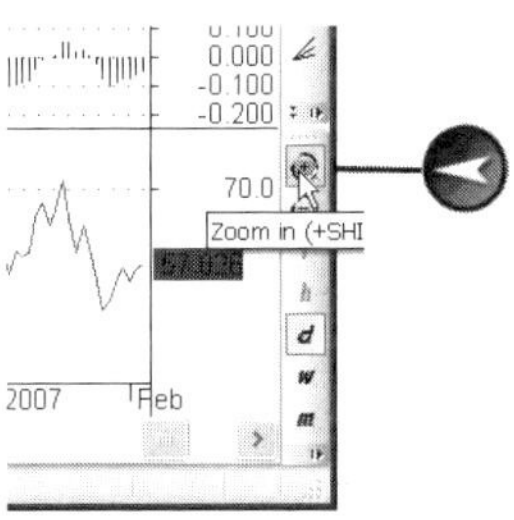

Zoom back out using the **Zoom Out** icon on the View toolbar. (There is no graphic for this step.)

To exit AmiBroker, using the **File** pull-down menu, select **Exit**.

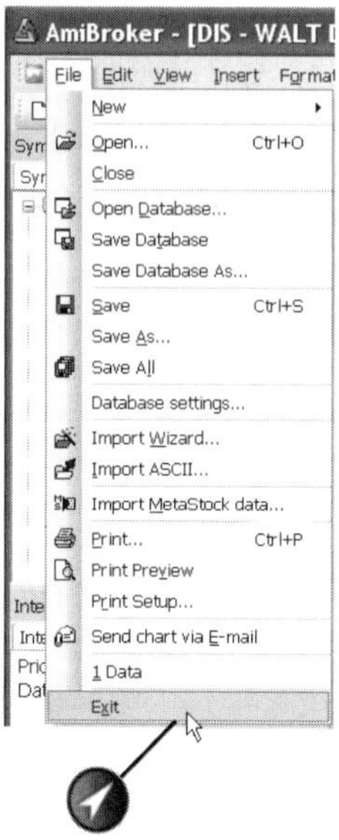

EXAMPLE 2 - APPLY A TRENDLINE

In this example, you will apply a trendline, resize panes, and move a trendline.

Start AmiBroker and plot the data for GE (General Electric) using Daily bars.

Resize the panes to give the chart more screen real estate.

1. Move your mouse slowly across the vertical bar between the top pane and the Symbols window. Watch for the cursor to change from a single large arrow to two small arrows on either side of two vertical lines.
2. When you have the new cursor, left-click, hold the mouse button down, drag the vertical divider to the left, release the mouse.

Pick the points you want to use for your trendline. One technique is to connect two or more bottoms. For this example, we will use the low on April 24, 2007 and the low on July 11, 2007. That line passes very close to the bottom on June 8, 2007, so the line is supported by three bottoms.

Use your mouse to select the Extended Trendline Tool from the Draw toolbar.

The cursor will change to a small crosshairs. Position the cursor at the low on April 24, 2007. The ToolTip box will display the information about the bar your cursor is hovering over. When it is in the correct place, left-click your mouse.

Move your mouse, with no buttons held down, to the low on July 11, 2007. The ToolTip will tell you where you are.

When you are satisfied with the position of your second point, left-click your mouse. The trendline will be drawn between the two points you selected and extended to both the right and left. You will see two small red squares at the points you used to define the trendline.

If you want to move one of the end points, hover your mouse over the red square until it becomes a two-headed arrow. Then left-click, drag the square to the position you want, and release the mouse button.

If you want to move the whole trendline, hover your mouse over the trendline between the two red squares until it becomes a four-headed arrow. Then left-click, drag the trendline to the position you want it, and release the mouse button. The trendline will maintain its angle and be parallel to its original position.

Scroll, zoom, change to weekly - do whatever you want to with the chart - the trendline will remain anchored at the two red squares and change with the chart.

If you have a registered version of AmiBroker, the trendline will be saved when you exit. If you are unregistered, no changes are saved.

The techniques for placing and moving a trendline apply to most of the tools on the Draw toolbar.

Exit AmiBroker.

Example 3 - Plot a Moving Average

In this example, you will insert a new pane with a new price series, overlay it with a moving average, and modify the moving average.

Start AmiBroker. You will see the normal chart window with three panes.

If necessary, resize the panes so that you can see the Charts tabbed menu.

Follow these steps to insert a price series in a new pane into the window:

1. Click the **Charts** tab.
2. Expand the Basic Charts category by clicking on the +.
3. Right-click **Price**, which brings up the context menu.
4. Left-click **Insert**.

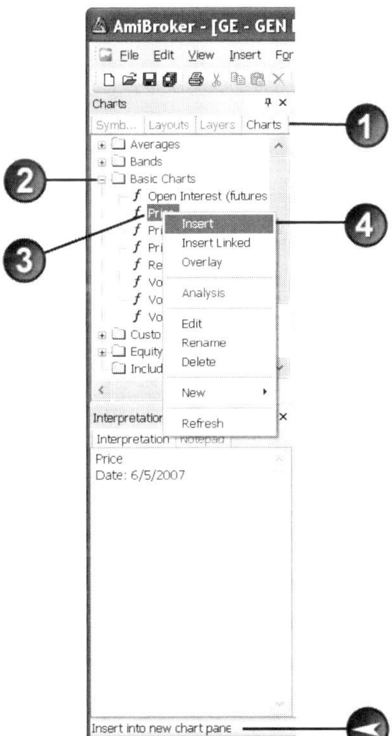

Note the tip at the bottom of the window that tells you what this command will do.

A new pane is opened as the bottom pane and the price series is plotted in candlestick format.

A properties dialog box is also opened. Click **OK** to close it.

Move your mouse slowly over the divider between the new pane and the one above it until the cursor changes to two parallel lines with two small arrows. Use this cursor to resize the new pane to make it bigger.

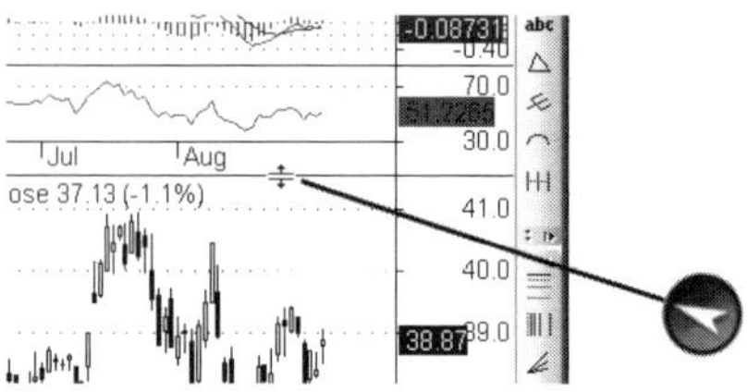

Left-click in the new pane to be certain that it is active (or selected, or has the focus).

Follow these steps to apply an Exponential Moving Average to the Price series:

1. Click the **Charts** tab.
2. Expand the **Averages** category.
3. Right-click **EMA - Exponential Moving Average,** which brings up the context menu.
4. Left-click **Overlay**.

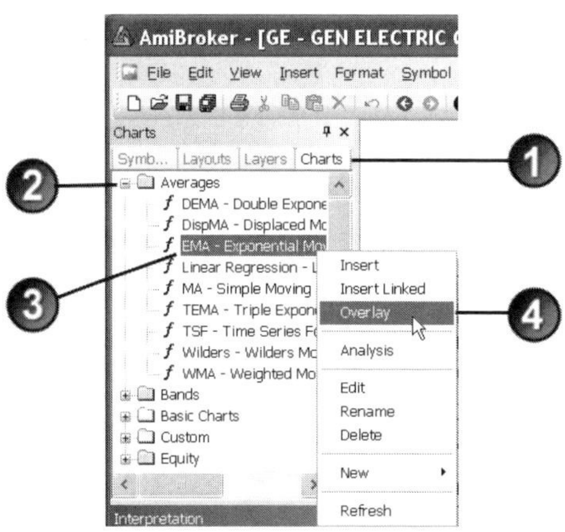

An exponential moving average, based on the price series, is plotted in the same pane and with the same scale as the price series.

A properties dialog box is also opened.

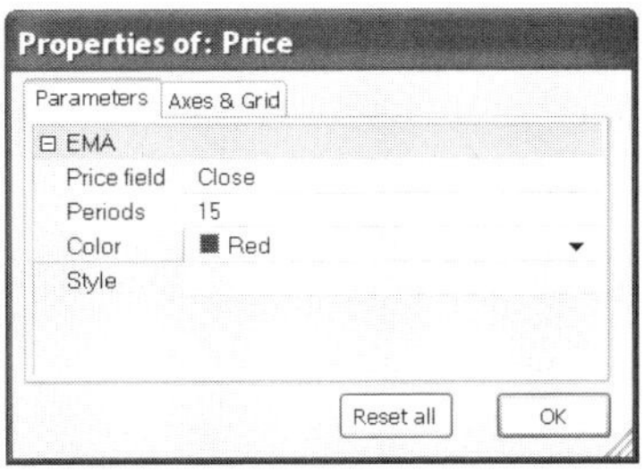

If you are satisfied with the parameter values, Click **OK**. If you want to change one or more of them, follow these steps.

To change the length of the moving average, click in the area to the right of the Periods field. Then either:

- Type a numeric value for the length.
- Use the slider to adjust the length.

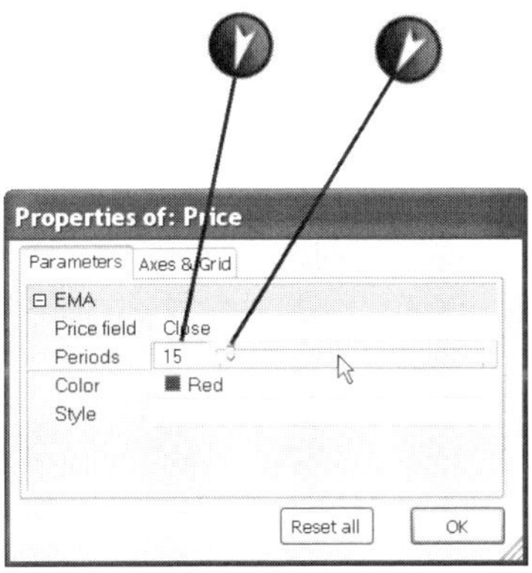

As you change the length of the moving average, the line that plots the moving average changes immediately to reflect the new length parameter. Move the slider and watch the red line. As the length is shorter, the moving average responds quickly and hugs the prices more closely. As the length increases, the moving average is smoother, but lags behind when the price series changes.

To change the color of the line used to plot the moving average, click in the area to the right of the Color field. A color chart will appear and you can choose the color you prefer.

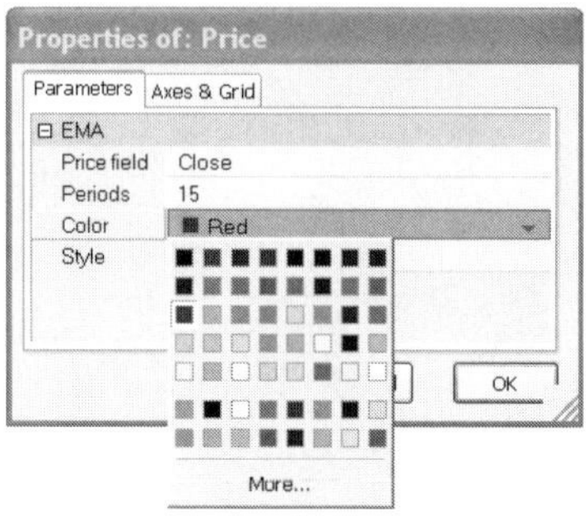

To change the type of line, click in the area to the right of the Style field. A pull-down menu will give you choices such as dashed, dotted, and thick.

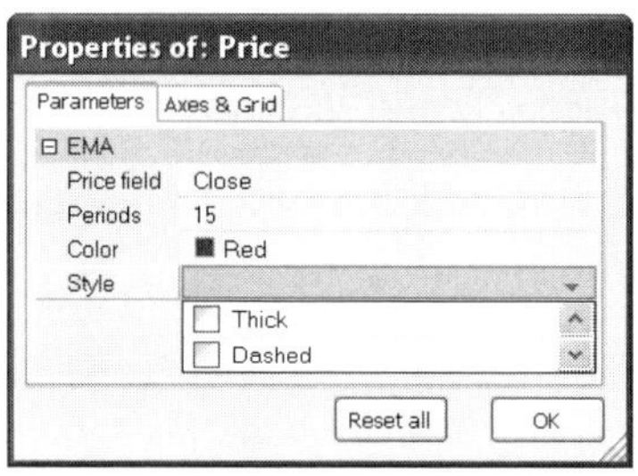

The Axes and Grid Tab also has some parameters that can be changed, but skip them for now.

If you have a registered version of AmiBroker, the window, including the new pane with the price series and moving average, will be saved when you exit. If you are unregistered, no changes are saved.

The techniques used to modify the moving average are also applicable to many of the indicators on the Charts tabbed menu.

Exit AmiBroker.

Example 4 - Make a Watchlist

In this example you will make a watchlist, modify it, and use it to display the charts of each member.

Start AmiBroker.

Follow these steps to learn about Watchlist Number 0:

1. Click on the **Symbols** tabbed menu.
2. Expand the **Watchlist** category.
3. Hover your mouse over **List 0**.

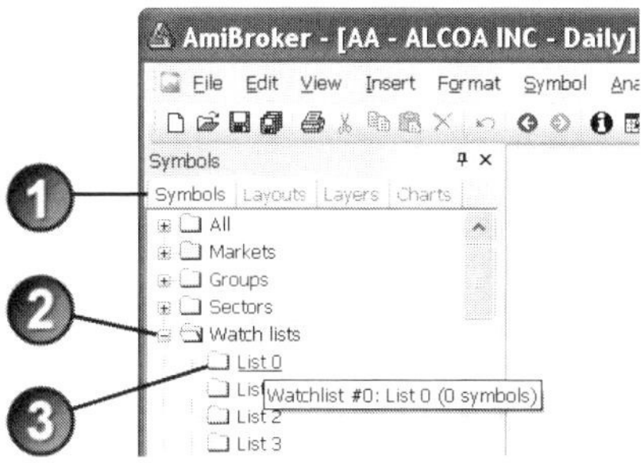

A message informs you that there are 0 symbols in List 0.

Follow these steps to add three ticker symbols to Watchlist 0:

1. Right-click **List 0**. The context menu will open.
2. Left-click **Type-in symbols**.

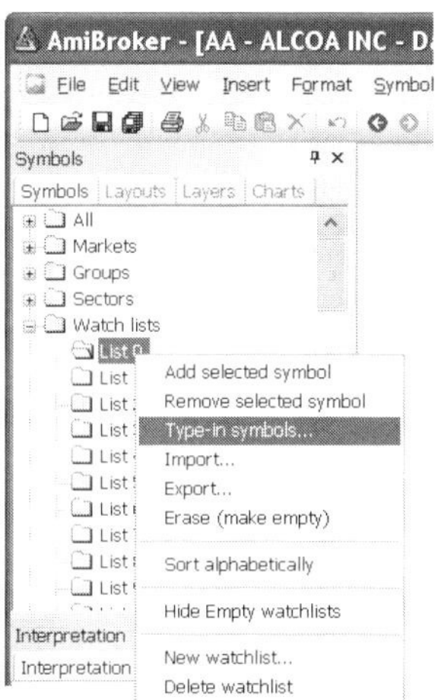

A dialog box will open, inviting you to Type symbols into watchlist.

1. Type in IP,DD,AA. Use all capital letters and separate the symbols with commas.
2. Click **OK**.

Expand **Watchlist 0** and note that it now has three members.

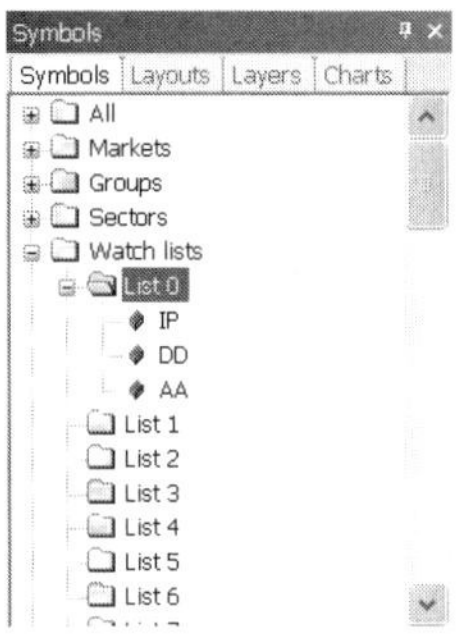

Rename **Watchlist 0** to something more meaningful, say Basic Materials:

1. Click the name, **List 0**.
2. Wait a few seconds.
3. Click **List 0** again. The name field will be selected.

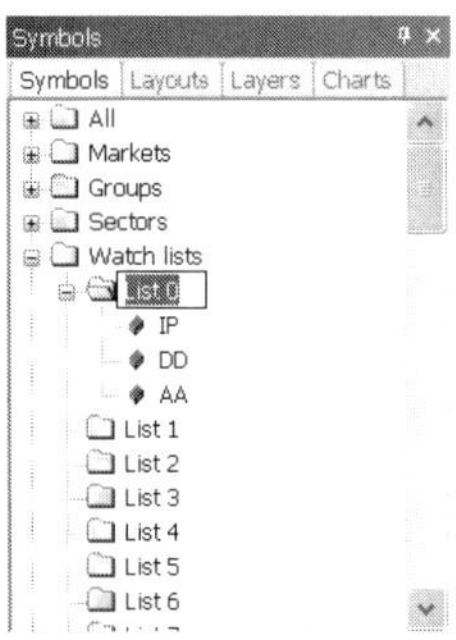

4. Type the new name, **Basic Materials**.
5. Press **Enter**. The watchlist has been renamed.

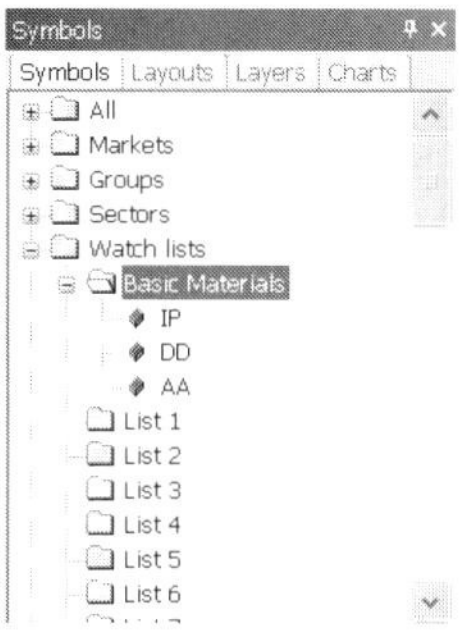

Add a symbol to the watchlist:

1. Right-click the name of the watchlist, **Basic Materials**. A context menu opens.
2. Left-click **Type in symbols**. A dialog box opens.
3. Type in the additional symbol(s), say XOM. The watchlist has four members.

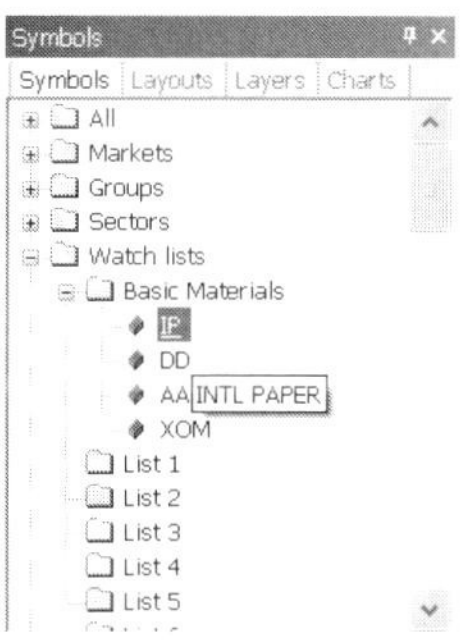

To use the watchlist to rapidly review the charts of its members:

1. Left-click the first member of the list, IP. The chart for International Paper will be displayed.
2. Press the **keyboard cursor-down-arrow key**. The chart of the next member, DuPont, will be displayed.
3. Continue through the watchlist.

Exit AmiBroker.

Example 5 - Run an Exploration

In this example, you will use the Formula Editor, and write and run an Exploration. For this exploration, the AFL program checks a watchlist to see how many stocks are at new 10 day highs or new 10 day lows. There is also a short introduction to Automatic Analysis.

Start AmiBroker.

Formula Editor

First, use the Formula Editor to write and save an AFL program.

Open the Formula Editor:

1. Click the **Analysis** pull-down menu.
2. Click **Formula Editor**. The Editor window will open.

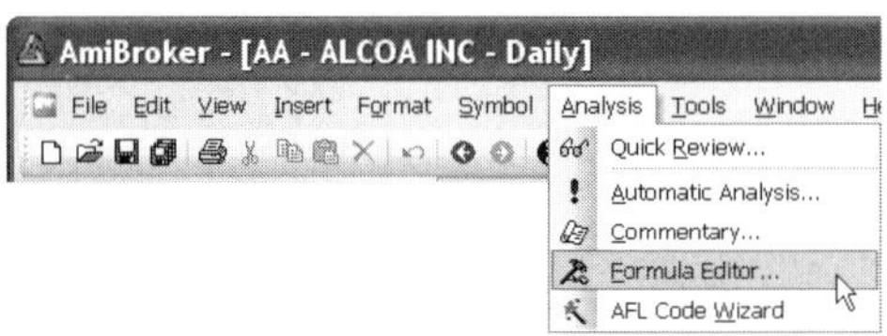

3. Expand the Editor window enough to give yourself room to work.
4. Type the AFL code into the window so that it matches the example below.

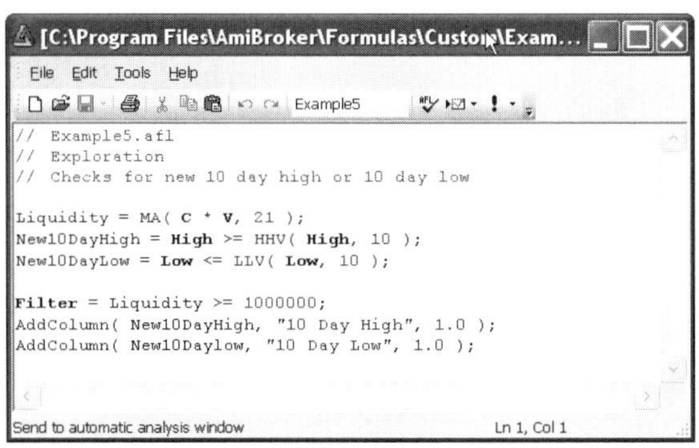

5. Using the Editor's **File** pull-down menu, select **Save As**.
6. The Save In directory should already be Custom. If it is not, navigate to: C:\Program Files\AmiBroker\Formulas\Custom.
7. For the File Name, type **Example5.afl**.
8. Click **Save**. (This works even if you are using an unregistered version of AmiBroker.)

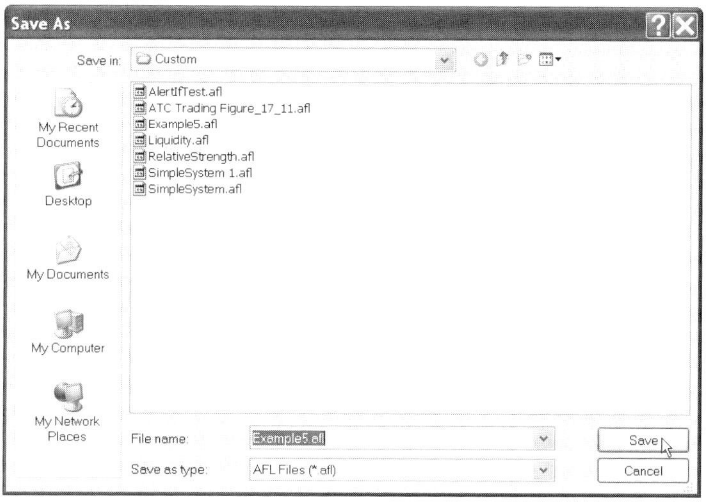

Any time you want to modify or edit this program:

1. Use the Formula Editor's **File** menu, select **Open**.
2. Choose **Example5.afl.**
3. Click **Open.**

Exploration

Next, use Example5.afl as an Exploration.

1. Using the **Analysis** pull-down menu, select **Automatic Analysis.**

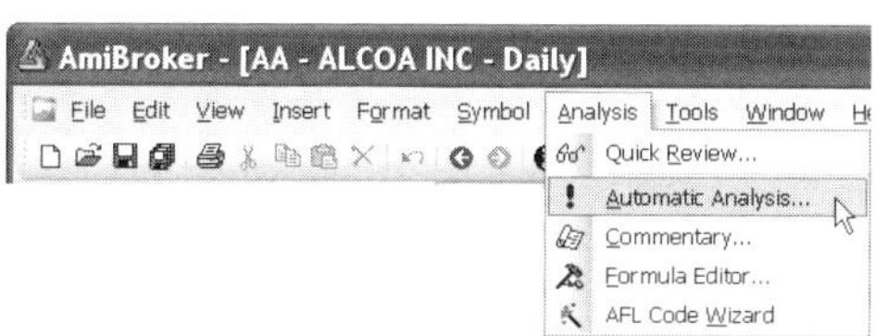

In the Formula File area:

(In this example, the program you want to use is already loaded, so the next few steps are not necessary. But, you need to know how to load an afl program into Automatic Analysis. These steps show how to load whatever program you want to use. We will re-load Example5.afl.)

1. Click **Pick**.

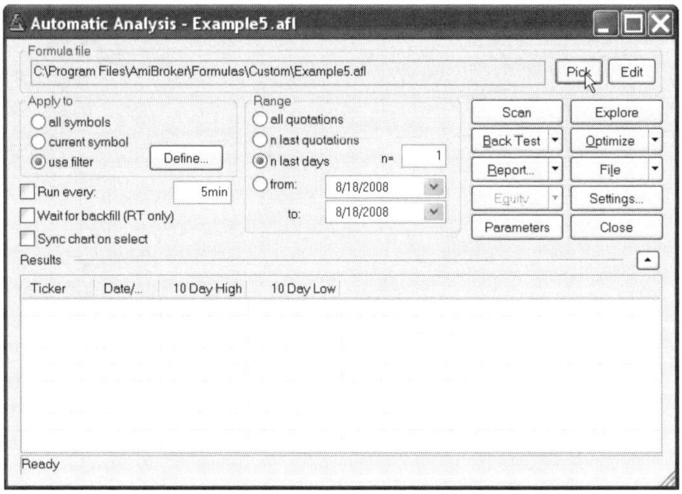

2. Navigate to the AmiBroker\Formulas\Custom directory. (You are probably already there, but use the usual techniques to move around in the directory structure.)
3. Select **Example5.afl.**
4. Click **Open.**

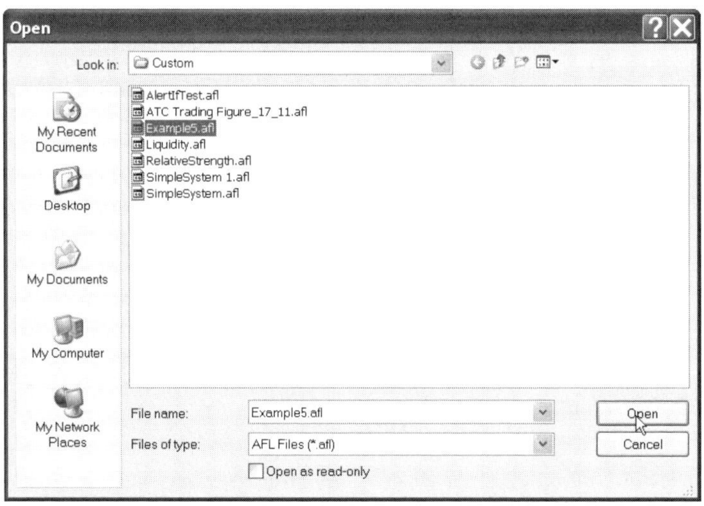

As you can tell from the Formula File box, you now have Example5.afl loaded into Automatic Analysis.

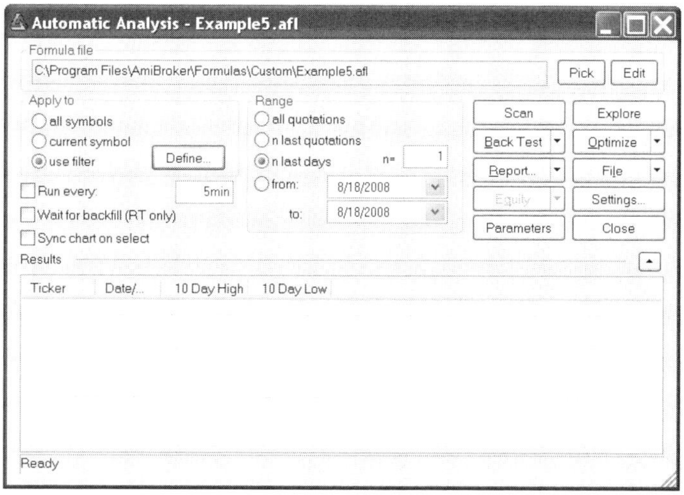

Automatic Analysis is the screen from which you will run the formula-based analysis techniques. These are the quantitative techniques, as compared with the visual and graphical techniques of applying trend-lines and looking for chart patterns. There are four major components of Automatic Analysis:

- Explore - used to search for conditions that are interesting, and produce reports with columns of data. For example, search for all instances of the stochastic oscillator being below 20 for two days. Compute and report the price change over the next three days.
- Backtest - used to test a trading system using historical data. Backtests can be performed on individual stocks or on portfolios of stocks. You have complete control over the account size, how many positions are held at any time, how much to invest in each position, when to buy, and when to sell. The output is a report, a plot showing arrows at the the buy and sell points, and a plot of the account equity.
- Optimize - used to select the best values for the parameters in the trading system. In a moving average crossover trading system, optimization could be used to select the best values for the lengths of the moving averages.
- Scan - after the system has been designed and is ready to be traded, scan through the symbols that are in the universe of possible holdings to see if there are new buy or sell signals.

Depending on what instructions you have written in your afl program, you may be able to run exactly the same program in all of the Automatic Analysis components. Chapter 9, Analysis, goes into each of these in much more detail.

For now, fill in just what is necessary to complete the Exploration.

In the Apply to area:

1. Click **use filter.**
2. Click **Define**. A Filter settings dialog box will appear.
3. Click the **Exclude** tab.
4. Click **Clear**.
5. Click the **Include** tab. Click **Clear** again.
6. Using the **Watchlist** pull-down menu, select the **Basic Materials** watchlist.
7. Click **OK**.

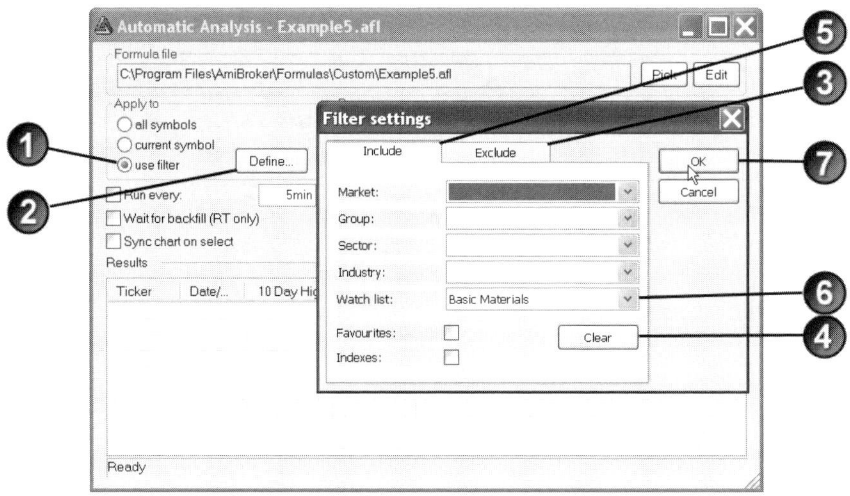

In the Range area:

1. Click **n last days**.
2. For n=, enter **2.**

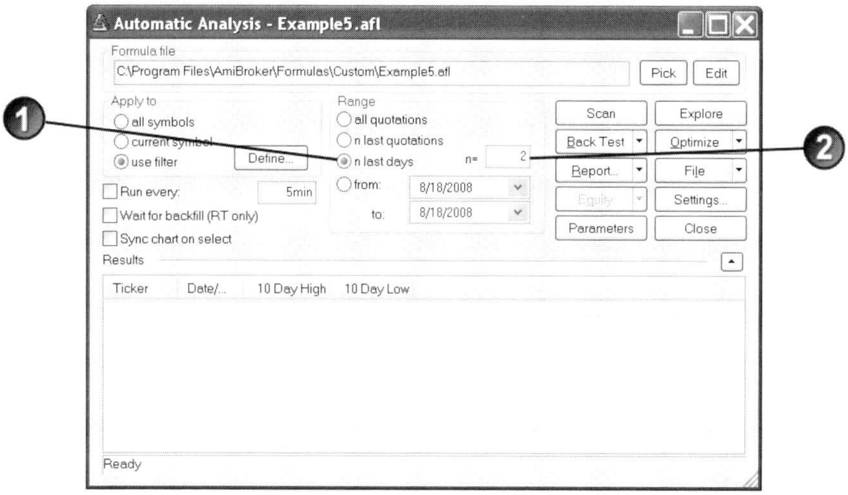

1. Click **Explore**.

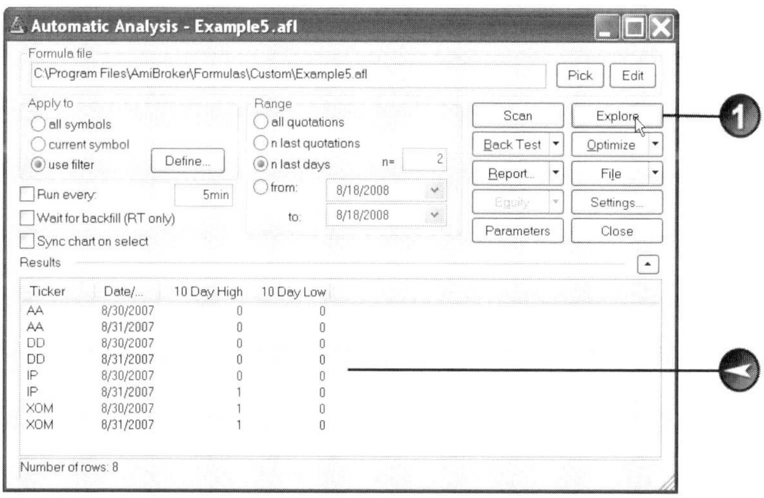

The results of the Exploration appear in the Results window. IP reached a new 10 day high on 8/31/2007 (the last day of data), and XOM reached a new high the final day and the day before.

Exit AmiBroker.

Example 6 - Run a Single Stock Backtest

In this example, you will use the Formula Editor to write the AFL code for a simple trading system, run the code as a Backtest on the historical data of one stock, review the results, plot the Buy and Sell arrows, plot the Equity Curve.

Start AmiBroker.

Using the Automatic Analysis pull-down menu, select the Formula Editor. The Formula Editor will open, ready to accept your new AFL program. Type it in so it matches this one:

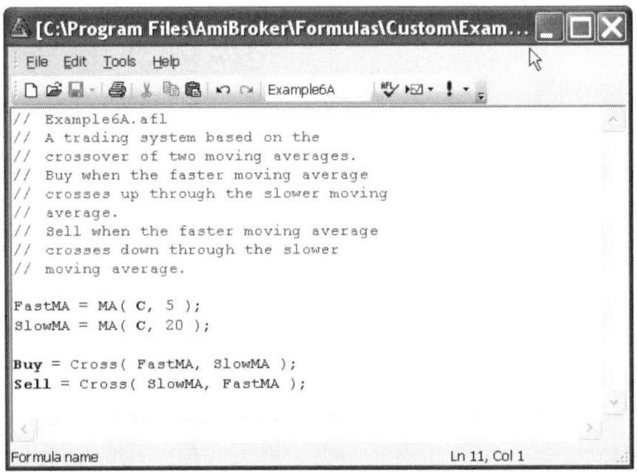

Save it in the Custom directory as Example6A.afl.

In setting up Automatic Analysis, you need to load the file you want processed. Example 5 showed one way to do that. Here is another - a shortcut that coordinates Formula Editor with Automatic Analysis.

Formula Editor has a toolbar. The rightmost icon in the toolbar is an exclamation point. If you hover your mouse over it, the tooltip says Analysis. When you click that icon, the file that is open in Formula Editor is loaded into Automatic Analysis and Automatic Analysis is opened. This makes for an easy cycle of editing and analyzing. After the edit, click the Analysis icon and go directly on with the analysis.

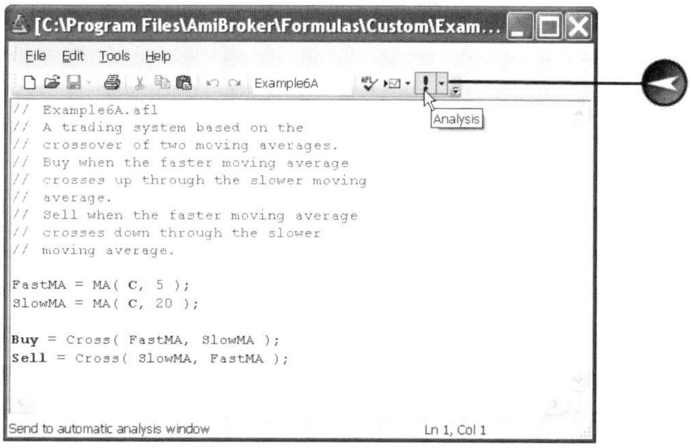

Backtest

In the **Formula file** area, load **Example6A.afl.**

Make CAT, Caterpillar Corporation, the active symbol and display it in the chart window with daily bars.

To run the backtest:

1. In the **Apply** to area, click **current symbol**.
2. In the **Range** area, click **all quotations**.
3. Click **Backtest** (ignore the pull-down menu for now).

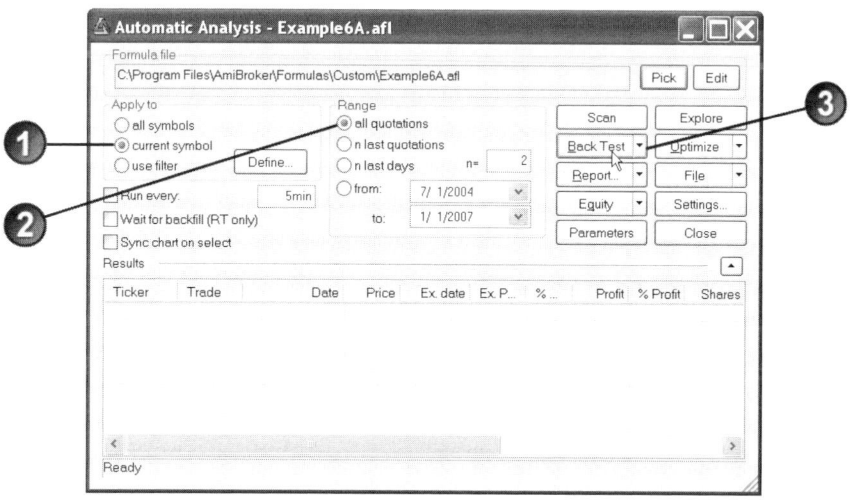

The trade-by-trade results appear in the Results window.

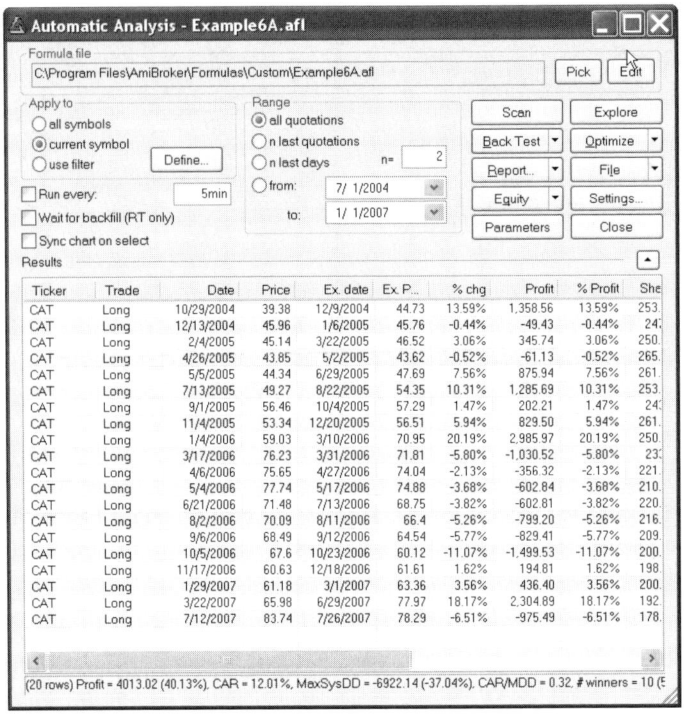

In addition to the trade-by-trade results, there are three ways you might like to review the results - the report, buy and sell arrows, and equity curve. Each will be discussed in turn.

REPORT

1. Click **Report.**

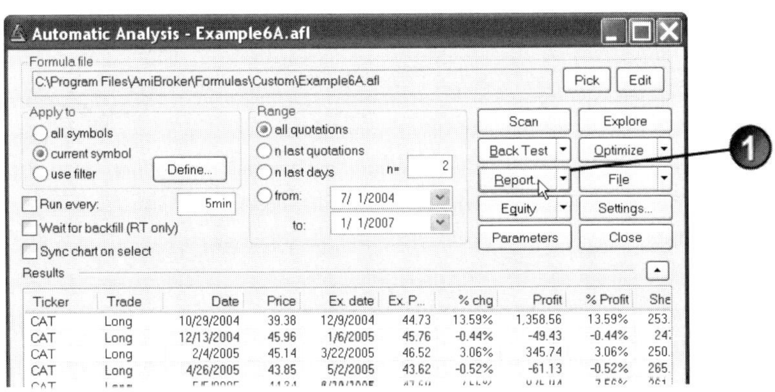

The report gives results summarized by all trades, long trades, short trades; all trades, winning trades, losing trades; and a series of overall fitness metrics, and risk and reward statistics.

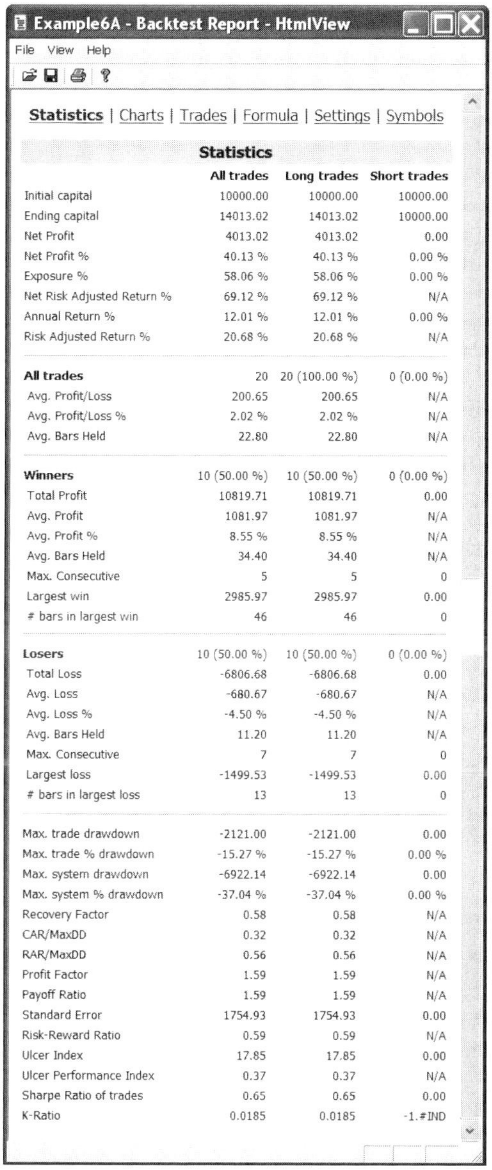

Example6A - Backtest Report - HtmlView

File View Help

Statistics | Charts | Trades | Formula | Settings | Symbols

Statistics

	All trades	Long trades	Short trades
Initial capital	10000.00	10000.00	10000.00
Ending capital	14013.02	14013.02	10000.00
Net Profit	4013.02	4013.02	0.00
Net Profit %	40.13 %	40.13 %	0.00 %
Exposure %	58.06 %	58.06 %	0.00 %
Net Risk Adjusted Return %	69.12 %	69.12 %	N/A
Annual Return %	12.01 %	12.01 %	0.00 %
Risk Adjusted Return %	20.68 %	20.68 %	N/A
All trades	20	20 (100.00 %)	0 (0.00 %)
Avg. Profit/Loss	200.65	200.65	N/A
Avg. Profit/Loss %	2.02 %	2.02 %	N/A
Avg. Bars Held	22.80	22.80	N/A
Winners	10 (50.00 %)	10 (50.00 %)	0 (0.00 %)
Total Profit	10819.71	10819.71	0.00
Avg. Profit	1081.97	1081.97	N/A
Avg. Profit %	8.55 %	8.55 %	N/A
Avg. Bars Held	34.40	34.40	N/A
Max. Consecutive	5	5	0
Largest win	2985.97	2985.97	0.00
# bars in largest win	46	46	0
Losers	10 (50.00 %)	10 (50.00 %)	0 (0.00 %)
Total Loss	-6806.68	-6806.68	0.00
Avg. Loss	-680.67	-680.67	N/A
Avg. Loss %	-4.50 %	-4.50 %	N/A
Avg. Bars Held	11.20	11.20	N/A
Max. Consecutive	7	7	0
Largest loss	-1499.53	-1499.53	0.00
# bars in largest loss	13	13	0
Max. trade drawdown	-2121.00	-2121.00	0.00
Max. trade % drawdown	-15.27 %	-15.27 %	0.00 %
Max. system drawdown	-6922.14	-6922.14	0.00
Max. system % drawdown	-37.04 %	-37.04 %	0.00 %
Recovery Factor	0.58	0.58	N/A
CAR/MaxDD	0.32	0.32	N/A
RAR/MaxDD	0.56	0.56	N/A
Profit Factor	1.59	1.59	N/A
Payoff Ratio	1.59	1.59	N/A
Standard Error	1754.93	1754.93	0.00
Risk-Reward Ratio	0.59	0.59	N/A
Ulcer Index	17.85	17.85	0.00
Ulcer Performance Index	0.37	0.37	N/A
Sharpe Ratio of trades	0.65	0.65	0.00
K-Ratio	0.0185	0.0185	-1.#IND

Buy and Sell Arrows

In order to see the green buy arrows and red sell arrows:

1. **Right-click** in the top pane of the chart window - the pane with the price series. A context menu will open.
2. Left-click **Parameters.**

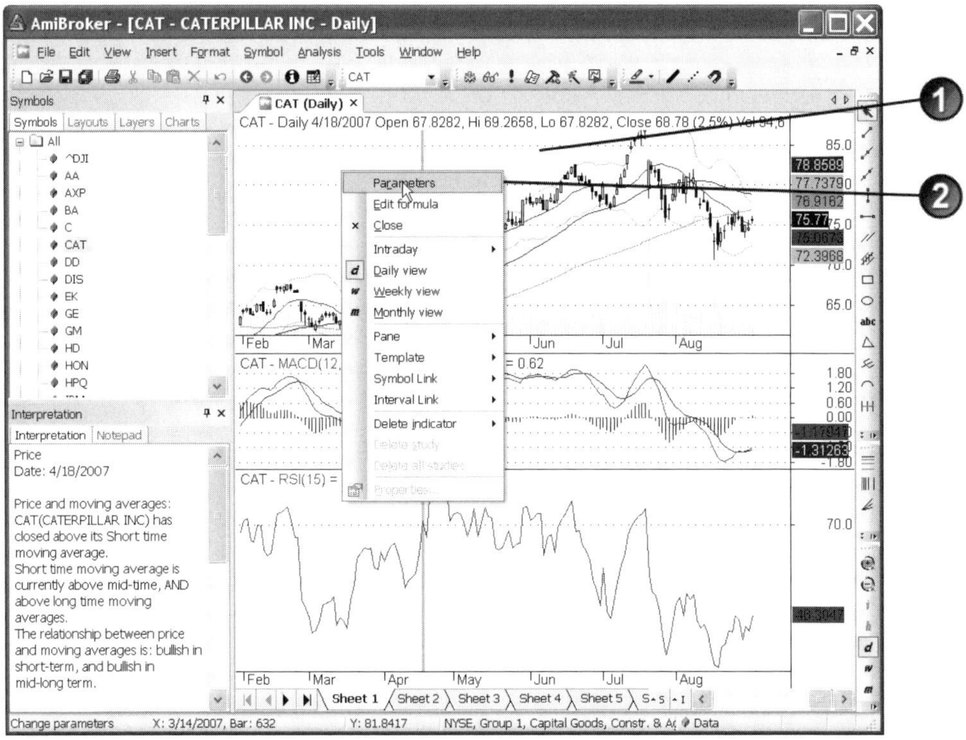

A parameter dialog box will open.

1. Click the **Axes & Grid** tab.
2. Scroll down until you find **Show trading arrows**. Click in the area to the right until it is set to **Yes**.
3. Click **OK**.

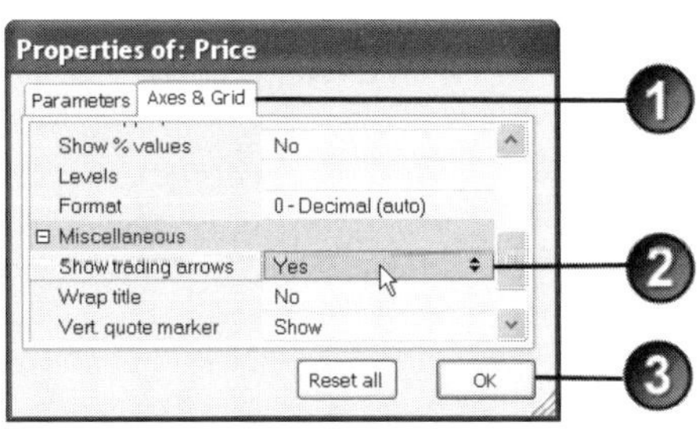

Return to the Results window.

1. Right-click **any row** in the results table. A context menu will open.
2. Left-click **Show arrows for actual trades**.

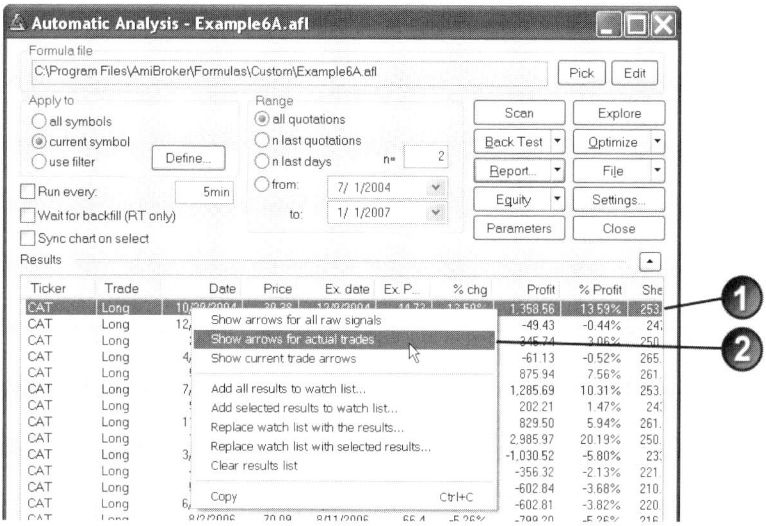

Move the Automatic Analysis window out of the way. You will see the green upward-pointing arrows at the bars where Buy signals occurred and red downward-pointing arrows at the bars where the sell signals occurred.

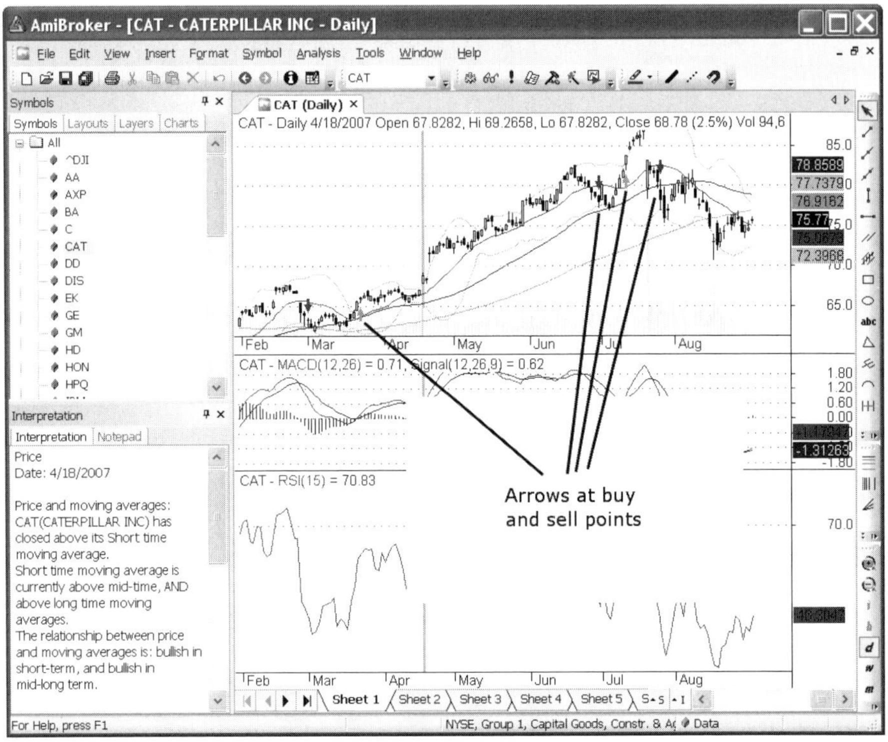

Equity Curve

1. In **Formula Editor**, open **Example6A.afl.**
2. Add the lines necessary to make it like the code shown below.
3. Save it as **Example6B.afl.**
4. Click the **Apply indicator** icon in the toolbar.

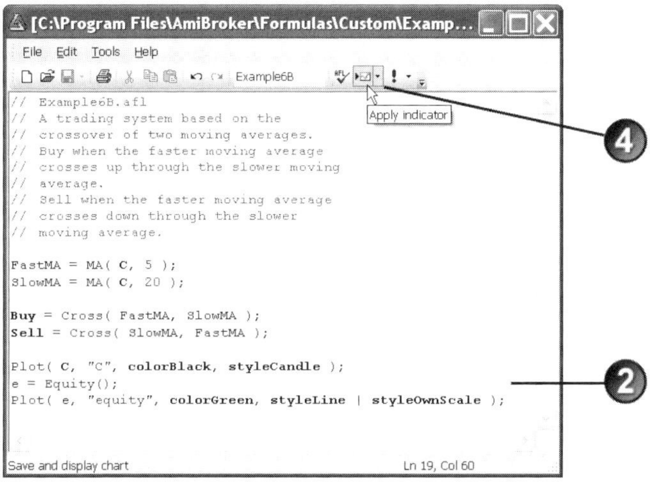

A new pane will appear as the bottom pane in the chart window. It contains two plots - the price series as black candlesticks, and the equity for an account that started at $10,000 as a green line. The final equity for CAT is $14,013.

Using the **Symbols** tabbed menu, click on **any symbol.**

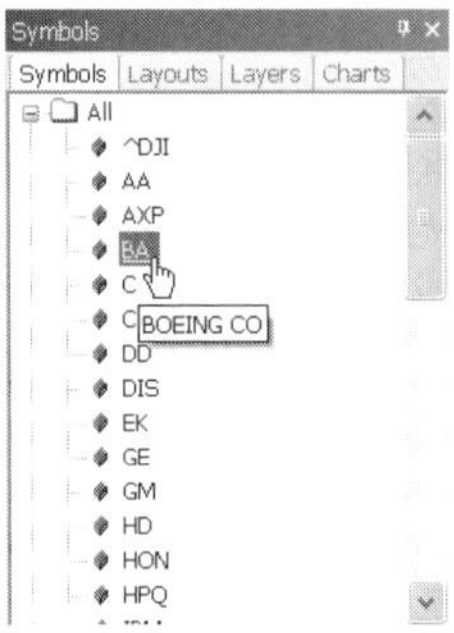

Note that the bottom pane will show the new price chart and the equity curve that results from applying that trading system to that symbol. It is not necessary to click Backtest - when the new symbol is selected, all of the indicators in all of the panes are recomputed and re-displayed, including the result of applying the trading system. The final equity is in the green box in the right-hand margin.

Exit AmiBroker.

Example 7 - Run a Portfolio Backtest

This example will apply a trading system to a portfolio and view the portfolio equity.

Start AmiBroker.

Using the **Formula Editor:**

1. Open **Example6A.afl.**
2. Change it to make it agree with the program shown below.
3. Save the new program as **Example7A.afl.**

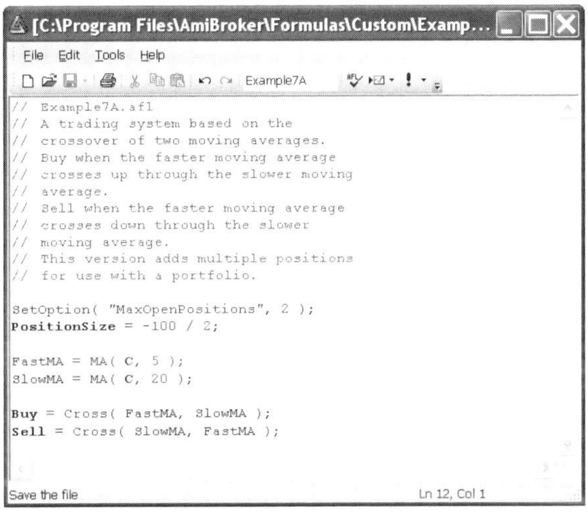

4. Click the **Analysis** icon. Example7A is loaded into Automatic Analysis as the Formula File.
5. In the **Apply to** area, check **Use filter**.
6. Click **Define**.
7. Clear all fields.
8. On the **Include** tab, **Watchlist** entry, select **Basic Materials**.
9. Click **OK**.
10. In the **Range** area, check **All quotations**.

11. Click the **Settings** button. The Backtester Settings dialog box will open.
12. Click the **Report** tab.
    1) Click **Trade list**.
    2) Click **OK**.

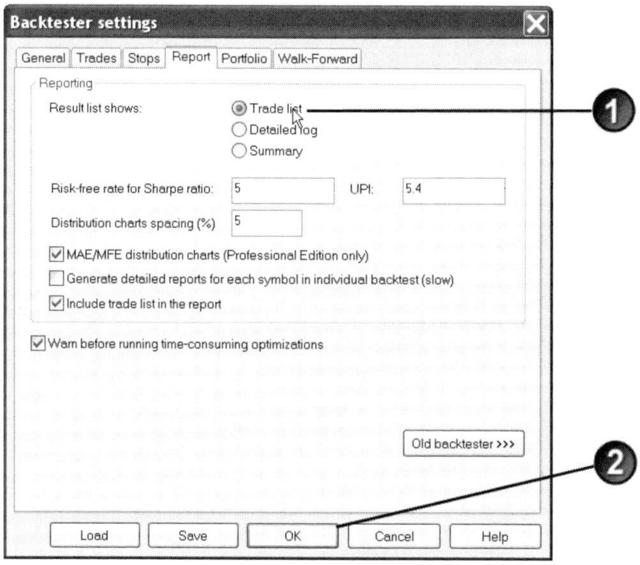

13. Click **Backtest**. The Results window shows trades.

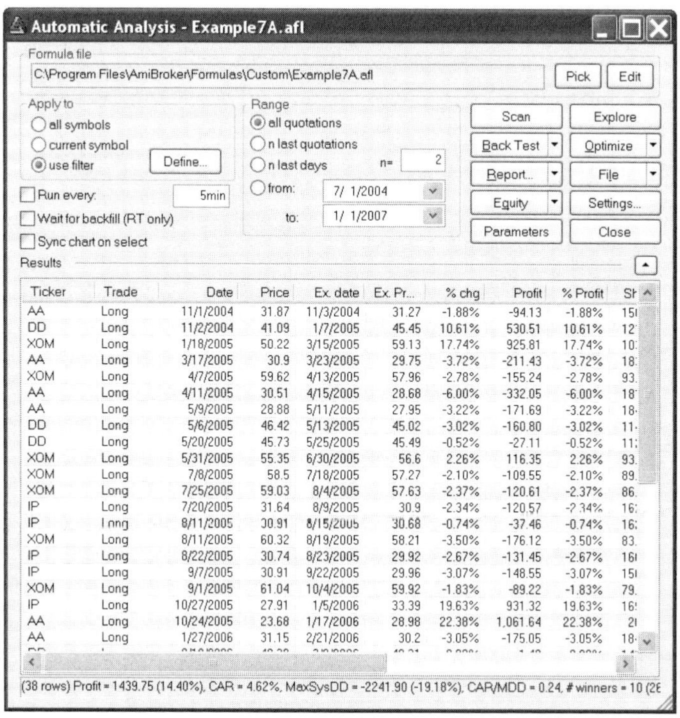

Looking carefully at the results, there are times when there are two positions, times when there is only one, and times when there are none. When processing a portfolio backtest, AmiBroker starts out with 100% cash and knows the maximum number of positions it can hold simultaneously (2 in this case). The code in Example7A tells AmiBroker to divide the available funds into two, giving each 50%. The trading system is applied to each of the ticker symbols in the watchlist. When the first (in chronological order) buy signal occurs, one position is taken and as many shares as possible are purchased with 50% of the funds. Whenever there is a sell signal for that symbol, those shares are sold and the cash made available for another purchase. In the mean time, when the next buy signal occurs, the remaining 50% is used to buy shares in that stock. The buying and selling, using funds and returning funds, continues for the length of time specified.

Plotting the portfolio equity gives a graphic view of the process.

1. Click the **Equity** button.

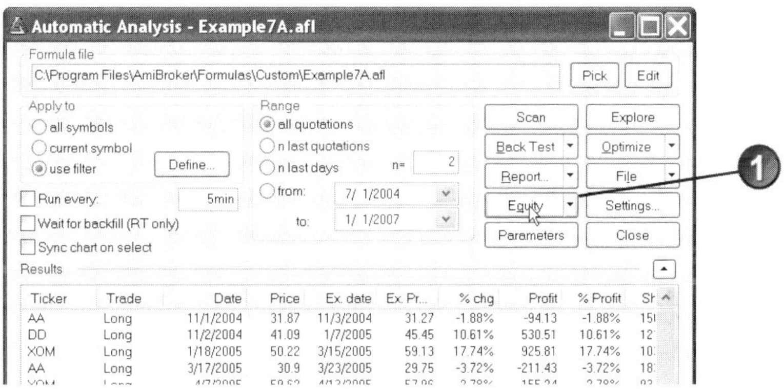

A new pane opens at the bottom of the chart window.

The two positions are evident, one above the other. When a stock position is held, the plot is blue. When cash is held, the plot is green. The chart shows the ebb and flow of positions - sometimes two, other times one, other times none. The dark brown area at the bottom shows the drawdown. For this run, the final equity was $11,439. The drawdown when the test period ended was $831. Drawdown is the decrease in equity from the highest high equity value.

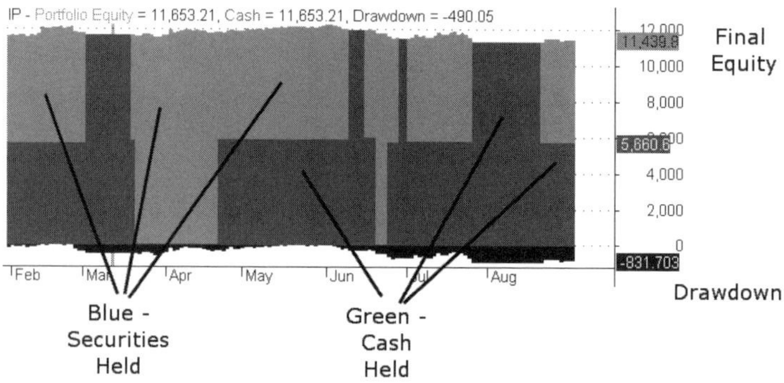

To read the report for this run, click the **Report** button.

This run was made allowing a maximum of two simultaneous positions. The code can be modified to study the effect of allowing fewer or more positions. Using Formula Editor, modify Example7A to agree with the code that follows, and save it as Example7B.afl.

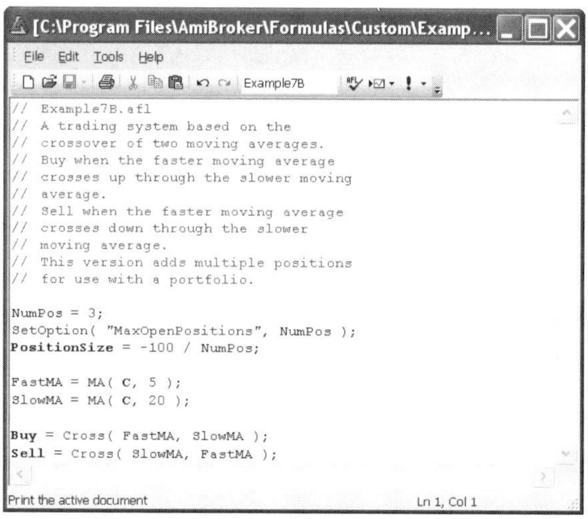

Now just change the value of NumPos, click Analysis, and look at the equity chart.

Exit AmiBroker.

Example 8 - Optimize a Trading System

In this example, the moving average crossover system introduced in Example 6 is studied in more detail. The values for the two moving average lengths were guesses. In this example they will be chosen through an optimization process. An optimization is an organized search, done in such a way that a large number of alternative values of parameters are considered. For each set of values, the trading system is tested. The report produced at the conclusion of the optimization lists the profitability and other statistics for each of the sets of values tested. The hope is that the best set of values will continue to be profitable in the future.

Start AmiBroker.

Using **Formula Editor**:

1. Open **Example6B.afl.**
2. Change it to agree with the code shown below.
3. Save the new program as **Example8A.afl**.

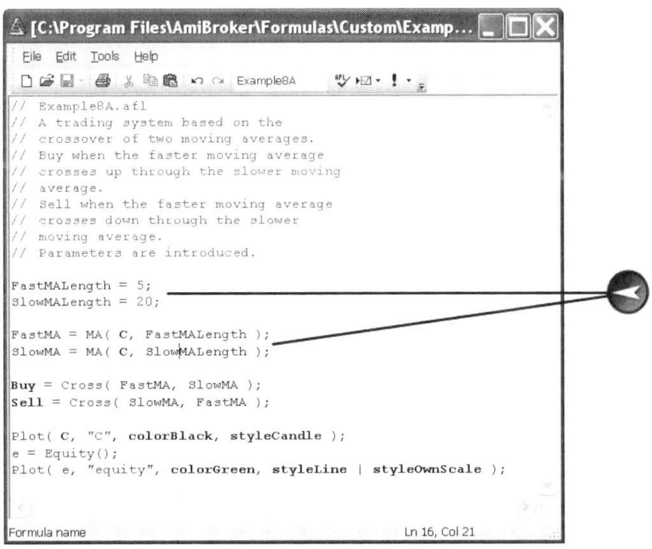

Compare the statements that were changed.

Example6B:
```
FastMA = MA ( C, 5 );
```

Example8A:
```
FastMALength = 5;
FastMA = MA ( C, FastMALength);
```

A numeric value is assigned to a variable FastMALength, then that variable is used to calculate the moving average. Computationally, Example6B and Example8A are the same. But using the variable gives some flexibility.

Optimize Function

AmiBroker has a built-in function, Optimize, that has this format:

```
V = Optimize ("Name", Default, Initial, Final,
                    Increment);
```

- V is a variable that will be assigned one value at a time, and a series of values as the search takes place.
- Name is the name of the variable as it will appear in the reports.
- Default is the value that will be assigned to V if the run is only a backtest (or Explore or Scan), not an optimization.
- Initial is the first value to be tested during the optimization.
- Final is the last value to be tested.
- Increment is the step taken from one iteration to the next.

For example, `V = Optimize ("Length", 5, 1, 20, 1);`

- If only a backtest is being run, V will be assigned the value 5.
- If an optimization is being run, V will be assigned 20 values, one for each optimization pass. The first will be 1, then 2, then 3, and so forth, with the final value assigned to V being 20. From 1 to 20 in steps of 1.

Example8B.afl

Using the Formula Editor, modify Example8A so that it agrees with the code shown below. Then save it as Example8B.afl.

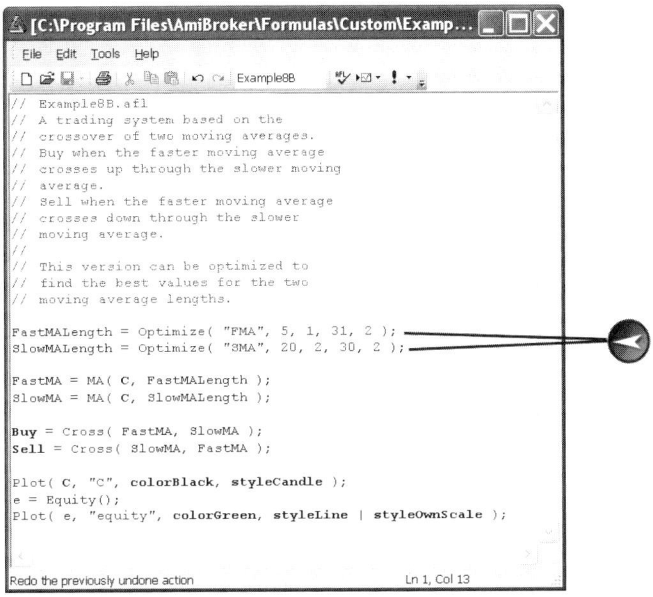

Note there are two Optimize statements. The first will assign values from 1 to 31 in steps of 2 to the variable named FastMALength. The second will assign values of 2 through 30 by steps of 2 to the variable named SlowMALength. There are 16 different values in the first statement, 15 different values in the second statement. To do the complete search, FastMALength will be set to 1, then all 15 values of SlowMA-Length tried; following that, FastMALength will be set to 3, then all 15 values of SlowMALength will be tried; and so forth until all 240 combinations have been tested.

To perform the Optimization test, in Automatic Analysis:

1. In **Formula File**, load **Example8B.afl**.
2. Load CAT as the current ticker symbol.
3. In **Apply to**, click **Current symbol.**
4. In **Range**, set the **From date to 7/1/2004**.
5. In **Range**, set the **To Date to 1/1/2007**.
6. Click **Optimize**.

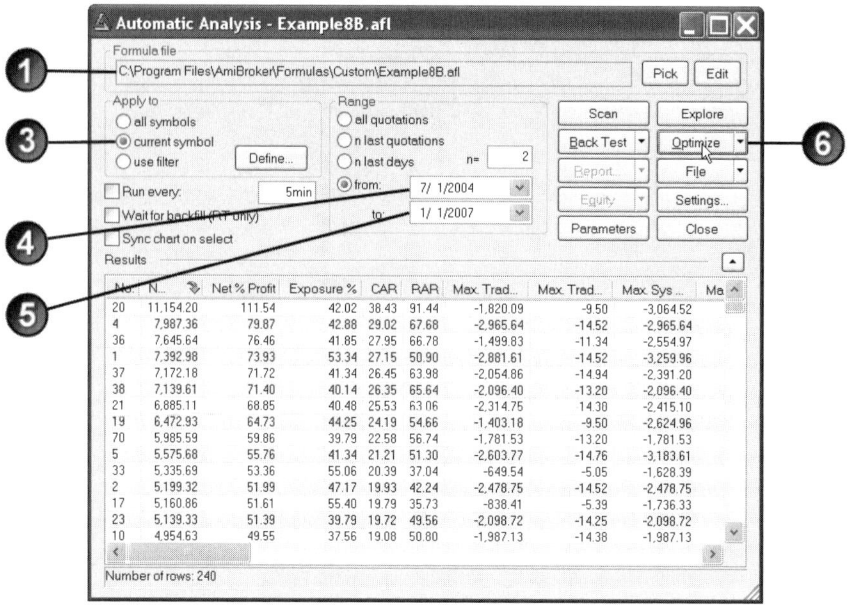

The Results window will fill with 240 rows, one for each combination of FastMALength and SlowMALength.

Sort the results according to some measure of the goodness that you like. In general, the measure of goodness is called a fitness function or an objective function. There are several fitness functions in the results that both reward equity growth and penalize drawdown. These include CAR/MDD, RAR/MDD, RRR, Ulcer Performance Index, and K-ratio. The results, sorted by RAR/MDD are shown in the next image.

Click the header of any column to sort by that column.

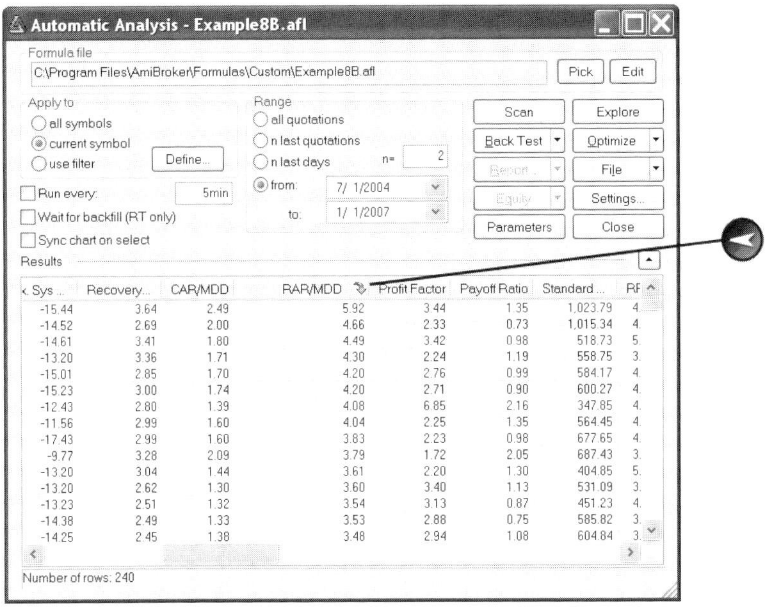

Scroll over to the far right and note the values of FMA and SMA that correspond to the best fitness value. They are FMA = 7, SMA = 4.

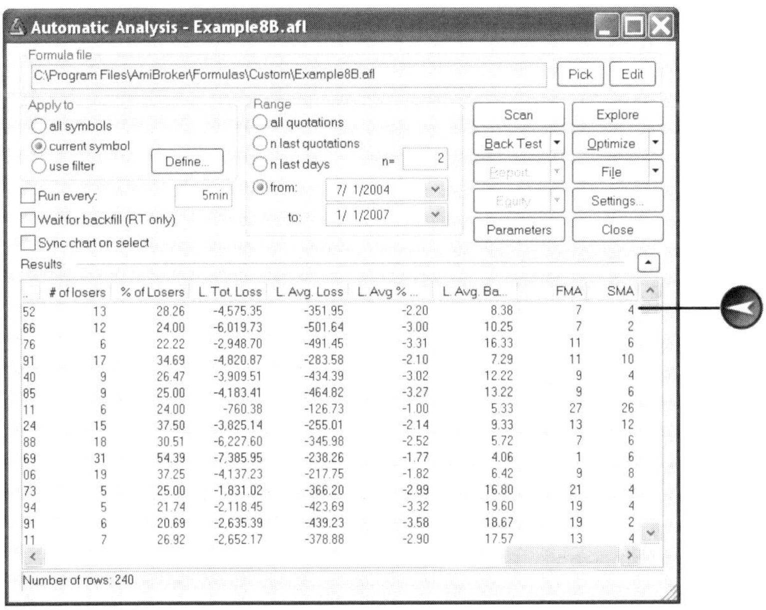

Return to Example8B.afl and enter those values as the defaults in the two optimize statements.

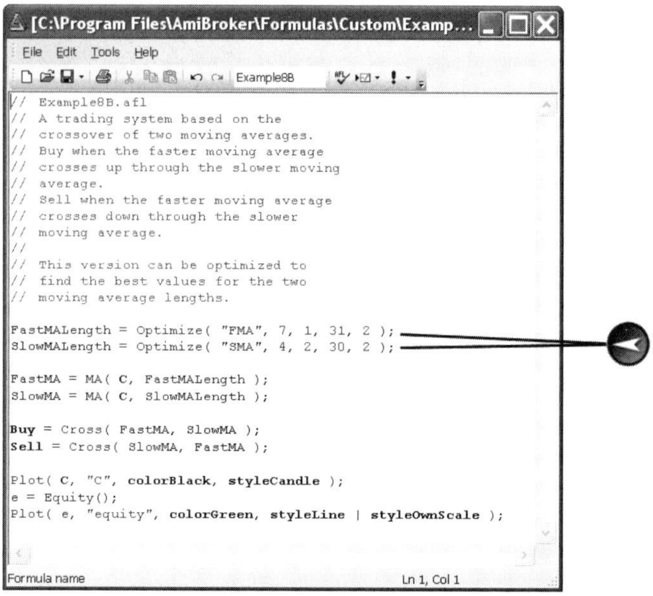

1. Save the program.
2. In Formula Editor, click Apply Indicator icon. Look at the chart showing the equity curve. It shows a final equity of $21,154.

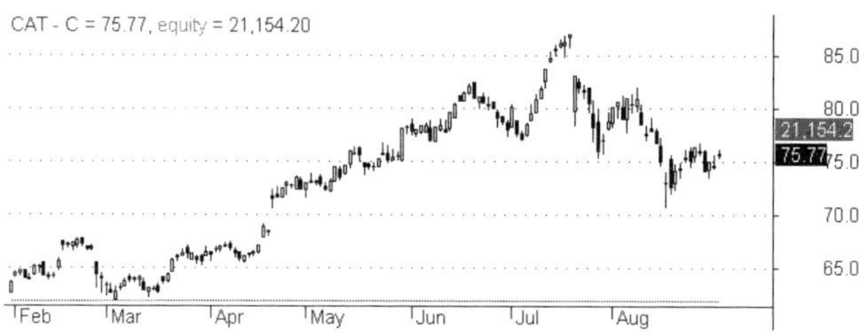

But the right side of the equity curve is flat. That is because the optimization was run up to 1/1/2007. The data from 1/1/2007 through the end of the file, 8/31/2007, was saved to do an out-of-sample test.

1. In **Automatic Analysis**, set the **To Date to 8/31/2007**.
2. Click **Backtest**. The final equity is $22,447.

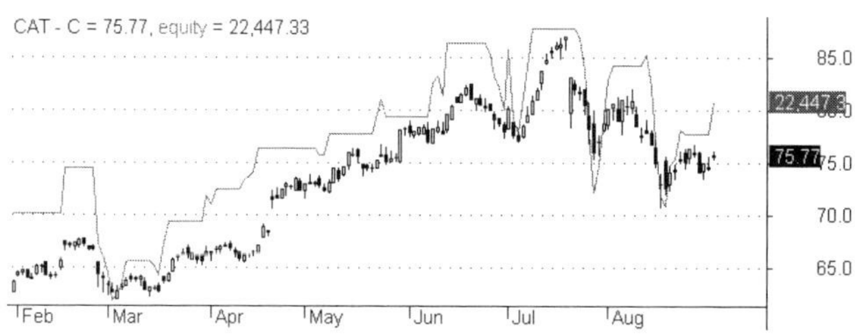

The system was optimized using in-sample data from 7/1/2004 through 1/1/2007. Those results are good. In-sample results are *always* good. We do not stop playing with the trading system until they *are* good.

The real test of a trading system is how well it performs on data that was not used during the optimization - the out-of-sample data. The results from this test are encouraging - the out-of-sample test was profitable.

An Important Observation

Take another look at the results of the optimization. The length of the "fast" moving average is 7; the length of the "slow" moving average is 4. Traditional technical analysis tells us that we should buy when the fast moving average crosses up through the slow moving average. The result of the optimization run in this example suggests that is not always the case. In this example, we are buying when the fast moving average crosses down through the slow moving average.

Buy when the fast moving average is rising is a trend following system - buy when recent prices are rising faster than older prices. This works well for very stable price series, such as high-yield bond funds.

Buy when the fast moving average is falling is a mean reversion system - buy when prices are weak, anticipating that they will return to their mean. This works well for very active price series.

Exit AmiBroker.

Example 9 - Perform Walk Forward Validation

In this example, you will use the walk-forward technique to validate a trading system.

In applying technical analysis, several assumptions are made:

- Patterns exist that precede profitable trading opportunities.
- The trading system can detect those patterns.
- The patterns persist beyond the in-sample period used to develop the system for a long enough time that we can trade profitably.

When any trading system is developed, the process involves searching through a set of data, looking for the patterns. The data that is searched is called the in-sample data. The results obtained by using the system on the in-sample data are always good. The system developer does not stop looking until the results are good.

The proof that a trading system has found a recognizable pattern, and has not just mined the data, is performance on data that has never been used to develop the system. That never-before-used data is called the out-of-sample data.

The walk forward process consists of several iterations of:

1. Developing a system over a set of in-sample data.
2. Testing the profitability over a set of out-of-sample data.
3. Stepping forward in time to a new set of in-sample data and a new set of out-of-sample data.

The combined results of all the out-of-sample data are used to decide whether the system recognizes profit potential or not.

There are two major advantages to using walk forward testing:

- The in-sample period can be relatively short, giving the system an opportunity to stay in synchronization with the underlying market.
- Each transition from in-sample to out-of-sample gives the developer one more data point. Eventually, when trades are made with real money, the decision to trade is a decision to trust the in-sample results. The greater the number of steps in the walk forward process, the greater the number of transitions from in-sample to out-of-sample the developer has seen. Each successful transition raises confidence that the system is a good one.

The following graphics might help understand the process.

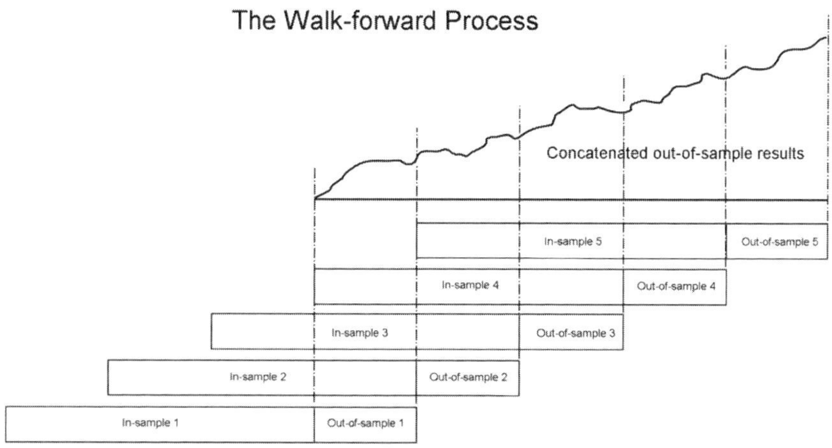

The decision whether to trade the system or go back to the drawing board is made after reviewing all the out-of-sample results.

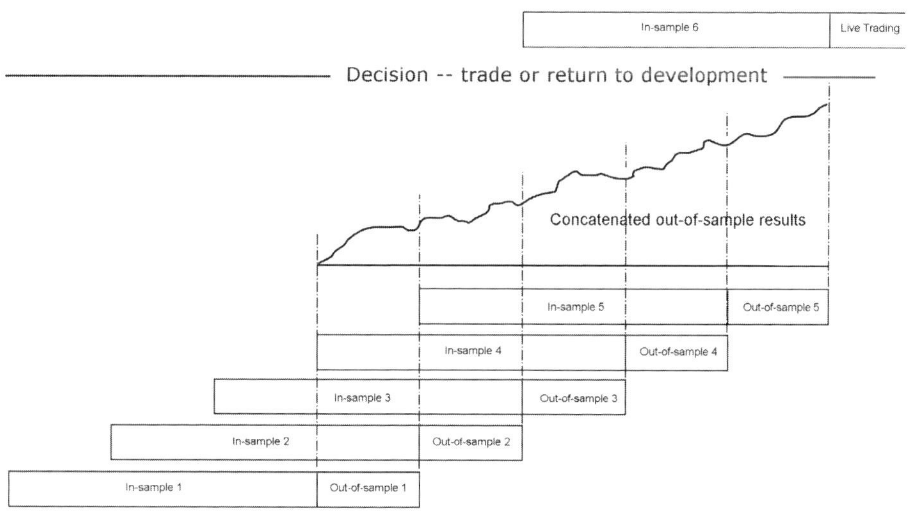

Start AmiBroker.

Load CAT using daily data.

Load Example8B.afl. No changes to the afl code are necessary.

In **Automatic Analysis**:

1. Click **Settings**.

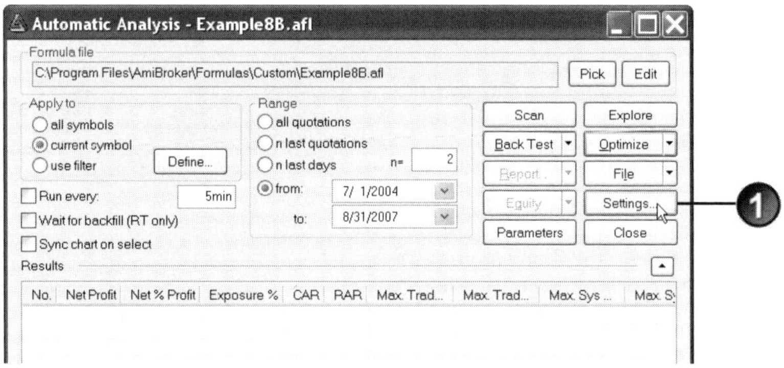

2. Click the **Walk-Forward** tab.
3. Click **Easy mode**.
4. Set **Start date to 7/1/2004**.
5. Set **End date to 1/1/2005**.
6. Set **Last date to 7/1/2007**.
7. Set **Step to 6**.
8. Use pull-down menu to select **Months**.
   Note that the in-sample and out-of-sample periods have been calculated and are listed in the window.
9. From the pull-down menu for **Optimization target**, select **RAR/MDD**.
10. Click **OK**.

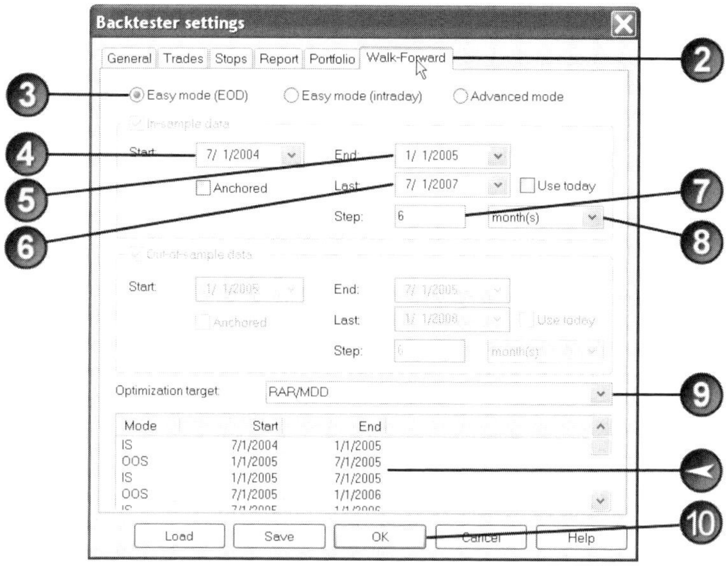

Back on Automatic Analysis:

1. Left-click the **arrow next to Optimize** to open the pull-down menu.
2. Click **Walk-Forward Optimization**.

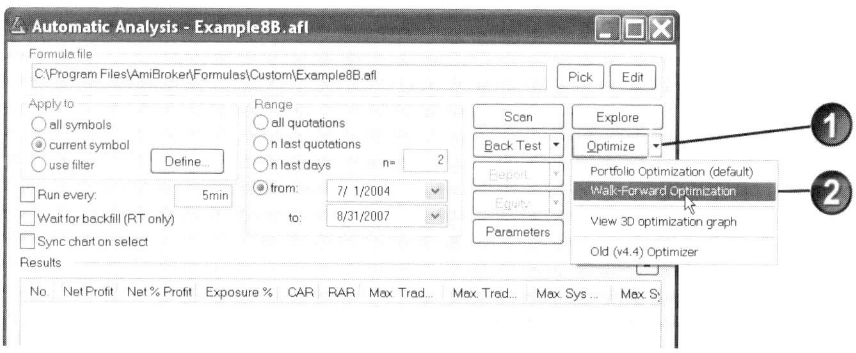

The optimization runs will start. There will be six steps. Each in-sample period is six months long. The first in-sample period starts 7/1/2004. The sixth in-sample period ends 7/1/2007. The out-of-sample periods are also six months long and each immediately follows an in-sample period. There are five full out-of-sample periods. The sixth out-of-sample period begins 7/1/2007 and ends with the end of the data on 8/31/2007.

As the walk forward runs progress, pairs of lines are created and displayed in a tabbed window. The first line of each pair gives the results for the in-sample period. The second line gives the results for the associated out-of-sample period.

CAT (Daily) Walk Forward ×

Address file:///C:/Program%20Files/AmiBroker/WalkForward.htm Go Sync

Completed.

Mode	Begin	End	No.	Net Profit	Net % Profit	Exposure %	CAR	RAR	Max. Sys % Drawdown	CAR/MDD	RAR/MDD	FMA	SMA
IS	7/1/2004	1/1/2005	189	456.77	4.57	3.75	15.52	413.85	-0.19	82.70	2205.33	25	24
OOS	1/1/2005	7/1/2005	1	435.50	4.35	42.86	9.08	21.19	-8.87	1.02	2.39	25	24
IS	1/1/2005	7/1/2005	2	1394.11	13.94	46.03	30.49	66.24	-5.81	5.24	11.39	3	2
OOS	7/1/2005	1/1/2006	1	2046.48	20.46	45.67	45.27	99.12	-9.06	5.00	10.94	3	2
IS	7/1/2005	1/1/2006	5	3170.10	31.70	35.43	73.71	208.04	-4.70	15.68	44.24	9	2
OOS	1/1/2006	7/1/2006	1	532.24	5.32	36.00	11.22	31.16	-14.76	0.76	2.11	9	2
IS	1/1/2006	7/1/2006	1	3400.91	34.01	54.40	82.26	151.22	-4.13	19.93	36.63	1	2
OOS	7/1/2006	1/1/2007	1	-1194.34	-11.94	45.24	-22.85	-50.50	-15.85	-1.44	-3.19	1	2
IS	7/1/2006	1/1/2007	19	1869.60	18.70	52.38	41.83	79.87	-5.03	8.33	15.89	5	4
OOS	1/1/2007	7/1/2007	1	517.73	5.18	41.94	10.97	26.16	-6.27	1.75	4.17	5	4
IS	1/1/2007	7/1/2007	159	645.06	6.45	9.68	13.76	142.17	-1.03	13.42	138.64	29	20
OOS	7/1/2007	1/1/2008	1	-273.43	-2.73	34.09	-15.52	-45.52	-6.75	-2.30	-6.74	29	20

Ignore the in-sample profitability.

Add up the Net Profit from all the out-of-sample periods: $435 + 2046 +532 -1194 + 517 - 273 = $2063. $10,000 became $12063 in 2.666 years. The average percentage of time a position was held was 41%. The annual percentage return while in a position is 17.8%. All out-of-sample.

Look at the values that the optimization chose for FMA and SMA. They are: 25/24, 3/2, 9/2, 1/2, 5/4, and 29/20. In five of the six periods, the system itself chose to be a mean reversion system. The one period it chose to be a trend following system was the period of its biggest out-of-sample loss. It appears that trend following using a moving average crossover to signal entries and exits does not work well for CAT, but mean reversion is promising.

Because of the limited number of securities and the limited length of the historical data, the results achieved were not spectacular. When you have installed a more complete database, you will find systems and symbols that give better results than these.

This is an example, not a ready-to-use trading system. Although the results of this example are reasonable there are many factors beyond those described that should be taken into consideration in system design, testing, and validation. Do Not trade this system without performing your own tests and validations.

Exit AmiBroker.

Example 10 - Scan for Buy and Sell Signals

In this example, you will use the Scan feature to check for buy or sell signals.

Due to the limitations of the trial mode, it will be difficult to demonstrate realistic results of the Scan feature. Assume that Example8B is a validated trading system for all of the symbols in watchlist Basic Materials.

Scan combines a trading system with a watchlist to give a report telling you what buy and sell signals were generated for the symbols in the watchlist. The period of time this report covers is under your control, but it is usually just one or two days.

Start AmiBroker.

Load IP using daily data.

Load **Example8B.afl.**

In **Automatic Analysis**:

1. **Use filter** and select the **Watchlist Basic Materials**.

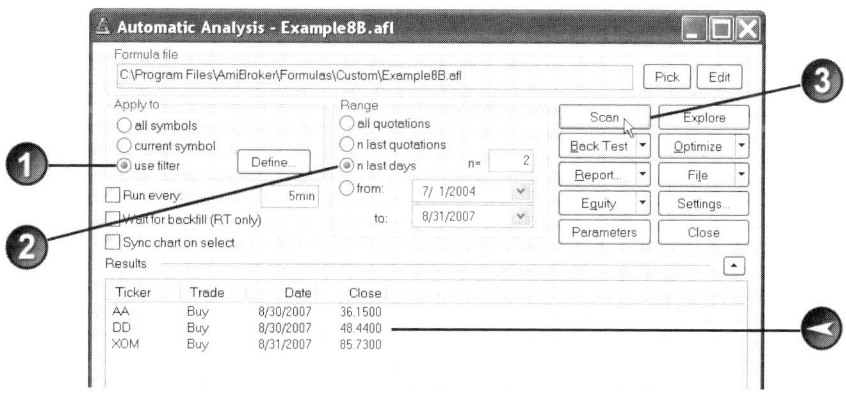

2. Set **n last days** with **n = 2.**
3. Click **Scan.**

The results appear in the results window. AA and DD had Buy signals on 8/30; XOM had a Buy signal on 8/31.

Exit AmiBroker.

Section II

Charting

Chapter 4

AmiBroker Chart Structure

In the earlier portion of this book, rather loose reference was made to databases, layouts, windows, charts, panes, drawing objects, and so forth. To fully understand AmiBroker, it is necessary to understand the structure into which these components fit.

- The top level component is a **Layout**.
- Each **Layout** is associated with a single **Database** when that layout is active.
- Each **Layout** consists of one or more **Windows**.
- Each **Window** has data for one **Symbol**.
- Each **Window** displays with one **Periodicity**.
- Each **Window** contains one or more **Sheets**.
- Each **Sheet** contains one or more **Panes**.
- Each **Pane** contains one or more **Chart**, **Formula**, or **Tool**.

You can have as many layouts as you wish. But only one layout can be active (open) at a time.

Layouts can be *local* or *global*. Local layouts are associated only with a specific database. Each local layout is stored in the database directory it is associated with, in the file named broker.workspace. Global layouts can be used with more than one database. Global layouts are stored in the AmiBroker\Layouts subdirectory.

Window Layouts

A window layout (that is, an AmiBroker window layout) is a complete set of one or more windows. Each window displays data for its own symbol, has its own display interval, its own size on the monitor, its own set of charts, its own panes, and its own charts and formulas.

The image below shows a 2-window layout. Each window has a different stock and a different set of indicator panes.

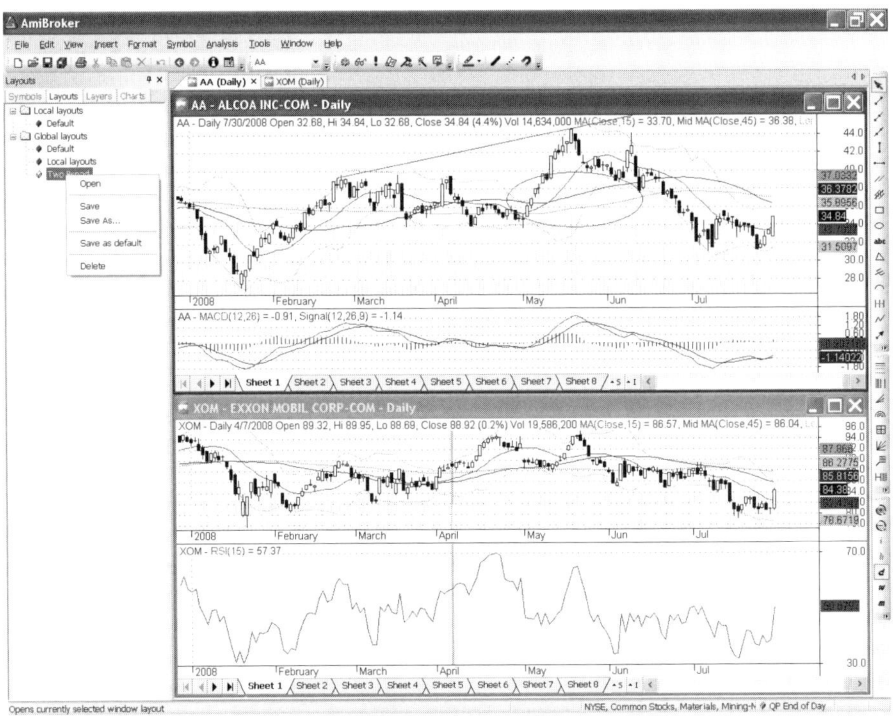

You can have an unlimited number of single or multiple-window layouts. Each can be a custom set up; they do not need to share anything. Switch between them by double clicking on the layout's name in the layouts tab.

The active layout can be automatically saved whenever the database is switched or AmiBroker is exited. To set this, use the Tools menu > Preferences > Miscellaneous. In the Auto-save area, Check the Layouts box. Information saved in layouts include: window sizes and positions, bar interval, symbol, chart sheets, panes, charts, formulas.

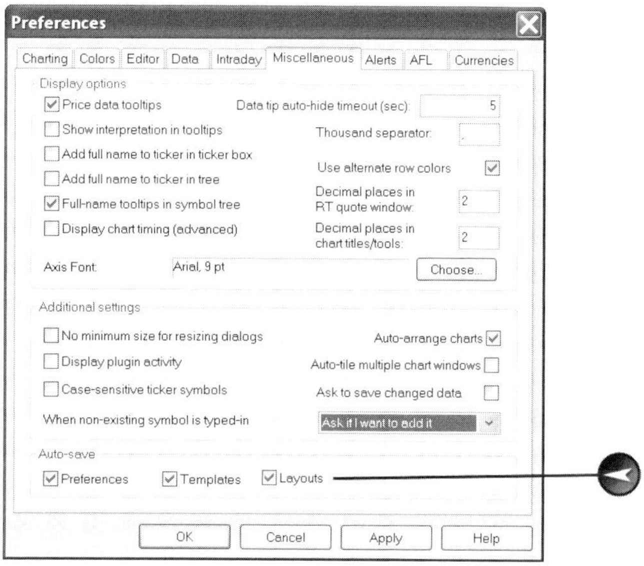

You can switch between multiple windows (within a layout) using either the Window menu and selecting the desired window from the list at the bottom of the menu, or using the new MDI tabs.

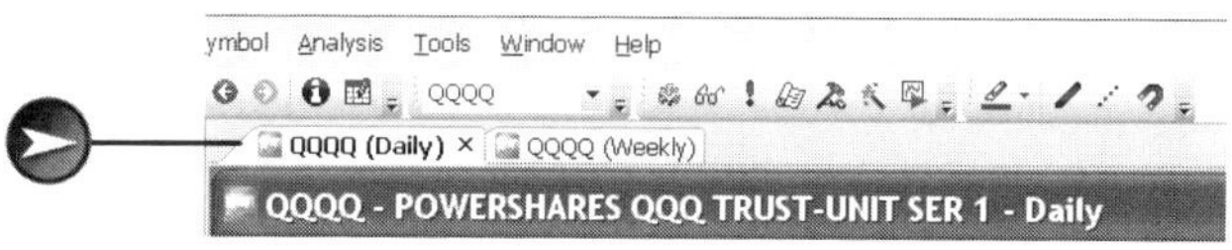

To begin with, a single window layout will probably be sufficient. You will need a multi-window layout if you want to :

- Display charts for more than one ticker symbol
- Display charts of different periodicity
- Display charts showing different range of bars.

While not necessary, you may want a multi-window layout in order to be able to float a window and move it to a second monitor.

Most of the concepts and techniques that are described in the pages that follow are applied to the active pane and are independent of the layout structure.

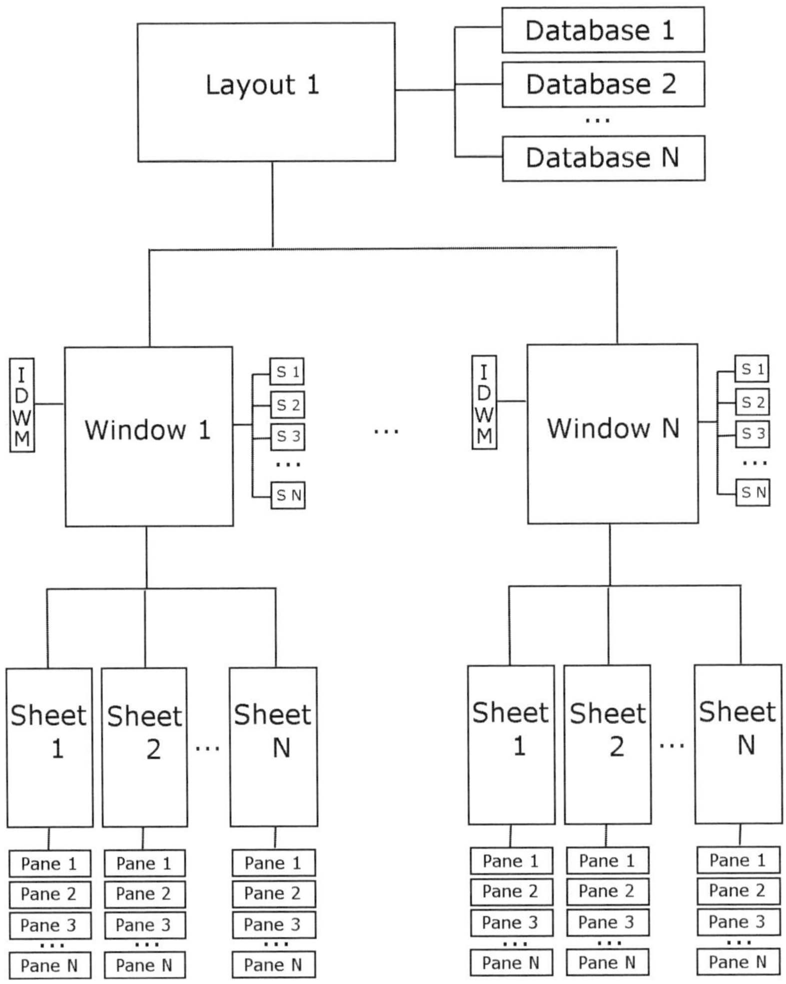
Layout 1
Database 1
Database 2
...
Database N
I D W M
Window 1
S 1
S 2
S 3
...
S N
...
I D W M
Window N
S 1
S 2
S 3
...
S N
Sheet 1
Sheet 2
...
Sheet N
Pane 1
Pane 2
Pane 3
...
Pane N

Block Diagram

On the left is a block diagram view of layouts, their components, and their relationship to databases.

One layout is shown. You can have as many layouts as you want. Only one layout can be open and active at a time. To make another active:

- Save the current database
- Open the new database
- Select the layout you want to use

Everything shown on the block diagram will change to reflect the new layout / database combination - all windows, sheets, panes, tools, watchlists.

To reiterate:

- The top level component of the AmiBroker structure is the layout.
- Each layout can be associated with any number of databases (there is no limit). Only one database is open and active when a layout is active.
- Some layouts - local layouts - are associated with only one database. Other layouts - global layouts - are associated with two or more databases, but only one at a time.
- Each layout consists of one or more windows. Only one window can be active at a time. All of the windows associated with the layout are listed in the windows menu. If you choose a multi-window layout, all the windows will be visible; otherwise only the active window is visible. You can change back and forth from window to window as you wish.
- Each window displays data for one symbol at a time.
- Each window displays data in one time frame at a time.
- Each window contains one or more sheets (there is no limit). Only one sheet can be active at a time. To make another sheet active, click its tab. All sheets display the same range of dates.
- Each sheet contains one or more panes (there is no limit).
- Each pane contains one or more displays of price data, manually applied tools, or formulas. Only one pane can be active at a time. To make another pane active, click anywhere in it.

Chapter 5

The GUI — Graphical User Interface

When you start AmiBroker using an end-of-day database, here is what you see.

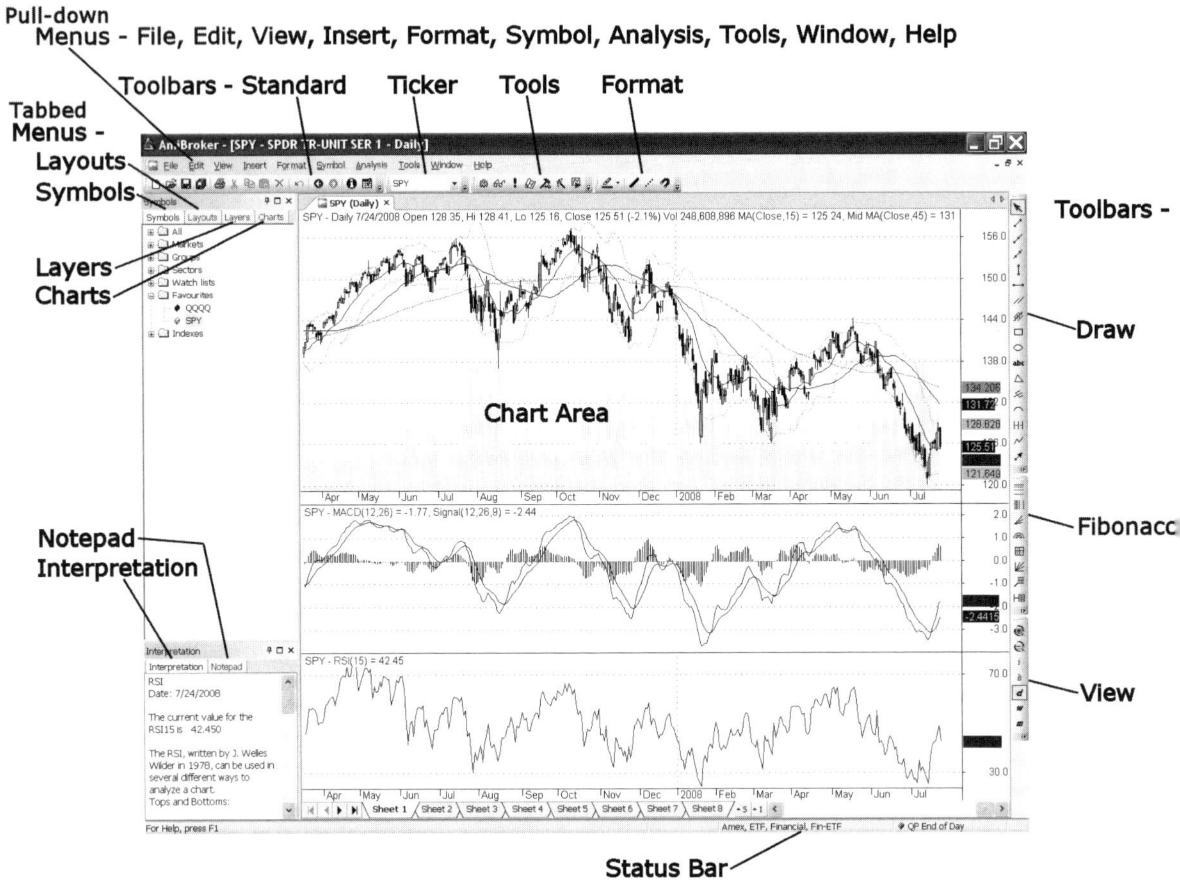

FIGURE 5.1 - AMIBROKER CHART WINDOW

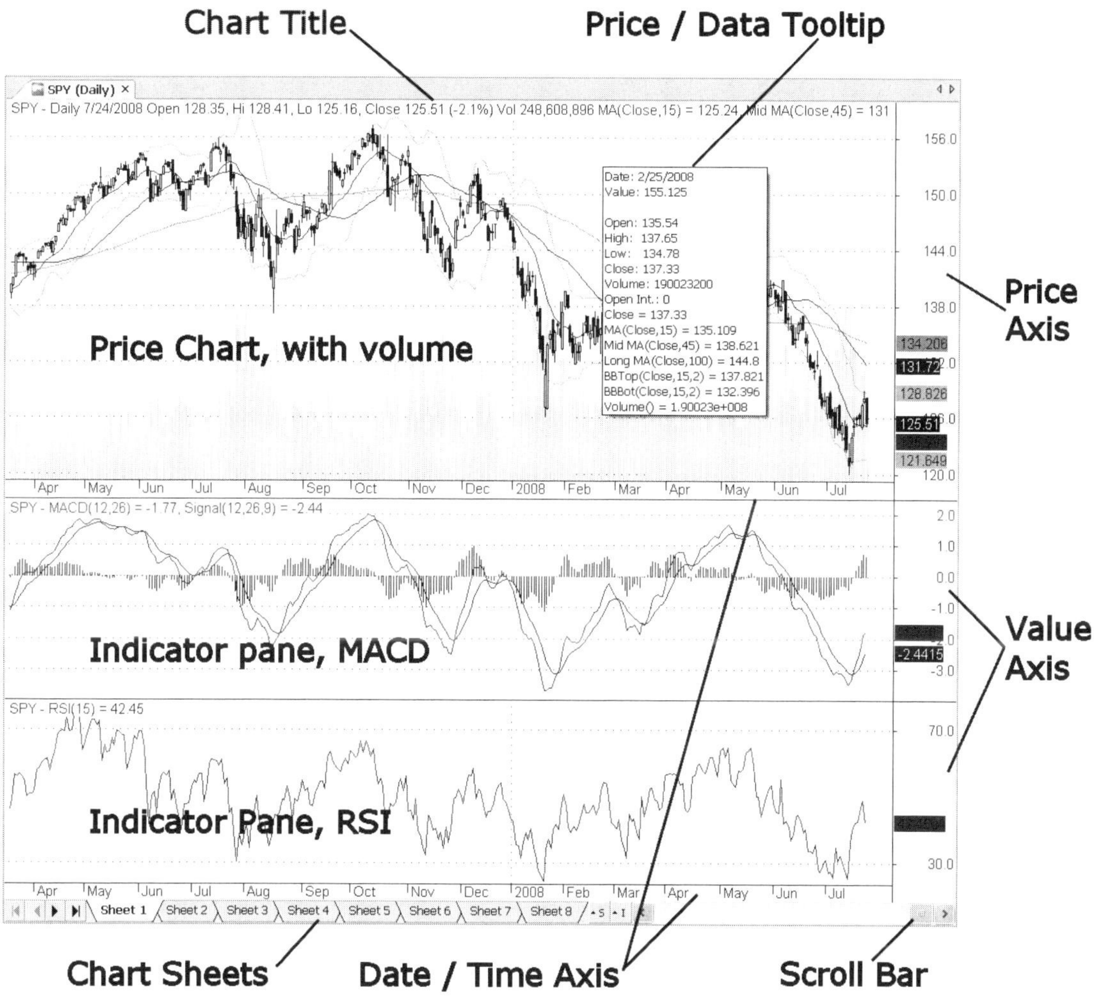

Figure 5.2 - Main Charting Area, End-of-Day Database

Charts

This chapter describes the AmiBroker Chart Window and the Chart Area, and the tools that are available. This is a beginners guide to charting. If an AmiBroker feature is missing from this book, it is either a new feature or an advanced topic. For more information, please see the AmiBroker User's Guide.

The AmiBroker charting engine uses object-oriented manipulation of all drawings, and standard Windows techniques. You can move, resize, cut, copy, paste, and delete all charts and drawing objects with ease.

Display a New Price Series

Use one of these methods:

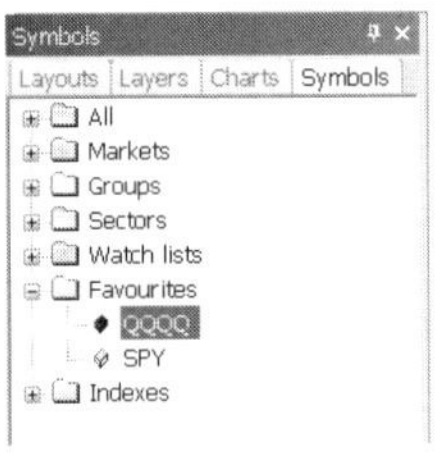

- Use the Symbols Tabbed menu. Find the symbol you want in any of the categories of which it is a member. (It will always be a member of "All".) Click the Ticker symbol. All panes in the active layout will be loaded with the data for the new symbol, and all indicators will be recalculated using that data.

- Using the Symbol pull-down menu, select **Find**. The Symbol Finder will open. Fill in either the ticker or the name. Select the ticker you want, click **OK**. The new symbol will be loaded.

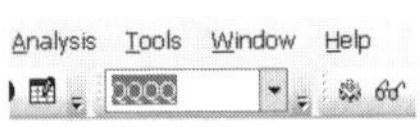

- Using the Ticker toolbar (see Figure 5.1), select all of the letters in the old ticker, type in the new ticker erasing the old one, press ENTER. The new symbol will be loaded.

For more details, see Chart Pane Context Menu, page 122.

Default Chart

Figure 5.2 shows a typical default chart window. Every chart window is a component of a Layout. You can have as many layouts as you wish. Figure 5.1 shows the chart window of a typical default layout. You have a great deal of control over what is included in your default charts and how they appear. Use the Tools > Preference menu to set your preferences. These two figures will be used as illustrations for this section.

This layout consists of a single window with eight chart sheets. Each window can have as many sheets as you wish. Using the tabs along the bottom edge, you can select which sheet you want to be active. In Figure 5.2, Sheet 1 is the active sheet and contains three panes. A sheet can have as many panes as you wish.

The upper pane contains the price in candlestick format, a simple moving average of the closing price with a short period, a simple moving average with a medium period, a simple moving average with a long period, a set of Bollinger bands, volume bars, an exponential moving average of the close with a short period, an exponential moving average with a long period, and interpretation code.

The middle pane contains the MACD indicator, an exponential moving average of the MACD indicator, and interpretation code.

The bottom pane contains the RSI indicator, an exponential moving average of the RSI indicator, and interpretation code.

Active Pane

At any time, you will have one active layout, of which one window is active, of which one sheet is active, of which one pane is active. Saying that a chart or pane is *active* is the same as saying it is *selected* or has the *focus*.

Price and Value Axis

At the right-hand side of each pane, there is a vertical axis. (See Figure 5.2.) It displays the price (if a price series is being plotted) or value (if an indicator or formula is being plotted). The colored boxes give the values of the last data point visible on the chart. They are color-coded to correspond with the color of the line that is used to plot them.

Unless you turn it off in the Tools > Preferences menu, a box containing

Tooltip (see Figure 5.2) will display information about that bar of that pane that is at the point of your cursor whenever the cursor is paused over any pane.

Date and Time Axis

At the bottom of some panes is a date and time axis. (See Figure 5.2.) You have control over whether the dates are displayed, but they are always there and are used to synchronize the data displayed in each of the panes. To toggle the display of the dates on and off, see Chart Pane Context Menu, page 122.

Scroll Through Dates

There are several ways to scroll (to change the date range of the data that appears in the pane):

- At the bottom, right-hand side you will see a scroll bar. (See Figure 5.2.) Clicking and holding the scroll bar, then moving your mouse, you will make different date ranges of data visible in the pane.
- You can use the right and left arrows next to the scroll bar. Each click of an arrow scrolls by a single bar.
- If your mouse has a wheel, rolling the wheel scrolls the window.

As the display scrolls, every pane of every sheet will be redrawn so that the date range displayed is the same in every one of them. Every pane will be rescaled so the data is displayed as efficiently as possible. (Just rescaled; all the calculation was done for all the dates before the panes were displayed the first time.)

Pane Size

As you move your mouse slowly up and down, you will cross pane boundaries. When the cursor changes from an ordinary arrow to a set of two parallel lines with small arrows pointing up and down, you can click and drag the boundary to change the sizes of the panes separated by that boundary.

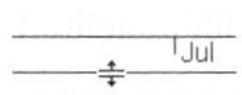

Zoom

There are several ways to Zoom (increase or decrease the number of bars of data being displayed).

- Use the icons in the View toolbar. (See Figure 5.1.)
- Using the View menu, select **Zoom**, then In or Out.
- View > Zoom > All will display all the quotes in your history file.
- View > Zoom > Range will zoom to the range you have set. (See Mark a Range, page 120.)
- Hold the Control key while rolling the wheel on your mouse. When you have the amount of zoom you want, click the mouse anywhere in the chart.

Bar Interval (Periodicity)

There are several ways to change periodicity.

- Use the icons in the View toolbar. (See Figure 5.1.)
- Using the View menu, select **Daily**, **Weekly**, or **Monthly**. If you have an intraday database, you can select any bar size that is the same as or longer than your base time interval. If the intraday bar size you want is not on the menu, you can define it using the Tools menu > Preferences > Intra-day.

When you change the periodicity for any pane, all panes on all sheets for the active chart window will be changed and synchronized.

If you want to have different periodicities for the same symbol, open a second chart window, creating a multi-window layout. (Use the File menu > New > Chart.) The new chart will open with the same ticker. Change the periodicity as you wish. You can tile the windows so that you can see, for example, both the daily chart and weekly chart. You can save the tiled view as a new layout. Whenever you open that layout, the daily and weekly display will be loaded.

Select a Quote

Move your mouse to the date you are interested in and click anywhere in any pane. A vertical line will appear through all panes at the bar you selected. If that is close to, but not exactly the one you wanted, use the Keyboard Left Arrow and Right Arrow (the cursor keys) to move one bar at a time. The chart title will display the date (and time) of the selected bar.

Mark a Range

Set a bar range by either:

- Double-click one end of the range, then double-click the other end of the range.
- Select the desired bar for the left (older) end. Press F12. Select the desired bar for the right end. Press SHIFT+F12.

The left end of the range will be marked with a vertical line and a small green bar at the bottom of that line. The right end will be marked by a vertical line and a small red bar at the bottom of that line. Once the range is established, double-clicking outside the range will extend the range in that direction. Double-clicking inside the range will move the closer end to the bar being double-clicked.

Date ranges can be zoomed-to by using the View menu > Zoom. Date ranges can also be referenced from an AFL program using the functions BeginValue and EndValue.

Remove the Range Markers

Either:

- Press CTRL+F12.
- Double-click either the left or right vertical line.

Add a New Pane

Use one of these methods:

- To have that pane display a price series or a formula, use the Charts Tabbed menu, select the formula you want, right click it, click Insert. If you are planning to apply an indicator to the price series, select Price as the formula.
- Follow the first method, but double-click the formula you want (instead of right-click and insert).
- Alternatively, you can insert a new blank pane and then fill it later. Use the File menu > New > Pane. The new pane will appear as the bottom pane of the active window and will have no price or formula in it.

Close Any Pane

Use one of these methods:

- Click on the pane you want to close to make it the active pane. Right-click, bringing up the context menu, choose **Pane**, then **Close**.
- Using the View menu, choose **Pane**, then **Close**.
- Using the View Toolbar:

1. Click in the pane you want to close.
2. Click the **Close Pane** icon.

Reorder the Panes

Right-click on the pane you want to move either up or down. From the context menu, choose **Pane**, then **Move Up** or **Move Down**. The pane will exchange places with the one next to it. To move a pane several locations, repeat the operation.

Chart Pane Context Menu

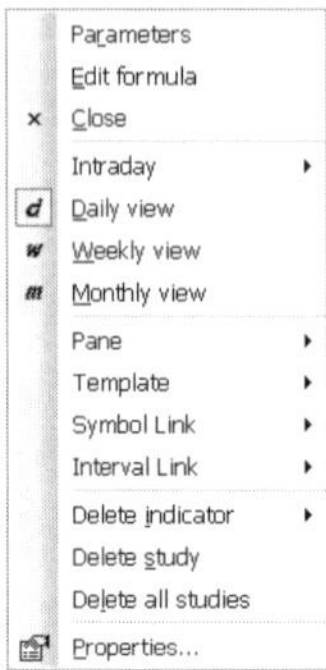

This context menu shows up when you right-click over any pane. It gives a great deal of control over the items shown in the pane.

The parameters submenu gives access to the formula-based indicators. The properties submenu gives access to the manually placed indicators. The content and level of detail of both these menus depends on what indicators have been placed in the pane.

Edit Formula opens the AFL Formula Editor with the formula loaded.

Parameters

- Parameters - Opens the Parameters dialog allowing you to modify parameters of indicators, as well as settings of colors, styles, scaling, and axes. Depending on the charts, formulas, and studies applied to the pane, there could be a lot of options. A pane was created and the formula Price (all in one) inserted into it. The context menu shown here is for that formula.

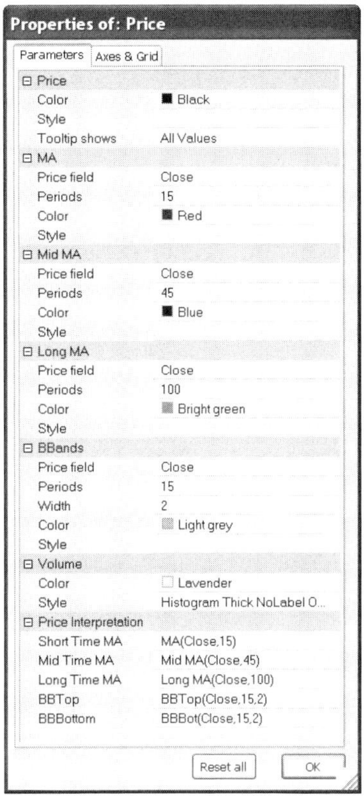

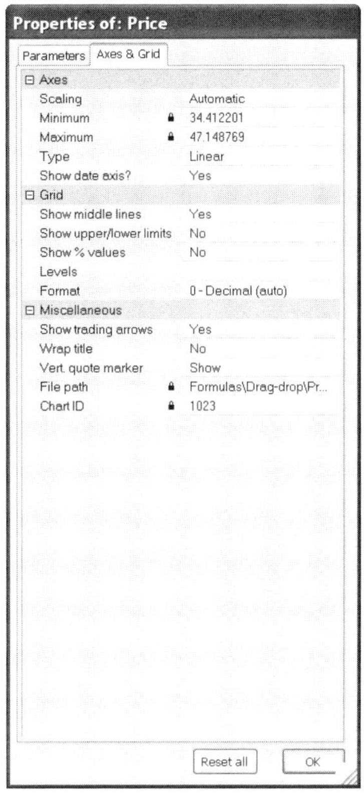

Scroll your mouse up and down and note that most of these parameters can be changed. Some of the more important ones are described here.

The parameters over which you have control are the parameters of the code in the formula. This is closely related to the Edit Formula menu described on page 127.

Colors

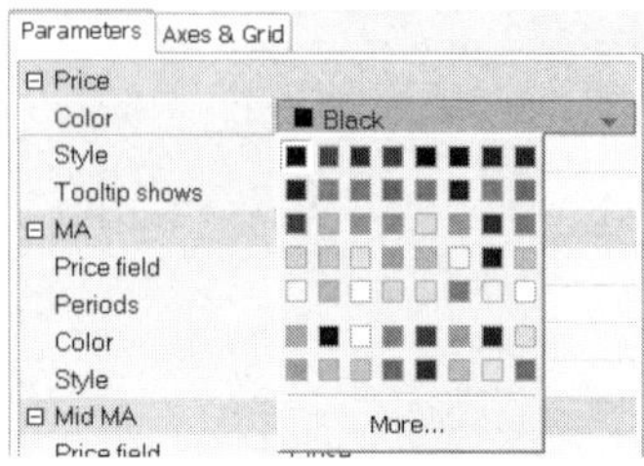

- Every color parameter will have a pull-down menu that brings up a color chart. You can select the color you want by clicking the sample. If you want more control over the color, click More and this window will open, allowing complete specification of the color.

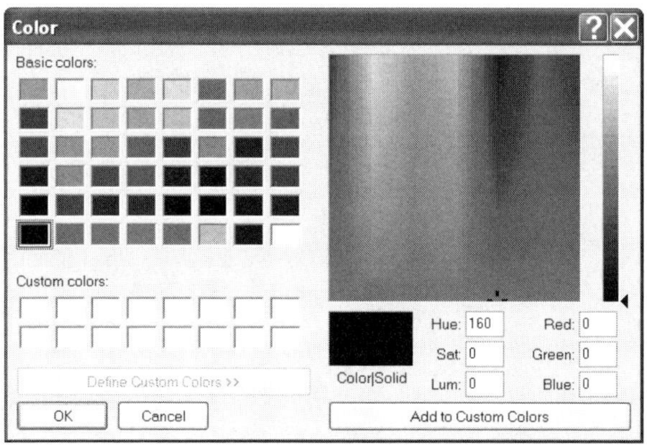

Periods

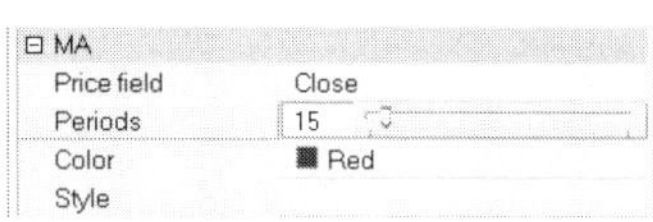

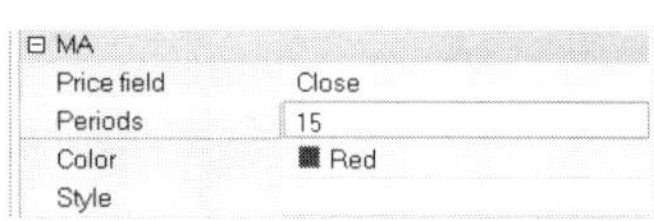

- Click in the middle of the field to the right of the word Periods. The box allowing you to change the length of the period will open to show a slider in the right portion and a text box in the left portion. Either use your mouse to slide the slider, or select and change the numeric value to the length you want. Watch the plot of the line change as you change the value of the period.

Price Field

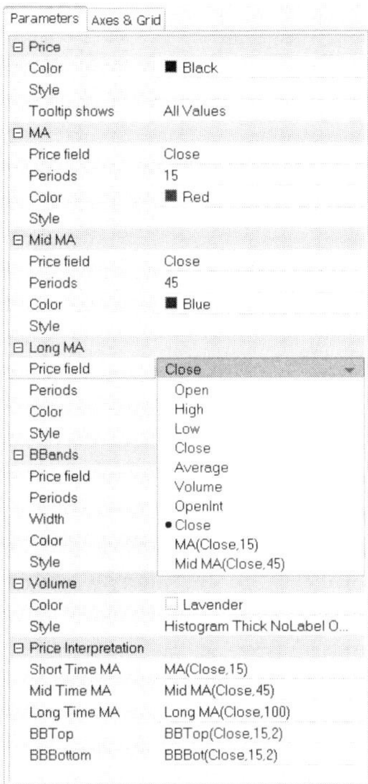

- When the Price Field sub-menu is dropped down (in this case for the Long MA formula), it allows you to choose the field to take the moving average of. Choices include everything that was placed in the pane before Long MA.

  Compare by dropping down the Price Field of the formula MA or Mid MA. Since MA was placed before Mid MA, and Mid MA was placed before Long MA, any of Close, MA, or Mid MA can be used as the Price Field.

Axes and Grid

- Axes gives control over the vertical scale used for plotting. If you click on Scaling, it will switch from automatic to custom. The locks will disappear from the Minimum and Maximum fields, allowing you to set whatever range you wish.

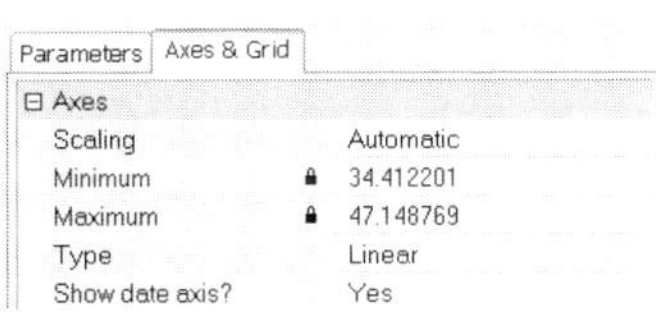

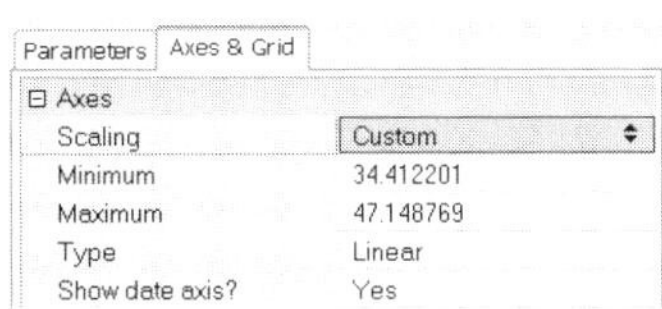

Type Linear alternates with Logarithmic.

Show Date Axis is either Yes or No. Set this to Yes if you want to display the date and time axis as part of the pane.

- Grid gives control of horizontal lines.

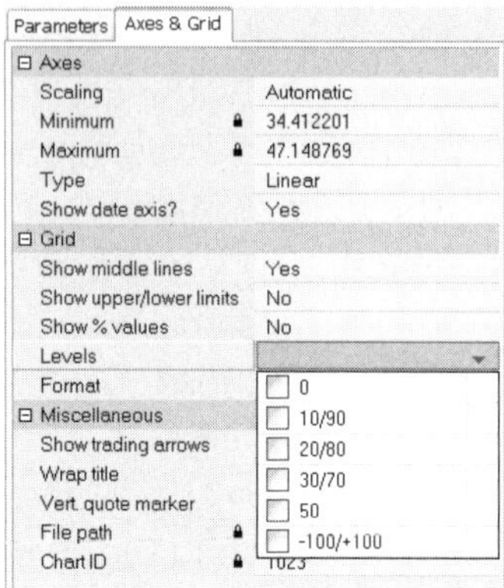

Levels pull-down menu allows you to select automatic horizontal lines at some standard levels. The choices include levels that are often used to evaluate indicators, particularly oscillator-type.

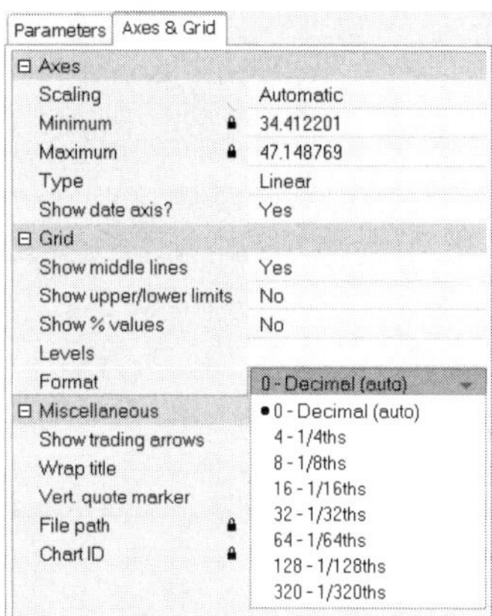

Format pull-down menu allows you to change between decimal and fractional display of prices.

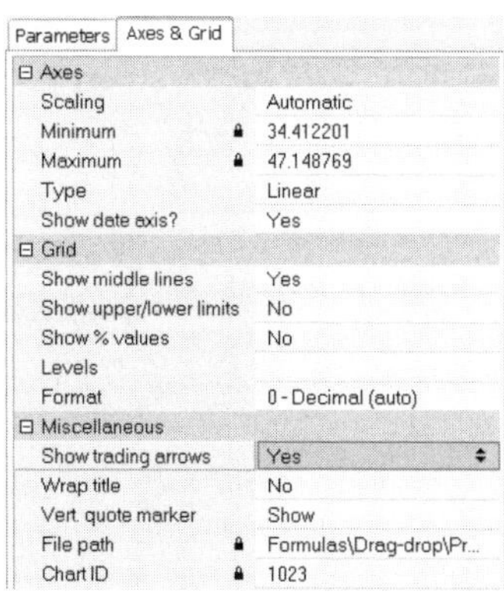

Show Trading Arrows must be set to Yes to have the green buy and red sell arrows display on the chart in the pane.

Edit Formula

- Edit Formula - Opens the Formula Editor allowing you to view or modify the AFL code of indicator. The Formula Editor is described in detail in another section. But it is instructive to look at a portion of the code for the formula Price (all in one) that was used to illustrate the Parameters entry above, page 122 and following.

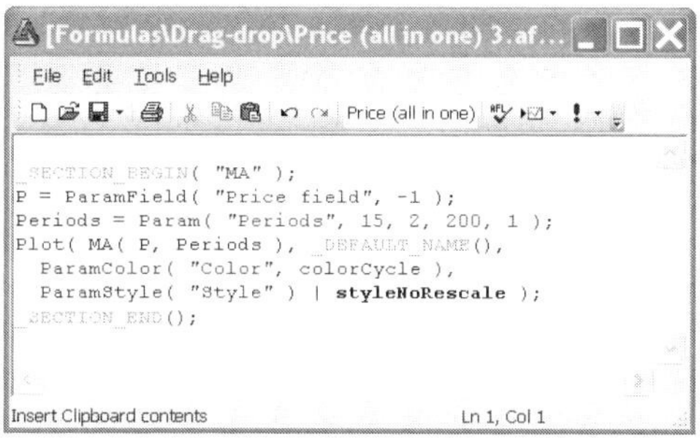

- Close - closes the chart pane.
- Intraday - Allows you to switch the periodicity or viewing time frame to one of the available intraday intervals.
- Daily view - Switches the viewing interval to daily.
- Weekly view - Switches the viewing interval to weekly.
- Monthly view - Switches the viewing interval to monthly.
- Pane

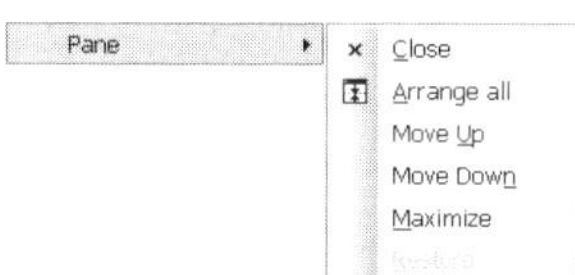

  - Close - Closes chart pane
  - Arrange all - Arranges all the panes to be equal height
  - Move up - Moves the selected chart pane up (switches pane vertical order)
  - Move down - Moves the selected chart pane down (switches pane vertical order)
  - Maximize - Maximizes the selected pane so it fills entire screen
  - Restore - Restores the selected pane to its previous size (after using maximize)

- Template - The complete set of chart sheets, together with their names, panes, sizes, locations, formulas is called a template.

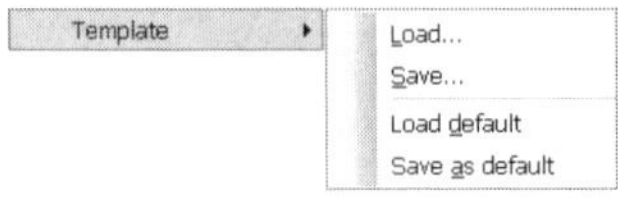

  - Load - Loads a single-window chart template from the selected file
  - Save - Saves a single-window chart template to the selected file
  - Load default - Loads the default single window template
  - Save as default - Saves the current single-window setup as the default template
- Symbol Link - Links two or more windows by symbol. When the symbol is changed in any one of these windows, it will change in all of them.
- Interval Link - Links two or more windows by display interval or periodicity. When the interval is changed in any one of these windows, it will change in all of them.
- Delete indicator - Deletes one of the drag-and-drop indicator sections found in the code. A submenu will expand to list the indicators that can be deleted.
- Delete study - Deletes the selected manually drawn study, such as trend line or Fibonacci.
- Delete All studies - Deletes all the manually drawn studies.

Properties

- Properties - Displays properties of the manually drawn studies.

The chart shows a regression channel applied to a price series.

Select the Regression study (move the cursor over the middle line until it becomes a four-direction arrow), and right-click, bringing up the context menu, then click Properties.

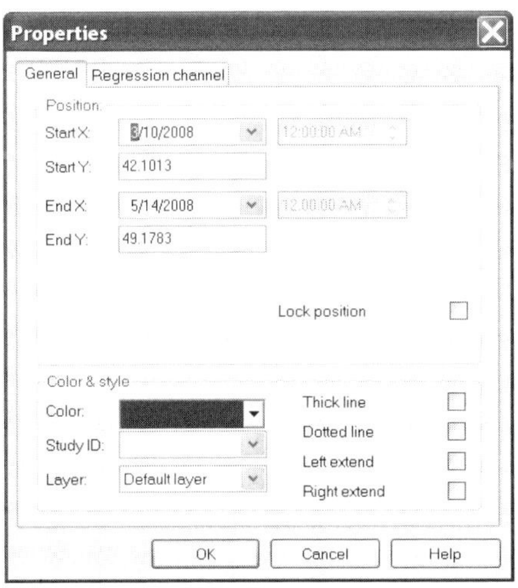

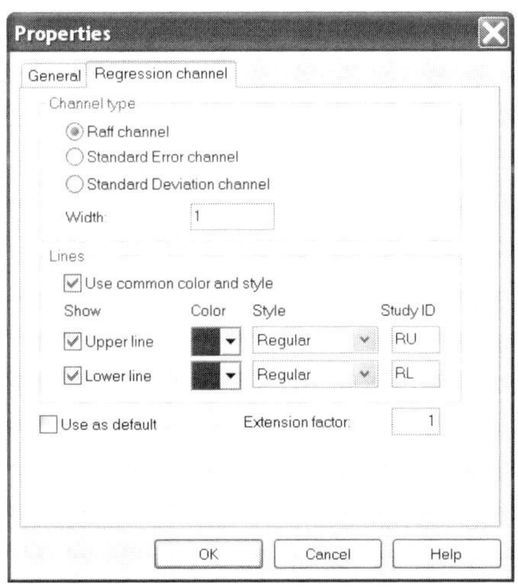

The General tab lets you refine the starting and ending point, place the study on a specific Layer (see Layers, page 163), extend the study to the left and right, change the color and thickness of the lines.

The Regression tab lets you control the type of the regression, the width of the channels, the color and thickness of the lines. It also lets you assign a study identifier to the upper and lower boundaries. The study identifier can be used to test for conditions such as prices moving above the upper boundary.

Pull-Down Menus

Pull-down menus, also called drop-down menus, are menus of commands or options that appear when you select an item with a mouse. The item you select is generally at the top of the display screen, and the menu appears just below it, as if you had pulled it down.

There are ten pull-down menus arranged across the top of the AmiBroker Chart Window (see Figure 5.1.)

File Menu

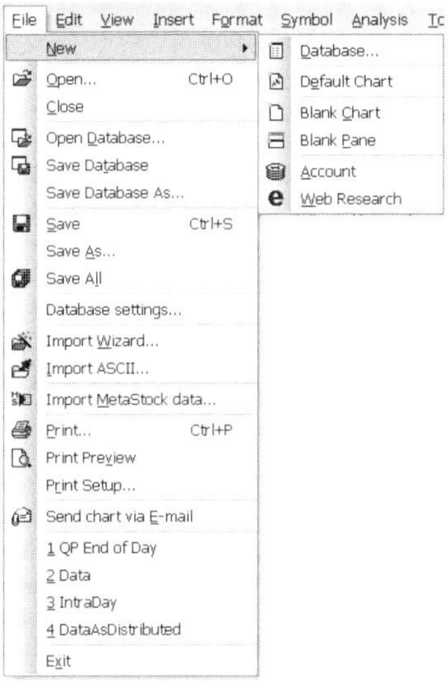

- New
  - Database — Creates a new AmiBroker database, and launches the database settings window.
  - Default Chart - Creates a new chart window, including all its sheets, using the default template. It's possible to select the symbols and time frame independently in each of the windows opened.
  - Blank Chart - Creates a new completely blank chart window, including all its sheets. This is useful if you want to create a multi-window layout. This is important if you want to have indicators that have independent parameters from the other windows that you have created. (See Window Layouts, page 108.)
  - Blank Pane - Creates a new blank chart pane in the active sheet.
  - Account - Creates a new Account Manager account.
  - Web Research - Creates a new web research window. Information about the current symbol will be automatically loaded.

- Open - Opens an existing document (account, database or HTML file). You can pick the document type from "Files of type" combo in the Open > File selector window.
- Close - Closes the current active document window.
- Open Database - Allows you to open an existing AmiBroker database. Select the database folder and press OK.
- Save Database - Saves the current database.
- Save Database As - Saves the current database with a new name in a new folder.
- Save - Saves the current document (account or HTML file).
- Save As - Saves the current document with a new name.
- Save All - Saves all documents currently open.
- Database settings - Opens the database settings dialog that allows you to specify database parameters when setting up a database; or change your database parameters or intraday settings for an existing database.
- Import Wizard - Launches the ASCII Import Wizard window, that allows you to easily import ASCII (text) files into your database.
- Import ASCII - Allows you to import ASCII files with use of

predefined import formats.

- Import MetaStock data - Launches the Metastock importer window. Note: The Metastock importer should be used only if you want to import MS data to a native, local AmiBroker database once. If you want AmiBroker to read the Metastock database directly on a regular basis, set up your database with the MetaStock Plugin.
- Print - Print the currently displayed charts.
- Print Preview - Displays how the information will look when printed.
- Print Setup - Opens the Print Setup dialog box.
- Send chart via e-mail - AmiBroker creates a .png image of the currently displayed chart and uses your default mailing program (e.g. Outlook Express) to send the file as an attachment.

- List of AmiBroker databases. Click on any database name to open it.
  - QP End of Day
  - Data
  - IntraDay
  - DataAsDistributed

- Exit - Closes the AmiBroker program.

Edit Menu

- Undo - Undo the last operation performed on chart studies such as trendlines. This option will be unavailable if no study has been drawn or moved.
- Cut - Cut a study from the chart and hold it in the clipboard.
- Copy - Copy a study from the chart to the clipboard.
- Paste - Paste the contents of the clipboard to the current chart.
- Delete - Delete a study from the chart without holding a copy in the clipboard.
- Delete All - Delete all objects from the current chart pane.
- Image
  - Copy as Bitmap - Copies the current chart window into the clipboard in .bmp format
  - Copy as Metafile - Copies the current chart window into the clipboard in metafile format
  - Export to file - Saves the current chart window in .png format to a disk location you choose
  - Send by e-mail - Create a .png image of the current chart window and send it as an e-mail using your default e-mail utility

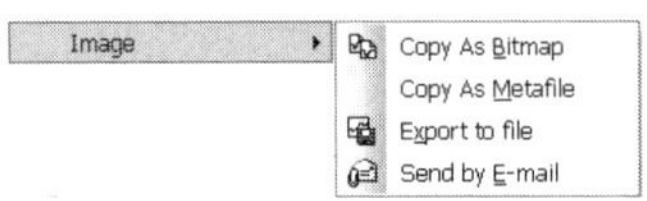

- Delete quotation - Deletes the currently selected bar from the database for the current ticker symbol.
- Delete session - Deletes the currently selected bar from all symbols in the database.
- Properties - Opens a study properties dialog. (See Chart Pane Context Menu, page 122.)

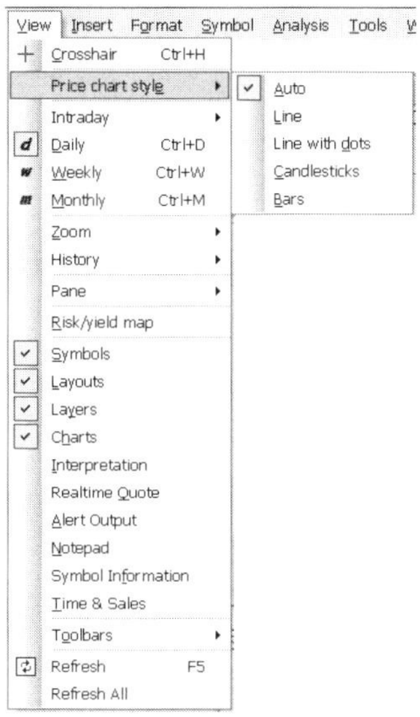

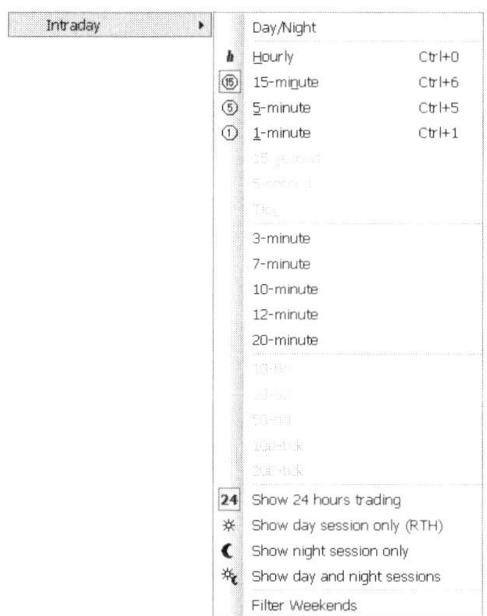

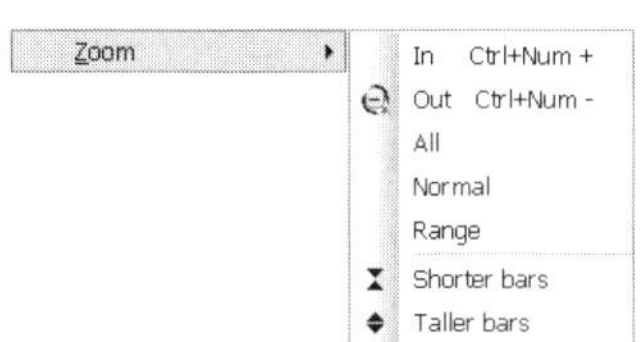

View Menu

- Crosshair — Turns crosshair on and off.
- Price chart style
  - Auto — Uses settings in Tools > Preference
  - Line — Line chart
  - Line with dots — Line chart with dots at closing price
  - Candlesticks — Candlestick chart
  - Bars — OHLC Bar chart
- Intraday — Controls size of intraday bars and day - night sessions.
- Daily — Displays daily bars.
- Weekly — Displays weekly bars.
- Monthly — Displays monthly bars.
- Zoom
  - In — Reduces number of bars displayed
  - Out — Increases number of bars displayed
  - All — Displays all available bars
  - Normal —Displays the default number of bars (Tools > Preference > Charting)
  - Range — Displays the bars in the selected range
  - Shorter bars — Reduces the vertical size of the bars
  - Taller bars — Increases the vertical size of the bars

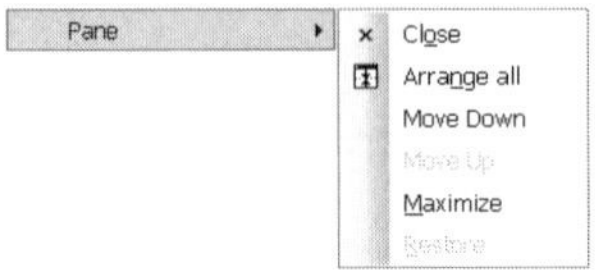

- History — Move back and forth between charts recently viewed in a browser-like way.
- Pane
  - Close — Closes the currently selected chart pane
  - Arrange all — Arranges all the displayed charts
  - Move down — Moves the currently selected chart down one pane
  - Move up — Moves the currently selected chart up one pane
  - Maximize — Maximizes the currently selected chart pane
  - Restore — Restores the chart layout after using maximize
- Risk / yield map — Displays Risk / yield map of all the symbols in the database. Risk / yield map calculates average the weekly return (the yield) and standard deviation of the weekly returns (the risk) over at least 12 weeks. It requires at least 60 bars worth of data for every stock. To zoom in, mark the area with the mouse. To zoom out, simply click on the map.
- Symbols — Displays or hides the symbol tree (the Symbols tabbed menu) with categories.
- Layouts — Displays or hides the Layouts tabbed menu.

- Layers — Displays or hides the Layers tabbed menu.
- Charts — Displays or hides the list of charts, formulas, and indicators (the Charts tabbed menu).
- Interpretation — Displays or hides the interpretation window
- Realtime Quote —Displays or hides the real-time quote window
- Alert output — Displays or hides the Alert Output window. The window displays messages generated by formula based alert.
- Notepad — Displays or hides the Notepad window that allows you to store free-text notes about the active ticker symbol.
- Symbol information — Displays or hides the Information window.
- Time & sales — Displays or hides the time & sales window.
- Toolbars

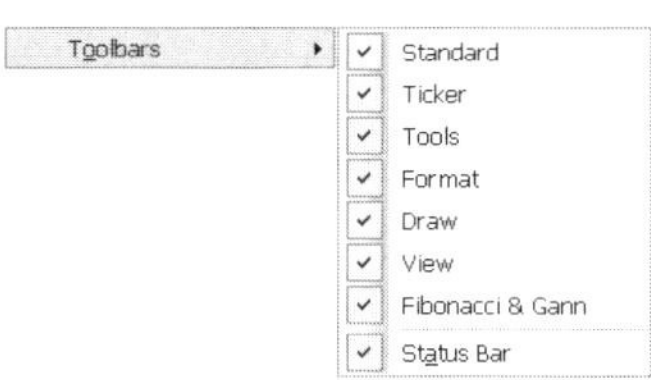

  - Standard — Display or hide the standard toolbar
  - Ticker — Display or hide the ticker toolbar
  - Tools — Display or hide the tools toolbar
  - Format — display or hide the format toolbar
  - Draw — display or hide the draw toolbar

    - View — displar or hide the view toolbar
    - Fibonacci & Gann — Display or hide the Fibonacci & Gann toolbar
    - Status Bar —Display or hide the status bar
- Refresh — Refreshes the chart window.
- Refresh all — Refreshes the chart window and re-reads the contents of all the categories in symbols tree.

Insert Menu

The insert menu and the draw toolbar duplicate each other for many features. For more detailed description, see Draw Toolbar, page 154.

- Trend line - Draws a trend line.
- Ray - Draws a ray - a right-extended trend line.
- Extended line - Draws a trend line that is extended on both right and left.
- Horizontal line - Draws a horizontal line.
- Vertical line - Draws a vertical line.
- Parallel lines - Draws parallel trend lines.
- Regression Channel - Draws Raff, standard deviation, and standard error channels.
- Andrews' Pitchfork - Draws an Andrews' pitchfork.
- Triangle - Draws a triangle.
- Rectangle - Draws a rectangle.
- Ellipse - Draws an ellipse.
- Arc - Draws an arc.
- Cycle - Draws time cycles.
- Text - Places custom text.
- Zig-zag - Draws a series of connected trend lines.
- Arrow - Draws a line that ends with an arrow.

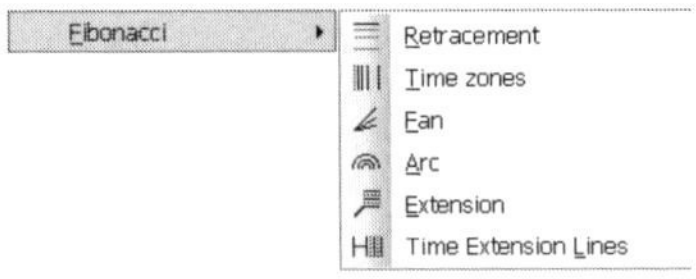

- Fibonacci studies
  - Retracement
  - Time zones
  - Fan
  - Arc
  - Extension
  - Time Extension Lines

- Gann studies
  - Fan
  - Square

Format Menu

This menu operates on the drawing tool that is active.

The format menu and the draw toolbar duplicate each other for many features. For more detailed description, see Draw Toolbar, page 154.

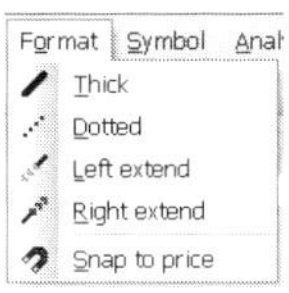

- Thick - Changes the formatting to thick.
- Dotted - Changes the formatting to dotted.
- Left extend - Extends the trendline to the left.
- Right extend - Extends the trendline to the right.
- Snap to price - Turns on the magnet that snaps the drawn studies to the prices. The snap to price % threshold can be set in the Preferences window. Snap to price % threshold defines how far price 'magnet' works - it will snap to price when the mouse is nearer than % threshold from H/L/C price.

Symbol Menu

- New - Add new symbols to the database. After selecting this function you will be prompted for new ticker symbol. Symbols should be 26 characters or shorter and entered in all capital letters.
- Delete - Removes the currently selected symbol from the database. Note that this operation can not be undone.
- Split - Allows you to perform a stock split. The program will try to determine the split date and ratio by analyzing the quotations. If there is just a single quotation after the split this should work, if not you will be asked for a split date and ratio. You can specify a split using following expression: x->y which means that x shares before split become y shares after it. For example 2->3 means that 2 shares become 3 after the split. It is also possible to perform a reverse-split. For example 2->1, which means that 2 shares are joined together into 1 share.
- Merge - This function allows you to merge two tickers. It is used when the ticker for the symbol is changed and in your database one symbol holds historical quotes and the second one holds newest quotes (after name change). Select the

new ticker (after name change) and use Symbol > Merge. Then choose the original ticker ("merge with") and optionally check the following fields:

  - overwrite duplicate quotes - checking this option will overwrite the quotes already existing in "new" ticker with those present in "old" ticker (this should really not be the case, but may happen).
  - delete "merge with" afterwards - checking this option will delete the "old" ticker after merging.
  - assign alias name - checking this option will copy the "old" ticker to the alias field of the "new" ticker.

- Find - Opens the Symbol Finder window that allows you to quickly search the database for a symbol by typing the first letters of its full name or its ticker.
- Information - Opens the Information window for the symbol, which allows you to change the information related to the symbol.
- Quote Editor - Opens the Quote Editor window that allows you to edit, delete and add quotations in your database. Note that you can edit the AmiBroker native database, but not the external database.

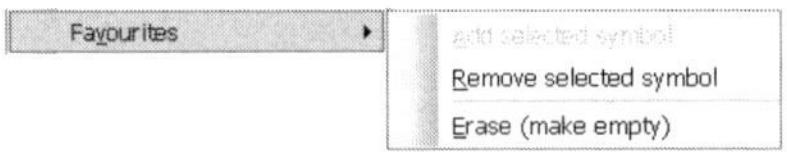

- Favorites
  - Add selected symbol - Adds the current symbol to the Favorites category.
  - Remove selected symbol - Removes the current symbol from the Favorites category.
  - Erase (make empty) - Removes all entries from the Favorites category.

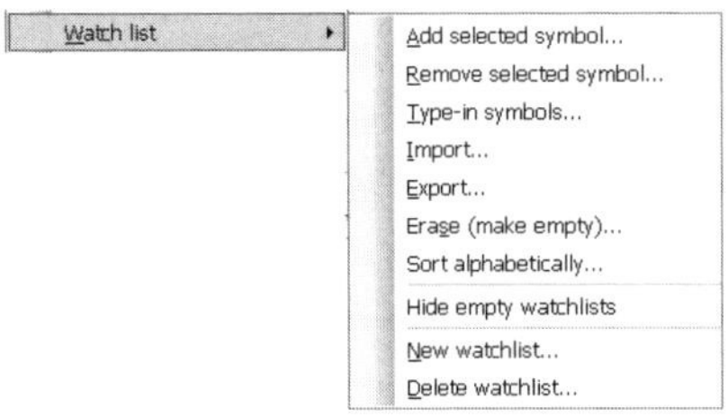

- Watch list
  - Add selected symbol - Adds the current symbol to the watchlist you select.
  - Remove selected symbol - Removes the current symbol from the watchlist(s) you select.
  - Type-in symbols - Add symbol(s) to a watchlist.
  - Import - Import symbols to a watchlist from a .tls file.
  - Export - Export the list of symbols in a watchlist to a .tls file.
  - Erase (make empty) - Remove all symbols from a watchlist.
  - Sort alphabetically - Sort the symbols in a watchlist into alphabetical order.
  - Hide empty watchlists - In the symbol tree, show only those watchlists that are not empty.
  - New watchlist - Create a new watchlist.
  - Delete watchlist - Removes

the selected watchlists. Does not delete the symbols from the database.

- See Watchlists, page 179.

- Real Time Quote

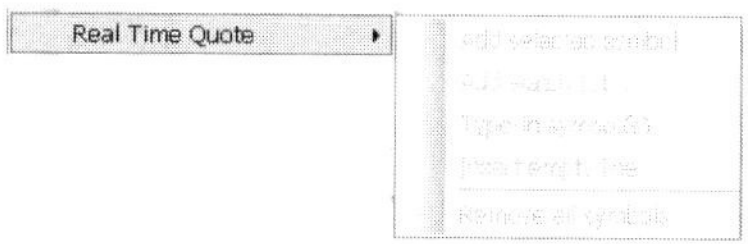

    - Add selected symbol - Add the current symbol to the real-time quote list.
    - Add watchlist - Add all the symbols in a watchlist to the real-time quote list.
    - Type in symbol(s) - Type the symbols to be added.
    - Insert empty line - Add an empty (separator) line.
    - Remove all symbols - Remove all symbols from the real-time quote list.
- Categories - Opens the Categories window that allows you to define the names of markets, groups, sectors, industries, and watchlists. (See Categories, page 177.)
- Organize assignments - Opens the Assignment organizer window that allows you to change the category assignments for symbols or to delete multiple symbols from the database.
- Calculate composites - Opens the Composite recalculation window that allows automatic calculation of number and volume of advancing/declining/unchanged issues or volume numbers for indices.

Analysis Menu

This is the workhorse menu of AmiBroker. After you have visually examined the chart and want to test the profitability of your ideas, you will use Analysis extensively. Each of these options has its own section in Chapter 9.

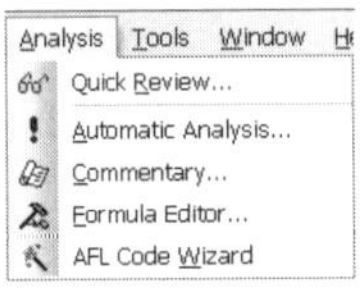

- Quick Review - Opens the Quick review window that provides overall market information like: daily symbol quotes, daily/weekly/monthly/quarterly/yearly returns comparison table.
- Automatic Analysis - Opens the Automatic Analysis window that enables you to perform explorations, backtests, optimizations, or scans.
- Commentary - Displays the Commentary window which allows you to read comments generated by the technical indicators and describing the current conditions.
- Formula Editor - Opens the Formula Editor window that enables you to write your own formulas.
- AFL Code Wizard - Opens the AFL Code Wizard - Creates trading system AFL code from plain English sentences.

Tools Menu

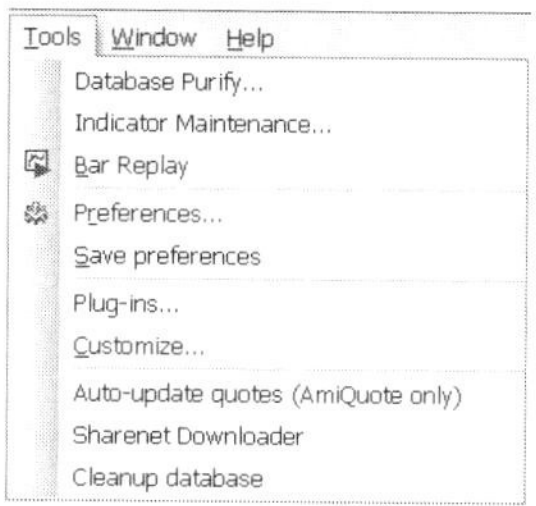

- Database Purify - Checks the database to detect missing or extra quotes, possible splits or invalid OHLC relationships.
- Indicator Maintenance - Opens the Indicator Maintenance wizard to clean up unused indicator space.
- Bar Replay - Opens the Bar Replay tool which allows replay of historical data.
- Preferences - Opens the Preferences window which allows you to configure the AmiBroker program.
- Save Preferences - Saves all the preferences changes (the information is stored in broker.prefs file).
- Plug-ins - Opens the Plugins window. It contains the lists of all loaded plug-in DLLs. It can be used for inspecting which plug-ins are active and unloading unnecessary plug-ins.
- Customize - Opens the Customize tools dialog which allows you to define custom tools that can be invoked from Tools menu.
- Auto-update quotes - Invokes AmiQuote to update the historical quotes from the latest data in the file up to today.

- Sharenet Downloader - Launches the script which downloads the quotations from Sharenet (South Africa only).
- Cleanup database - Launches the script that allows you to find non-traded stocks in the database. The script automatically scans the database and checks the latest quotation date. If it is old enough, the script will display warning message and let you decide whether the stock should be deleted or not. Additionally, the script can generate a list of "old" stocks and save it to the text file. The detailed information is available in the 05-2000 issue of the newsletter. (See Appendix C, Resources, for newsletter references.)

Window Menu

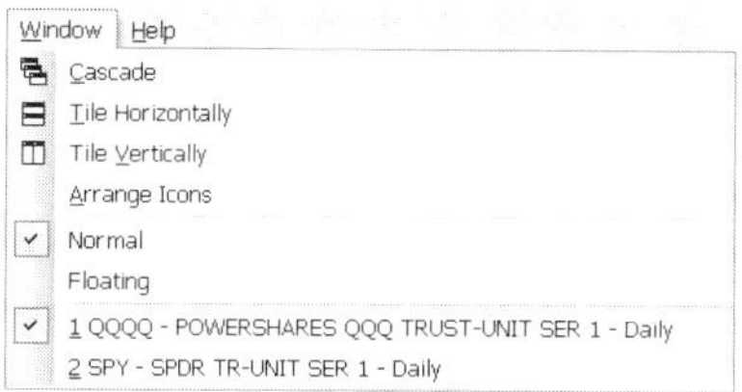

- Cascade - Cascades the open chart windows.
- Tile Horizontally - Tiles the open chart windows horizontally.
- Tile Vertically - Tiles the open chart windows vertically.
- Arrange Icons - Aligns the windows nicely at the bottom of the AmiBroker window. Arrange icons works only if:
  - You created more than two windows (via Window > New or Window > New Linked)
  - You have minimized them
  - You moved the minimized boxes
- Normal - Switches the chart window to "normal" (non-floating) state.
- Floating - Switches the chart window to floating state.

- List of open windows. Click any entry to make it active.
  - QQQQ
  - SPY

Help Menu

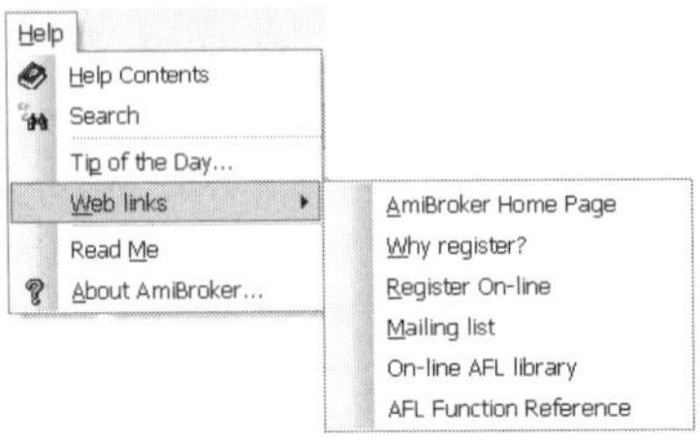

- Help Contents - Displays the Contents page of the AmiBroker User's Guide.
- Search - Allows you to search the User's Guide.
- Tip of the Day - Shows Tip of the Day dialog where many useful usage tips are displayed.
- Web Links - All open your default web browser
    - AmiBroker Home Page - AmiBroker Home Page.
    - Why Register - Purchasing and registering information.
    - Register On-line - Purchasing and registering information.
    - Mailing list - Opens Yahoo AmiBroker Forum.
    - On-line AFL Library - Library of AFL code, mostly contributed by users.
    - AFL Function Reference - On-line reference for AFL functions.
- Read Me - Using your browser, displays the contents of the Readme file describing features of the latest version of AmiBroker.
- About AmiBroker - Shows the 'About' window, which contains the information about program version and user details.

Toolbars

A toolbar is a narrow panel in a graphical user interface where buttons and icons can be placed. The icons are associated with menus and programs, and the toolbar gives a convenient way of keeping commonly used tools handy.

All of the tools on all of the toolbars are available from other menus. The toolbars are strictly for your convenience. The icons and programs shown in the screen capture images are the defaults. Add and remove icons to simplify your use of AmiBroker.

Toolbars can be modified by the user: adding and removing icons as desired; undocked and re-docked in a more convenient location; in view or hidden.

To set any of the toolbars to be in view or hidden, use the View menu, select Toolbars.

Tools for general use

Standard Toolbar

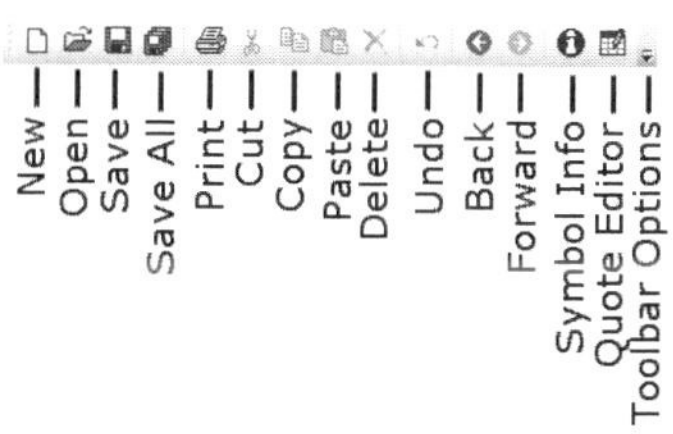

There are a lot of icons that can be added to the Standard Toolbar. Click the Toolbar Options icon to open the Add or Remove Buttons menu.

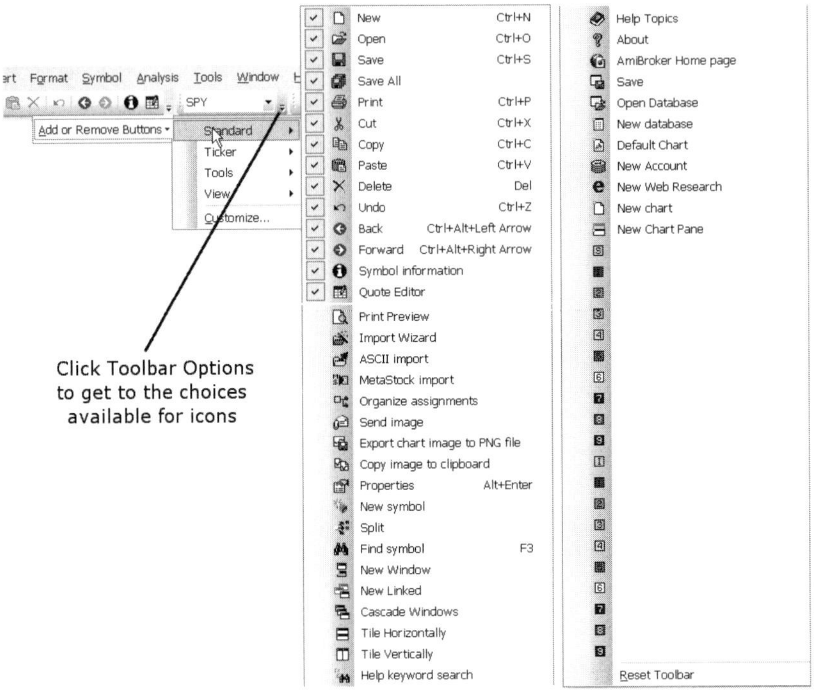

Ticker Toolbar

The ticker toolbar is one of the quickest ways to load a new symbol into the existing charts.

Tools Toolbar

View Toolbar

Icons can be added to the View Toolbar.

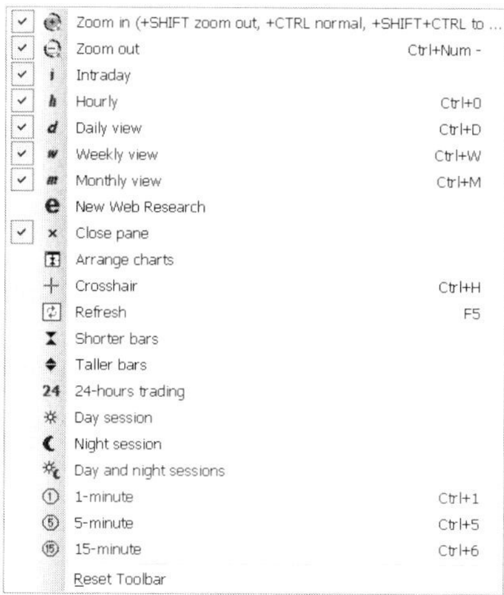

Tools for drawing

There are three toolbars that are used to place studies on price charts. They are the Drawing Tools, Fibonacci and Gann Tools, and Formatting Tools. They make placement and modification of studies very easy, and are much more efficient than using the Insert and Format pull-down menus where they also reside.

Toolbar Docking

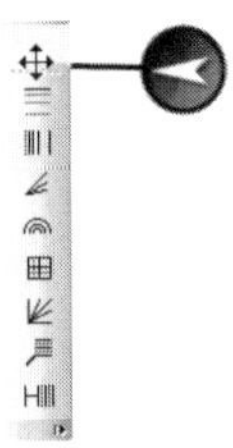

You can un-dock these from their original positions and re-dock them anywhere you wish. To do that, move your cursor over the string of dots at the top of the toolbar; it will change to a four-direction arrow. Using normal drag and drop technique, place the toolbar wherever you want it.

Draw Toolbar - Fibonacci Toolbar - Format Toolbar

The Drawing and Fibonacci Toolbars let you select and place a tool; the Formatting Toolbar lets you modify the properties of the study tool, such as color and line style.

Select Arrow is the first tool - at the top, or left if you have docked the toolbar horizontally, shown as a Red Arrow. It is used to select objects that have already been drawn so that they can be moved or resized.

To draw a study object on the chart:

1. Select the desired tool.
2. Move the mouse to the position you want to start drawing.
3. Left-click the mouse.
4. If the drawing needs only one point, you will see the lines appear. If it needs a second point, move the mouse to the position you want the second point. You can either hold the left button down while moving the mouse, or not; either works.
5. Left-click again (or release the mouse button).

To modify a study object on the chart:

1. Select the study. Usually, just hovering your mouse around the object is adequate. If there are multiple studies in close proximity, using the Select Arrow to select the study. The control points will appear as small squares. These are used to resize the object.
2. If your cursor is near one of the control points, it will change to a two-direction arrow, meaning that the object can be resized. If your cursor is in the middle of the object, it will change to a four-direction arrow, meaning that the object can be moved.

The Format Toolbar has icons to:

- Change the color of the study.
- Make the lines thick.
- Make the lines dotted.
- Snap the study to the nearest price. Set the price using the Tools menu, select Preferences, on the Charting tab.
- Extend the study to the left.
- Extend the study to the right.

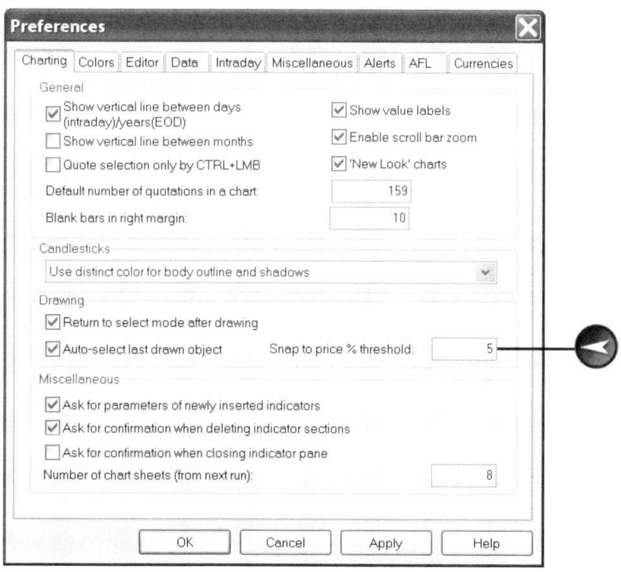

Techniques used to manipulate the study and drawing tools follow Windows.

- To select the object, move the mouse over the object so the four-directional arrow cursor appears. Click once. The sizing handles will appear.
- To de-select the object, click in any blank chart space.
- To re-size the object, click on the sizing handle and drag it to the desired location.
- To move the object, click on any part of the object other than the sizing handles and move it to the desired location.
- To delete object, select it, then press the Delete key on the keyboard. Alternatively, use the Edit menu and select Delete.
- To copy the object to the clipboard, select it, then press Ctrl+C. Alternatively, use the Edit menu and select Copy; or use the Copy toolbar button.
- To cut the object, select it, then press Ctrl+X. Alternatively, use the Edit menu and select Cut; or use the Cut toolbar button.
- To paste the object from the clipboard, press Ctrl+V. Alternatively, use the Edit menu and select Paste; or use the Paste toolbar button. The pasted object will be drawn in the same location as copied one and will be selected automatically so you can move it to a new location.
- To apply color or style to the object select it and use Format menu or Format tool bar buttons to change color, thick, dotted and snap to price styles. You can select the color and style of the object before drawing a new object. Deselect previous object (if any), change color / style selections, and draw new object.
- To modify the properties of an object, first select it, then open the Properties dialog box.
- To delete all objects in the pane, use the Edit menu and Delete All.

Study Tools

Trend line, Ray, Extended, Vertical, Horizontal

These tools give different flavors of the basic trend line. Trend line gives a line segment, Ray gives right-extended trend line, Extended gives trend line that is extended automatically from both left- and right- sides. Vertical and Horizontal are self-explaining.

Arrow

Similar to Trend line but ends with an arrow

Zig-zag

Draws a series of connected trend lines. To end drawing press the ESC key.

Parallel

This tool draws a series of parallel trend line segments. First you draw a trend line as usual. A second line parallel to the first is automatically created and you can move it around with the mouse. Once you click on the chart it is placed in that position. A third parallel line appears that can be placed somewhere else. And so forth. When you have all the parallel lines you need, either press ESC key or choose the Select tool.

Regression channels

Three kinds of regression channels are available:

- Raff regression channel.
- Standard error channel.
- Standard deviation channel.

All these channels are based on linear regression trend line. They differ in the method used for setting the distance from the trend line to the upper and lower channel lines.

"Study ID" column defines study identifier that can be used in your custom formulas to detect crossovers. If necessary, you can change these IDs by simply editing these fields. For more information on Study IDs check the Tutorial: Using studies in AFL formulas.

More information on regression channels is available from the AmiBroker User's Guide.

Fibonacci and Gann studies

There are many options, parameters, and preferences. Please refer to the AmiBroker User's Guide for details.

Triangle

Triangle tool is self-explanatory. To draw a triangle:

1. Left-click at the first point.
2. Hold the left mouse button and drag to the second point.
3. Release the mouse button.
4. Move the cursor to the third point.
5. Click once.

Andrews' Pitchfork

Andrews' pitchfork is a study using parallel trendlines. To construct the study, choose three starting points. The first is a major peak or trough on the left side of the chart display. The second and third are chosen to be a major peak and a major trough to the right of the first point. Left-click at the first point, hold down and drag to the second point, then release mouse button and drag to the third point and click once. After all starting points have been decided, AmiBroker draws a trendline from the first point (the most left) so that it passes directly between the right most points. This line is called the handle of the pitchfork. The second and third trend lines are drawn by AmiBroker beginning at the starting points and parallel to the handle.

Cycles

Click at the starting point of the cycle and drag to the end of the cycle. Vertical lines will be drawn on the chart extending that cycle length to both the right and left.

Add Icons to Toolbar

If you do not see an icon you want on a toolbar, you can turn it on. For example, assume you want the close pane icon on the view toolbar.

1. Click the Toolbar Options icon at the bottom of the View Toolbar. It will open the Add or Remove Buttons menu.
2. Select View.
3. Select Close Pane.

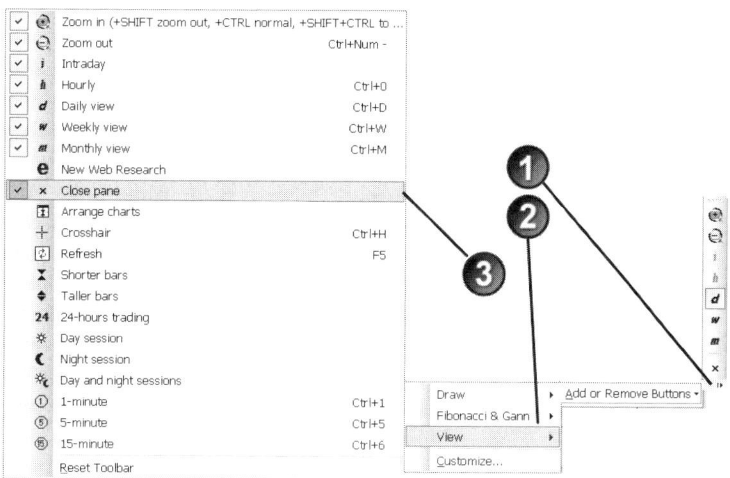

Because the View Toolbar is at the right edge of the screen, these menus open right to left.

Tabbed Menus

AmiBroker has several "tabbed" menus. These can be "torn off" from their present location and re-docked wherever you want them. And they can be set to slide to the side of the window (in an auto-hiding technique) giving more screen real estate to the charts.

The next few pages describe the "tabbed" menus and windows. They include menus Layouts, Symbols, Layers, Charts, Notepad, and Interpretation, and windows Symbol Information, Real-time Quote, Alert Output, Time and Sales.

Re-dockable menus

All of these tabbed menus are implemented as "tear-off tabs" and can be re-docked wherever you wish. To re-dock a menu into any side of the application or as a tab simply click on docking window's caption bar and drag it. Docking stickers will appear. Drag the pane until the cursor is over one of the docking stickers, then release. The pane will dock in that position. (See figure on next page.)

When you re-dock the pane back into its original location, it may not be in the same order relative to the other tabs.

Auto-hiding sliding menus

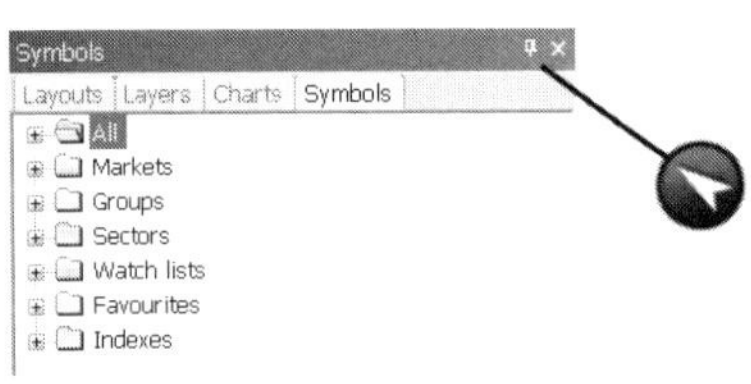

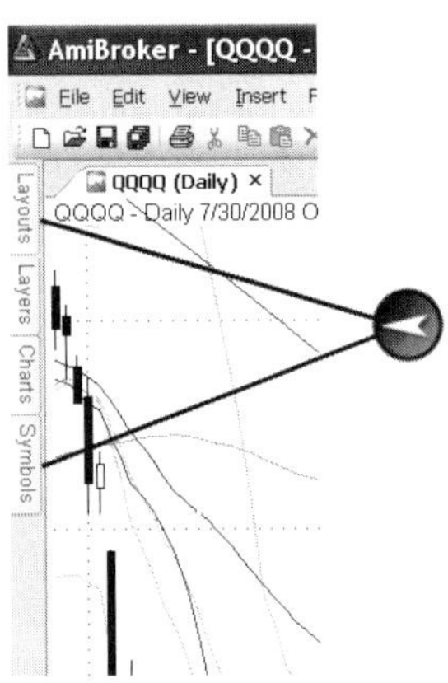

If there is a pin in the upper right hand corner of a tabbed menu, that menu may be set to auto-hide. Auto-hiding brings the menu out when you want it, and lets it slide out of the way and off the chart's real estate when you do not need it.

To set Auto-hiding On, just click the pin. The pin icon will turn from upright to sideways and the menu will be auto-hiding, as in the illustration to the left. Click the tab and the menu will slide out.

AmiBroker - [QQQQ - POWERSHARES QQQ TRUST-UNIT SER 1 - Daily]
Cursor
Docking stickers
QQQQ - Daily 4/18/2008 Open 46.51, Hi 46. 46.22, Close 46.71 (3.2%) Vol 133,022,400 MA(Close,15) =
Symbols
All
Markets
Groups
Sectors
Watch lists
Favourites
QQQQ
SPY
Indexes
For Help, press F1
Nasdaq, ETF, Financial, Fin-ETF
QP End of Day

Layouts, Layouts Tabbed Menu, Layouts Context Menu

Layouts are the highest level of the AmiBroker chart structure. They are described in Chapter 4, AmiBroker Chart Structure.

Layouts Tabbed Menu

The Layouts tabbed menu shows which layouts are available for use with the database that is open (local layouts), and which are available with any database (global layouts).

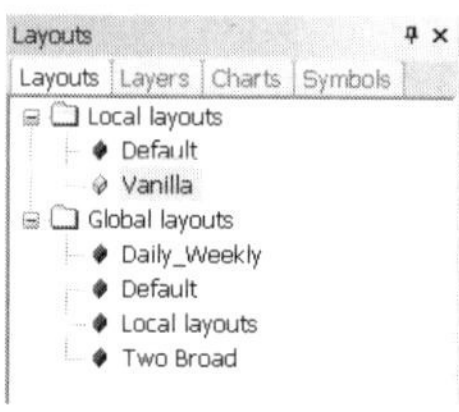

Show or hide the Layouts tabbed menu using View > Layouts.

The Yellow icon shows which layout is currently open and active.

Double-click any entry to open it and make it the active layout.

Layouts Context Menu

The Layouts context menu opens when you right-click in the Layouts tabbed menu.

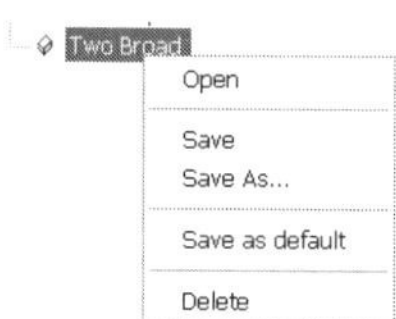

- Open - loads selected layout .
- Save - saves current window layout under current name.
- Save As... - save current window layout under new name.
- Save as default - save current window layout as default (startup) layout for given database.
- Delete - delete selected layout.

Layers, Layers Tabbed Menu, Layers Context Menu

Layers are like pieces of transparent plastic. You can put drawings on them. Showing or hiding a layer allows you to display or hide the drawings placed on that layer without affecting the drawings placed on other layers.

Layers Tabbed Menu

The Layers tab lists the pre-defined layers.

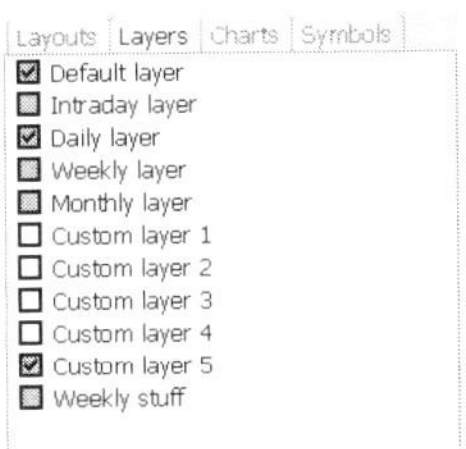

The checkboxes on the left side of each layer control layer visibility. If the box is checked, then that layer is visible; if it is unchecked, that layer is invisible.

Show or hide the Layers tabbed menu using View > Layers.

The first five layers are built-in and special. They are:

1. Default layer - always visible.
2. Intraday layer - visible only when viewing intraday charts.
3. Daily layer - visible only when viewing daily charts.
4. Weekly layer - visible only when viewing weekly charts.
5. Monthly layer - visible only when viewing monthly charts.

The visibility of these five is controlled by the charting interval selected, and cannot be changed using the checkboxes. The remaining layers can be shown or hidden by marking the checkbox.

To draw a study on a given layer:

1. Select the layer by clicking on its name.
2. Draw the study as usual.

You can move a study from one layer to another using the Properties menu of the study (not the Properties of the layer). That is, right-click the study, choose Properties, select the layer you want this study to be on.

Layers Context Menu

When you right-click on a layer name, you will see the context menu containing the following options:

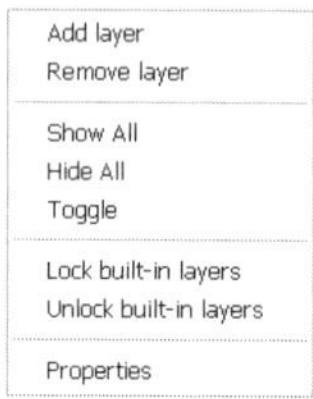

- Add layer - Adds a new layer.
- Remove layer - Removes the selected layer. Note that you cannot remove any of the first five, built-in layers.
- Show all layers - Shows all non-locked layers.
- Hide all layers - Hides all non-locked layers.
- Toggle - Toggles the visibility of all non-locked layers.
- Lock built-in layers - Lock the first five, built-in layers. When these layers are locked, their visibility changes when the charting interval changes.
- Unlock built-in layers - Unlocks the first five layers. The visibility now depends on the checkbox.

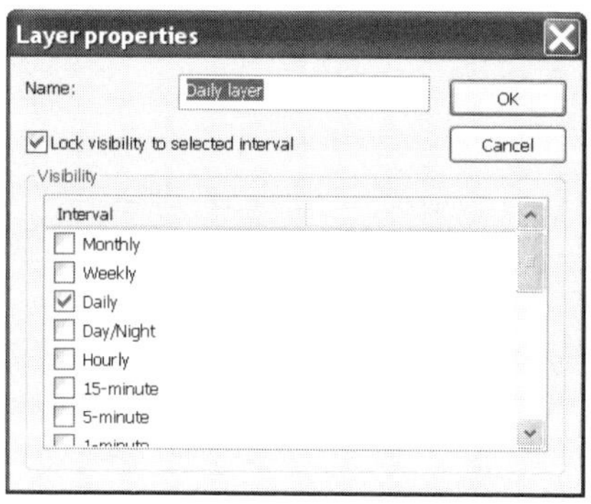

- Properties - Launches the properties box that allows you to rename layers, and decide if the layer should be locked to the charting interval displayed. There is a *separate* visibility setting for each interval. Check the boxes where you want the layer to be visible and uncheck those where you do not.

Symbols, Symbols Tabbed Menu, Symbols Context Menu

The Symbols Tabbed menu displays the ticker symbol of all issues in the active database. Each symbol may be a member of several categories. The ticker will be listed in every category to which it belongs. (See Categories, page 177.)

Show or hide the Symbols tabbed menu using View > Symbols.

Symbols Context Menu

The Symbols context menu opens when you right-click in the Symbols tabbed menu.

- Add to favorites - Add the active symbol to the Favorites category.
- Remove from favorites - Remove the active symbol from the Favorites category
- Erase favorites - Remove all members of the Favorites category from that category (not from the database).
- Web research - Open a new window in the AmiBroker Chart window, and use the built-in browser to display a page of information about the active symbol. (See figure next page.)

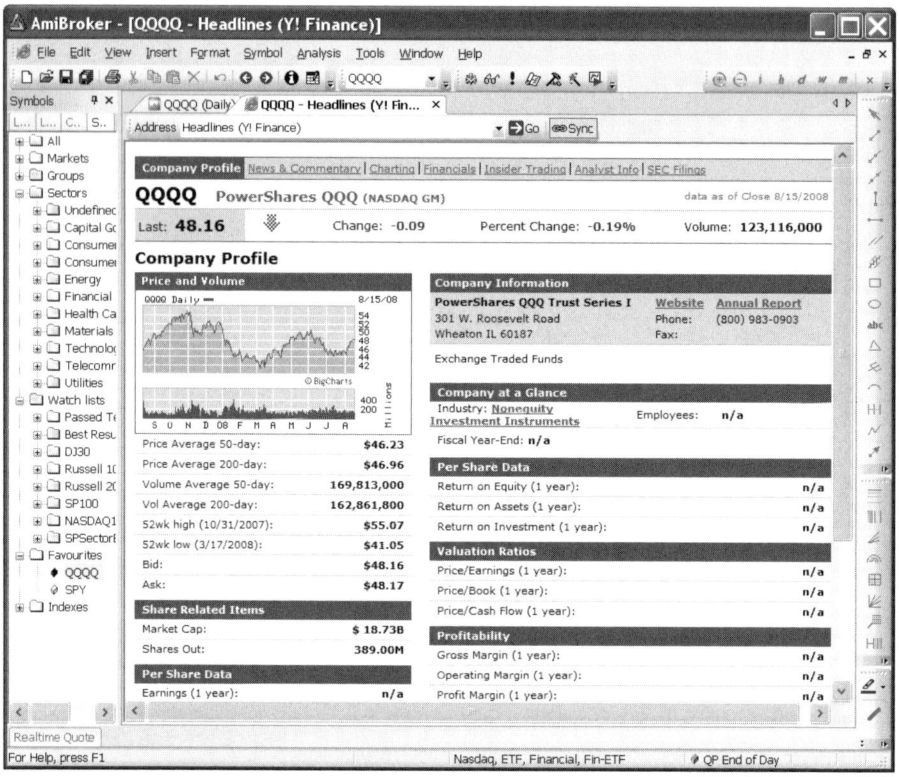

- Watchlist - The expanded menu is shown on the next page.
- Add to Real-time quote window - Add the active symbol to the real-time quote window.
- Delete - Delete the active symbol from the database. Use with care - this action cannot be "undone".

Watchlist Submenu

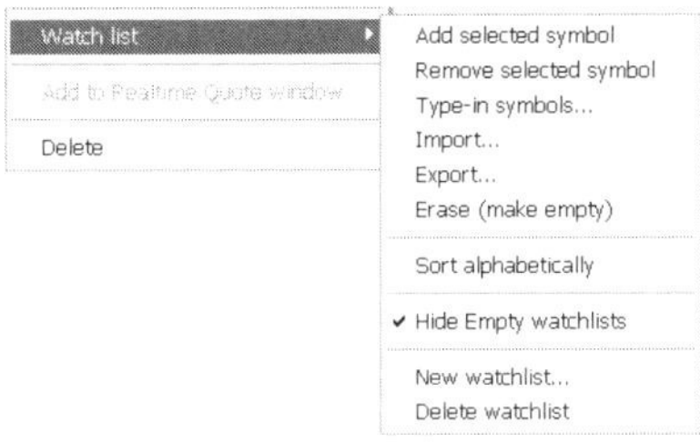

- Add selected Symbol - Add the active symbol to a watchlist. A dialog box will open so you can choose which watchlist.
- Remove selected symbol - Remove the active symbol from one or more of the watchlists of which it is a member.
- Type in symbols - Opens a dialog box and allows you to type in a comma separated list of symbols to add to a watchlist.
- Import - Opens a dialog box and allows you to specify a list of symbols to be added to a watchlist.
- Export - Export the tickers of a watchlist to a text file.
- Erase (make empty) - Remove all entries from a watchlist.
- Sort Alphabetically - Sort the symbols in a watchlist into alphabetical order.
- Hide Empty Watchlists - A toggle to either hide or display watchlists that have no members.
- New Watchlist - Establishes a new watchlist at the end of the list of existing watchlists. Uses a name you specify.
- Delete Watchlist - Deletes the watchlists that are selected.

(See Watchlists, page 179.)

Charts (Formulas) Tabbed Menu, Charts Context Menu

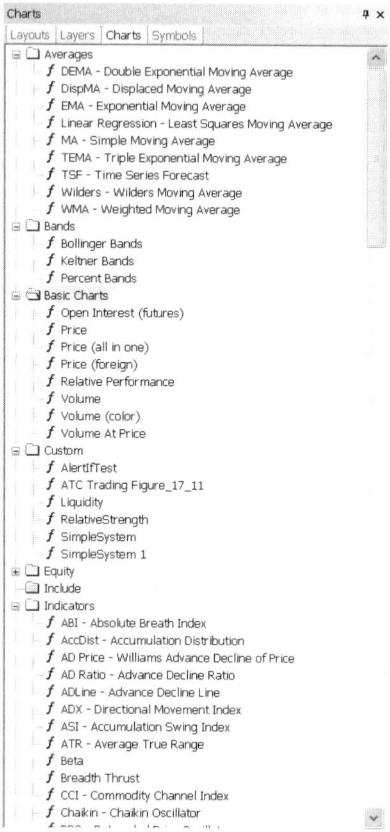

The Charts Tabbed Menu gives access to the charts, formulas, and indicators that can be applied to the chart panes.

Show or hide the Charts tabbed menu using View > Charts.

A later section, Charts (Formulas), page 190, lists the formulas and indicators, explains them, and shows how to apply them in more detail.

Charts Context Menu

Right-click any entry to display the context menu.

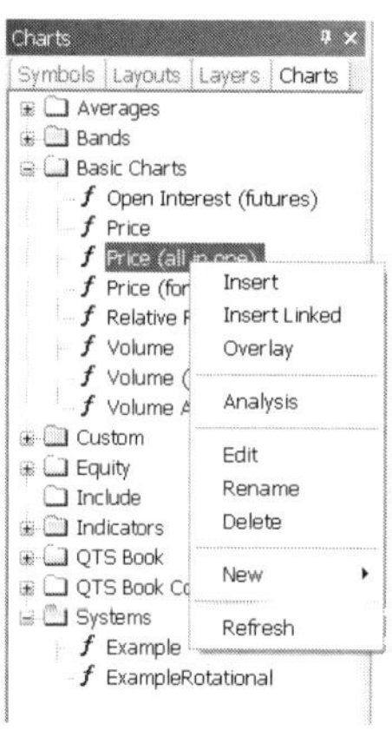

- Insert - inserts a copy of the selected indicator into a new pane. The copy of the original formula file is created and placed in a hidden drag-drop folder. The original formula will not be affected by subsequent use or editing, and other formulas can be applied to the same chart without conflict. Double clicking on a formula name is equivalent to choosing Insert from the menu.
- Insert Linked - Inserts the selected indicator into a new pane directly. Insert Linked does not create a copy of the formula. Instead, it cre-

ates a new pane that is directly linked to the original formula. Any modifications to the original formula will be applied to the one being inserted.

- Overlay - Overlay the selected indicator into the selected (active) pane. The overlay command appends additional code to the formula used by the pane. If the given pane was created using Insert Linked, it will modify the original (linked) formula. If there are several data series in the pane being overlaid, a dialog box will appear and you will be able to select which one is to be overlaid.
- Analysis - Opens the Automatic Analysis window with the selected formula chosen.
- Edit - Opens the Formula Editor with the code for the selected formula loaded.
- Rename - Rename the selected formula.
- Delete - Delete the selected formula.
- New
    - Formula - Creates a new formula file in the selected folder.
    - Folder - Creates a new subfolder under the selected folder.
- Refresh - Re-reads the Formula directory and re-displays the formula tree.

See the section Charts (Formulas), page 190.

Notepad, Notepad Tabbed Menu, Notepad Context Menu

Notepad window

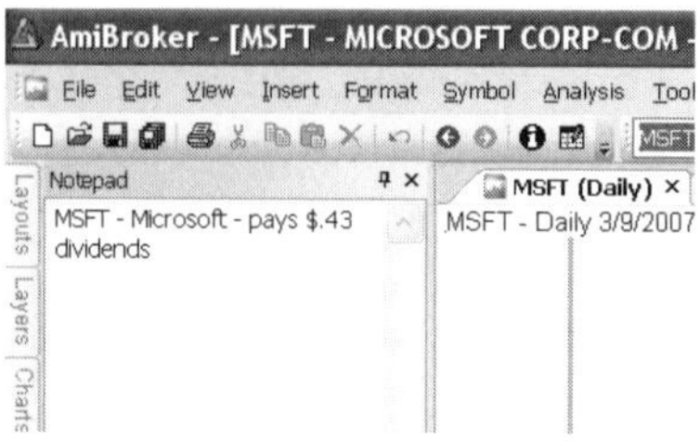

The Notepad window allows you to store free-text notes about a particular security. Type any text into the Notepad window (no editor required). It will be associated with whatever ticker symbol is in the active window and automatically saved. The text will appear in the Notepad window whenever that symbol is in the active window.

Notes are global, not database specific, and are saved in C:\Program Files\AmiBroker\Notes subfolder as ordinary text files.

Notes can be also written and read using AFL langauge NoteSet and NoteGet functions.

AmiBroker Notepad, one of the Tabbed menus, should not be confused with Microsoft Notepad, a general purpose text editor that is a component of Microsoft Windows.

Show or hide the Notepad tabbed menu using View > Notepad.

Notepad Context Menu

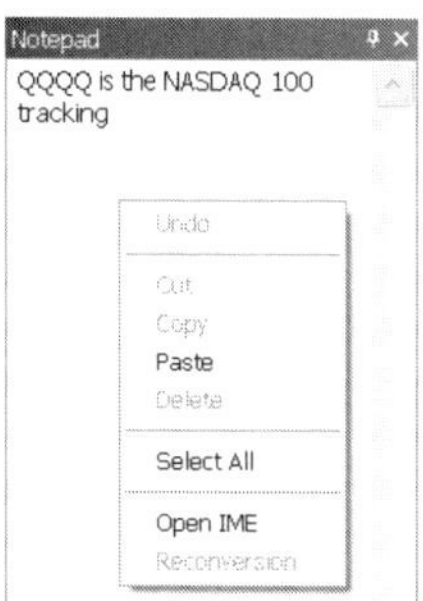

The Notepad context menu opens when you right-click over the Notepad window. The menu is a basic editing menu with options to cut, copy, paste.

Interpretation, Interpretation Tabbed Menu, Interpretation Context Menu

Interpretation Window

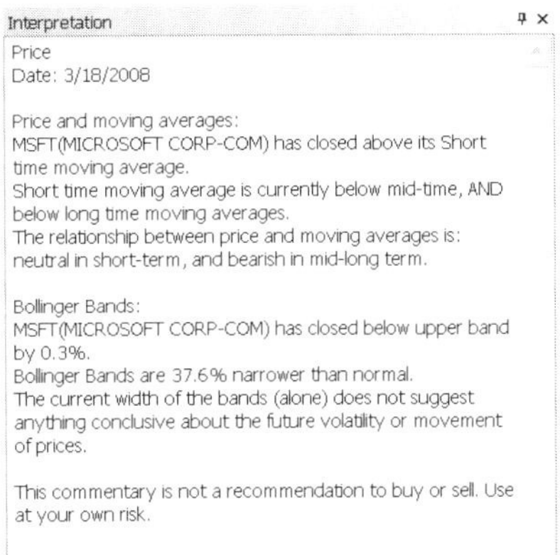

The Interpretation window shows chart-sensitive commentaries that are created by the execution of an AFL program. To add an interpretation, see Commentary and Interpretation, page 524.

Show or hide the Interpretation tabbed menu using View > Interpretation.

Interpretation Context Menu

The Interpretation context menu opens when you right-click over the Interpretation window. The menu is a basic editing menu with options to cut, copy, paste.

Alert Output, Alert Output Context Menu

Alert Output Window

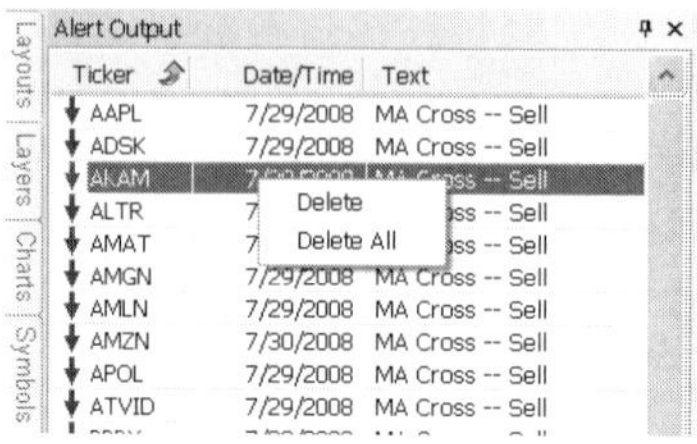

The Alert Output Window receives the messages sent by the AlertIf function as an AFL program runs.

Show or hide the Alert Output window using View > Alert Output.

Alert Output Context Menu

The Alert Output Context menu gives only two choices:

- Delete - Delete the selected row
- Delete All - Delete all rows in the window.

Real-Time Quote, Real-Time Quote Context Menu

Real-Time Quote Window

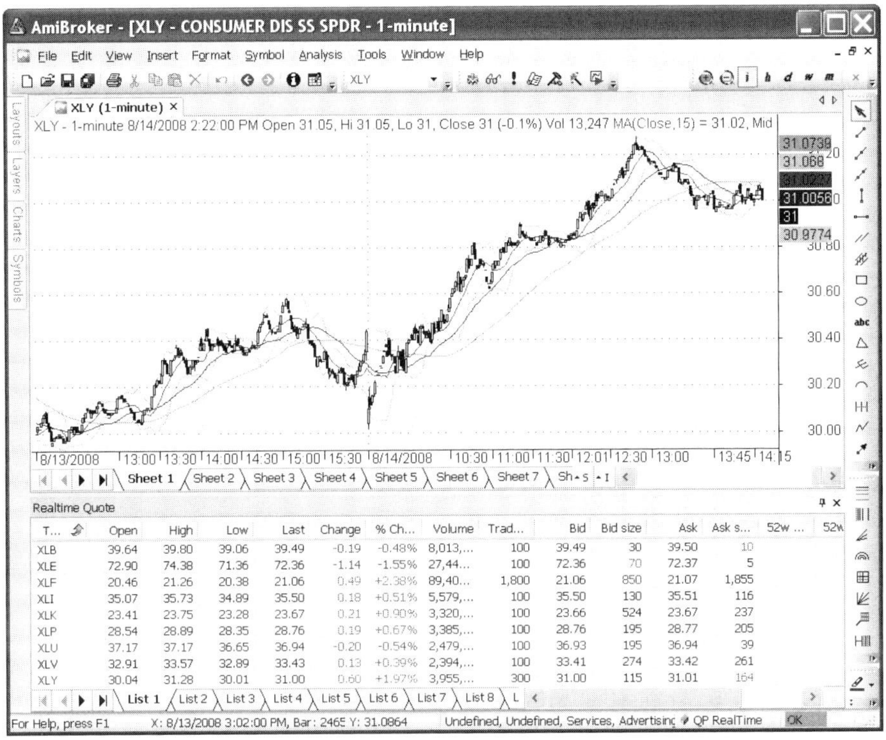

The Real-Time Quote window shows the tick-by-tick information about the symbols that have been added to the window. Fields depend somewhat on the data provider, but include:

- Prices for the session - Open, High, Low, Last.
- Change from previous close.
- Percent change from previous close.
- Volume for the session.
- Last trade volume.
- Bid price and size.
- Asked price and size.

Show or hide the Real-Time Quote window using View > Real-Time Quote.

Real-Time Quote Context Menu

The Real-Time Quote context menu opens when you right-click in the Real-Time Quote window.

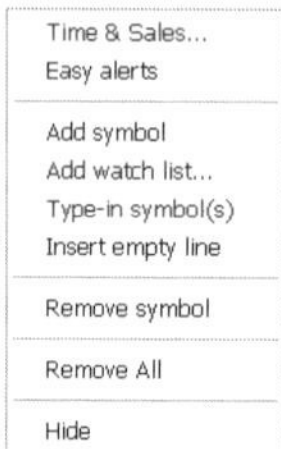

- Time and Sales - Opens the Time and Sales window that provides information about every bid, ask, and trade.
- Easy Alerts - Opens the Easy Alerts window that provides a way to define real-time alerts executed when bid, ask, or last hit user-defined levels.
- Add Symbol - Adds the current symbol to the Real-Time Quotes list.
- Add Watchlist - Adds all the symbols in a watchlist to the Real-Time Quotes list.
- Type in Symbol - Opens a dialog so you can type in a symbol to add.
- Insert Empty Line - Inserts a blank row in the Real-Time Quote window to help visual organization of the window.
- Remove Symbol - Removes the symbol in the highlighted line from the Real-Time Quote window.
- Remove All - Removes all symbols from the Real-Time Quote list.
- Hide - Hides the Real-Time Quote list and window.

Time and Sales

The Time and Sales window displays information about every bid, ask and trade streaming from the market. Each row displayed represents either a new trade, a new bid, or a new ask that is sent by the streaming data source.

Each line in the time and sales window is marked with color to make it easier to distinguish between various conditions.

Coloring rules are:

- Light green background means a new ask.
- Light red background means a new bid.
- Normal (white) background means a new trade.
- Red text for the bid price, ask price, or size means that the value is less than the previous value of the same category. For example, if the bid price is written in red letters, that means that the new bid is lower than the previous bid.
- Green volume field means that the volume of last trade, or ask or bid size, is greater than the last.
- Black text for the bid/ask price/size/volume means that the value is the same.
- Red last trade price means the trade occurred at or below the current bid.
- Green last trade price means the trade occurred at or above the current ask.
- Black last trade price means the trade occurred inside the current bid-ask range.

Time and Sales Context Menu

The Time and Sales Context Menu appears when you right-click in the Time and Sales Window.

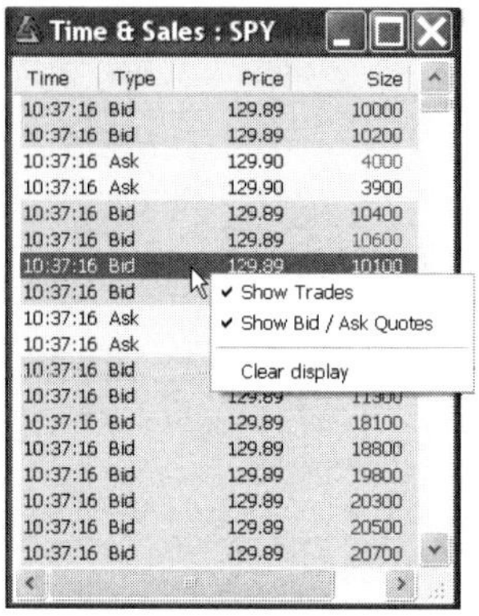

- Show Trades - When checked, displays trades.
- Show bid / ask Quotes - When checked, displays bid and ask prices.
- Clear display - Clears the window.

Categories

AmiBroker has the ability to assign ticker symbols to different categories, and then use categories as filters, selecting symbols based on membership in a particular category.

There are two types of categories:

1. Those with mutually exclusive membership: groups, markets, sectors, and industries. This means that a symbol must belong to exactly one group, one market, one sector, and one industry at a time.
2. Those with free membership: watchlists, favorites, and indexes. This means that a symbol may belong to any number (including zero) of watchlists, and, optionally, belong or not belong to the favorite and index categories.

Group - Market - Sector - Industry

For stocks, each stock belongs to one industry. It belongs to one sector based on its industry and on an assignment table - each industry belonging to exactly one sector. For example: GM (General Motors) belongs to the "Auto & Truck Manufacturers" industry, and this implies that GM belongs to "Consumer/Cyclical" sector.

AmiBroker can handle up to 32 sectors and up to 256 industries. The predefined list of industries and sectors is in Appendix B. You can define your own sectors and industries to use in place of those. For more details, see the AmiBroker User's Guide.

Category Membership

Categories are displayed under the Symbols Tabbed menu.

Although the icons look like normal folders used by Windows Explorer, categories do Not work like folders.

The difference is fundamental. In the Windows file structure, a file appears only once in a given tree as a leaf. In the AmiBroker symbol trees, any symbol may show up multiple times - once as a leaf in every category to which it belongs.

A single symbol belongs to many categories at the same time. For example AAPL (Apple Inc.) will belong to these categories:

- All
- Stocks group
- Nasdaq market
- Information sector
- Comp-Computer Mfg industry

And it may belong to these categories:

- Any number of watchlists
- Perhaps the favorite category
- Perhaps the index category

The special category called *All* lists all symbols present in the database.

Category Assignment

You can assign a symbol to an industry using either:

- Symbol Pull-down menu > Information, then edit the Categories you wish to change.
- Symbol Pull-down menu > Organize assignments, then use the Assignments Organizer.

The first method is fine if you want to change single symbol settings. The latter is better if you want to move multiple symbols from one category to another.

WATCHLISTS

Watchlists are lists of symbols that have something in common. Watchlists are used to define the universe of symbols that should be used when procedures are run. You will use them a lot, and there are many techniques for managing them. Examples of watchlists you might use are:

- Components of the S&P 100.
- Components of the NASDAQ 100.
- Sector ETFs.
- Commodity ETFs.
- Stocks that passed your favorite filter.

Watchlists differ from other kinds of categories (groups, markets, industries, sectors) in that you can assign a single symbol to more than one watchlist - in fact, to as many watchlists as you want to.

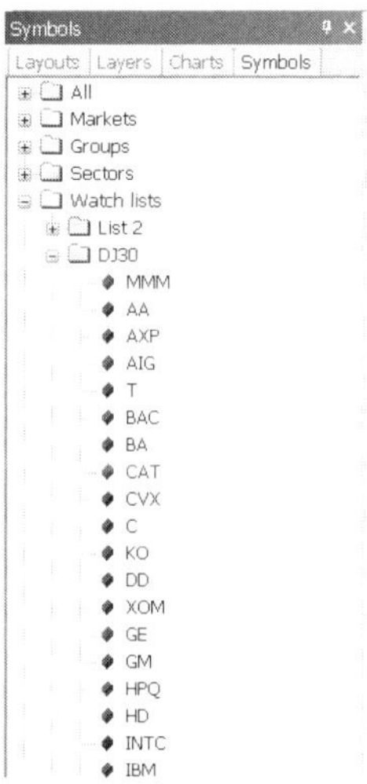

The members of each watchlist are shown in the symbol tree. Open the Symbol Tabbed menu and expand Watch lists.

Watchlists are associated with a single database. They are one symbol per line, and have the file extension .tls. The .tls files can also be opened by AmiQuote. They are stored as text files in the Watchlists folder in the subdirectory of the database they are used with. The folder contains any number of .tls files defining watchlists themselves; and it also contains the file named index.txt that defines the order of watchlists. You can create as many watchlists as you want, and name them whatever you want. You add your own .tls files to that subdirectory, and AmiBroker will automatically update index.txt, and add any new watchlists it finds.

All watchlists are local, there are no global watchlists. If you want to use the same watchlist with several databases, copy the .tls files to those database subdirectories.

When you open the default symbol tree and expand the watchlist category, you will see 64 watchlists, numbered 0 through 63, all initially empty. You can populate these and rename them, or you can add new watchlists.

Adding Watchlists

You can add watchlists in several ways:

- Use the Symbol menu > Watch List > New Watchlist.
- From the watchlist context menu.

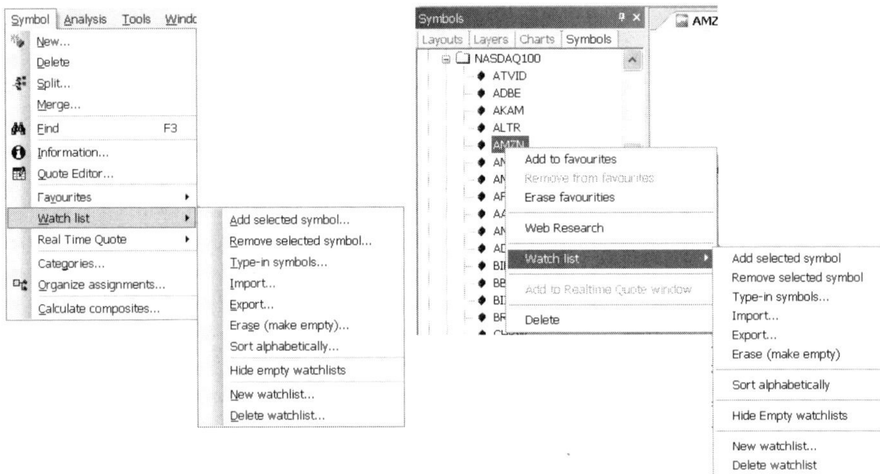

Removing Watchlists

Similarly, you can remove watchlists in those same ways using the Delete watchlist option.

If these menu items do not appear, use the Tools > Customize > Options, then press the Reset button for new menu items to appear.

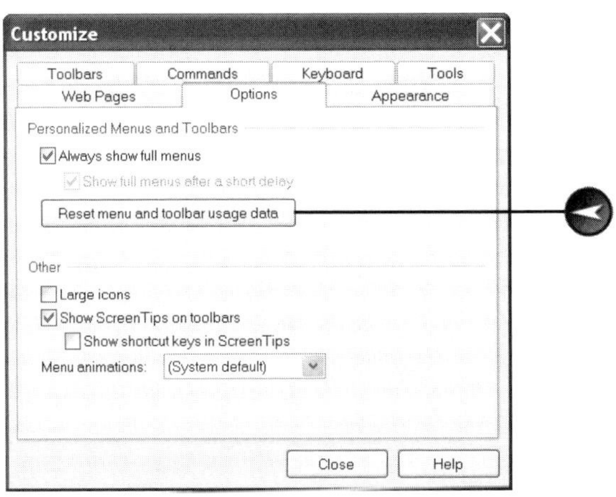

ADDING SYMBOLS TO WATCHLISTS

You can add a single symbol to a watchlist by right-clicking the symbol in the symbol tree (in any of the categories except watchlist) and choosing Watch List > Add selected symbol.

A watchlist selector window will appear.

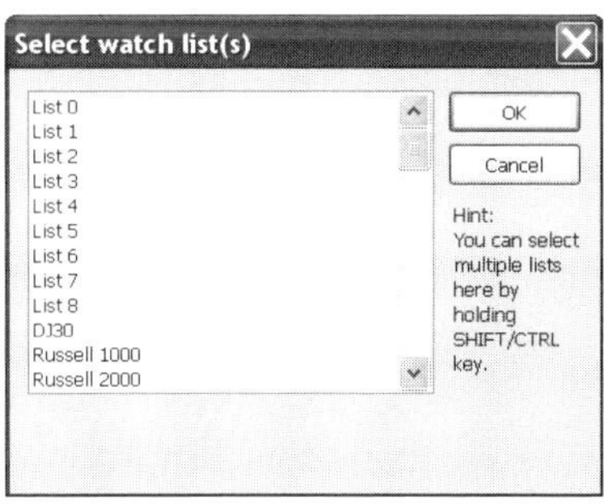

Select the list you want to add the symbol to. Note that you can add one symbol to multiple lists in one operation by holding the CTRL key while clicking on the list items. After clicking OK the selected symbol appears in the watchlist(s).

You can also type-in symbols directly into the watchlist using Symbol > Watch list > Type-in. You will be asked to select a watchlist, then to type in the list of symbols, each symbol separated from the next by a comma. Use uppercase letters.

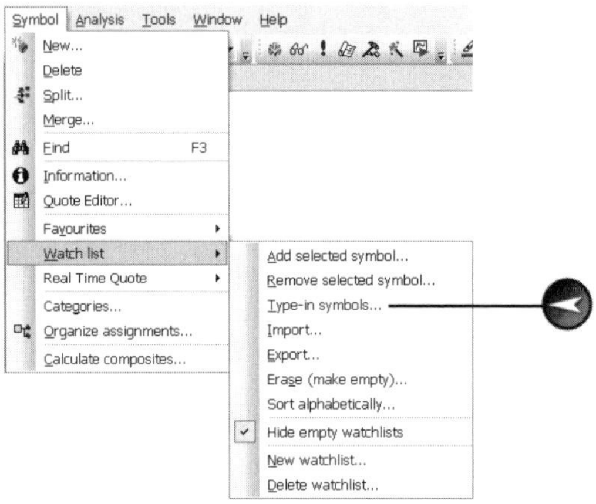

You can also right click the watchlist name in the workspace tree to type in symbols directly into the watchlist.

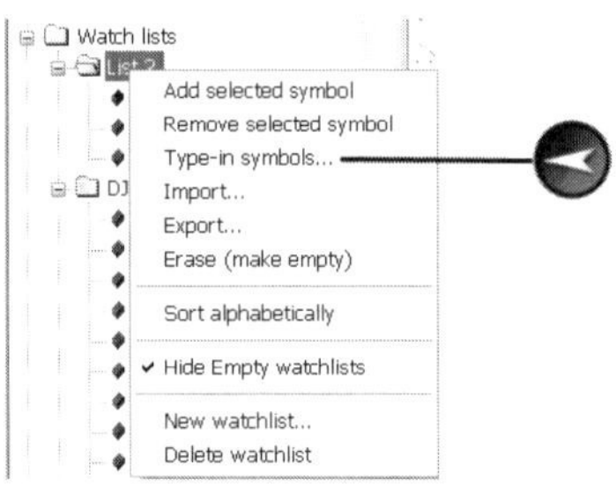

Sorting Symbols in a Watchlist

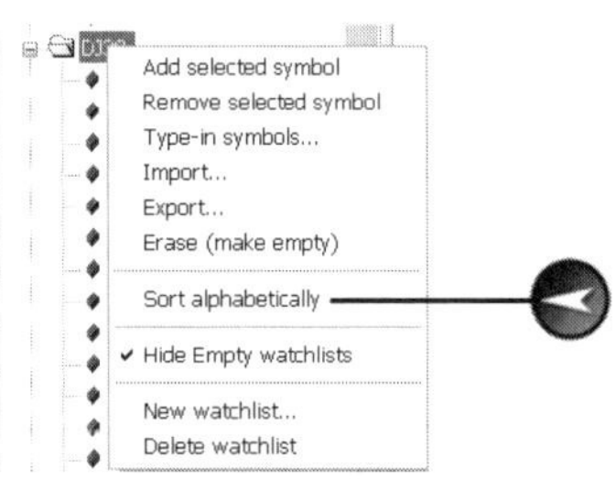

Watchlists remember the order in which symbols were added. If you sort a result list in some order and then you "add symbols to watchlist" the order will be kept in the watchlist.

You can ask AmiBroker to sort the watchlist into alphabetic order. Select the watchlist, right-click, and select Sort alphabetically.

Removing Symbols from Watchlists

Removing symbols from the watchlist is as easy as adding them. Right-click the Watchlist name and select Remove Selected Symbol.

Erasing Watchlists

Sometimes you may want to clear (or erase) the whole watchlist. Using the Symbol menu, Watch list, Erase (make empty) option. In the watch-list selector window mark the list(s) you want to clear and click OK. You will be asked to confirm.

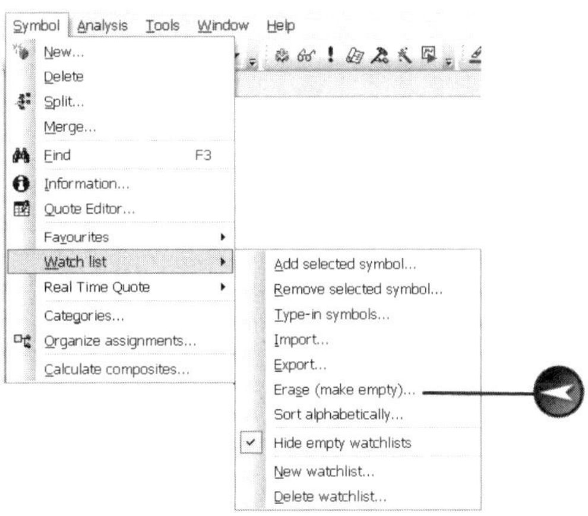

Hiding and Unhiding Empty Watchlists

By default all watchlists, including those that have no symbols in them, are shown in the symbol tree. You can hide empty lists. Right-click on any symbol or watchlist name in the symbol tree, and select "Hide Empty watchlists". To un-hide, use the same menu and remove the check mark.

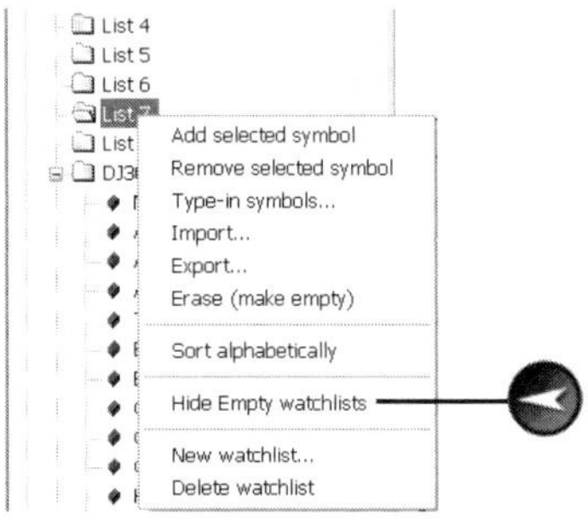

Using Watchlists in Automatic Analysis Window

The results of scanning, backtesting, and exploration can be added to a watchlist. After running your analysis, you will have a list of results. Sort those results as you wish. Select the lines of the symbols you want in a watchlist. (The lines do not need to be contiguous. Hold the CONTROL key while clicking the mouse on any lines in any order.) Right-

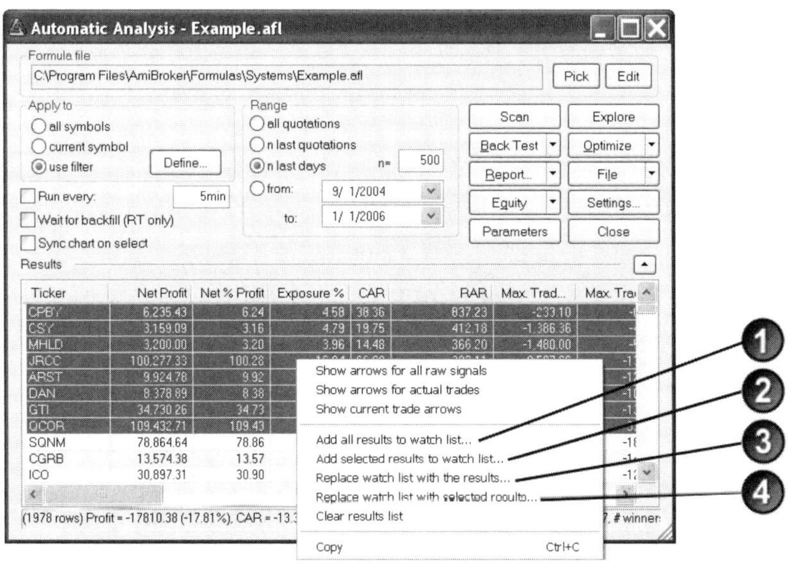

clicking brings up a dialog box that gives several choices. The four we are interested in at this time are:

- Add all the results to watch list. There are 1978 rows. Selecting this option will add the symbols for all 1978 rows to the watchlist. Duplicates will be eliminated.
- Add selected results to watch list. This option will add eight symbols to the watchlist. Duplicates will be eliminated.
- Replace watch list with the results. Make the watchlist empty, then save the 1978 symbols in it. Keep the symbols in the order they are in the results window.
- Replace watch list with selected results. Make the watchlist empty, then save the eight symbols in it.

After you have made your choice from among these four options, you will have an opportunity to select the watchlist(s) to receive the symbols.

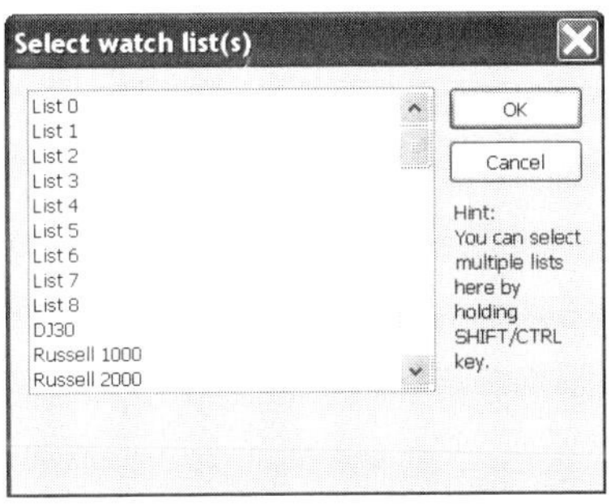

Import a Watchlist from a File

Using the Symbol menu, choose Watchlist, then Import. Select the watchlist you want to use. Ignore the file button - you cannot change it.

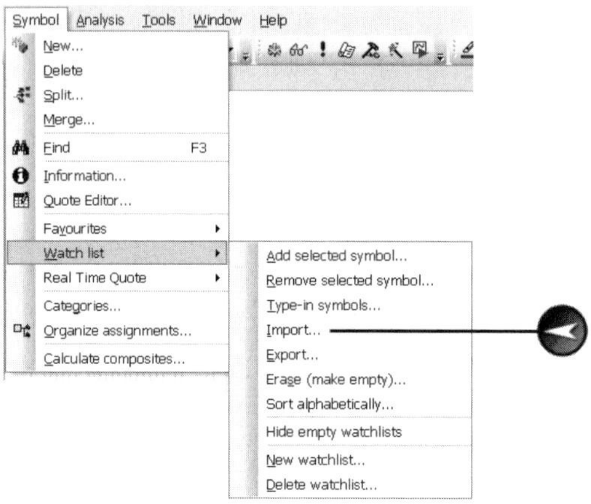

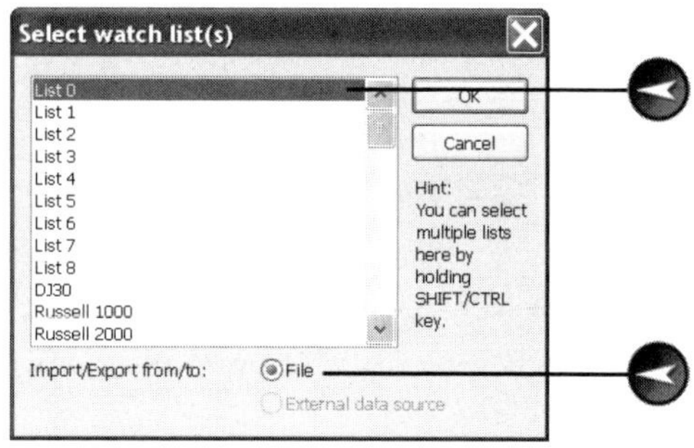

1. Navigate to the file you want to import.
2. Select that file.
3. Click Open.

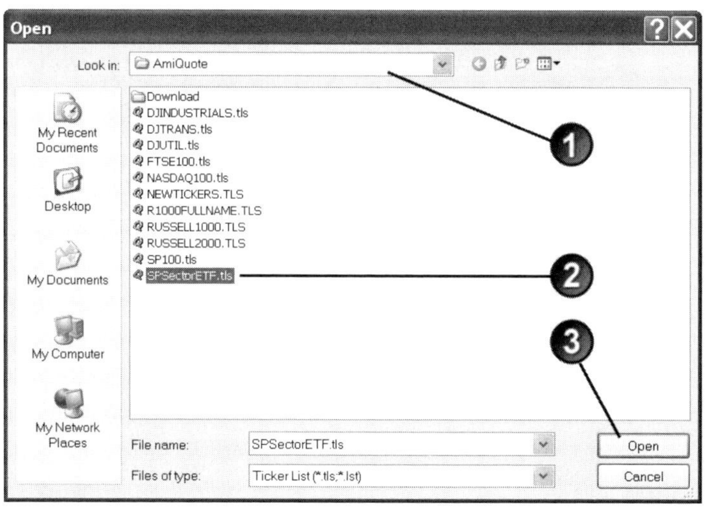

The file type dialog shows the file type that can be imported without need to convert them first - .tls, .txt, .csv, and .lst. The first three should have one ticker symbol per line and no other fields. .lst files are Quotes-Plus standard, comma separated list files that have the ticker symbol in the first column and some additional data in remaining columns. AmiBroker reads just first column and ignores the rest.

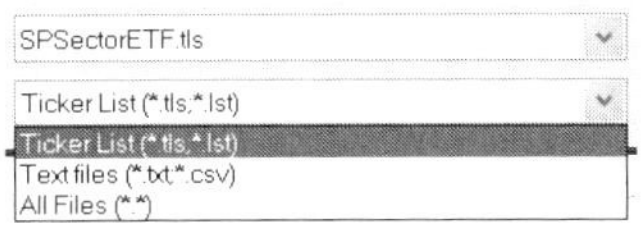

You can also start the import process by right-clicking the name of a watchlist in the symbols tree. The menu that comes up has an "Import" option.

Export a Watchlist to a File

Choose Symbol > Watchlist > Export. Select the watchlist you want to export. Select the directory, file name, and file extension for the exported data. The file format will be ASCII, with one ticker symbol per line.

You can also start the export process by right-clicking the name of a watchlist in the symbols tree. The menu that comes up has an "Export" option.

Renaming Watchlists

The formal way begins by pulling down the Symbols menu and selecting Categories.

In the categories box:

1. Select the Watch lists tab.
2. Select the list to be renamed.
3. Click Edit Name.
4. Type in the name you want, say Passed Test.
5. Click OK.

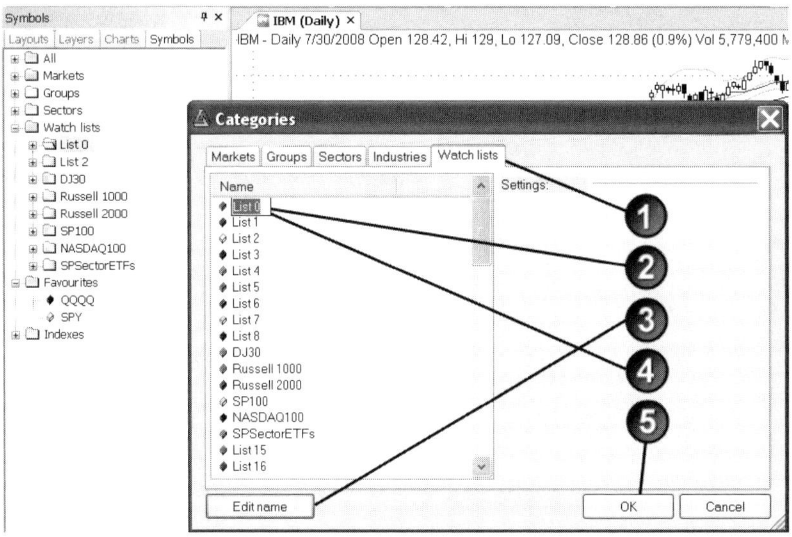

The watchlist is renamed.

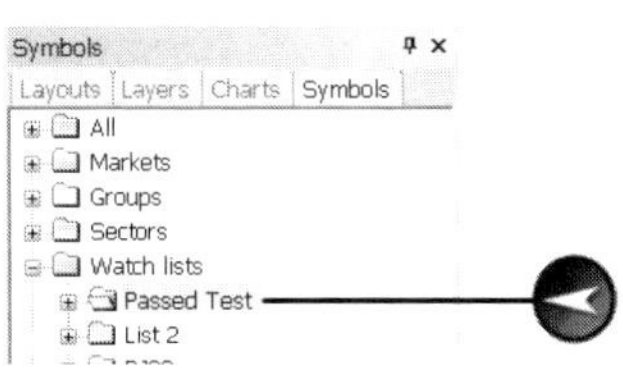

The informal way uses no menus, just Windows techniques.

1. Using the Symbol Tabbed menu, expand Watchlists.
2. Left-click the list you want to rename.
3. Left-click again, but not so quickly that Windows interprets it as a double-click.
4. The name of the watchlist will be selected.

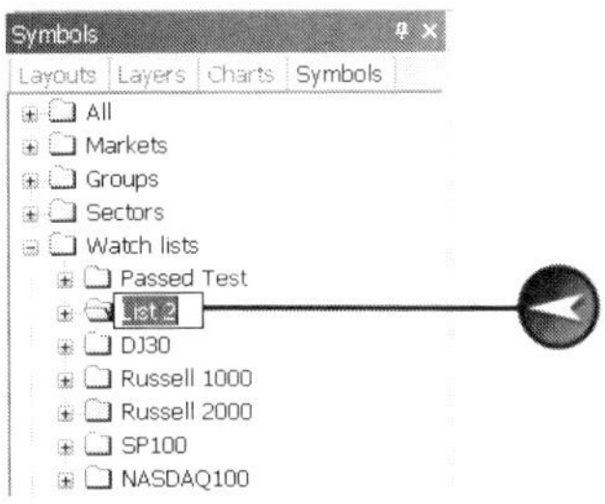

5. Type in the name you want.
6. Press Enter or click on any other watchlist name.
7. The watchlist is renamed.

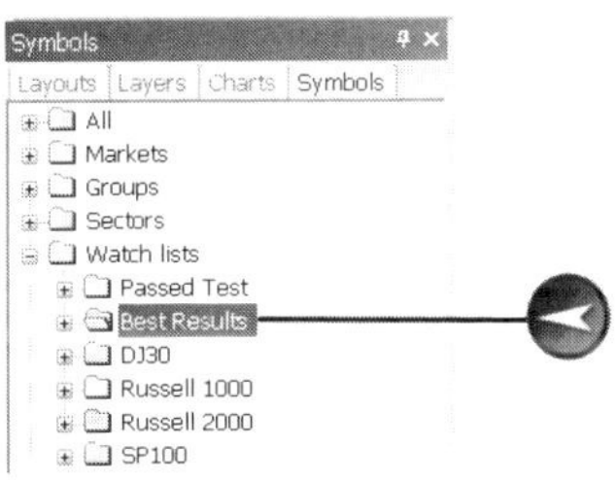

Charts (Formulas)

There are two types of tools that can be placed on charts:

- Those that can be placed and adjusted manually. They appear on the Toolbars and on the Insert menu, and were discussed in the previous section.
- Those that are based on formulas, are computed, have parameters that specify their relationship to the charts they are applied to, and are adjusted using their parameters rather than manually. A set of these tools has been pre-programmed, is ready-to-use, and appears on the Charts tabbed menu. To minimize confusion, the tools located on the Charts tabbed menu will be referred to in general as formulas and indicators. This section discusses basic operations of these tools.

An earlier section (page 190) briefly described the Charts tabbed menu and its context menu. And a later section (page xxx) will describe creating your own formulas and indicators using the AFL language.

Basic Operations

Insert - Insert a New Indicator

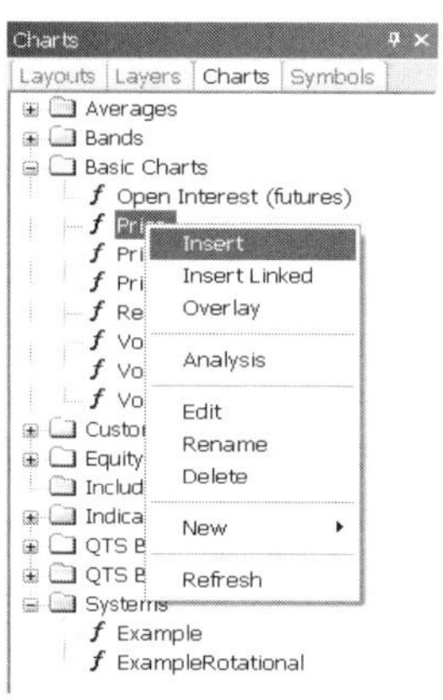

To display a new indicator in a separate pane, either:

- Using the Charts tabbed menu, locate the indicator you want, then double-click the indicator's name.
- Using the Charts tabbed menu, locate the indicator you want, then right-click the indicator's name bringing up the context menu. Click Insert.

Using either method, a new pane will be created, the indicator inserted and displayed, and a parameters dialog opened. If you wish, you can change the properties of the indicator, such as the color of its plot or the values of the parameters used in its calculation.

See Example 3, page 65, for more information and screen capture images.

Insert Linked

The difference between Insert and Insert Linked is:

When the Insert method is used to place an indicator in a pane, a *copy* of the indicator is placed. Any changes made to the original of the indicator will not affect the copy already placed.

When the Insert Linked method is used, the *original* code is placed. Any changes made to the original code will be reflected in the indicator already placed.

Delete an Indicator

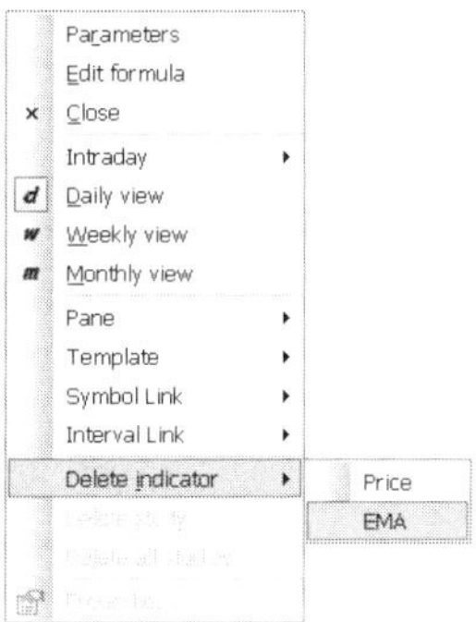

Right-click the pane the indicator is in, bringing up the context menu. Choose Delete indicator, then Click the name of the indicator to be deleted.

Drag and Drop

1. Load the price series you want to study in a pane.
2. Make that pane the active pane.
3. Open the Charts tabbed menu. Locate the indicator or formula you want to use.
4. Drag that indicator onto the price series and drop it. The cursor turns into a drag and drop cursor whenever it passes over any pane where dropping it would be meaningful.
5. Adjust the placement, properties, and parameters as necessary.

Overlay One Indicator on Another

Locate the indicator you want to overlay in the Charts tabbed menu. Left-click the name of the indicator, drag the indicator to the desired pane, hover over the series you want the indicator applied to, and drop. A properties dialog box will open. Verify that the indicator is being applied properly.

For example, create a 15 day moving average of the 14 day RSI:

1. Using the Charts tabbed menu, select Price, double-click, creating a new pane with the price series in candlestick format.
2. Using the Charts tabbed menu, select RSI, drag it to the pane with the new price series, drop it.

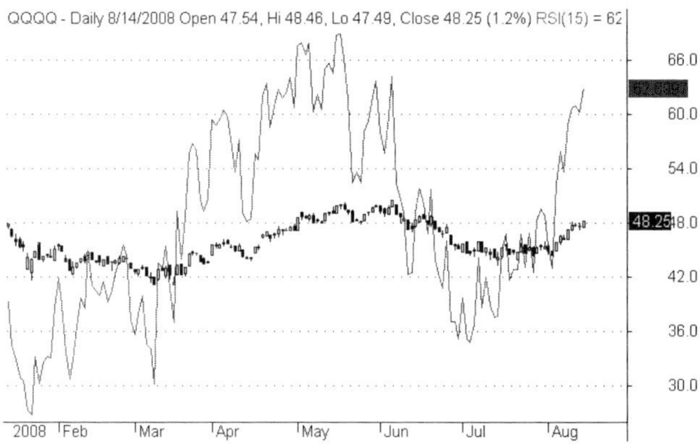

3. Using the Charts tabbed menu, select EMA, drag it to the pane with the price and RSI, drop it. A Properties dialog box will open. There are two series that the moving average could be applied to - Close and RSI. Select RSI.

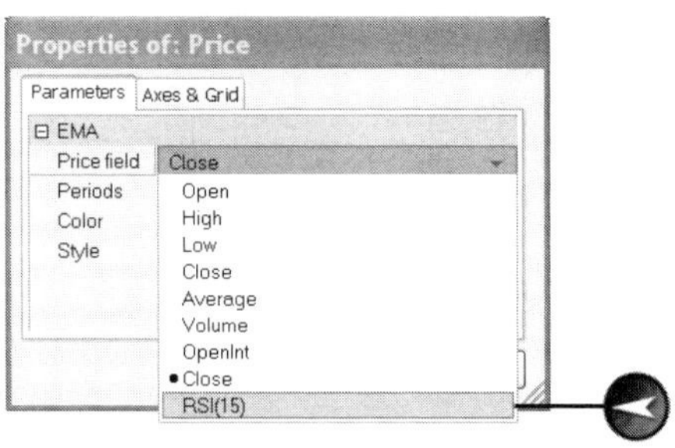

The pane shows the price, the RSI, and the moving average of the RSI.

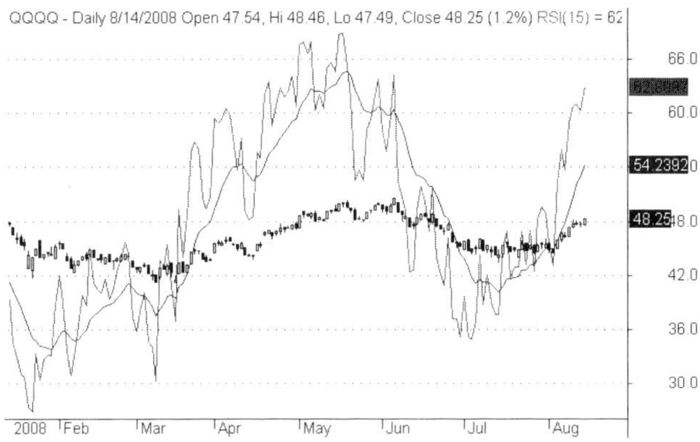

Also see Example 3, page 65.

Change Parameters

Right-click the pane the indicator is in. The context menu will appear, click Parameters. The Properties box will appear. Find the parameter you want to change, and change it.

For example, to change the example just above to an 11 day RSI with a 3 day moving average:

The properties box shows the indicators in that pane that have changeable parameters.

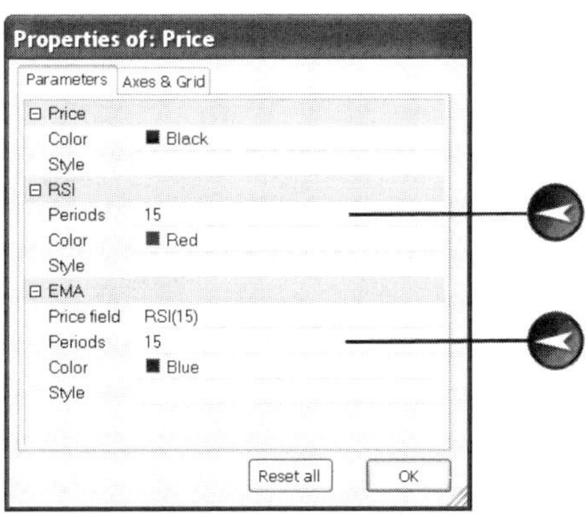

Change the Period associated with RSI to 11, and the Period associated with EMA to 3.

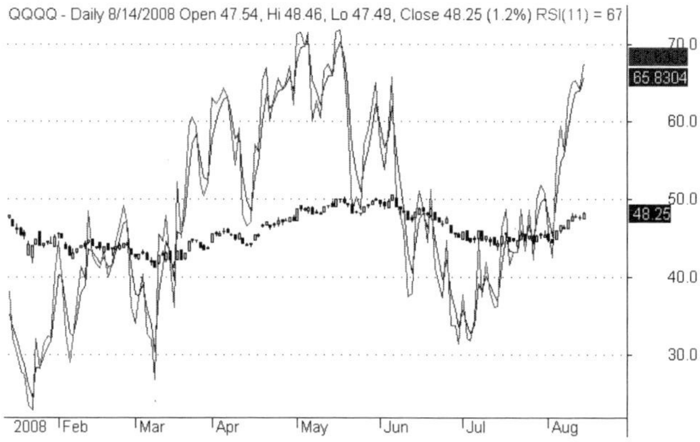

Also see Example 3, page 65.

Adjust the scale of an indicator

If you have a pane with two (or more) indicators, and they use different scales, one of them will be difficult to interpret. To give an indicator its own scale:

1. Right-click in the pane with the indicators. The context menu will appear.
2. Click Parameters. The Properties box will appear. Resize the box so you can see the details of all the indicators.
3. Click Style - the Style parameter has an option to give each indicator its own scale.
4. Click OwnScale for each of the indicators you want to change.

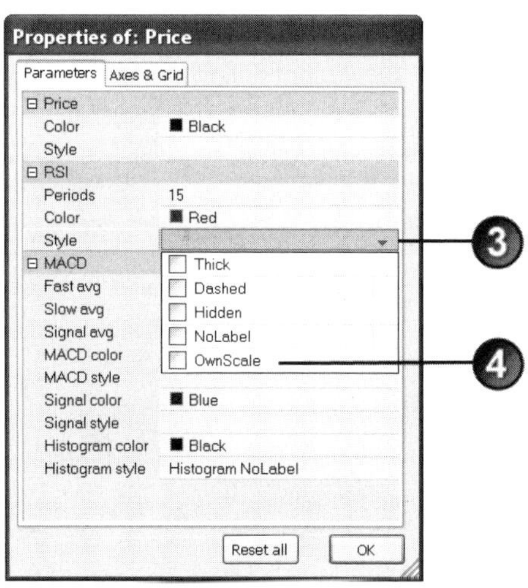

Averages

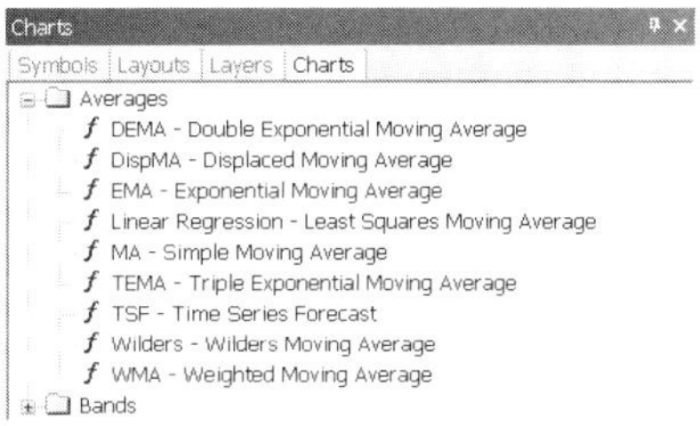

MA - Simple Moving Average

The simple moving average is the average of as many bars as are specified by the Period. This moving average has a lag of half of the length of the period. That is, a 15 day simple moving average is the average of 15 days, centered 8 days ago.

DispMA - Displaced Simple Moving Average

The displaced simple moving average is a simple moving average displaced in time. If the displacement is positive, the average is moved forward in time and plotted to the right of where the undisplaced simple moving average would be. If the displacement is negative, the average is moved backward in time and plotted to the left of the undisplaced moving average. The screen capture shows a 15 day simple moving average and a 15 day moving average displaced by -8 days. This illustrates the effect of lag.

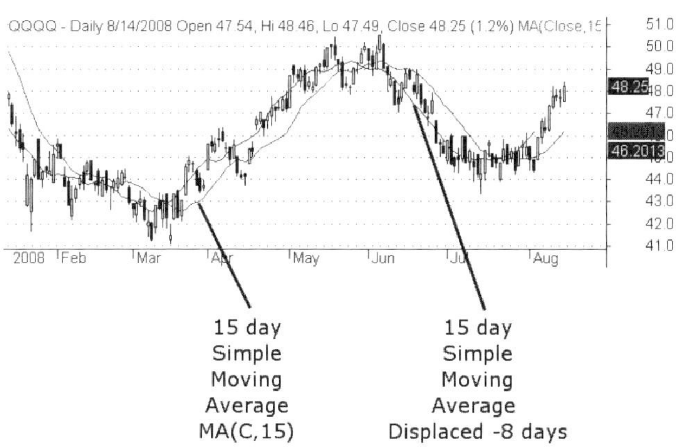

EMA - Exponential Moving Average

The exponential moving average is the sum of two terms - one the contribution of the latest bar of data, the other the contribution of the value of the indicator at the previous bar. The definition is recursive. The smoothing factor, a, determines how important the most recent data is and how fast the effect of earlier data dies away.

Today's value = a * Today's data + (1-a) * Yesterday's value

We can talk about exponential moving averages having a length just as simple moving averages do. The relationship between the number of days, n, in the exponential average and the smoothing factor, a, is:

$$a = 2 / (n + 1).$$

$$EMA[i] = a * C[i] + (1-a) * EMA[i-1].$$

For a 15 day exponential moving average, a = 2/(15+1) = 0.125. Today's new data is weighted 12.5% and the value the exponential moving average had yesterday is weighted 87.5%. The chart below illustrates.

DEMA - Double Exponential Moving Average

The DEMA uses a differencing technique to remove lag from the indicator. Note that it follows the changes in price more quickly (that is, it has less lag), but it is less smooth. There is a trade-off between lag and smoothness.

TEMA - Triple Exponential Moving Average

The TEMA uses a more extreme technique to remove even more lag.

The screen image compares the three exponential moving averages, all of which use 15 as the value for the period.

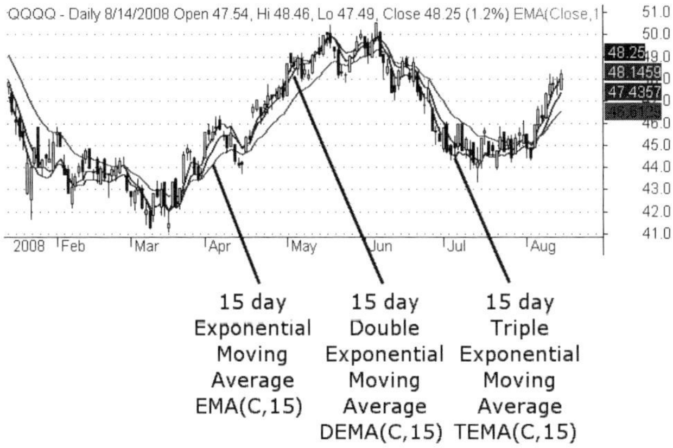

Linear Regression - Least Squares Moving Average

The linear regression indicator computes and plots the end point of a linear regression using the number of data points given as a parameter. The image shows a 15 period linear regression.

TSF - Time Series Forecast

The time series forecast indicator computes and plots the end point of a time series forecast using the number of data points given as a parameter. The technique is very similar to the linear regression method. The image shows a 15 period time series forecast.

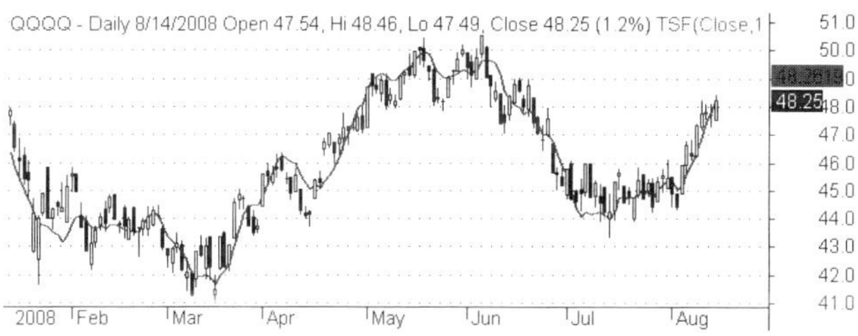

Wilders - Wilders Moving Average

Wilders moving average for a given period, n, is equivalent to an exponential moving average with period 2*n-1. The image shows a 15 period Wilders moving average.

WMA - Weighted Moving Average

The n-period weighted moving average gives the most recent data point a multiplying weight of n, the next older a weight of n-1, and so on to the nth older point getting a value of 1. The sum of all the terms is divided by the sum of all the weights. The image shows a 15 period weighted moving average.

Bands

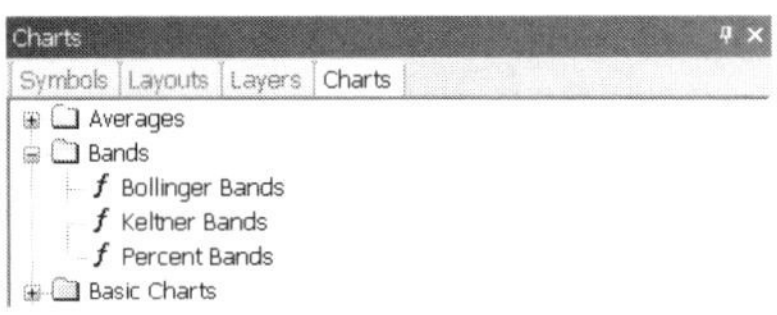

Bollinger Bands

Bollinger bands, developed and popularized by John Bollinger, are envelopes that surround the price bars on a chart. They are plotted some number of standard deviations (often 2) away from a simple average (often 15 bars). The length of the moving average is also the number of data points in the standard deviation. Because standard deviation is a measure of volatility, the Bollinger bands adjust themselves to the market conditions. They widen during volatile market periods and contract during less volatile periods. Bollinger bands become moving standard deviation bands. The image shows Bollinger bands 2.0 standard deviations away from a 15 day simple moving average.

Keltner Bands

Keltner bands, developed by Chester Keltner, are similar to Bollinger bands in that they measure and respond to volatility. Keltner bands are set some multiple (often 2) of the ATR (Average True Range) from a simple moving average (often 15 bars). (See ATR in the description of functions.) The number of bars in the ATR and the number of bars in the average are usually the same. The image shows Keltner bands 2 times the 15 day ATR away from the 15 day simple moving average.

Percent Bands

Percent bands are set a given percentage of the average above and below that average. The image shows percent bands set 2 percent above and below the 15 day simple moving average.

Basic Charts

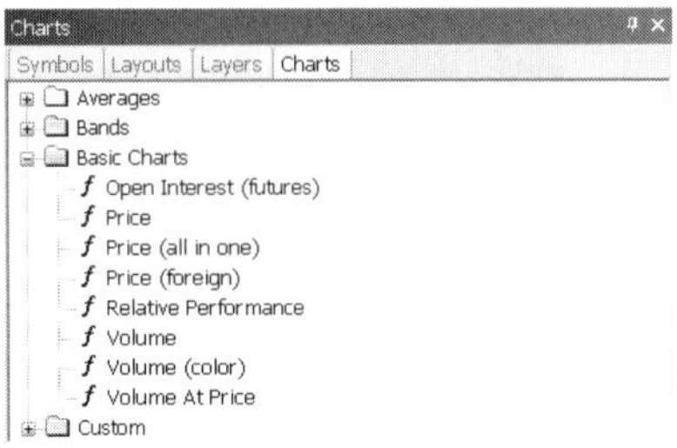

Open Interest

Plots the open interest field. Mainly used with futures contracts.

Price

Plots the price series as candlesticks.

Price (all in one)

Plots the price series, Bollinger bands, and moving averages.

Price (foreign)

Plots the price series using the Foreign function. When the price series is plotted using the Price function (as the two above) and the active symbol changes, the plot will change to reflect the new symbol. When the price series is plotted using the Price (foreign) function, it will not change. This is useful for plotting a reference symbol, then cycling through a watchlist of symbols and viewing the comparison.

In the image, SPY was plotted using Price (foreign), and given its own scale. Then the active ticker was changed to QQQQ.

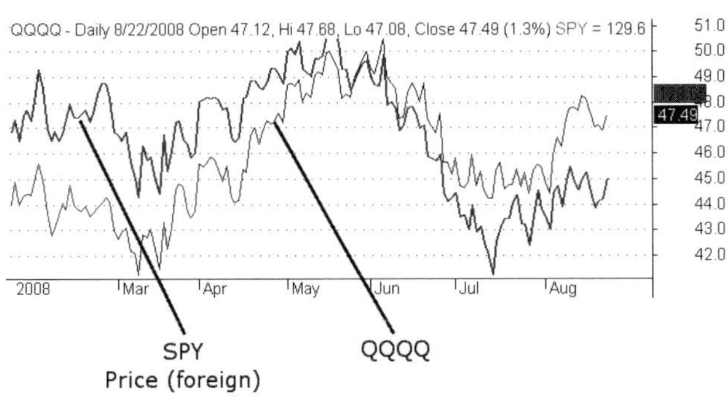

Relative Performance

Plots the relative performance of the issues plotted. Double-click Relative Performance. A Properties box will open. Type in the symbols you want to compare. The active symbol will be automatically added to the list. Click OK.

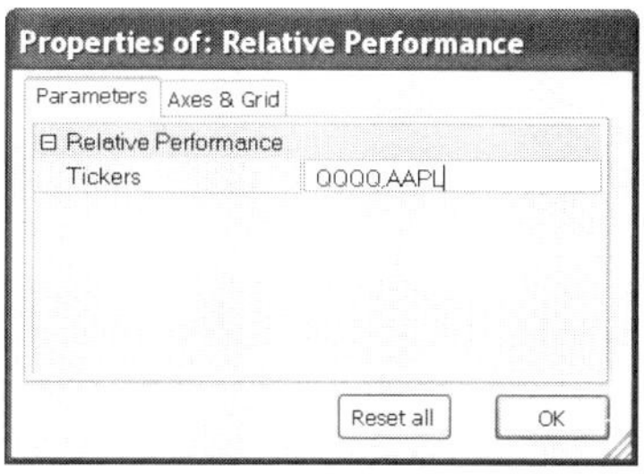

A new pane will open and the prices of the symbols you entered plotted. All prices will be normalized to 1.00 at the left side of the pane. The lines show the relative performance for the period displayed in the pane. Scroll to see other time periods. Click through a watchlist to see other issues relative to those symbols you entered.

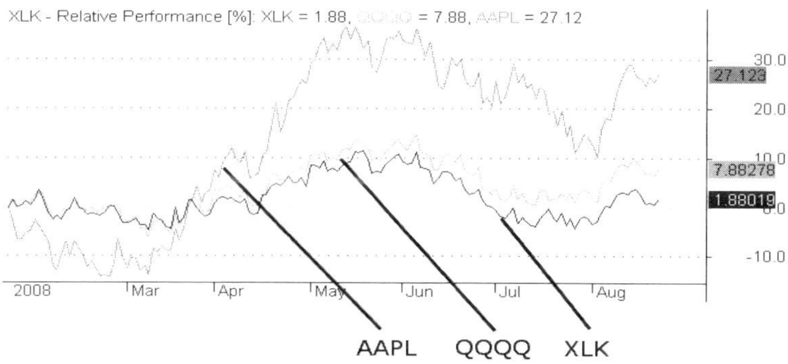

Volume

Volume opens a new pane and plots the volume.

Volume (color)

Volume (color) opens a new pane and plots the volume using colored bars. If the close was higher than the open, the bar is green, otherwise red.

Volume at Price

Plots a histogram of volume per price.

The pane needs to have both price and volume. This already exists in the top pane, but that is crowded. To display volume at price in a pane of its own:

1. Double-click Price. A new pane will open with the price plotted.
2. Right-click Volume, then click Overlay. The volume will be added to the pane.
3. Right-click Volume at Price, then click Overlay. A properties box will open.

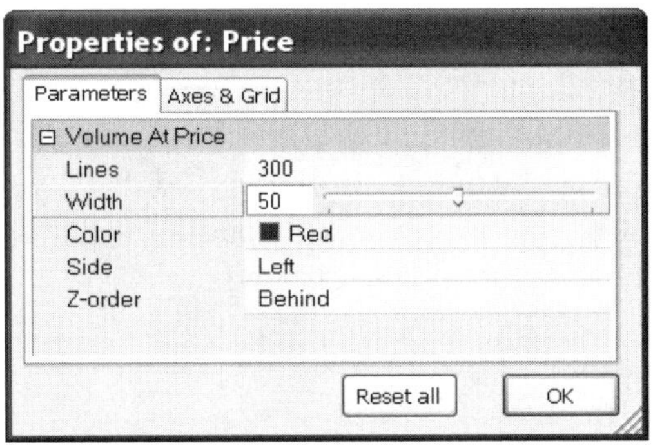

4. Adjust the parameters as you want them. Lines specifies the number of histogram bars. Width specifies how far across the pane the longest histogram bar reaches. Click OK.

Custom

The Custom category is a category that you can use to store whatever formulas you want. The Customs category was used to keep the examples used in chapter 3 of this book organized.

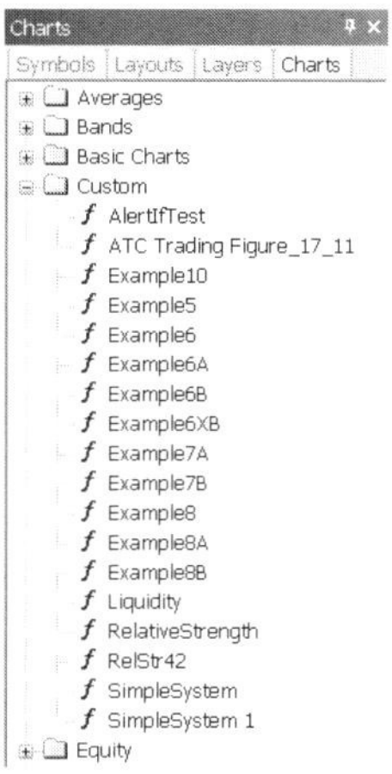

Equity

Individual

Individual Equity plots the equity curve using the data from the most recently run trading system.

Double-click Individual. A properties box will open asking if you want to display Buy and Hold. Click OK. The formula plotted here has been changed to show the equity as a line. The default plots as an area.

IS and OOS Equity

This formula is used with the walk forward testing. Two lines are plotted. One is the equity curve that results from taking all the In-Sample trades. The other is the equity curve that results from taking all the Out-of-Sample trades.

Use of this formula is described in Chapter 9, Analysis.

Portfolio

Portfolio Equity plots the equity curve from the most recent backtest. The plot shows when positions are held (blue color), when cash is held (green color), and drawdown (brown color). Also see Example 7, page 87.

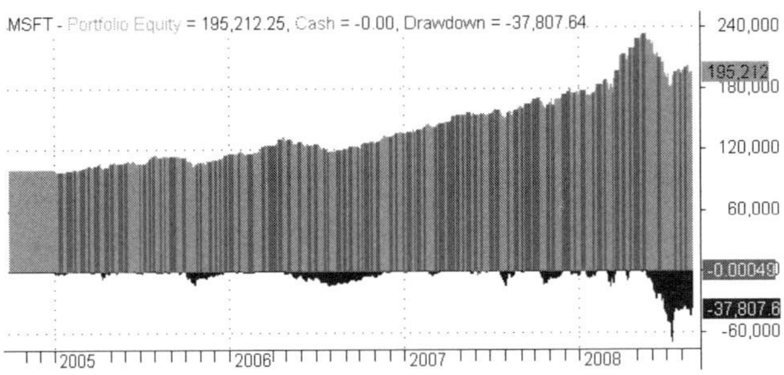

Include

The Include category holds code that can be included with an AFL program at the time it is run.

Indicators

An extensive list of formulas and indicators that can be applied to charts.

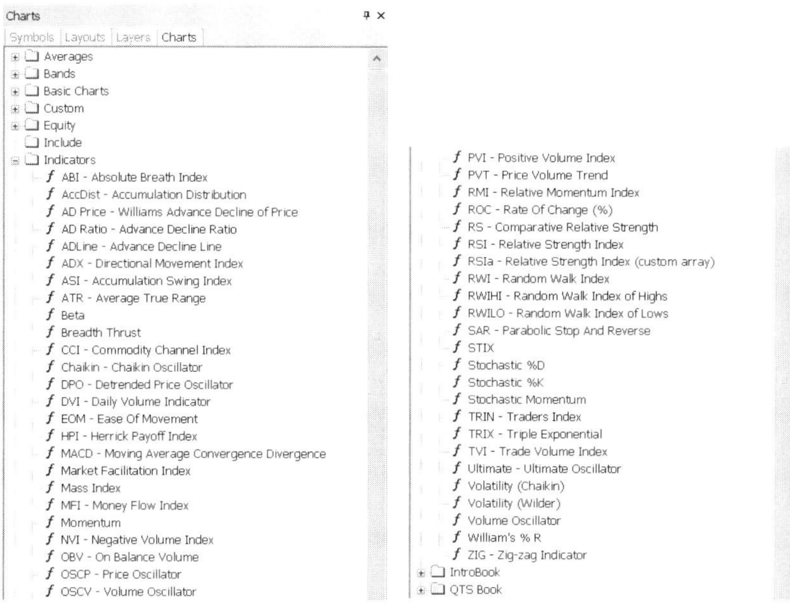

ABI - Absolute Breadth Index

Absolute Breadth Index is an indicator developed by Norman Fosback. It is calculated by taking the absolute value of the difference between the number of advancing issues and the number of declining issues. Any universe may be used. Large numbers suggest volatility is increasing, which may precede significant changes in stock prices in the coming weeks.

The formula shown below has been adapted to use the Quotes Plus symbols for the NYSE number of advancing issues and number of declining issues.

```
function AbsoluteBreadthIndex()
{
  return abs((Foreign("!NY-A","C") - Foreign("!NY-D","C")));
}

Plot( AbsoluteBreadthIndex(), _DEFAULT_NAME(),
ParamColor("Color", ColorCycle ) );
```

The chart shows the ABI plotted along with !NYA, the NYSE Composite Index.

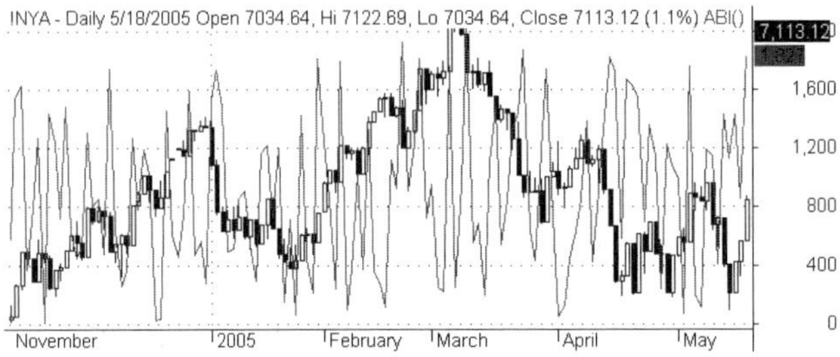

AccDist - Accumulation Distribution

A momentum indicator that attempts to gauge supply and demand by determining whether investors are generally *accumulating* (buying) or *distributing* (selling) a certain stock. It is calculated using the following formula:

AccDistFn = ((Close – Low) – (High – Close)) / (High – Low) * volume;

AD Price - Williams Advance Decline

The Williams Advance Decline, developed by Larry Williams, compares today's price and yesterday's price, adjusted by the true range and summed into a cumulative indicator. Practitioners suggest looking for divergences.

AD Ratio - Advance Decline

Advance Decline ratio divides the number of advancing issues by the number of declining issues.

ADLine - Advance Decline

ADLine is a summation of the net daily difference between the number of advancing issues and the number of declining issues. AmiBroker uses a slightly improved formula that also takes into account the number of unchanged issues. The AFL formula for AmiBroker's ADLine is:

```
Difference = ( AdvIssues() - DecIssues() )/ ( UncIssues() + 1 );
DiffSqrt = IIF( Difference > 0, sqrt( Difference ),
            - sqrt( - Difference ) );
ADLine = Cum( DiffSqrt );
```

ADX - Directional Movement

ADX, average directional movement index, was developed by Welles Wilder and is intended to indicate the market trend. When used with the up and down directional indicator values, +DI and -DI, ADX can be used as a trading system. The standard interpretation for using the ADX (blue line) is to establish a long position whenever the +DI (green line) crosses above the -DI (red line).

ADX is widely referenced. Be certain to test it carefully before using it to trade. The ADX calculation introduces a lot of lag into the signals, and the trading system suggested is not profitable on most issues.

The image shows ADX, PDI, MDI and a price series.

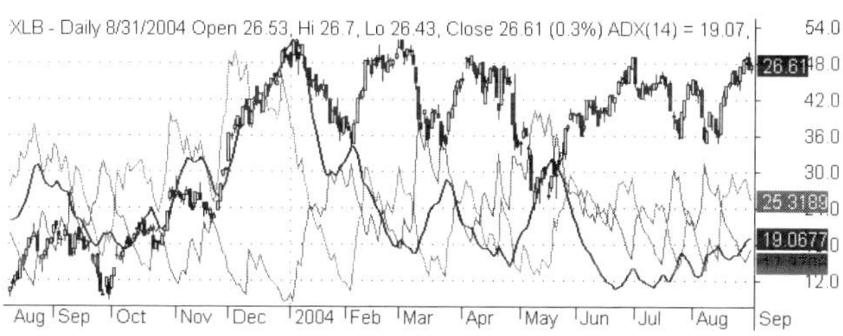

ASI - Accumulation Swing

The accumulation swing index (ASI) is a variation of Welles Wilder's swing index. It plots a running total of the swing index value of each bar. The swing index is a value from 0 to 100 for an up bar and 0 to -100 for a down bar. The swing index is calculated by using the current bar's open, high, low and close, as well as the previous bar's open and close.

ATR - Average True Range

Average True Range is a measure of volatility. The daily (or single bar) measure is the difference between *true high* and *true low*. True high is defined as the maximum of this bar's high and the previous bar's close. True low is defined as the minimum of this bar's low and the previous bar's close. The daily ATR values are typically averaged over a number of bars. For example, ATR(15) is the average of the most recent daily ATR and the previous 14 values.

The image shows a price series and the ATR(15) indicator.

Beta

Beta is the slope of the regression line between the issue being studied and a base issue. It is the multiplier that gives the ratio of the change in the issue being studied for every change in the base issue. When beta is greater than 1.00, the issue being studied moves a greater percentage than the base issue. When beta is less than 1.00, the issue being studied moves a smaller percentage than the base issue. A useful analysis technique is to build a trading system using a base issue that is relatively smooth and easy to model. Then make the trades in some other issue, usually in the same industry or sector, that has a beta greater than 1.00.

Here is the code to compute beta. The base issue has been set to XLE, the S&P Sector ETF tracking the energy sector.

```
// betatest.afl

function Beta( BaseSymbol, N )
{
 Chg = ROC( C, 1 );
 ChgBase = ROC( Foreign( BaseSymbol, "C" ), 1 );
```

```
    return ( N * Sum( Chg * ChgBase , N ) - Sum( Chg, N)
             * Sum( ChgBase, N ) ) /
           ( N * Sum( ChgBase ^ 2 , N ) -  Sum( ChgBase, N ) ^ 2 );
}

symbol = ParamStr( "Symbol", "XLE" );

Plot( Beta( symbol, Param("Periods", 21, 2, 100 ) ),
         _DEFAULT_NAME(), ParamColor( "Color", ColorCycle ) );
```

The image shows a plot of beta for the symbol DNR, Denbury Resources, which has had a beta of greater than 1.00 relative to XLE for most of the last two years.

Breadth Thrust

The Breadth Thrust indicator is a market momentum indicator developed by Dr. Martin Zweig. The Breadth Thrust is calculated by taking a 10-day exponential moving average of the advancing issues divided by the advancing plus declining issues.

Here is the NYSE composite and the breadth thrust indicator.

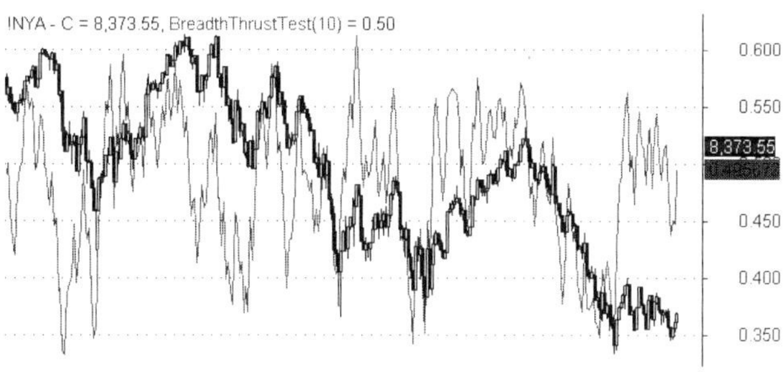

CCI - Commodity Channel Index

The Commodity Channel Index, developed by Donald Lambert, is based on the relationship between the asset's price, a moving average of the asset's price, and normal deviations from that average.

There are 4 steps involved in the calculation of a 20 period CCI:

1. Calculate the last period's Typical Price (TP) = (H+L+C)/3 where H = high, L = low, and C = close.
2. Calculate the 20-period Simple Moving Average of the Typical Price (SMATP).
3. Calculate the Mean Deviation. First, calculate the absolute value of the difference between the last period's SMATP and the typical price for each of the past 20 periods. Add all of these absolute values together and divide by 20 to find the Mean Deviation.
4. The final step is to combine the Typical Price (TP), Simple Moving Average of the Typical Price (SMATP), Mean Deviation, and a Constant (.015) in the following formula:

   CCI = (Typical Price - SMATP) / (.015 X Mean Deviation)

Here is a plot of the CCI and the NYSE Composite.

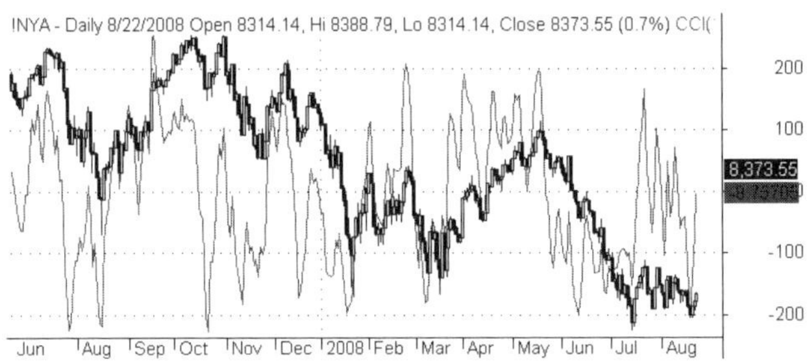

Chaikin - Chaikin Oscillator

The Chaikin Oscillator was developed by Marc Chaikin in the 1970s when opening prices were not widely available. It begins with an accumulation - distribution, then takes two moving averages.

DPO - Detrended Price Oscillator

The AmiBroker formulation of the detrended price oscillator is the closing price divided by the moving average of the price, with the moving average shifted by half its period (to center it).

DVI - Daily Volume Indicator

The daily volume indicator begins by computing the midpoint of the day's price as half the high plus low. It multiplies the difference between the close and the midpoint by the volume and accumulates that.

EOM - Ease of Movement

The Ease of Movement indicator begins by computing the midpoint of the day's prices as half the high plus low. A ratio of the volume to the difference between the high and low is computed and called the box size. Ease of movement is the midpoint change divided by the box size.

HPI - Herrick Payoff Index

The Herrick Payoff Index indicator, developed by John Herrick, determines the amount of money flowing into or out of a futures contract. The value increases and decreases with the average price for each day, with the trading volume, changes in the number of open contracts, and changes in the average price. The value of each new day is combined with the value of the previous day using the multiplying factor.

MACD - Moving Average Convergence Divergence

The MACD was developed by Gerald Appel in the 1960s. It is constructed in steps.

1. Take the difference between two exponential moving averages, often 12 days (or bars) and 26 days. This is the MACD line.
2. Compute an exponential moving average, often 9 days, of the MACD. This is the Signal line.
3. Compute the difference between the MACD line and the Signal. This is the MACD Histogram.
4. Plot the two lines and the histogram.

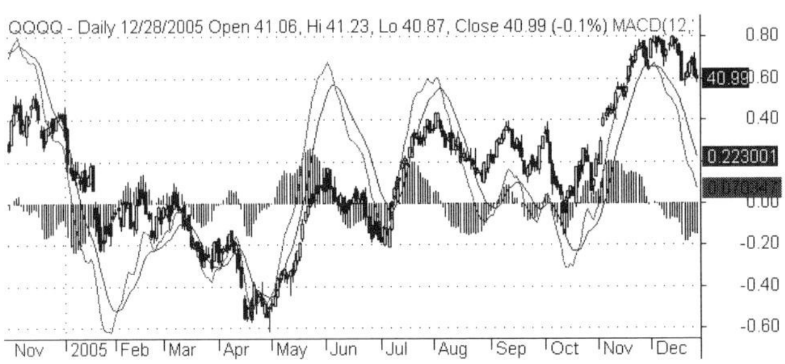

Market Facilitation Index

The Market Facilitation Index was developed by Bill Williams. It is computed as the price difference (high minus low), that divided by volume. AmiBroker plots it as it would plot volume, but with the bars colored by the value of the Market Facilitation Index.

Mass Index

Mass Index begins by computing the difference between the high and low, taking an exponential moving average of that, then taking another exponential moving average, and finally accumulating those values.

MFI - Money Flow Index

Money Flow Index is essentially a volume-weighted RSI. The code to compute MFI is:

```
NumDays = 14;
Typical = ( H + L + C ) / 3;
MF = Typical * V;
PMF = Sum( IIf( Typical > Ref( Typical, -1 ), MF, 0 ), NumDays );
NMF = Sum( IIf( Typical < Ref( Typical, -1 ), MF, 0 ), NumDays );
MFITest = 100 * PMF / ( PMF + NMF );
Plot ( MFITest, "MFITest", colorGreen, styleLine );
```

Momentum

Momentum is the difference between the price today and the price some number of days ago.

NVI - Negative Volume Indicator

Negative Volume Indicator, developed by Norman Fosback, is an accumulating indicator that adds to its running total when today's volume is less than yesterday's volume.

OBV - On Balance Volume

On-balance volume, developed by Joe Granville in 1963, is a momentum indicator that measures positive and negative volume flow.

- If today's close is greater than yesterday's close, then today's volume is added to yesterday's OBV, and is considered up volume.
- If today's close is less than yesterday's close, then today's volume is subtracted from yesterday's OBV and it is considered down volume.
- And if today's close is equal to yesterday's close then today's OBV is equal to yesterday's OBV.

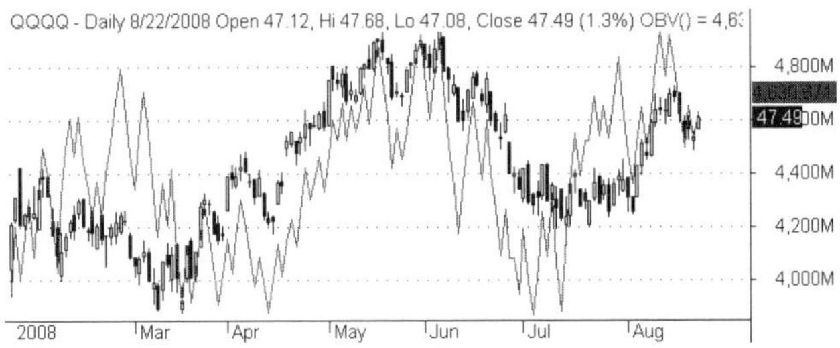

OSCP - Price Oscillator

Price Oscillator is the difference of two exponential moving averages of price. The lengths used for this image are 9 and 18.

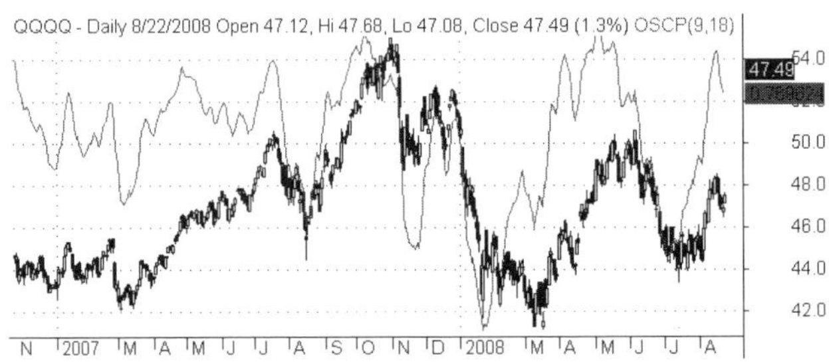

OSCV - Volume Oscillator

Volume Oscillator is the difference of two exponential moving averages of volume. The lengths used for this image are 9 and 18.

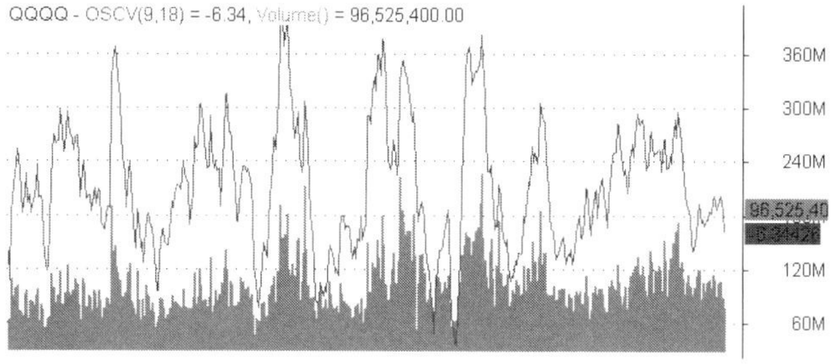

PVI - Positive Volume Index

Negative Volume Indicator, developed by Norman Fosback, is an accumulating indicator that adds to its running total when today's volume is greater than yesterday's volume.

PVT - Price Volume Trend

Price Volume Trend is a summation index that adds the volume times the one-day percentage change in the price to its running total.

RMI - Relative Momentum

Relative Momentum Index, developed by Roger Altman in 1993, is a modification of the Relative Strength Index (see below). While the relative strength index always compares price changes 1 day apart, the relative momentum index compares changes any number of days apart. That number of days is a parameter to the index. For a given lookback period, say 14, RMI(14,1) is identical to RSI(14). Change the second parameter and watch the change in the index.

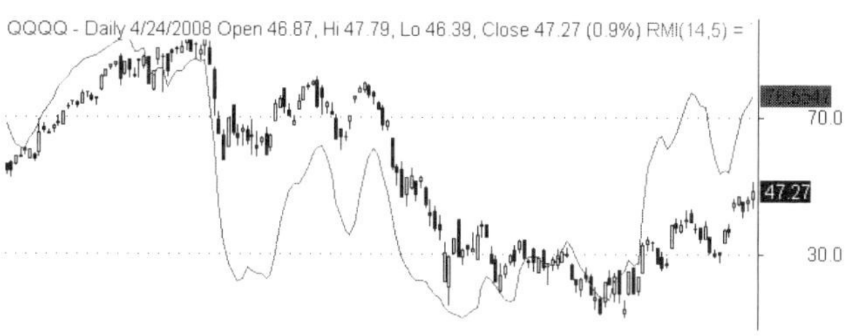

ROC - Rate of Change

Rate of Change compares the price to the price some number of days ago. For example, ROC(C,15) gives the percentage price change from 15 days ago to today.

RS - Comparative Relative Strength

Comparative Relative Strength compares a security's price change with that of a base security. When the Comparative Relative Strength indicator is moving up, it shows that the security is performing better than the base security. When the indicator is moving down, it shows that the security is performing worse than the base security.

In this image, XLK is the current symbol and QQQQ is the base. The plot shows that XLK is performing worse than QQQQ.

RSI - Relative Strength Indicator

Relative Strength Index is an oscillator that compares the upward strength with the downward strength over a lookback period.

To calculate the RSI:

1. Decide on the lookback period, call it N.
2. For each day, calculate the upward change, U, and the downward change, D over a one day period:
   If C > Ref(C,-1), U = C - Ref(c,-1), D = 0
   If C < Ref(C,-1), U = 0, D = Ref(C,-1) - C
   If C == Ref(C,-1), U = 0, D = 0
3. Compute the N day exponential moving average of the U series, call it EU.
4. Compute the N day exponential moving average of the D series, call it ED.
5. RSI = 100 * EU / (EU + ED)

This image shows the 14 day RSI.

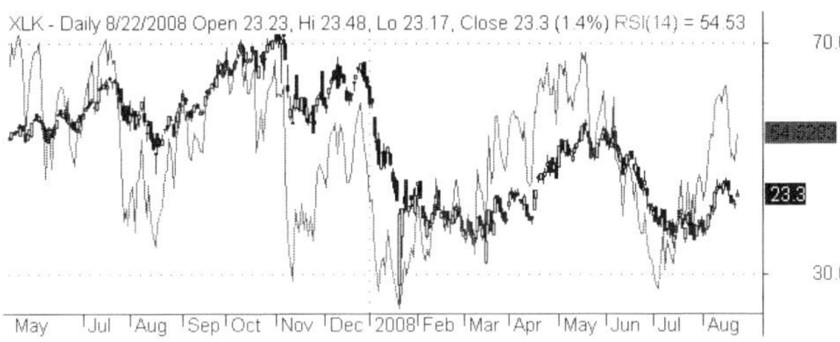

RSIa - Relative Strength Indicator

The RSI formula always uses the closing price. The RSIa formula allows you to specify the series.

RWI - Random Walk Index

The Random Walk Index measures the difference between a straight line connecting two prices and the path taken by the trades between the two. This RWI has parameters 9 and 40.

RWIHI - Random Walk Index

RWI using high prices.

RWILO - Random Walk Index

RWI using low prices.

SAR - Parabolic Stop and Reverse

SAR is a generic term meaning Stop And Reverse. Some trading systems are designed so that they always have a position, either long or short. The exit from a long position is the entry to the short position, and vice versa. Hence the name stop and reverse.

The Parabolic Stop and Reverse system is a combination of two ideas - a stop and reverse system, and a parabolic trailing exit or stop.

The parabolic trailing exit is plotted by the series of dots that follow below a long position and above a short position. The dots establish exit points. And, if the system is being used as a stop and reverse system, entry points in the other direction.

The formula has two variables: the step and the maximum step. The higher the step is set, the more sensitive the indicator will be to price changes. The maximum step controls the adjustment of the SAR as the price moves. The lower the maximum step is set, the further the trailing stop will be from the price. Wells Wilder, developer of the indicator, recommends setting the step at .02 and the maximum step at .20. Those values are used in the plot that follows.

STIX

STIX is the exponential moving average of the advance-decline ratio.

Stochastic %K

Stochastic is a term meaning random in the more general sense, a poor name for this indicator which is not random at all, but is a position-in-range indicator (PIR). There is some controversy over who developed the indicator, but George Lane is usually given credit. The work was done in the 1960s.

Position-in-range indicators have a lookback period, say it is N days or bars. Within the lookback period, identify the lowest of the values of interest and the highest of the values of interest. The PIR is the position the current value has within the range of lowest to highest. The general formula is:

PIR = (current - lowest) / (highest - lowest)

The PIR can be unscaled (so it ranges from 0.00 to 1.00), scaled so that it is a percentage (ranging from 0 to 100), scaled as an oscillator around 0 (ranging from -1 to + 1), and so forth.

The Stochastic %K has two parameters - the lookback period and a smoothing factor (the series is the close). Say they are 15 and 3. The calculation starts out computing a PIR of the close using a 15 day look-back. It then takes a 3 day moving average.

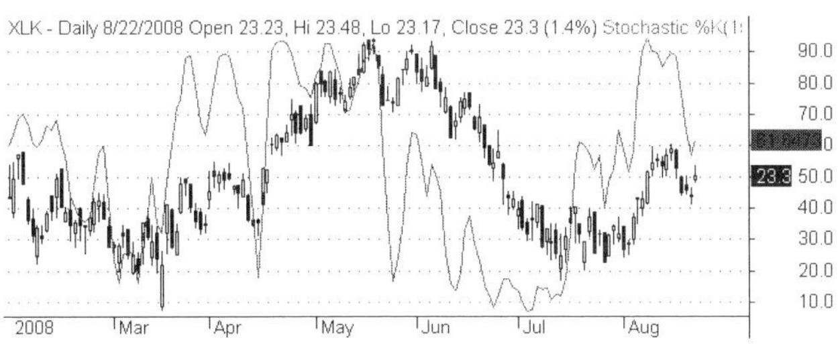

Stochastic %D

The Stochastic %D adds an additional smoothing to the Stochastic %K. There are three parameters - the lookback, the first smoothing, the second smoothing. Say they are 15, 3, and 3. Here is the plot showing both the %K (lighter line) and %D (heavier line).

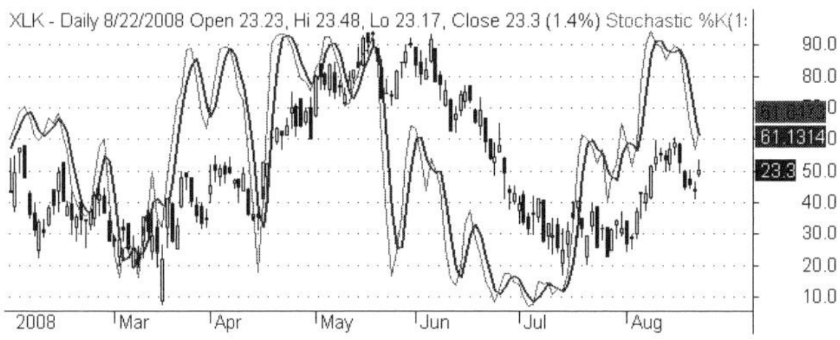

Stochastic Momentum

Stochastic Momentum is a position-in-range indicator. It is formed by subtracting the current value from the midpoint of the highest high and lowest low, and dividing that by the difference between the highest high and lowest low. Both numerator and denomination are smoothed twice. Here is the plot of stochastic momentum with parameters 15, 3, and 3.

TRIN - Traders Index

Trin, Traders Index, is sometimes called the Arms' Index after its developer, Richard Arms. It measures the advancing and declining volume and compares that with the number of advancing and declining issues. It can be used with any universe of issues, but is most often used for a broad market.

The formula for the NYSE TRIN using Quotes Plus symbols is:

```
ArmsIndex = ( Foreign("!NY-A", "C") / Foreign("!NY-D", "C") )
/ ( Foreign("!NY-AV", "C") / Foreign("!NY-DV","C" ) );
Plot( ArmsIndex, "Trin", colorRed );
Plot (1.0,"",colorBlue,styleLine);
```

Note two unusual features of TRIN:

- High values are associated with weakness.
- The indicator is not symmetric around 1.0.

Here is a plot of TRIN and the NYSE Composite Index.

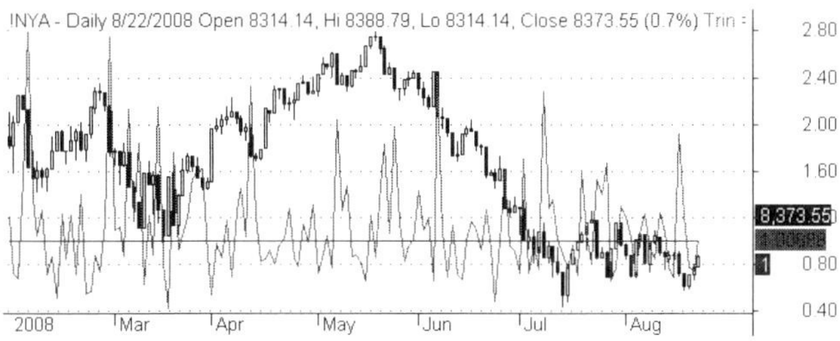

TRIX - Triple Exponential

TRI-ple eXponential. TRIX is calculated as a one period rate of change of the third exponential moving average pass of the closing price. The image is TRIX applied to monthly data for the XLF ETF.

Ultimate - Ultimate Oscillator

Ultimate Oscillator, developed by Larry Williams in 1985, is the weighted sum of three oscillators, each looking back a different time period. Commonly used lookbacks are 7, 14, and 28. The oscillators used can be simple stochastic oscillators; or they can more complex, using concepts similar to true range and measuring buying pressure in each time period. Here is the Ultimate Oscillator with parameters 7, 14, and 28 and the SPY ETF.

Volatility (Chaikin)

Chaikin Volatility is calculated by first taking an exponential moving average of the difference between the high and low, using an n day period. Then taking a rate of change between the current value and the one n days ago. Here is the 10 day Chaikin Volatility.

Volatility (Wilder)

Wilder Volatility is simply ATR - Average True Range. Here is Wilder Volatility for 10 days.

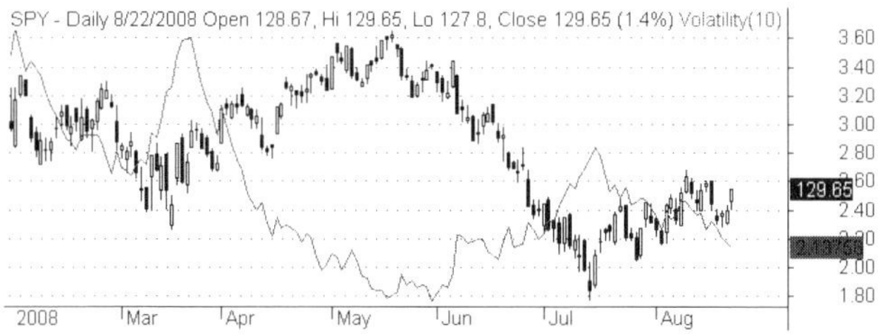

Volume Oscillator

Volume Oscillator is the difference between two exponential moving averages of the volume.

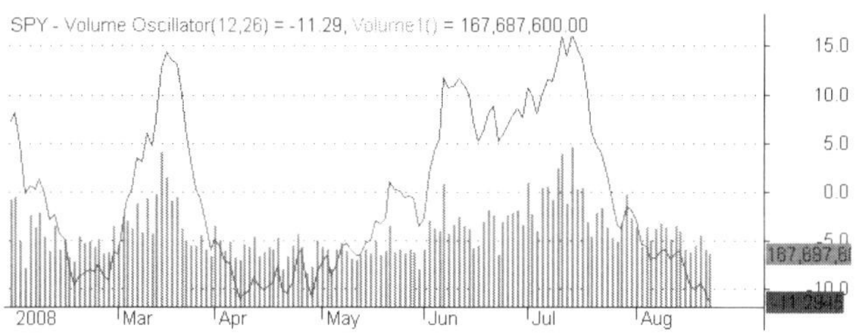

William %R

Williams %R, developed by Larry Williams, is an unsmoothed position-in-range indicator. Note that the scale is inverted relative to the other PIR indicators. There is one parameter, the lookback period - 14 days for this example.

ZIG - ZigZag Indicator

The Zig Zag indicator has a single parameter - a percentage value, say 5. It connects highest values (of the close, in this case) and lowest values in such a way that there is no price change greater than 5 percent between two connected points.

The zig-zag indicator looks into the future, therefore cannot be used in trading systems. It is, however, an excellent tools for studying the profit potential of an issue.

Systems

You can store any formulas you want to in any subdirectory you want to. But, for convenience and organizational value, the Systems directory is used for formulas that are trading systems. That is, they have Buy and Sell (and perhaps Short and Cover) statements. Two trading system examples are installed when AmiBroker is installed.

Example

Example.afl uses the MACD indicator to signal when to buy and when to sell. Here is the code:

```
Buy = Cross( MACD(), Signal() );
Sell = Cross( Signal(), MACD() );

// trade on next bar open
SetTradeDelays( 1, 1, 1, 1 );
BuyPrice = SellPrice = Open;

// trade size: 25% of current portfolio equity
SetPositionSize( 25, spsPercentOfEquity );
```

The first two lines generate the buy and sell signals. Buy when the MACD line rises through the Signal line. Sell when the two lines cross the other direction. Refer back for descriptions of these two functions.

The next two lines determine when the trades will take place. Signals are calculated after trading has completed for the day. The trades are to be taken after a 1 bar delay, and at the Opening price.

And the final two lines state that a maximum of 25% of available capital should be used to take any single position.

Trading systems will be discussed in more detail in Chapter 9, Automatic Analysis.

Example Rotational

ExampleRotational.afl uses a technique called rotational trading. In your research and testing, you have found some metric that can be computed for every symbol every day, where larger values of that metric indicate larger gains in price in the future. Call that metric PositionScore. For this example, issues that have done poorly over the past year are given high scores. Every day, compute PositionScore for all the issues you want to trade. Take initial positions in the four issues that have the highest scores. Sell any issue that is not one of the top six, replacing it with the highest ranking issue that you do not already hold.

```
// Simple example of rotational trading system
// This is contrarian strategy -
// it buys 4 "worst" stocks - the ones that suffered the most
in last year
// (4 stocks having worst 252-bar rate-of-change)
//
// 4 positions
MaxPositions = 4;
SetOption("MaxOpenPositions", MaxPositions  );
SetOption("WorstRankHeld", MaxPositions + 2 );
SetPositionSize( 100 / MaxPositions, spsPercentOfEquity );

// trade on next day open
SetTradeDelays( 1, 1, 1, 1 );
BuyPrice = Open;

SetBacktestMode( backtestRotational );

// offsetting by large positive number
// makes sure that our score is always positive and we don't
enter short trades
PositionScore = 10000 - ROC( C, 252 );
```

Section III

Analysis

Chapter 6

Technical Analysis

Decisions to buy and sell anything - stocks, mutual funds, cars, houses, jewelry - are made for a variety of reasons and use a variety of decision making techniques. When it comes to securities, there are three broad categories of decision making:

- Fundamental analysis
- Chart analysis
- Quantitative analysis

Fundamental analysis uses information about the financial health of the organization, derived from financial statements, reports by the management, estimates of future revenue and expenses, and so forth. The efficient market hypothesis postulates that all the information that can be known about an organization has already been taken into account and is always already reflected in the price of its shares. Trading decisions are made using one of the models based on the market being efficient, such as the Capital Asset Pricing Model.

The two branches of technical analysis - chart analysis and quantitative analysis - believe that the markets are somewhat inefficient, and that there is information in the historical price and volume data that can be recognized and can lead to profitable transactions. For both, several things must be true in order to be profitable trading:

- The markets must be inefficient.
- There must be patterns in the price and volume that precede profitable trading opportunities.
- The patterns must occur often enough to be profitable enough to overcome trading costs.
- The analyst must be able to recognize those patterns, either visually or through computer programs.
- The patterns must persist long enough beyond the period being analyzed so that trades can be made.

Chart analysis uses visual examination of the price and volume searching for patterns such as head-and-shoulders, trendlines, support and resistance levels. Often, the recognition of important patterns is a subjective judgement of the analyst. As demonstrated in the earlier chapters, AmiBroker has an outstanding complement of charting tools to aid the chart analysts.

Quantitative analysis, used in the sense of analysis of price and volume information, relies on writing a set of rules into a computer program, then running that program as a component of a trading system development platform. Trading system programs have the same characteristics as general purpose computer programs, in that they have variables and constants, read and write data, can perform numeric calculations and string manipulation, have flow control statements, have subroutines and functions, and so forth. In addition, trading system programs have special features to deal with financial data and trading. They can process the data streams with the daily sets of open, high, low, close, and volume. They have special functions to handle the buying of shares, selling of shares, and accounting for the profits.

AmiBroker is a trading system development platform. It has special features and specialized functions to deal with the price data, the purchase and sale of shares (or whatever is being analyzed and traded), the accounting and reporting related to the trading account.

Of particular importance is a trading system development platform's ability to search for patterns (backtest), its ability to automatically search for the best sets of rules (optimize), and its ability to perform statistical tests to measure the likelihood of a set of rules being profitable in the future (validation). AmiBroker excels at all these tasks, and each will be discussed in the chapters to come.

Chapter 7

Trading System Development

All traders need confidence that their system will be profitable when traded. For any trader, the way to build confidence is to practice.

One advantage that traders who use mechanical systems have over those who use graphical methods is that the mechanical system is (or, at least, can be) objective, rule-based, judgement free, and testable.

You will be writing a trading system, testing it using historical data, then following the rules to place actual trades. The period of time, and the data associated with that time, that you use to develop and test your system is called the in-sample period and the in-sample data. The period of time, and the data associated with that time, that follows the in-sample period and has never been tested or evaluated by the system is called the out-of-sample data. Actual trades are always out-of-sample.

The process of validating a trading system is one of observing the profitability and behavior of the system in the out-of-sample period after it leaves the in-sample period.

The transition you make going from testing your system in-sample to trading it out-of-sample is one data point in the validation of your system. Your confidence level will be much higher if you have observed many of these transitions.

The ten step outline presented here is designed to build your confidence that your system will be profitable. For a more extensive discussion of trading system development, including expansion of the topics presented in this outline, please see *Quantitative Trading Systems.*

1. Define the Objective Function

An objective function is a metric of your own choosing that you use to rank the relative performance of two or more alternative trading systems. The phrase "of your own choosing" is critical. Your objective function must accurately reflect what is important to you. If you prefer long holding periods and infrequent trading, your objective function must rate systems that hold for weeks to months higher than systems that hold for a few days. If you prefer high equity gain without regard to drawdown over lower, but smoother, gain your objective function must reflect that.

I believe the psychology of trading experts who try to help traders become comfortable with the systems they trade have it backwards. If you decide ahead of time what you want, and design trading systems that satisfy your wishes, and if you have the confidence built through the validation process, you are guaranteed to be comfortable with your system.

AmiBroker reports the score for many metrics with each test run. If one of these standard, built-in metrics meets your needs, use it. If you want something else, you can create a custom metric and use it. For many people, rewarding equity growth while penalizing drawdown is important. If you agree, consider using one of the standard metrics that does that: RAR/MDD (risk adjusted annual rate of return / maximum drawdown), CAR/MDD (compound annual rate of return / maximum drawdown), K-ratio, Ulcer Performance Index, RRR (risk-reward ratio).

2. Decide What to Trade and How to Trade It

If you have a day job, you probably want to use daily data, run your trading system in the evening, and place your trades the next day. Or, you may be able to watch the market during the day and want to place your trades intra-day or at the close. You may have a preferred group of stocks or mutual funds. Be certain your system works well with your choices.

3. Design the Trading System

A trading system is a combination of a model and a set of data. The model is contained in the AFL code you write. The data is the price data of the ticker symbol your code processes. The model contains the intelligence. It is looking for the patterns in the data and testing the profitability of buying and selling.

A model consists of several parts: filter or setup, entry, exit, trailing stop, position size, portfolio composition, and so forth. In much of the literature, the entry is emphasized. But the other components are more important.

A model is a static representation of a dynamic process. Once you are done coding and testing, the model does not change. It may be cleverly designed and have self-adapting parameters, but it is still static. The market being modeled is dynamic and ever changing. Your model is looking for a particular pattern or set of conditions, after which it expects a profitable trade. As long as the model and the market remain in synchronization, the system will be profitable. When the two fall out of sync, the system will be less profitable or unprofitable.

It is useful to think of the data as comprised of two components - signal and noise. The pattern your model is looking for is the signal portion of the data. Everything your model does not recognize is the noise portion of the data. Your goal, as a designer of trading systems, is to accurately recognize the signal and ignore the noise.

Our hope is that:

- We can build a model,
- That recognizes some inefficiency,
- And use that model to trade profitably,
- As long as the model and reality stay in sync.

4. Determine the Length of the In-Sample Period

There are two views about how much time and data should be used to develop the system.

Some want a long time. They feel that the system will experience a variety of conditions and be better able to handle changes in the future. The risk is that conditions vary so much in the in-sample period that the system will not learn any of it well.

Some want a short time. They feel that the system will be better able to synchronize itself and learn very well. The risk is that the system may learn a temporary pattern that does not persist beyond the in-sample period. Another way to view this is that the system has fit itself to the noise because the signal is too weak. A system that has fit to the noise, performs well in-sample, but does not perform well out-of-sample is sometimes described as a system that is curve-fit, or over-fit, to the data.

The proper length of the in-sample period is impossible to state in general. It is very much a function of both the model and the data. The only way to determine the length of the in-sample period is to run some tests.

5. Determine the Length of the Out-Of-Sample Period

The length of the out-of-sample period is: As long as the model and the market remain in sync and the system remains profitable. There is no general relationship between the length of the out-of-sample period and the length of the in-sample period.

6. Decide What to Optimize

To optimize means to search a lot of alternatives and choose the best of them. Optimization is not a bad thing; in fact, it is a necessary step in system development. If you were to think up a new trading system and write the AFL code for it, it would include logic and parameters that were first guesses. You could test that system as it stands, and then either trade it or erase it and start over. But you are unlikely to do that. More likely, you will try other logic and other parameters values. If you are trying a few hand-picked alternatives, you might as well run an optimization and try thousands of alternatives. Give yourself a chance to find the best system.

Anything you would consider changing in your system - a different parameter value or an alternative logic statement - is a candidate to be optimized.

7. Perform Walk Forward Runs

While there is nothing special about optimizing, there is something very special about a walk forward run. You saw these diagrams in Chapter 3, Example 9, but they are worth looking at again.

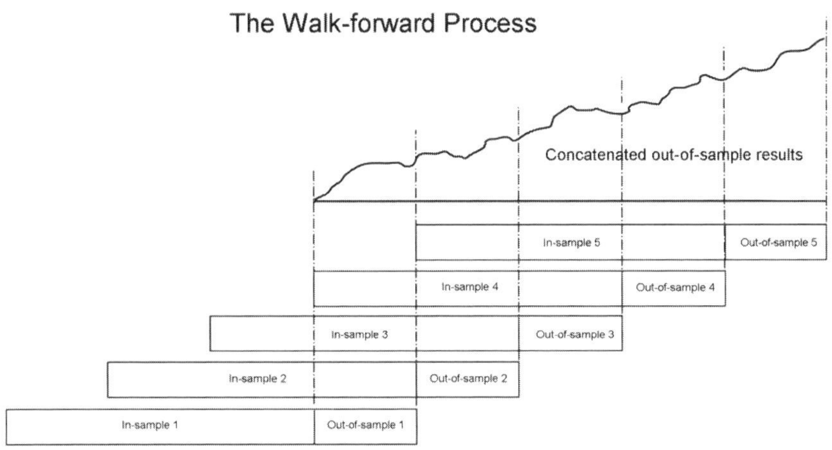

The walk forward process is several iterations of:

1. Optimize in-sample.
2. Choose the best according to your objective function.
3. Use those values and test out-of-sample.
4. Step forward by the length of the out-of-sample period.

Continue this process until you have used the last full in-sample period.

8. Evaluate the Out-Of-Sample Results

Either trade the system or send it back to development.

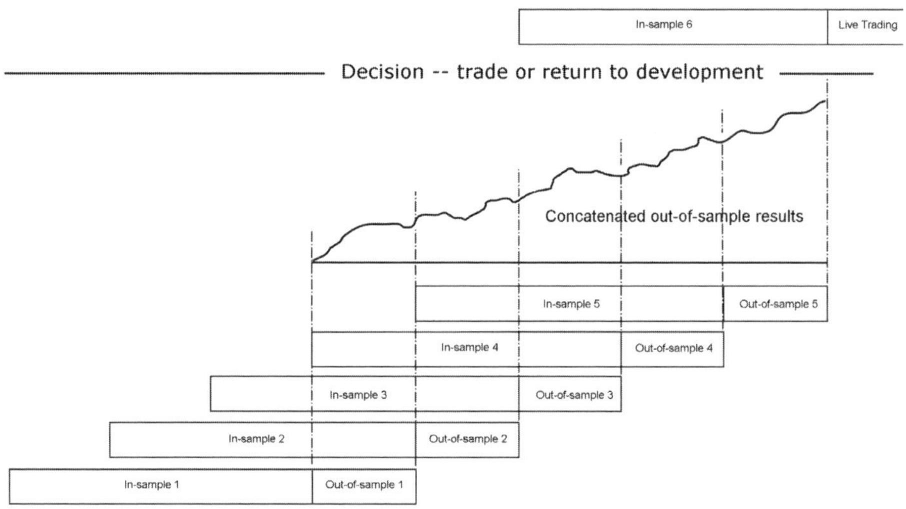

Note the importance of having an objective function you trust. The set of parameters used to test out-of-sample are the parameters that are at the top of the results list, after the list has been sorted by your objective function. The process is automatic and objective. All the decisions were made in earlier steps. You will never even see what the second choice is; the first choice is always used.

Each walk forward step is one data point you will use in the validation of your system.

9. Trade the System

Using the set of parameters that are at the top of the list after the last optimization, buy and sell when the system gives signals.

Take all the signals. If you have some way to decide which signals to take and which to skip, that logic belongs in the trading system and should go through the validation process.

On the last day of what would have been the out-of-sample period, re-optimize. Pick the top-ranked parameter values and continue to trade.

10. Monitor the Results

Each trade signaled after development has finished, and each trade you actually take, is an out-of-sample trade. You can compare the statistics for your trades with statistics for the out-of-sample results from the walk forward runs. If your results drop below what is statistically expected, stop trading the system. Either paper-trade it to see if it recovers; or re-optimize ahead of schedule, then paper-trade it and observe its performance.

In Summary

There are no guarantees. The best we can hope for is a high level of understanding and confidence gained through the validation process.

Chapter 8

AFL

AmiBroker Formula Language

AFL is AmiBroker Formula Language - the code that takes your ideas and puts them in the form that AmiBroker understands. Formulas, indicators, explorations, and trading systems are all written in AFL.

AFL is a component of AmiBroker, and is installed automatically in all versions of AmiBroker.

AFL is a procedural programming language, similar to Visual Basic, C, C++, Pascal, and Fortran. As such, it has language features for:

- Computation of numerical expressions.
- Evaluation of logical expressions.
- Declaration and use of data storage.
- Definition of data structures.
- Reading data into the program.
- Writing data out from the program.
- File manipulation.
- Program control.
- Built-in and user-defined functions.

AFL could be used for general purpose computing. But its unique capabilities come from the additional features designed to work with financial time series and trading systems. These include:

- Language and procedures to deal with financial quotations, such as open, high, low, close, volume, and open interest.
- Language and procedures to deal with trading system orders, such as buy, sell, short, and cover.
- The ability to plot or chart financial data, such as price, technical indicators, and buy and sell arrows.
- Powerful array processing capabilities. Much of the data used in trading systems is organized in time-ordered series, which AmiBroker stores in arrays and manipulates with array-oriented procedures.

AFL files are clear-text files, not proprietary or encoded in any way. While any text editor can be used to create and modify them, the AFL Formula Editor is designed specifically to work with AFL files. This chapter begins with a discussion of the AFL Editor, the Formula Editor.

Following that is a description and discussion of the AFL Language, including the language features and built-in functions.

AFL Editor (Formula Editor)

The AFL Editor, or Formula Editor, is the editor that is built-in to AmiBroker. It is used to write AFL programs that will display custom indicators and test trading systems. It has four pull-down menus, a toolbar, and a context menu of its own.

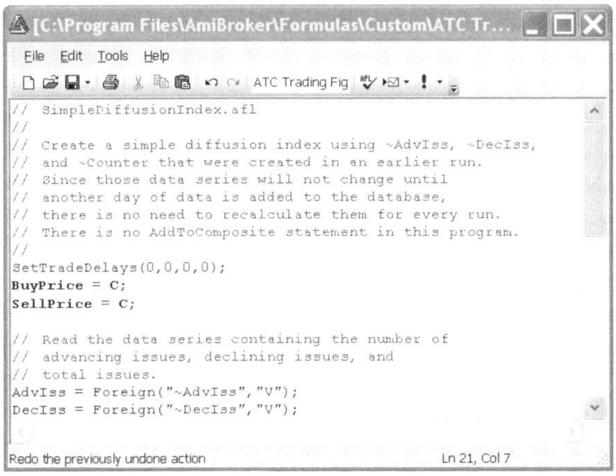

Pull-down Menus

- File Menu

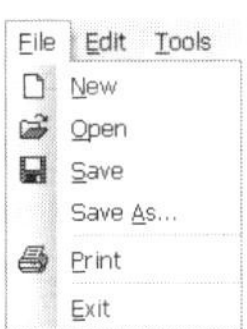

- New - Clears the AFL window
- Open - Opens an existing AFL file
- Save - Saves the contents of the window under the current name
- Save As - Saves the contents under a new name
- Print - Opens the Print dialog box to send the AFL to a printer
- Exit - Close the editor

- Edit Menu

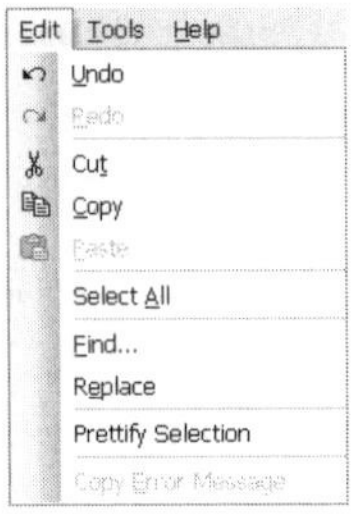

- Undo - un-does last action (multi-level)
- Redo - re-does recent action (multi level)
- Cut - Moves selected text to the clipboard
- Copy - Copies selected text to the clipboard
- Paste - Copies clipboard to cursor location
- Select All - Selects the entire file
- Find - Opens search dialog
- Replace - Opens search and replace dialog
- Prettify Selection - Reformats selected text to a consistent standard; adjusts indents and spacing
- Copy Error Message - After checking AFL syntax, if there is an error, copies that error message to the clipboard

If you get the error message shown below when trying to run prettify, get AStyle.dll from this url:
http://www.amibroker.com/bin/astyle.dll
and copy it to the AmiBroker directory:
C:\\Program Files\AmiBroker

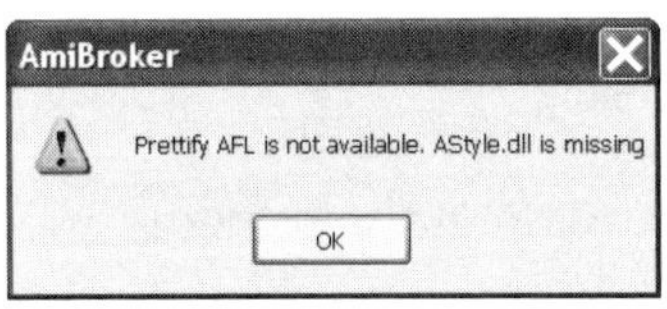

- Tools Menu

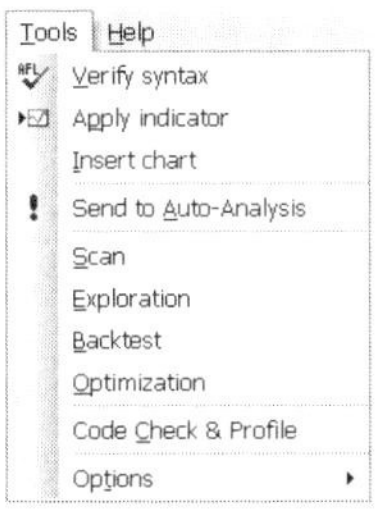

- Verify Syntax - Check AFL code for errors
- Apply Indicator - Saves the file, then applies it one time. (If you click again, no new pane is opened.)
- Insert Chart - Saves the file, then applies it many times. (If you click again, another new pane is opened.)
- Send to Auto-Analysis - Saves the file, makes it the selected file for Automatic Analysis, opens Automatic Analysis, and waits for your action.
- Scan - Saves the file, makes it the selected file for Automatic Analysis, and runs the Scan process
- Exploration - Saves the file, makes it the selected file for Automatic Analysis, and runs the Explore process
- Backtest - Saves the file, makes it the selected file for Automatic Analysis, and runs the Backtest process
- Optimization - Saves the file, makes it the selected file for Automatic Analysis, and runs the Optimize process
- Code Check & Profile - Saves the file, makes it the selected file for Automatic Analysis, and runs the Code Check and Profile process. Code Check tests for "future leaks" where the code peaks into the future. Profile lists the operations required to run the code and estimates the execution time.
- Options - There is only one option - Auto-save formula. When checked, the file will be saved before being sent to Automatic Analysis for processing.

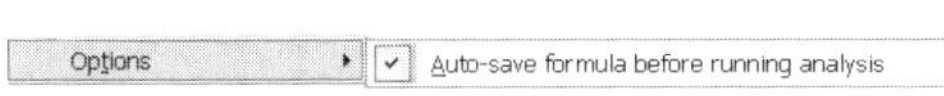

- Help Menu

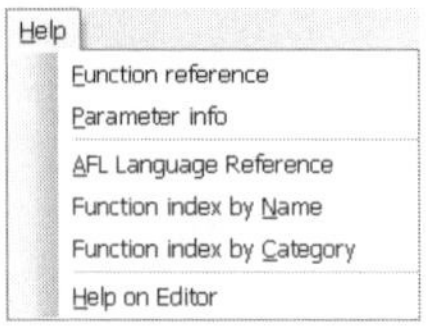

- Function Reference - Displays the AFL reference page for the function highlighted. Pressing the F1 key is equivalent.
- Parameter info - Display a Tooltip containing the complete function prototype, including parameters.
- AFL Language Reference - Displays the AFL Language Reference section of the User's Guide, describing AFL in general.
- Function index by name - Displays the available AFL functions, sorted alphabetically.
- Function Index by Category - Displays the available AFL functions, grouped by category.
- Help on Editor - Displays User's Guide entry for the AFL Editor

AFL Editor Toolbar

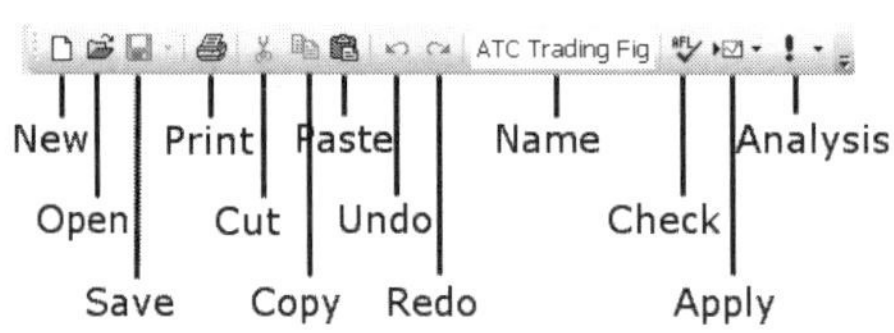

- New - Clears the AFL window
- Open - Opens an existing AFL file
- Save - Saves the contents of the window under the current name. Pull-down menu gives a choice of the default "save" or "save as".

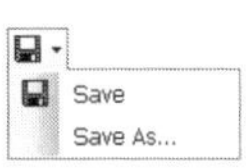

- Print - Opens the Print dialog box to send the AFL to a printer
- Cut - Moves selected text to the clipboard

- Copy - Copies selected text to the clipboard
- Paste - Copies clipboard to cursor location
- Undo - Un-does last action (multi-level)
- Redo - Re-does recent action (multi-level)
- Name - An edit field to allow you to name the formula. Save will use this name.
- Check - Check AFL code for errors. Same as Verify Syntax.
- Apply - Saves the file, then applies it to the chart. Usually a plot. Pull-down menu gives choice of the default "apply" (to an existing pane) or "insert" (into a new pane).

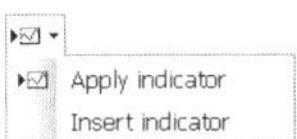

- Analysis - Saves the file, makes it the selected file for Automatic Analysis. Pull-down menu selects action.

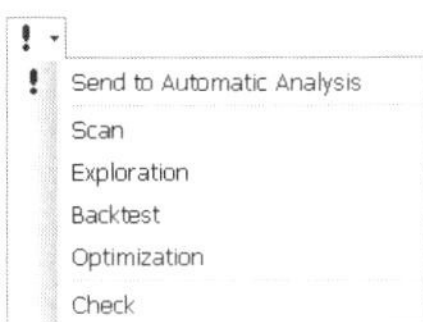

  - No specific choice (the default) - AA performs in the mode it last performed.
  - Scan - Perform a Scan
  - Exploration - Perform an Exploration
  - Backtest - Perform a Backtest
  - Optimization - Perform an Optimization
  - Check - Check for future leak.

AFL Editor Context Menu

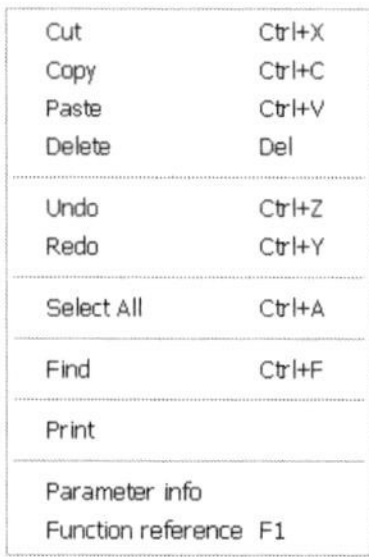

- Cut - Moves selected text to the clipboard
- Copy - Copies selected text to the clipboard
- Paste - Copies clipboard to cursor location
- Delete - Deletes selected text
- Undo - Un-does last action (multi-level)
- Redo - Re-does recent action (multi-level)
- Select All - Selects the entire file
- Find - Opens search dialog
- Print - Opens the Print dialog box to send the AFL to a printer
- Parameter info - Display a Tooltip containing the complete function prototype, including parameters.
- Function reference - Displays the AFL reference page for the function highlighted. Pressing the F1 key is equivalent.

AFL Language

Arrays

In computer science an array is a data structure consisting of a group of elements that are accessed by indexing. Each element has the same data type and the array occupies a contiguous area of storage.

Arrays are so important to AmiBroker that they will be introduced first - before other data structures and before the general description of the AFL language.

In AmiBroker, the Open, High, Low, Close, Volume, and Open Interest are stored in arrays. All other formulas and indicators that are used must be computed using the OHLCVI data.

Take a look at the data. Make IBM the selected issue. Its price chart will appear. Using the **Symbol** menu, select **Quote Editor**.

There is a row for each bar and a column for each data field. When plot-

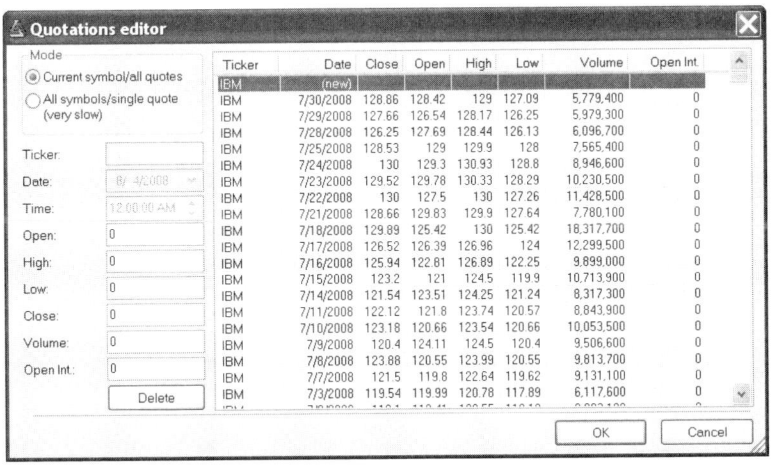

ted on a chart, the date axis has the oldest at the left of the chart and most recent at the right.

When the data is read from the database into memory, an array is created for each field - Date, O, H, L, C, V, OI. The array for each of them has one element for each bar. The elements are referenced (identified) by their position in the array - their index. The oldest element is stored in the first array element and has index 0. Each newer bar (newer element) has an index number 1 greater than its left neighbor. The set of all seven data fields for a given bar form a data record. All elements of a record have the same index number. When using end-of-day data, each bar holds the data for one day; the number of bars and the number of days will be the same.

BarCount

Look at the entire array, say for the closing price. When the data is loaded into memory, the number of data points is counted. That number is stored in a special variable named BarCount. The elements of the Close array are numbered from 0 to BarCount-1. There is no element whose index is BarCount. Trying to refer to an element whose index number is less than 0, or BarCount or greater, results in an "index out of bounds" error.

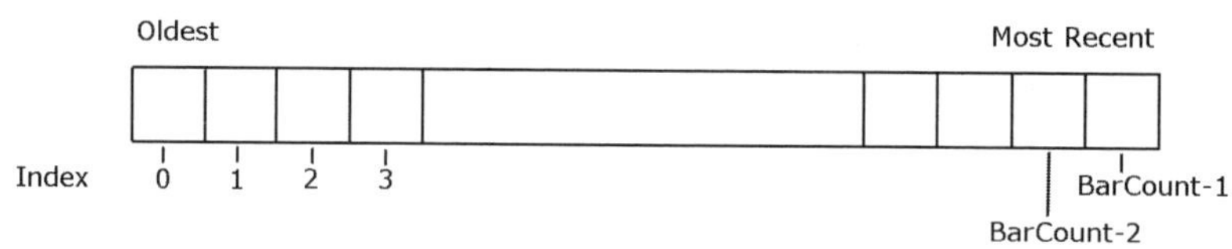

A total of BarCount elements, indexed from 0 to BarCount-1

When the price series is loaded from the database to memory, that established not only the length of those OHLCV arrays, but of all arrays. The default number of elements in every array is BarCount. When you compute an array indicator, such as the simple moving average, the resulting array also has BarCount elements; and they are also indexed from 0 through BarCount-1. When you program AFL and use looping, you will need to be aware of the array indexing and of the BarCount variable.

Array Operations

In order to use an indicator, like the 25-day moving average, the value of that average must be computed for each day.

The average is the sum of the 25 days up to (earlier than) and including the day being processed, divided by 25. Beginning with index number 24, every day has a 25-day moving average. For elements 0 through 23 there is not enough data to compute a 25 day average.

AmiBroker is unique in that it uses a very efficient array-processing technique to compute the 25-day moving average, giving the value for all the data elements in a single array in a single processing step. Computed once, they are available whenever they are needed for further analysis.

The formula to compute the moving average and store it so it can be used is:

```
MyAverage = MA ( C, 25 );
```

- MA is the AFL function that computes the simple moving average.
- C, or Close, tells the function to take the moving average of the Closing price.
- 25 is the number of bars (days) in the average.
- MyAverage is the location where the result is stored.

The key point is that this is an array operation. Close and MyAverage are arrays, and MA is a function that works with arrays (and only with arrays).

When people get confused with AFL, it is often over whether a function works with arrays or scalars (single values).

The description of MA, the function that computes the simple moving average, called the syntax of the function, tells us what it uses as input and what it returns as results.

Syntax:

MA (ARRAY, *periods*);

Returns:

ARRAY

Description:

Calculates a Simple Moving Average of length *periods* of ARRAY. Returns the result as an array.

For example:

```
MAofClose = MA ( Close, 20 );
```

Close is an array. MA is an array operation that computes the moving average for every element in the Close array. The result is also an array. The result returned from the function must be stored in a variable that is an array. All of these arrays have the same length - the length that was established when the data was read from the database and stored in the Close array.

Language Basics

Keep in mind that this is an introductory explanation. There are features of AmiBroker and AFL that are not explained, or even mentioned, here. For more information, please see the AmiBroker AFL Reference, which is a component of the AmiBroker User's Guide.

An AFL program consists of the following elements:

Tokens are word-like units recognized by the AFL language processor.

Whitespace is the collective name given to spaces, tabs, line breaks, and comments. Whitespace serves to separate tokens. Excess whitespace is discarded. That means that if a single whitespace character is permitted, you can have any number of them, including extra line breaks to aid program readability.

Comments are text used to document a program. They are for the programmer's use only - they are stripped out of the code before it is processed. There are two ways to denote text as being a comment:

- // - two adjacent slashes - the remainder of the line is a comment.
- /* */ - two, two-symbol pairs - everything between the opening /* and the closing */ is a comment.

Comments may not be nested.

Tokens. AFL recognizes five classes of tokens:

- identifiers
- constants
- string-literals
- operators
- punctuators

Identifiers are arbitrary names, of any length, given to variables and functions. Identifiers must begin with a letter, may contain letters (a-z, A-Z), digits (0-9), and the underscore ("_"). AFL identifiers are not case sensitive. The identifiers MyMovingAverage and mymovingaverage are treated as being the same.

Constants are tokens representing fixed numeric or character values. Numeric constants consist of decimal integer and, optionally, decimal point and decimal fractional part. Negative numeric constants are preceded by the minus sign.

String literals, or string constants, are a sequence of any characters surrounded by double quotes ("). "This is a string literal"

Operators are the arithmetic, relational, and assignment operators, such as +, -, <. They will be covered in more detail below.

Punctuators are any of the following characters: (),;=.

TERMS are constants, variables, or other terms that are operated upon by operators.

EXPRESSIONS are combinations of constants, variables, terms, and operators that can be evaluated and result in a single value -- a scalar (single number), string, or array.

STATEMENTS consist of one or more expressions, an assignment operator, and a variable. The expressions are evaluated and assigned to the variable. Each statement must be terminated by a semicolon.

Operators

COMPARISON OPERATORS are used to test the relation between two expressions. The result of the test will be either True (1) or False (0). The operators are:

- < Less than
- > Greater than
- <= Less than or equal to
- >= Greater than or equal to
- == Equal to
- != Not equal to

ASSIGNMENT OPERATOR is used to store the value on the right side in the variable on the left side. The operator is the = character. For example:

B = A + 14;

The right hand side is evaluated to a single result by adding A and 14 together. The result is stored in the variable B.

Note the difference between "=" and "==". The single = is an assignment. The double == tests equality.

Arithmetic operators combine one or more terms to produce a term or expression. They include:

- + Addition
- - Subtraction (including unary minus)
- * Multiplication
- / Division
- % Modulus (remainder)
- ^ Exponentiation (raise to a power)
- | Bit-wise Or
- & Bit-wise And

Logical operators work with logical constants and logical variables. They include:

- NOT Logical Not of a single operand
- AND Logical And of two operands
- OR Logical Or of two operands

Logical constants are True and False.

- **False** is represented by numeric zero .
- **True** is represented by numeric 1. Actually any non-zero value, positive or negative, evaluates to True.

Compound assignment operators perform an arithmetic operation followed by an assignment operation. The most commonly used are:

- ++ Post increment (increment the variable and store it back) i++ means add 1 to i. More completely, it means take the value of i, add 1, assign the result to i.
- -- Post decrement (decrement the variable and store it back) i-- means subtract 1 from i.
- += Add the value of the operand (variable) on the left plus the value of the operand on the right, then store the result back in the variable on the left. j += 2; Add 2 to j.
- -= Subtract the value of the operand on the right from the value of the operand (variable) on the left, then store the result in the variable on the left. k-= 5; Subtract 5 from k.
- *= Multiply the value of the operand (variable) on the left by the value of the operand on the right, then store the result back in the variable on the left. m *= i; Multiply m by i.

- /= Divide the value of the operand on the left (variable) by the value of the operand on the right, then store the result back in the variable on the left. x /= y; Divide x by y.

When in doubt, write out the calculation you want using ordinary arithmetic operators. The possible confusion is not worth the execution efficiency.

Operator Precedence

Parentheses can be used to control the order in which the operations take place. Those operations that are in the innermost parentheses are done first, then working outward. When there are no parentheses to explicitly define the order, this precedence is followed (highest ranked are listed first and done first):

1. ++ Post increment
2. -- Post decrement
3. [] Array element operator
4. ^ Exponentiation
5. - Unary minus
6. * Multiplication
7. / Division
8. % Modulo
9. + Addition
10. - Subtraction
11. < Less than
12. > Greater than
13. <= Less than or equal to
14. >= Greater than or equal to
15. == Equal to
16. != Not equal to
17. & Bit-wise And
18. | Bit-wise Or
19. NOT Logical Not
20. AND Logical And
21. OR Logical Or
22. = Assignment
23. *= Compound assignment (all operators)

In addition to having ++ be a post increment operator, it can be a pre increment operator. j = i++ uses ++ as a post increment operator. j is assigned the value of i, then i is incremented. j = ++i uses ++ as a pre increment operator. i is incremented, then the new value of i is assigned to j.

Use parentheses to insure that the calculations are carried out in the order you intend.

If H is 110 and L is 106, (H+L)/2 is 108. H+L/2 is 163, because the division takes place before the addition.

Array Subscript Operator

An entire array is referenced by using its name without qualification, as in MM = O;

To reference a particular element of an array, use the [] operator. For example, to reference the most recent closing price, use C[BarCount-1].

BarCount, as you will recall from the earlier discussion, is the number of elements in the OHLCV arrays, and all other arrays derived from those. The first element of every array is index 0, the final element is index BarCount-1.

Compound Statements (Blocks)

A compound statement consists of zero or more statements within curly brackets {}. A compound statement can be used anywhere a statement can be used.

Built-in Functions

In addition to the arithmetic operators, AmiBroker has over 70 built-in functions that perform mathematical operations. Functions accept zero or more arguments enclosed in parentheses, and return zero or one values. The built-in functions will be discussed later in this chapter.

Conditional If

The conditional if function has the form IIF(exp, Tp, Fp); Note that IIF is a function - it returns a value. The expression exp is evaluated to either True or False. If True, return Tp, if False, return Fp.

Note that IIF is Not a program flow control statement. That is, it does not operate like the traditional IF statement. IIF is a function and it returns a value.

Variables

A variable is an identifier and its associated data structure and storage.

- You can define and use as many variables as you wish; there is no limit.
- Each variable must be assigned a value before it can be used further.
- Variables used in the main program cannot be assigned values in functions.
- User-defined variables may not duplicate names already defined by built-in functions (such as EMA), predefined arrays (such as Open), keywords (such as If), or reserved words (such as Buy).
- It is good programming practice to define variables, give them meaningful names, assign values to the variables, then use the variables in subsequent calculations and function calls.

Reserved Variables

AmiBroker uses some variable names and reserves those. You may not use these identifiers for variables you define:

- buy
- sell
- short
- cover
- buyprice
- sellprice
- shortprice
- coverprice
- title
- tooltip
- graphxspace
- graphzorder
- exclude
- roundlotsize
- ticksize
- pointvalue
- margindeposit
- positionsize
- positionscore
- numcolumns
- filter
- maxgraph
- columnN, where N is a digit
- columnNformat
- columnNname
- graphN, where N is a digit
- graphNname
- graphNcolor
- graphNbarcolor
- graphNstyle

USER-DEFINED FUNCTIONS, PROCEDURES, SCOPE

User-definable functions make it possible to encapsulate user code into easy-to-use modules that can be used in many places without the need to copy the same code over and over again.

Functions must have a definition. The function definition includes the function body — the code that executes when the function is called.

The function definition establishes the name and parameters of a function. The function must be defined prior to the call to the function. The definition is a single line of code that begins with the keyword *function,* is followed by the function name, and then the list of parameters enclosed in parentheses. The function body, enclosed in curly braces, follows using as many statements as you wish.

When the function is invoked or called by the calling program, control passes to the called function. Variables are passed for the arguments. Each argument corresponds to a parameter. The function performs its calculations, including executing the *return* statement. If there is a result to be returned, it is passed back to the calling program.

If the function does not have any return statement (does not return anything) then we call it a procedure.

Following is an example of a function, a 2nd order smoother:

```
// the first line is the definition of the function
function IIR2( input, f0, f1, f2 )
// the remaining lines are the body of the function
{
    result[ 0 ] = input[ 0 ];
    result[ 1 ] = input[ 1 ];

    for( i = 2; i < BarCount; i++ )
    {
       result[ i ] = f0 * input[ i ] +
                     f1 * result[ i - 1 ] +
                     f2 * result[ i - 2 ];
    }
   // this function returns an array
   return result;
}

// this is the main, or calling, program
Plot( Close, "Price", colorBlack, styleCandle );
Plot( IIR2( Close, 0.2, 1.4, -0.6 ), "function example", col-
orRed );
```

IIR2 is a user-defined function. There are four formal parameters: input, f0, f1, f2.

The calling program prepares actual arguments, one argument corresponding to each format parameter. At the time of the function call the values of arguments are passed (by value, not by name or by reference). Formal parameters behave like local variables and have the numeric values that were passed to them. They are undefined (have no numeric values) until the function is called. And when the return statement is executed, they become undefined again. They have no memory.

Within the body of the function, local variables named *result* and *i* are defined and used. Local variables are visible inside the function only. If any other function uses the same variable name the two will not interfere with each other.

Local, Global

AFL does not require that variables be declared before they are used. The first use of a variable determines whether it is *local* or *global.*

If a given identifier appears first inside a function, then it is treated as a local variable to that function.

If a given identifier appears first outside the function, but is used within the function, then it is treated as a global variable and it carries whatever value it had at the time of the call into the function.

Since this can cause problems that are difficult to debug, there are two keywords, local and global, that can be used to force the scope. See the following example.

```
k = 4; // this is a global variable because of its first use

function f( x )
{
   z = 3; // this is LOCAL variable
   return z * x * k; // 'k' here references global variable k
(first used above outside function)
}

z = 5; // this is GLOBAL variable with the same name
       // as the local variable in function f

"The value of z before function call :" + WriteVal( z );

// Calling the function will not affect the
// the value of our global variable z
// because the global variable z and
```

```
// local variable z are separate and
// arguments are passed by value (not by reference)

"The result of f( z ) = " + WriteVal( f( z ) );

"The value of z after function call is unchanged : " + Write-
Val( z );
```

Example 2: Using local and global keywords to override default visibility rules:

```
VariableA = 5; // implict global variable
function Test()
{
   local VariableA;  // explicit local variable
                     // with the same identifier as global
   global VariableB; // explicit global variable
                     // not defined earlier
                     // may be used to return more
                     // than one value from the function

   VariableA = 99;
   VariableB = 333;
}

VariableB = 1; // global variable

"Before function call";
"VariableA = " + VariableA;
"VariableB = " + VariableB;

Test();

"After function call";
"VariableA = " + VariableA + " (not affected by function call
)";
"VariableB = " + VariableB + " (affected by the function call
)"
```

At the end of the function we can see the *return* statement that is used to return the result to the caller. Currently the return statement must be placed at the very end of the function.

It is also possible to write a procedure (a function that returns nothing (void))

```
procedure SinePlotter( Freq, ColorIndex )
{
   pname = "Line"+WriteVal(ColorIndex,1.0);
   array = sin( Cum( Freq * 0.01 ) );
   Plot( array, pname , colorRed + ColorIndex, styleThick );
}

for( n = 1; n < 10; n++ )
{
```

```
        SinePlotter( n/2+Cum(0.01), n );
    }
```

Although there are two separate keywords *function* and *procedure,* AmiBroker currently treats them the same (they both accept return values but do not require them), but in the future the rules might be enforced. That will require use of the return statement only in functions. So it is advisable to use the function keyword in the case where your function returns any value and the procedure keyword if it does not.

Note that recursion (having a function call itself from within itself) is not presently supported.

Flow Control

If you are using the array-oriented features of AFL, then most of the code you write will start at the top of the program and flow to the bottom of the program without interruption. None of the flow control statements or tests accept arrays as arguments. The flow control statements are:

- do ... while
- for
- if ... else
- switch
- while

There are two typical uses for flow control statements:

1. You want to perform some task that may or may not operate on entire arrays for each of several values of a variable. For example, write to a file the results of running tests with values for a particular argument of 5, 7, 9, and 11.
2. You want to step through the data that is in one or more of the arrays, such as the array of closing prices, and make some decision based on what you find. To do this requires that the program use looping.

Each of the five flow control statements will be illustrated with an example. The optional statements that can be used with the flow control are also explained.

break

The break keyword is a part of switch statement and an optional part of looping for, do-while, and while statements.

The break keyword terminates the smallest enclosing do, for, switch, or while statement in which it appears.

The syntax is:
break;

The break statement is used to exit an iteration or switch statement. It transfers control to the statement immediately following the iteration substatement or switch statement.

The break statement terminates only the most tightly enclosing loop or switch statement. In loops, break is used to terminate before the termination criteria evaluate to 0. In the switch statement, break is used to terminate sections of code — normally before a case label. The following example illustrates the use of the break statement in a for loop:

```
i = 0;
while ( i < 10 )
{
  i++;
  // break at step 5
  if( i == 5 )
  {
    break;
  }
  printf("Step " + i );
}
```

continue

The continue statement is an optional part of for, do-while, and while statements.

It stops the current iteration of a loop, and starts a new iteration.

The syntax is:
continue;

You can use the continue statement only inside a while, do...while, or for loop. Executing the continue statement stops the current iteration of the loop and continues program flow with the beginning of the loop.

This has the following effects on the different types of loops:

- while and do...while loops test their condition, and if true, execute the loop again.
- for loops execute their increment expression, and if the test expression is true, execute the loop again.

The following example illustrates the use of the continue statement:

```
i = 0;
while ( i < 10 )
{
  i++;
  // Skip 5
  if( i == 5 )
  {
    continue;
  }
  printf("Step " + i );
}
```

do ... while

The syntax (general form) of the do ... while statement is:

do
{ statements }
while (expression);

do and while are keywords. They are always spelled exactly the same way and used in the same way.

{ statements } is any executable statement or statements, enclosed in a set of curly brackets. The curly brackets are mandatory.

(expression) is any expression that can be evaluated to either True or False. The parentheses are mandatory. The final semicolon is mandatory.

When this part of the program is reached, the statements are executed in order. There may be flow control statements included. Eventually the end of the statement code will be reached.

The expression is evaluated. If the result is True, then the statements in the body will be executed again, starting from the beginning, with the variables retaining their most recent values. If the result is False, then the do ... while is finished and program flow continues to the statement following it.

```
// initialize control variables to prepare for the do ... while
length = 5;
// the do ... while
do
{
  printf (" something interesting " + NumToStr(length) + \"n");
  length = length + 2;
}
while (length <= 13);
// whatever code comes after the do ... while
```

The output of the printf will have lines for lengths of 5, 7, 9, 11, and 13.

for

The syntax of the for statement is:

for (initial; conditional; loop-expression)
{ statements; }

for is a keyword.

(initial; conditional; loop-expression) control the loop. Before the first execution of the statements in the body, initial is executed. Immediately, and before every execution of the body, conditional is tested. If the result of the test is True, execute the statements in the body of the loop. If the result is False, then program flow continues to the statement following the for. After each execution of the statements in the body, execute the loop-expression.

```
// prepare for the for loop
myema[0] = Close[0];
// the for loop
for ( i=1; i < BarCount; i++ )
{
    myema[i] = 0.1 * Close[i] + 0.9 * myema[i-1];
}
// whatever code comes after the for loop
Plot (C, "C", colorBlack, styleCandle);
Plot (myema, "MyEma", colorRed,styleLine);
```

if ... else

The syntax for the if ... else statement is:

if (expression)
    statement1
[**else**
    statement2]

or, more symetrically:

if (expression)
{
    statement1;
}
else
{
    statement2;
}

if and else are keywords. The portion in the [ ] in the first explanation is optional (the brackets are not meant to indicate an array index). The else is optional. The second explanation includes the else portion, which will have an empty statement if there is no action to take.

(expression) is evaluated. If it is True, statement1 is executed. If it is False and there is an else clause, statement2 is executed. If it is False and there is no else clause, no action is taken.

For example:

```
i = 1;
if (i > 1)
    printf ("i is big \n");
else
    printf ("i is small \n");
```

if ... else statements can be nested. For example:

```
i = 2;
j = 4;
if (i > 1)
    if (j > i)
        printf ("i is big \n");
else
    printf ("i is small \n");
```

The question immediately arises: "which if gets the else?" The best answer, from good programming practice, is to use a full complement of braces so the question never arises. The answer to the question as it stands is: the else goes with the closest if that does not already have an else. The spacing on the page does not enter into the discussion at all. Don't let ambiguity into your programs - use a full set of braces. The fully braced equivalent to the example above is:

```
i = 2;
j = 4;
if (i > 1)
{
    if (j > i)
    {
        printf ("i is big \n");
    }
    else
    {
        printf ("i is small \n");
    }
}
else
{
}
```

Run each of these. (Use the Commentary window for quick and dirty testing.) First as they stand, then with j set to 0.

Important note. The values being compared in the expression part of the if ... else are scalars - single values. If ... else can only be used on scalars, not on arrays. You can test to determine whether H[i] > H[i-1]. But you cannot test whether H > Ref(H,-1). The first is testing two single numbers, and the result is clearly either True or False. The second is testing two arrays, and the result is not defined.

switch

The syntax of the switch statement is:

switch (expression)
{
    case constant-expression1: statement;
    case constant-expression2: statement;
    ...
    case constant-expressionN: statement;
    default: statement:
}

Control passes to the statement whose case constant-expression matches the value of switch (expression). The switch statement can include any number of case instances, but no two case constants within the same switch statement can have the same value. Execution of the statement body begins at the selected statement and proceeds until the end of the body or until a break statement transfers control out of the body.

You can use the break statement to end processing of a particular case within the switch statement and to branch to the end of the switch statement. Without break, the program continues to the next case, executing the statements until a break or the end of the statement is reached. In some situations, this continuation may be desirable.

The default statement is executed if no case constant-expression is equal to the value of switch (expression). If the default statement is omitted, and no case match is found, none of the statements in the switch body are executed. There can be at most one default statement. The default statement, if exists, must come at the end. Otherwise it may be executed before hitting conditions defined below it. A case or default label is allowed to appear only inside a switch statement.

The type of switch expression and case constant-expression can be any. The value of each case constant-expression must be unique within the statement body, otherwise the first match will be used.

Example:

```
for( n = 0; n < 10; n++ )
{
printf("Current n = %f\n", n );
switch(n) {
    case 0:
      printf("The number is zero.\n");
      break;
    case 3:
    case 5:
    case 7:
      printf("n is a prime number\n");
      break;
    case 2: printf("n is a prime number\n");
    case 4:
    case 6:
    case 8:
      printf("n is an even number\n");
      break;
    case 1:
    case 9:
      printf("n is a perfect square\n");
      break;
    default:
      printf("Only single-digit numbers are allowed\n");
    break;
   }
```

while

The while statement lets you repeat a statement until a specified expression becomes false.

The syntax of the while statement is:

while (expression)
    statement;

The expression must have an arithmetic (numeric or logical) type. Execution proceeds as follows:

1. The expression is evaluated.

A. If the expression is initially false, the body of the while statement is never executed, and control passes from the while statement to the next statement in the program.

B. If the expression is true (nonzero), the body of the statement is executed and the process is repeated beginning at step 1.

This is an example of the while statement:

```
i = 10;
while( i < 20 )
{
  Plot( MA( Close, i ), "MA" + WriteVal( i, 0 ),
            colorBlack + i );
  i = i + 1;
}
```

The example plots 10, 11, 12, 13, 14, 15, 16, 17, 18, 19 - bar moving averages.

Flags

In order to reduce the size of computer programs, early computer scientists devised the use of flags to allow one computer storage location (originally a byte or word, now a byte, word, or generic variable) to store the on or off state of many variables.

For example, assume the mouse has three buttons: left, right, and center. Each button can be either up or down (unclicked or clicked), and more than one may be clicked at one time. The state of any button could be stored by assigning 0 if that button is up or unclicked, 1 if that button is down or clicked. The state of all three buttons could be stored in three variables, for example:

LeftButton = 0;

RightButton = 1;

CenterButton = 0;

By using flags, the states of all three buttons can be stored in one variable.

Imagine a storage scheme to be a series of bits (binary digits). Let the first bit (right-most, when actually using bits) represent the state of the left button, the second bit represent the state of the right button, and the third bit represent the state of the center button.

Continuing with the bit analogy, the value or weight of each position increases by a factor of 2 moving right to left. The right-most bit posi-

	Third bit Center Button	Second bit Right Button	Right most bit Left Button	Flag Value
No buttons clicked	0	0	0	0
Right button clicked	0	1	0	2
Center button clicked	1	0	0	4
Left and Right buttons clicked	0	1	1	3
The "Value" of each bit position	4	2	1	

tion has a position value of 1, the next a value of 2, then 4, 8, 16, and so on. Combining the up or down state with the value of the bit position, the left button is coded as 1 (the value of its bit position) times either 0, if it is up, or 1, if it is down. The right button is coded as 2 (the value of its bit position) times either 0 or 1. The center button is coded as 4 (the value of its bit position) times either 0 or 1. So the state of all three buttons is stored in one variable, say MouseButtons, by adding together the values for the three individual buttons.

To describe the states of three buttons in terms of flags, we say that:

0 means no button is down

1 means the left button is down

2 means the right button is down

4 means the center button is down

The possible combinations range from 0 (no buttons down) to 7 (all three buttons down). If both the left and right buttons are down, we can store this using the statement:

```
MouseButtons = 3;
```

If we want to test that only the right mouse button is down, we might use this statement:

```
RightDown = MouseButtons == 2;
```

or

```
IIF (MouseButtons == 2, sometruething, otherfalsething);
```

The flag concept can be used for both storing values and retrieving them. It is often used to specify the desired states of a large number of binary variables. See Graph Styles, for example.

AFL Function Reference

AmiBroker has several hundred functions available for you to use as you write your AFL programs. This section of the book lists all of them, and describes some of the ones you might find most useful. For more information, including descriptions of those not fully described here, please see the AmiBroker User's Guide, AFL Function Reference.

The functions have been grouped together according to their primary use. Note carefully what data structure each function returns. Most are arrays.

Lowest/Highest

HHV - Highest high value

Syntax:
HHV (ARRAY, periods)

Returns:
ARRAY

Function: Calculates the highest value in the ARRAY over the preceding periods (periods includes the current day).

Example: The formula "HHV(close, 4)" returns the highest closing price over the preceding four periods. "HHV(high, 8)" returns the highest high price over the preceding eight periods.

HHVBars - Bars since highest high

Syntax:
HHVBars (ARRAY, periods)

Returns:
ARRAY

Function: Calculates the number of periods that have passed since the ARRAY reached its periods period peak.

Example: The formula "HHVBars(close, 30)" returns the number of periods that have passed since the closing price reached its 30-period peak.

Highest - Highest value

Syntax:
Highest (ARRAY)

Returns:
ARRAY

Function: Calculates the highest value in the ARRAY since the first day loaded in the chart.

Example: The formula Highest(MFI(14)) returns the highest Money Flow Index value. Highest (Close) returns the highest closing price.

HighestBars - Bars since highest value

Syntax:
HighestBars (ARRAY)

Returns:
ARRAY

Function: Calculates the number of periods that have passed since the ARRAY's highest value.

Example: The formula "HighestBars(close)" returns the number of periods that have passed since the closing price reached its highest peak.

HighestSince - Highest value since condition met

Syntax:
HighestSince(EXPRESSION, ARRAY, Nth = 1)

Returns:
ARRAY

Function: Returns the highest ARRAY value since EXPRESSION was true on the Nth most recent occurrence.

Example: HighestSince(Cross(macd(), 0), Close, 1) returns the highest close price since macd() has crossed above zero.

HighestSinceBars - Bars since highest value since condition met

Syntax:
HighestSinceBars(EXPRESSION, ARRAY, Nth = 1)

Returns:
ARRAY

Function: Returns the number of bars that have passed since highest ARRAY value since EXPRESSION was true on the Nth most recent occurrence.

Example: HighestSinceBars(Cross(macd(), 0), Close, 1) returns the number of bars passed since the highest close price was detected from the time when macd() has crossed above zero.

LLV - Lowest low value

Syntax:
LLV(ARRAY, periods)

Returns:
ARRAY

Function: Calculates the lowest value in the ARRAY over the preceding periods (periods includes the current day).

Example: The formula "LLV(close, 14)" returns the lowest closing price over the preceding 14 periods.

LLVBars - Bars since lowest low

Syntax:
LLVBars(ARRAY, periods)

Returns:
ARRAY

Function: Calculates the number of periods that have passed since the ARRAY reached its periods period trough.

Example: The formula "LLVBars(close,50)" returns the number of periods that have passed since the closing price reached its 50 period trough.

Lowest - Lowest value

Syntax:
Lowest(ARRAY)

Returns:
ARRAY

Function: Calculates the lowest value in the ARRAY.

Example: The formula Lowest(RSI(14)); returns the lowest Relative Strength Index value. Lowest (close) returns the lowest closing price.

LowestBars - Bars since lowest

Syntax:
LowestBars(ARRAY)

Returns:
ARRAY

Function: Calculates the number of periods that have passed since the ARRAY's lowest value.

Example: The formula "LowestBars(Close)" returns the number of periods that have passed since the closing price reached its lowest point.

LowestSince - Lowest value since condition met

Syntax:
LowestSince(EXPRESSION, ARRAY, Nth = 1)

Returns:
ARRAY

Function: Returns the lowest ARRAY value since EXPRESSION was true on the Nth most recent occurrence.

Example: LowestSince(Cross(MACD(), 0), Close, 1) returns the lowest close price since MACD() has crossed above zero.

LowestSinceBars - Bars since lowest value since condition met

Syntax:
LowestSinceBars(EXPRESSION, ARRAY, Nth = 1)

Returns:
ARRAY

Function: Returns the number of bars that have passed since lowest ARRAY value since EXPRESSION was true on the Nth most recent occurrence.

Example: LowestSinceBars(Cross(MACD(), 0), Close, 1) returns the number of bars passed since the lowest close price was detected from the time when MACD() has crossed above zero.

Math functions

abs - absolute value

Syntax:
abs(NUMBER)
abs(ARRAY)

Returns:
NUMBER
ARRAY

Function: Calculates the absolute value of the NUMBER or ARRAY.

Example: The formula "abs(-15)" will return +15. The formula "abs(15)" also returns +15. The formula "abs(C-Ref(C,-1))" will return the array containing the absolute value of the day to day point change.

acos - arccosine function

Syntax:
acos(x)

Returns:
NUMBER, ARRAY

Function: Returns the arccosine of NUMBER or ARRAY. The acos function returns the arccosize of x in the range 0 to pi radians. If x is less than -1 or greater than 1, acos returns an indefinite.

Example: The formula "acos(0.916)" returns 0.413.

AlmostEqual - Rounding error insensitive comparison

Syntax:

AlmostEqual(x, y, ulps = 5)

Returns:

NUMBER

ARRAY

Function: This is a helper function for comparing floating point numbers. It returns True if x and y are equal or almost equal up to defined accuracy (ulps). It is recommended to use this function instead of equality check (==) as it leads to more reliable comparisons and less headache caused by IEEE floating point accuracy issues.

Parameters: x, y - the numbers or arrays to be compared, ulps stands for "units in last place" and represents maximum relative error of the comparison. Since 32 bit IEEE floating point numbers have accuracy of 7 significant digits, 1 unit in last place(ulp) represents relative error of 0.00001 %. The default value of ulps parameter is 5 which gives roughly 0.00005% "comparison sensitivity".

Thanks to Bruce Dawson for his fast routine.

Example:

```
if( 1/3 == 0.333333 )
{
  printf("32-bit Floating point IEEE exact equality\n");
}
else
{
  printf ("The numbers are not exactly equal \n");
}

if( AlmostEqual( 1/3, 0.3333333 ) )
{
  printf("Numbers are almost equal\n");
}
```

Run it again with: if(4/2 == 2)

asin - arcsine function

Syntax:
asin(x)

Returns:
NUMBER, ARRAY

Function: Returns the arcsine of NUMBER or ARRAY. The asin function returns the arcsine of x in the range -pi/2 to pi/2 radians. If x is less than -1 or greater than 1, asin returns an indefinite

Example: The formula "asin (0.5)" returns 0.524.

atan - arctangent function

Syntax:
atan(NUMBER)
atan(ARRAY)

Returns:
NUMBER
ARRAY

Function: Returns the arc tangent of NUMBER or ARRAY. The value is returned in radians

Example: The formula "atan (1.00)" returns 0.785, Pi/4.

atan2 - arctangent of y/x

Syntax:
atan2(y, x)

Returns:
NUMBER or ARRAY

Function: atan2 returns the arctangent of y/x. If x is 0, atan2 returns 0. If both parameters of atan2 are 0, the function returns 0. atan2 returns a value in the range -PI to +PI radians, using the signs of both parameters to determine the quadrant of the return value.

Example:
```
ffc = FFT(data,Len);
for( i = 0; i < Len - 1; i = i + 2 )
{
   amp[ i ] = amp[ i + 1 ] = sqrt(ffc[ i ]^ 2  +  ffc[ i + 1
]^2);
   phase[ i ] = phase[ i + 1 ] = atan2( ffc[ i + 1], ffc[ i ]
);
}
```

ceil - ceiling value

Syntax:

ceil(NUMBER)
ceil(ARRAY)

Returns:

NUMBER
ARRAY

Function: Calculates the lowest integer that is greater than NUMBER or ARRAY.

Example: The formula ceil(6.2) returns 7; the formula ceil(-6.2) returns -6.

cos - cosine function

Syntax:

cos(NUMBER)
cos(ARRAY)

Returns:

NUMBER
ARRAY

Function: Returns the cosine of NUMBER or ARRAY. Assumes that the NUMBER or ARRAY values are in radians.

Example: The formula "cos(0.5)" returns 0.878.

cosh - hyperbolic cosine function

Syntax:
cosh(NUMBER)
cosh(ARRAY)

Returns:
NUMBER
ARRAY

Function: Returns the hyperbolic cosine of NUMBER or ARRAY. This function assumes that the ARRAY values are in radians.

Example: cosh (0.5) returns 1.128.

exp - exponential function

Syntax:
exp(NUMBER)
exp(ARRAY)

Returns:
NUMBER
ARRAY

Function: Calculates e raised to the NUMBER or ARRAY power.

Example: exp (0.5) returns 1.649.

floor - floor value

Syntax:
floor(NUMBER)
floor(ARRAY)

Returns:
NUMBER
ARRAY

Function: Calculates the highest integer that is less than NUMBER or ARRAY.

Example: The function floor(18.9) returns 18. The formula floor(-19.9) returns -20.

frac - fractional part

Syntax:
frac(NUMBER)
frac(ARRAY)

Returns:
NUMBER
ARRAY

Function: Eliminates the integer portion of NUMBER or ARRAY and returns the fractional part.

Example: The formula frac(12.4) returns 0.4. The formula frac(-15.7) returns -0.7.

int - integer part

Syntax:
int(NUMBER)
int(ARRAY)

Returns:
NUMBER
ARRAY

Function: Removes the fractional portion of NUMBER or ARRAY and returns the integer part.

Example: The formula "int(10.7)" returns 10. The formula "int(-19.8)" returns -19.

log - natural logarithm

Syntax:
log(NUMBER)
log(ARRAY)

Returns:
NUMBER
ARRAY

Function: Calculates the natural logarithm of NUMBER or ARRAY.

Example: log (9.5) returns 2.251.

log10 - decimal logarithm

Syntax:
log10(NUMBER)
log10(ARRAY)

Returns:
NUMBER
ARRAY

Function: Calculates the decimal logarithm of NUMBER or ARRAY.

Example: log10 (9.5) returns 0.978.

Max - Maximum value of two numbers / arrays

Syntax:
Max(NUMBER1, NUMBER2)
Max(ARRAY1, ARRAY2)

Returns:
NUMBER
ARRAY

Function: Returns the largest of the two parameters.

Example: The formula "Max(Close, 10)" returns either the closing price or 10, whichever is greater. The formula "Max(-14, 13)" always returns 13.

Min - Minimum value of two numbers / arrays

Syntax:
Min(NUMBER1, NUMBER2)
Min(ARRAY1, ARRAY2)

Returns:
NUMBER
ARRAY

Function: Returns the smallest of the two parameters.

Example: The formula "min(Close, 10)" returns the closing price or 10, whichever is less. The formula "min(-14, 13)" always returns -14.

Prec - Adjust number of decimal places

Syntax:
Prec(NUMBER, precision)
Prec(ARRAY, precision)

Returns:
NUMBER
ARRAY

Function: Truncates NUMBER or ARRAY to precision decimal places.

Example: The formula "prec(10.12981, 2)" returns 10.120. The formula "prec(10.12981, 4)" returns 10.12980.

round - Round number to nearest integer

Syntax:
round(NUMBER)
round(ARRAY)

Returns:
NUMBER
ARRAY

Function: Rounds NUMBER or ARRAY to the nearest integer.

Example: The formula "round(+11.5)" returns +12. The formula "round(-11.4)" returns -11.

sign - Returns the sign of the number or array

Syntax:
sign(x)

Returns:
ARRAY
NUMBER

Function: The sign function returns 1 if x value is greater than zero, -1 if the x is less than zero and 0 if x equals zero. x can be a number or array.

Example: sign (-2.5) returns -1.

sin - sine function

Syntax:
sin(NUMBER)
sin(ARRAY)

Returns:
NUMBER
ARRAY

Function: Returns the sine of NUMBER or ARRAY. This function assumes that the NUMBER or ARRAY values are in radians.

Example: You can plot a sine wave using the formula "sin(cum(0.05))." Increasing the value in this formula (i.e., "0.05") will increase the frequency of the sine wave.

sinh - hyperbolic sine function

Syntax:
sinh(NUMBER)
sinh(ARRAY)

Returns:
NUMBER
ARRAY

Function: Returns the hyperbolic sine of NUMBER or ARRAY. This function assumes that the NUMBER or ARRAY values are in radians.

Example: sinh (0.92) returns 1.055.

sqrt - square root

Syntax:
sqrt(NUMBER)
sqrt(ARRAY)

Returns:
NUMBER
ARRAY

Function: Calculates the square root of NUMBER or ARRAY. The square root of a negative number returns NAN (Not a Number).

Example: The formula "sqrt(16)" returns 4

tan - tangent function

Syntax:
tan(NUMBER)
tan(ARRAY)

Returns:
NUMBER
ARRAY

Function: Returns the tangent of NUMBER or ARRAY. This function assumes that the NUMBER or ARRAY values are in radians

Example: tan (1.0) returns 1.557.

tanh - hyperbolic tangent function

Syntax:
tanh(NUMBER)
tanh(ARRAY)

Returns:
NUMBER
ARRAY

Function: Returns the hyperbolic tangent of NUMBER or ARRAY. This function assumes that the NUMBER or ARRAY values are in radians.

Example: tanh (0.8) returns 0.664.

Moving Averages, Summation

AMA - Adaptive moving average

Syntax:
AMA(ARRAY, SmoothingFactor)

Returns:
ARRAY

Function: Calculates adaptive moving average - similar to EMA() but smoothing factor could be time-variant (array).

Example: The example of volatility-weighted adaptive moving average formula:

```
Plot (C,"C", colorBlack,styleCandle);
Plot(EMA( Close, 15 ), "EMA", colorRed,styleLine);
fast = 2/(2+1);
slow = 2/(30+1);
dir=abs(Close-Ref(Close,-10));
vol=Sum(abs(Close-Ref(Close,-1)),10);
ER=dir/vol;
sc =( ER*(fast-slow)+slow)^2;
Plot(AMA( Close, sc ), "AMA", colorBlue,styleLine);
```

AMA2 - Adaptive moving average

Syntax:
AMA2(ARRAY, SmoothingFactor, FeedBackFactor)

Returns:
ARRAY

Function: Calculates adaptive moving average - simliar to EMA() but smoothing factor could be time-variant (array).

AMA2 has a separate control of FeedBackFactor which is normally (1-SmoothingFactor). Internally this function works like this: today_ama = SmoothingFactor * array + FeedBackFactor * yesterday_ama

Example: The example of volatility-weighted adaptive moving average formula:

```
Plot (C,"C", colorBlack,styleCandle);
Plot(EMA( Close, 15 ), "EMA", colorRed,styleLine);
fast = 2/(2+1);
slow = 2/(30+1);
dir=abs(Close-Ref(Close,-10));
vol=Sum(abs(Close-Ref(Close,-1)),10);
ER=dir/vol;
sc =( ER*(fast-slow)+slow)^2;
Plot ( AMA2( Close, sc, 1-sc),"AMA2", colorBlue,styleLine);
```

Cum - Cumulative sum

Syntax:

cum (NUMBER)

cum(ARRAY)

Returns:

NUMBER

ARRAY

Function: Calculates a cumulative sum of the ARRAY from the first period in the chart.

Example: The formula cum(1) calculates an indicator that rises one point for each day since the beginning of the chart - this is an equivalent of bar number - especially useful if you want to detect the last bar: ThisIsLastBar = cum(1) == lastvalue(cum(1));

DEMA - Double exponential moving average

Syntax:

DEMA(ARRAY, periods)

Returns:

ARRAY

Function: Calculates double exponentially smoothed average - DEMA. The function accepts time-variable periods.

Example: DEMA(Close, 5)

EMA - exponential moving average

Syntax:
EMA(ARRAY, periods)

Returns:
ARRAY

Function: Calculates a periods exponential moving average of ARRAY.

Example: EMA(close, 5)

MA - Simple moving average

Syntax:
MA(ARRAY, periods)

Returns:
ARRAY

Function: Calculates a periods simple moving average of ARRAY.

Example: MA(CLOSE, 5)

Sum - Sum data over specified number of bars

Syntax:
Sum(ARRAY, periods)

Returns:
ARRAY

Function: Calculates a cumulative sum of the ARRAY for the specified number of lookback periods (including today).

Example: The formula "Sum(Close, 14)" returns the sum of the preceding 14 closing prices. A 14-period simple moving average could be written "sum(C,14) / 14."

TEMA - Triple exponential moving average

Syntax:
TEMA(ARRAY, periods)

Returns:
ARRAY

Function: Calculates triple exponentially smoothed average - TEMA. The function accepts time-variable periods.

Example: TEMA(Close, 5)

Wilders - Wilder's smoothing

Syntax:
Wilders(ARRAY, periods)

Returns:
ARRAY

Function: Calculates Wilder's average of the ARRAY using periods averaging range

Example: Wilders(close, 10);

WMA - Weighted moving average

Syntax:
WAM(ARRAY, periods)

Returns:
ARRAY

Function: Calculates weighted average. 5 day weighted average gives weight of 5 to the most recent quote, 4 to the previous quote, down to 1 for the 5-bar back quote. The function accepts time-variable periods.

Example: WMA(Close, 5)

Statistical functions

Correlation - Correlation

Syntax:
Correlation(ARRAY1, ARRAY2, periods)

Returns:
ARRAY

Function: Calculates correlation between ARRAY1 and ARRAY2 using periods range.

Example: Calculate the 25 period correlation between Close price and Close price 5 days back with this statement, Correlation(Close, Ref(Close, -5), 25);

```
// Built-in correlation can be re-coded with
// basic AFL functions like MA (moving average) - which
// is equivalent for "expected value" statistic term
// and few basic arithmetic operations

function Correl( x, y, number )
{
nom = MA( x * y, number ) - MA( x, number ) * MA( y, number );
denom = sqrt( MA( x ^ 2, number ) - MA( x, number ) ^ 2 ) *
sqrt( MA( y ^ 2, number ) - MA( y, number ) ^ 2 );
return nom / denom;
}

Plot (Correlation( C, Ref( H, -2 ), 10 ), "built-in",
    colorRed,styleLine);

Plot (Correl( C, Ref( H, -2 ), 10 ), "re-coded",
    colorBlue,styleLine);
```

LinearReg - Linear regression end-point

Syntax:
LinearReg(ARRAY, periods)

Returns:
ARRAY

Function: Calculates linear regression line end-point value according to a + b * x (where a and b are intercept and slope of linear regression line) from the ARRAY using periods range.

Example: LinearReg(Close, 10);

LinRegIntercept - Intercept of the linear regression line

Syntax:
LinRegIntercept(ARRAY, periods)

Returns:
ARRAY

Function: Calculates intercept of linear regression line - the "a" coefficient in a + b*x (LinRegSlope calculates b) from the ARRAY using periods range.

Example:

```
DaysBack = 10;
Lri = LinRegIntercept(C, Daysback);
Plot( Close, "Close", colorBlack, styleCandle );
Plot (Lri, "LRI", colorRed,styleLine|styleOwnScale);
```

LinRegSlope - Linear regression slope

Syntax:
LinRegSlope(ARRAY, periods)

Returns:
ARRAY

Function: Calculates linear regression line slope from the ARRAY using periods range.

Example:

```
DaysBack = 10;
Lrs = LinRegSlope(C, Daysback);
Plot( Close, "Close", colorBlack, styleCandle );
Plot (Lrs, "LRS", colorBlue,styleLine|styleOwnScale);
```

Median - Calculate median (middle element)

Syntax:
Median(ARRAY, period)

Returns:
ARRAY

Function: The Median function - finds median (middle element) value of the ARRAY over period elements.

Example:

```
// list only symbols which volume is greater than
// median Volume from past 50 days
Filter = Volume > Median( Volume, 50 );
AddColumn( V, "Volume" );
```

mtRandom - Mersene Twister random number generator (single number version)

Syntax:
mtRandom(seed = Null)

Returns:
NUMBER

Function: mtRandom(seed = Null) - returns a single random number (scalar) in the range [0,1)

seed is the random generator seed value. If you don't specify one, the random number generator is automatically initialized with current time as a seed that guarantees unique sequence. If you want a repeatable sequence, you must supply your own seed.

Both functions use Mersene Twister mt19973ar-cok algorithm. (Copyright (C) 1997 - 2002, Makoto Matsumoto and Takuji Nishimura.)

Mersene Twister has a period of 2^19973 (approximately 2.9*10^6012) and is vastly superior to C-runtime pseudo-random generator available via Random() function.

mtRandomA - Mersene Twister random number generator (array version)

Syntax:
mtRandomA(seed = Null)

Returns:
ARRAY

Function: mtRandom(seed = Null) - returns an array of random numbers in the range [0,1)

Percentile - Calculate percentile

Syntax:
Percentile(ARRAY, period, rank)

Returns:
ARRAY

Function: The Percentile function gives rank percentile value of the array over last period bars.

rank is 0..100 - defines percentile rank in the array

Performance note: the implementation of percentile function involves sorting that is a relatively slow process even though the quicksort algorithm is used.

Examples:

```
// Example 1:
// show bars when 'current' Day Volume ranks within
// TOP 30% of volumes of last 100 bars
// (is above 70th Percentile)
Filter = Volume > Percentile( Volume, 100, 70 );

// Example 2:
// show bars when 'current' Day Volume ranks within
// BOTTOM 30% of volumes of last 100 bars
// (is below 30th percentile)
Filter = Volume < Percentile( Volume, 100, 30 );
```

Random - Random number

Syntax:
Random(seed = Null)

Returns:
ARRAY

Function: Returns an array of random values in 0..1 range. To get a single random value use LastValue(Random()).

Seed initializes the random number generator. This allows either a reproducible series of pseudo-random numbers - the same seed always produces the same random number series - or a random series. If the seed is not specified, the series is random. If the seed is the number 1, the series is reproducible. Any other value for seed sets the generator to a random starting point.

Examples:
```
RN = Random(); // generates different sequences
RM = Random(1); // generates the same sequence
```

StdErr - Standard error

Syntax:
StdErr(ARRAY, periods)

Returns:
ARRAY

Function: Calculates the standard error function (standard error of linear regression estimate) of the ARRAY over periods bars.

Example: StdErr(close, 10);

StDev - Standard deviation

Syntax:
StDev(ARRAY, periods)

Returns:
ARRAY

Function: Calculates the moving standard deviation of the ARRAY over periods bars

Example: StDev(close, 10);

TSF - Time series forecast

Syntax:
TSF(ARRAY, periods)

Returns:
ARRAY

Function: Calculates the time series forecast indicator (similar to LinearReg but differs by the value of lin reg slope)

Example:

```
Plot( Close, "Price", colorBlue, styleCandle );
Plot( TSF(Close,5), "Time Series Forecast", colorRed );
```

Basic Price Pattern Detection

FFT - Performs Fast Fourier Transform

Syntax:
FFT(array, len = 0)

Returns:
ARRAY

Function: The function performs the FFT (Fast Fourier Transform) on the last 'len' bars of the array. If len is set to zero, then FFT is performed on entire array. The len parameter must be even.

Result: The function returns an array that holds FFT bins for the first 'len' bars. There are len/2 FFT complex bins returned, where bin is a pair of numbers (complex number): first is real part of the complex number and second number is the imaginary part of the complex number.

result = FFT(array, 256);

where:

0th bin (result[0] and result[1]) represents DC component, 1st bin (result[1] and result[2]) represents real and imaginary parts of lowest frequency range and so on up to result[len - 2] and result[len - 1]

The remaining elements of the array are set to zero.

```
// FFT.afl
SetBarsRequired(100000,100000);

Len = Param("FFT Length", 1024, 64, 10000, 10 );
Len = Min( Len, BarCount );

x = BarIndex();
x1 = x - BarCount + Len;

input = C;
a = LastValue( LinRegIntercept( input, Len - 1 ) );
b = LastValue( LinRegSlope( input, Len - 1 ) );

Lr = a + b * x1;

data = input - Lr;// de-trending

ffc = FFT(data,Len);


for( i = 0; i < Len - 1; i = i + 2 )
{
   amp[ i ] = amp[ i + 1 ] = sqrt(ffc[ i ]^ 2  +  ffc[ i + 1
]^2);
   phase[ i ] = phase[ i + 1 ] = atan2( ffc[ i + 1], ffc[ i ]
);
}

auto = ParamToggle("Auto dominant cycle", "No|Yes", 1 );
sbar = Param( "Which FFT bin", 1, 0, 50 );

skipbin1 = ParamToggle("Skip 1st FFT bin", "No|Yes", 1 );

if( auto )
{
   sbar = int( LastValue(ValueWhen( amp
        == LastValue(Highest( IIf( skipbin1 AND x < 4, 0 , amp )
)), x / 2 )) );
}

fv = Status("firstvisiblebar");

thisbar = Ref( int(x/2) == sbar, -fv);
Plot( Ref(amp,-fv),
    "amplitude (bin " + Ref( int(x/2), -fv ) +")",
    IIf( thisbar, colorRed, colorBlack ),styleArea);

Plot( IIf( BarCount - BarIndex() < Len, data, Null ) ,
    "de-trended input ("+Len+" bars)", colorOrange, styleLef-
tAxisScale );
Plot( cos( phase[ sbar * 2 ] + (sbar) * x1 * 2 * 3.1415926 /
Len ),
    " dominant cycle "+ Len/(sbar)
    + "(" + sbar + " bin) bars", colorBlue, styleOwnScale );

GraphZOrder=1;
GraphXSpace = 10;
```

GapDown - Gap down

Syntax:
GapDown()

Returns:
ARRAY

Function: Returns a "1" or "true" on the day a security's prices gap down. Otherwise the result is "0". A gap down occurs if yesterday's low is greater than today's high.

Example: GD = GapDown();

GapUp - Gap up

Syntax:
GapUp()

Returns:
ARRAY

Function: Returns a "1" or "true" on the day a security's prices gap up. Otherwise the result is "0". A gap up occurs if yesterday's high is less than today's low.

Example: GU = CapUp();

Inside - Inside day

Syntax:
Inside()

Returns:
ARRAY

Function: Returns a "1" or "true" when an inside day occurs. Gives "0" otherwise. An inside day occurs when today's high is less than yesterday's high and today's low is greater than yesterday's low.

Example: ID = Inside();

Outside - Outside day

Syntax:
Outside()

Returns:
ARRAY

Function: Returns "true" (or 1) when an outside day occurs. An outside day is when today's high is greater than yesterday's high and today's low is lower than yesterday's low.

Example: Outside()

Peak - Peak

Syntax:
Peak(ARRAY, change, n = 1)

Returns:
ARRAY

Function: Returns the value of ARRAY n-th peak(s) ago. This uses the Zig Zag function (see Zig Zag) to determine the peaks. n =1 would return the value of the most recent peak. n =2 would return the value of the 2nd most recent peak.

Example: Peak(Close,5,1)

Notes:

- **Zig, Peak, and Trough functions work correctly for arrays containing data greater than zero.**
- **This function is based on Zig-Zag indicator and may look into the future.**

PeakBars - Bars since peak

Syntax:
PeakBars(ARRAY, change, n = 1)

Returns:
ARRAY

Function: Gives the number of bars that have passed from the n-th peak. This uses the Zig Zag function (see Zig Zag) to determine the peaks. n =1 would return the number of bars that have passed since the most recent peak. n =2 would return the number of bars that have passed since the 2nd most recent peak.

Example: PeakBars(Close,5,1)

Notes:

- **Zig, Peak, and Trough functions work correctly for arrays containing data greater than zero.**
- **This function is based on Zig-Zag indicator and may look into the future.**

Trough - Trough

Syntax:
Trough(ARRAY, change, n = 1)

Returns:
ARRAY

Function: Gives the value of ARRAY n-th trough(s) ago. This uses the Zig Zag function (see Zig Zag) to determine the troughs.

Example: Trough(Close,5,1)

Notes:

- **Zig, Peak, and Trough functions work correctly for arrays containing data greater than zero.**
- **This function is based on Zig-Zag indicator and may look into the future.**

TroughBars - Bars since trough

Syntax:
TroughBars(ARRAY, change, n = 1)

Returns:
ARRAY

Function: Returns the number of bars that have passed from the n-th trough. This uses the Zig Zag function (see Zig Zag) to determine the troughs.

Example: TroughBars(Close,5,1)

Notes:

- **Zig, Peak, and Trough functions work correctly for arrays containing data greater than zero.**
- **This function is based on Zig-Zag indicator and may look into the future.**

Zig - Zig-zag indicator

Syntax:
Zig(ARRAY, change)

Returns:
ARRAY

Function: Calculates the minimum % change Zig Zag indicator. Caveat: this function is based on Zig-Zag indicator and may look into the future - this means that you can get unrealistic results when back testing trading system using this indicator. This function is provided rather for pattern and trend recognition formulas.

Example: Zig(Close,5)

Notes:

- **Zig, Peak, and Trough functions work correctly for arrays containing data greater than zero.**
- **This function is based on Zig-Zag indicator and may look into the future.**

Composites

AddToComposite - Add value to composite ticker

Syntax:
AddToComposite(array, "ticker", "field", flags = atcFlagDefaults)

Returns:
NOTHING

Function: Allows you to create composite indicators with ease.

The parameters are:

- array - the array of values to be added to "field" in "ticker" composite symbol
- "ticker" - the ticker of composite symbol. It is advised to use tilde as the first character of the symbol (~comp)
- "field" - newly added composites are assigned to group 253 by default and have "use only local database" feature switched on for proper operation with external sources possible field codes: "C" - close , "O" - open, "H" - high, "L" - low, "V" - volume, "I" - open interest, "X" - updates all OHLC fields at once
- flags - contains the sum of following values
  - atcFlagDeleteValues = 1 - deletes all previous data from composite symbol at the beginning of scan (recommended)
  - atcFlagCompositeGroup = 2 - put composite ticker into group 253 and EXCLUDE all other tickers from group 253 (avoids adding composite to composite)
  - atcFlagTimeStamp = 4 - put last scan date/time stamp into FullName field
  - atcFlagDefaults = 7 (this is a composition of atcFlagResetValues | atcFlagCompositeGroup | atcFlagTimeStamp flags)
  - atcFlagEnableInBacktest = 8 - allow running AddToComposite in backtest/optimization mode
  - atcFlagEnableInExplore = 16 - allow running AddToComposite in exploration mode
  - atcFlagResetValues = 32 - reset values at the beginning of scan (not required if you use atcFlagDeleteValues)
  - atcFlagEnableInPortfolio = 64 - allow running AddToCom-

posite in custom portfolio backtester phase

- atcFlagEnableInIndicator = 128 - allow running AddTo-Composite in indicator mode

AddToComposite function also detects the context in which it is run. It works only in scan mode, unless atcFlagEnableInBacktest or atcFlagEnableInExplore flags are specified. And it does not affect composite ticker when run in Indicator or Commentary mode, so it is possible to combine scan and indicator into a single formula.

Example: AddToComposite(MACD() > 0, "~BullMACD", "V");

AddToComposite is an extremely powerful function. An extensive discussion of it is beyond the scope of this book. There is an excellent reference and tutorial, Introduction to the AmiBroker AddToComposite(), a 32 page pdf document, written by Herman van den Bergen in 2002. You can find it at: http://www.amibroker.org/3rdparty/IntroToAtc.pdf.

ADLine - Advance/decline line

Syntax:
ADLine()

Returns:
ARRAY

Function: Calculates the Advance/Decline line indicator

Example: ADLine()

AdvIssues - Advancing issues

Syntax:
AdvIssues()

Returns:
ARRAY

Function: Returns the number of advancing issues for a given market (the one that the current stock belongs to)

Example: AdvIssues()

AdvVolume - Advancing issues volume

Syntax:
AdvVolume()

Returns:
ARRAY

Function: Returns the volume of advancing issues for a given market (the one that the current stock belongs to)

Example: AdvVolume()

DecIssues - Declining issues

Syntax:
DecIssues()

Returns:
ARRAY

Function: Returns the number of declining issues for a given market (the one that the current stock belongs to)

Example: DecIssues()

DecVolume - Declining issues volume

Syntax:
DecVolume()

Returns:
ARRAY

Function: Returns the volume of declining issues for a given market (the one that the current stock belongs to)

Example: DecVolume()

Trin - Traders (Arms) index

Syntax:
Trin()

Returns:
ARRAY

Function: Calculates TRIN (Arms Index) indicator.

Example: Trin()

NOTE: All built-in a/d indicators (AdLine/Trin) work only with composites calculated inside AmiBroker.

If you are using the Quotes Plus database for example you should use QP2's own symbols for advances and declines.

!NY-A, !NY-D, !NY-AV, !NY-DV

The formula for NYSE Trin using the QP2 database is:

```
ArmsIndex = ( Foreign("!NY-A", "C") / Foreign("!NY-D", "C") ) /
( Foreign("!NY-AV", "C") / Foreign("!NY-DV","C" ) );
Plot( ArmsIndex, "Trin", colorRed );
```

UncIssues - Unchanged issues

Syntax:
UncIssues()

Returns:
ARRAY

Function: Returns the number of unchanged issues for a given market (the one that the current stock belongs to)

Example: UncIssues()

UncVolume - Unchanged issues volume

Syntax:
UncVolume()

Returns:
ARRAY

Function: Returns the volume of unchanged issues for a given market (the one that the current stock belongs to)

Example: UncVolume()

INDICATORS

AccDist - Accumulation/distribution

Syntax:
AccDist()

Returns:
ARRAY

Function: Calculates the Accumulation/ Distribution indicator.

Example: AccDist()

ADX - Average directional movement index

Syntax:
ADX(period = 14)

Returns:
ARRAY

Function: Calculates the Average Directional Index indicator

Example: ADX(), ADX(20)

ATR - Average true range

Syntax:
ATR(period)

Returns:
ARRAY

Function: Calculates the Average True Range indicator

Example: ATR(7)

BBandBot - Bollinger band - bottom

Syntax:
BBandBot(ARRAY, periods = 15, width = 2)

Returns:
ARRAY

Function: Calculates the bottom Bollinger Band of ARRAY.

Example: BBandBot(Close, 10, 2)

BBandTop - Bollinger band - top

Syntax:
BBandTop(ARRAY, periods = 15, width = 2)

Returns:
ARRAY

Function: Calculates the top Bollinger Band of ARRAY.

Example: BBandTop(Close, 10, 2)

CCI - Commodity channel index

Syntax:
CCI(periods = 14)
CCIa(ARRAY, periods = 14)

Returns:
ARRAY

Function: Calculates the Commodity Channel Index (using periods averaging range).

Second version (CCIa) accepts an input array, so CCI can be applied to an array different than close.

Example: CCI(14), CCIa(High, 14);

Chaikin - Chaikin oscillator

Syntax:
Chaikin(fast = 9, slow = 14)

Returns:
ARRAY

Function: Calculates the Chaikin Oscillator with averaging parameters: fast, slow

Example: Chaikin (9, 14);

GetCursorMouseButtons - Get current state of mouse buttons

Syntax:
GetCursorMouseButtons()

Returns:
NUMBER

Function: This function returns mouse button state at the time when chart formula is executed.

Example:

```
if( GetCursorMouseButtons() & 1 )
{
printf("left mouse button is pressed down" );
}
```

For more information, read the AmiBroker User's Guide.

GetCursorXPosition - Get current X position of mouse pointer

Syntax:
GetCursorXPosition(mode = 0)

Returns:
NUMBER (datetime)

Function: Retrieves the current mouse pointer X co-ordinate (i.e. datetime of bar under the mouse pointer).

Example:

```
ToolTip = "X=" + DateTimeToStr( GetCursorXPosition() ) +
          "nY=" + GetCursorYPosition();
```

GetCursorYPosition - Get current Y position of mouse pointer

Syntax:
GetCursorYPosition()

Returns:
NUMBER

Function: Retrieves the current mouse pointer Y co-ordinate (i.e. value in dollars or other Y-axis unit).

Example:

```
ToolTip = "X=" + DateTimeToStr( GetCursorXPosition() ) +
"nY=" + GetCursorYPosition();
```

MACD - Moving average convergence/divergence

Syntax:
MACD(fast = 12, slow = 26)

Returns:
ARRAY

Function: Calculates the MACD indicator using fast and slow averaging periods.

Example: The formula "MACD()" returns the value of the MACD indicator (i.e., the red line). The formula "SIGNAL()" returns the value of the MACD's signal line (i.e., the blue line).

MDI - Minus directional movement indicator (-DI)

Syntax:

MDI(period = 14)

Returns:
ARRAY

Function: Calculates the Minus Directional Movement Indicator (-DI line)

Example: MDI()

MFI - Money flow index

Syntax:

MFI(periods = 14)

Returns:
ARRAY

Function: Calculates the Money Flow Index with period range

Example: MDI(16)

NVI - Negative volume index

Syntax:
NVI()

Returns:
ARRAY

Function: Calculates the Negative Volume Index.

Example: NVI()

OBV - On balance volume

Syntax:
OBV()

Returns:
ARRAY

Function: Calculates the On Balance Volume indicator.

Example: OBV()

OscP - Price oscillator

Syntax:

OscP(fast , slow)

Returns:
ARRAY

Function: Calculates the price oscillator based on exponential moving averages

Example: OscP(9, 18)

OscV - Volume oscillator

Syntax:
OscV(fast, slow)

Returns:
ARRAY

Function: Calculates the volume oscillator based on exponential moving averages

Example: OscV(9, 18)

PDI - Plus directional movement indicator

Syntax:
PDI(period = 14)

Returns:
ARRAY

Function: Calculates the Plus Directional Movement Indicator (-DI line)

Example: PDI(14)

PlotText - Write text on the chart

Syntax:
PlotText("text", x, y, color, bkcolor = colorDefault)

Returns:
NOTHING

Function: This function writes text in specified co-ordinates. Where:

x - is x-coordinate in bars (like in LineArray)

y - is y-coordinate in dollars

color is text color

bkcolor is background color

If bkcolor is not specified (or equal to colorDefault) text is written with transparent background, any other value causes solid background with specified background color.

Example:

```
Plot(C,"Price", colorBlack, styleLine );
Plot(MA(C,20),"MA20", colorRed );

Buy=Cross( C, MA(C,20 ) );
Sell= Cross( MA( C, 20 ), C );

dist = 1.5*ATR(10);

for( i = 0; i < BarCount; i++ )
{
if( Buy[i] ) PlotText( "Buy\n@" + C[ i ], i,
       L[ i ]-dist[i], colorGreen );
if( Sell[i] ) PlotText( "Sell\n@" + C[ i ], i,
       H[ i ]+dist[i], colorRed, colorYellow );
}

PlotShapes( Buy * shapeUpArrow + Sell * shapeDownArrow,
       IIf( Buy, colorGreen, colorRed ) );
```

PVI - Positive volume index

Syntax:
PVI()

Returns:
ARRAY

Function: Calculates the Positive Volume Index.

Example: PVI ()

RequestTimedRefresh - Forces periodical refresh of indicator pane

Syntax:
RequestTimedRefresh(interval, onlyvisible = True)

Returns:
NOTHING

Function: The function causes the given indicator window to refresh automatically every interval seconds regardless of data source used or connection state.

The interval parameter defines timeout in seconds between refreshes. AmiBroker attempts to align refreshes to second boundary so if you call it RequestTimedRefresh(5) you should get refreshes at 0, 5, 10, 15, 20, 25, 30, 35, 40, 45, 50 and 55 second of the minute. Due to the way regular (low overhead) timers are implemented in Windows they have accuracy of +/-55ms provided the CPU is not very busy. Don't expect to get the first line of your code to execute exactly at .000 milliseconds. This varies depending on machine load, number of quotes, system time slice, and tens of other factors. Usually (on my testing machines) the first line of the code executes anywhere in the first 100 ms of the second, provided that other processes do not interfere. Windows is not a real-time operating system and it does not guarantee any fixed execution/reaction times.

The onlyvisible parameter set to True (default value) means that refreshes are triggered only for visible and not minimized windows. This applies also to the main AmiBroker window - when it is minimized charts are not refreshed by default. To force refreshes when a window is minimized you need to set this parameter to False. Note that this visibility applies mostly to the 'minimized' state or the situation when you move the chart outside the boundary of the physical screen so it is not visible (to an eye) but still open. It does not apply to chart windows that are placed on inactive sheets, as they do not really exist until they are shown (this way AmiBroker conserves memory and CPU) and as non-existing, chart windows can not be refreshed.

Hint: to detect whenever a given refresh comes from timer or user action you can use the Status("redrawaction") function. It returns 0 for regular refresh (user action) and 1 for timer-refresh.

Example: RequestTimedRefresh(5);

// automatically refresh this particular chart every 5 seconds

RMI - Relative Momentum Index

Syntax:

RMI(periods = 20, momentum = 5)

Returns:

ARRAY

Function: Calculates Altman's Relative Momentum Index (S&C Feb 1993)

Example: RMI(20, 5)

ROC - Percentage rate of change

Syntax:
ROC(ARRAY, periods = 12, absmode = False)

Returns:
ARRAY

Function: Calculates the periods rate-of-change of ARRAY expressed as percentage.

if absmode = False the value returned is (array - ref(array, -periods))/ref(array, -periods)

if absmode = True the value returned is (array - ref(array, -periods))/abs(ref(array, -periods))

Example: The formula roc(Close, 14) returns the 14-period percent rate-of-change of the closing prices.

RSI - Relative strength index

Syntax:
RSI(periods = 14)
RSIa(ARRAY, periods = 14)

Returns:
ARRAY

Function: Calculates the RSI indicator of the close using periods range

The second version, RSIa, accepts an input array so RSI can be applied to other arrays than close.

Example: RSI(12)

RSIa(High, 12);

RWI - Random walk index

Syntax:
RWI(minperiods, maxperiods)

Returns:
ARRAY

Function: Calculates the Random Walk Index indicator as a difference between Random Walk Index from Highs (RWIHI() function) and Random Walk Index from Lows (RWILO() function.

Example: RWI(9, 40);

RWIHi - Random walk index of highs

Syntax:
RWIHi(minperiods, maxperiods)

Returns:
ARRAY

Function: Calculates the Random Walk Index from Highs.

Example: RWIHi(9, 40);

RWILo - Random walk index of lows

Syntax:
RWILo(minperiods, maxperiods)

Returns:
ARRAY

Function: Calculates the Random Walk Index from Lows.

Example: RWILo(9, 40);

SAR - Parabolic stop-and-reverse

Syntax:
SAR(accel = 0.02, max = 0.2)

Returns:
ARRAY

Function: Calculates the Parabolic SAR indicator. Acceleration is given by accel argument and maximum acceleration level is given by max argument.

Example: SAR()

SetBarFillColor - Set bar/candlestick/cloud chart fill color

Syntax:
SetBarFillColor(colorarray)

Returns:
NOTHING

Function: SetBarFillColor(colorarray) allows independent control of candlestick, bar, cloud, and area chart fill color

SetBarFillColor must precede the Plot() function call it applies to.

When applied to:

- styleCandle - SetBarFillColor controls the color of the interior of the candle body. Shadows and outline are controlled by the color passed in Plot statement
- styleArea - SetBarFillColor controls the color of interior of histogram bars
- styleBar - SetBarFillColor controls the color of the bar (H-L). Open and close ticks color is controlled by Plot statement
- styleCloud - SetBarFillColor controls the color of interior of the cloud. Outline is controlled by the color passed in Plot statement
- Other styles are not affected

Example:

```
SetBarFillColor( IIf( MACD()>Signal(),
        colorYellow, colorBlue ) );
Plot( C, “Price”, IIf( C > O, colorGreen, colorRed ),
        styleCandle );
```

SetChartBkColor - Set background color of a chart

Syntax:
SetChartBkColor(color)

Returns:
NOTHING

Function: Sets chart background to user-specified color

Example: SetChartBkColor(colorBlue);

SetChartBkGradientFill - Set background gradient color fill in indicators

Syntax:
SetChartBkGradientFill(topcolor, bottomcolor,
titlebkcolor = default)

Returns:
NOTHING

Function: Enables background gradient color fill in indicators.

Please note that this is independent of chart background color (background color fills entire pane, gradient fill is only for actual chart interior, so axes area is not affected by gradient fill)

- topcolor - specifies the top color of the gradient fill
- bottomcolor - specifies the bottom color of the gradient fill
- titlebkcolor - (optional) the background color of title text. If not specified then top color is automatically used for title background.

Example: SetChartBkGradientFill(ParamColor("BgTop", colorWhite),
ParamColor("BgBottom", colorLightYellow));

Signal - MACD signal line

Syntax:
Signal(fast = 12, slow = 26, signal = 9)

Returns:
ARRAY

Function: Calculates the Signal line of MACD indicator.

Example: Signal(14, 28, 10);

StochD - Stochastic slow %D

Syntax:
StochD(periods = 14, Ksmooth=3, Dsmooth=3)

Returns:
ARRAY

Function: Calculates the %D line of Stochastic Oscillator (with internal slowing KSmooth, DSmooth).

Example: The formula "stochd(5)" returns the value of a 5-period %D double smoothed by 3 periods

StochK - Stochastic slow %K

Syntax:
StochK(periods = 14, ksmooth=3)

Returns:
ARRAY

Function: Calculates the %K line of Stochastic Oscillator (with internal slowing KSmooth).

Example: The formula "stochk(5)" returns the value of a 5-period %K slowed down 3 periods.

Trix - Triple exponential smoothed price

Syntax:
Trix(periods = 9)

Returns:
ARRAY

Function: Calculates the TRIX indicator (with averaging range of periods).

Example: Trix(12)

Ultimate - Ultimate oscillator

Syntax:
Ultimate(fast = 7, med = 14, slow = 28)

Returns:
ARRAY

Function: Calculates the Ultimate Oscillator indicator using the three cycle lengths supplied as parameters. Note that each of the three parameters must be greater than the preceding parameter.

Example: The formula "ultimate(7, 14, 21)" returns the default Ultimate Oscillator.

Exploration / Indicators

AddColumn - Add numeric exploration column

Syntax:

AddColumn(array, name, format = 1.2, textColor = colorDefault, bkgndColor = colorDefault, width = -1)

Returns:

NOTHING

Function: Adds a new column to the exploration result list. The column shows array values and has a caption of name. The values are formatted using format specification.

By default all variables are displayed with 2 decimal digits, but you can change this by assigning a different value to this variable: 1.5 gives 5 decimal digits, 1.0 gives no decimal digits. (Note for advanced users: the integer part of this number can be used to pad formatted number with spaces - 6.0 will give no decimal digits but a number space-padded to 6 characters.)

The next two parameters modify the text and background colors.

special format constants:

- formatDateTime - produces date time formatted according to your system settings

  ```
  AddColumn( DateTime(), "Date / Time", formatDateTime );
  ```

- formatChar - allows output of single ASCII character codes:

  Example (produces signal file accepted by various other programs):

  ```
  Buy=Cross(MACD(),Signal());
  Sell=Cross(Signal(), MACD());
  Filter=Buy OR Sell;
  SetOption("NoDefaultColumns", True );
  AddColumn( DateTime(), "Date", formatDateTime );
  AddColumn( IIf( Buy, 66, 83 ), "Signal", formatChar );
  ```

- width parameter allows control of the pixel width of the column

Example 1: Simple column showing close price

```
addcolumn( Close, "Close price", 1.4 );
```

Example 2: Colorful output

```
Filter =1;
AddColumn( Close, "Close", 1.2 );
AddColumn( MACD(), "MACD", 1.4 , IIf( MACD() > 0,
       colorGreen, colorRed ) );
AddTextColumn( FullName(), "Full name", 77 ,
       colorDefault,
       IIf( Close < 10, colorLightBlue, colorDefault ) );
```

AddTextColumn - Add text exploration column

Syntax:
AddTextColumn(string, name, format = 1.2,
textColor = colorDefault,
bkgndColor = colorDefault, width = -1)

Returns:
NOTHING

Function: Adds a new text column to the exploration result list. The column shows text and has a caption of name.

The next two parameters allow modification of text and background color.

Width parameter allows control of pixel width of the column.

Example: AddTextColumn(GroupID(1), "The name of the group");

Please note that AddTextColumn takes a single string as a parameter, so you can only display text that does not vary on bar-by-bar basis.

EncodeColor - encodes color for indicator title

Syntax:
EncodeColor(colorIndex)

Returns:
STRING

Function: Converts color index to a string escape sequence that changes the color of text output in chart title. Color escape sequence uses cXX sequence where XX is a 2 digit number specifying color index. For example, c38 defines violet. There is a special sequence c-1 that resets to the default axis color.

Example: Title = "This is written in " + EncodeColor(colorViolet) + "violet color " + EncodeColor(colorGreen) + "and this in green";

GetChartID - Get current chart ID

Syntax:
GetChartID()

Returns:
NUMBER

Function: Returns the chart ID of current indicator formula. Returns 0 if used in Automatic analysis.

Example: Cross(graph0, Study("RE", GetChartID()));

GetPriceStyle - Get current price chart style

Syntax:
GetPriceStyle ()

Returns:
NUMBER

Function: Returns the price chart style value to be used in Plot statement. Returned value depends on selection in View > Price chart style menu.

Example: Plot(C, "Close", ParamColor("Color", colorBlack),
styleNoTitle | ParamStyle("Style") | GetPriceStyle());

LineArray - Generate trend-line array

Syntax:

LineArray(x0, y0, x1, y1, extend = 0, usebarindex = False)

Returns:

ARRAY

Function: The LineArray function generates array equivalent to trend line drawn from point (x0, y0) to point (x1, y1). x coordinates are in bars (zero based), y coordinates are in dollars.

Note: x0 must be smaller than x1.

Note: The function accepts only numbers, therefore generates a single line. To produce multiple lines you have to call it multiple times with different coordinates.

extend parameter controls automatic extension of the trend line. If extend is 1 then line is right extended. If extend is 2 then line is left extended. If extend is 3 then line is left and right extended

usebarindex parameter controls if x coordinates are interpreted as current array indexes (from 0..BarCount-1) (when usebarindex = False) or as absolute bar indexes (returned by BarIndex() function) when usebarindex = True. These two may differ if QuickAFL feature is turned on.

Example:

```
y0=LastValue(Trough(L,5,2));
y1=LastValue(Trough(L,5,1));
x0=BarCount - 1 - LastValue(TroughBars(L,5,2));
x1=BarCount - 1 - LastValue(TroughBars(L,5,1));
Line = LineArray( x0, y0, x1, y1, 1 );
Plot(C, "C", colorWhite, styleCandle);
Plot( Line, "Trend line", colorBlue );
```

Param - Add user-definable numeric parameter

Syntax:

Param("name", defaultval, min, max, step, sincr = 0)

Returns:

NUMBER

Function: Adds a new user-definable parameter, which will be accessible via the Parameters dialog :

right click over chart pane and select "Parameters" or press Ctrl+R allows change of chart parameters - changes are reflected immediately.

"name" - defines parameter name that will be displayed in the parameters dialog

defaultval - defines default value of the parameter

min, max - define minimum and maximum values of the parameter

step - defines minimum increase of the parameter via slider in the Parameters dialog

sincr - automatic section increment value (used by drag-drop interface to increase default values for parameters)

Note: default/min/max/step parameters have to be constant numbers. This is because these values are cached and are not re-read during subsequent formula evaluations.

Note that Parameters are independent for each chart pane and for Automatic Analysis window.

In Automatic Analysis window parameters can be modified using "Parameters" button and they are independent from ones you use for any chart.

To change the parameters for the indicator, please right-click over chart pane and select "Parameters" from the menu.

Example: Sample code 1:

```
ticker = ParamStr( "Ticker", "MSFT" );
sp = Param( "MA Period", 12, 2, 100 );
PlotForeign( ticker, "Chart of "+ticker,
       ParamColor( "Price Color", colorLightYellow ),
       styleCandle );
Plot( MA( Foreign( ticker, "C" ), sp ),
       "MA(" + WriteVal( sp, 1.0 ) + ")",
       ParamColor( "MA Color", colorRed ) );
```

Sample code 2:

```
sp = Param( "RSI Period", 12, 2, 100 );
r = RSI( sp );
Plot( r, "RSI("+WriteVal(sp,1.0)+")",
       ParamColor("RSI Color", colorRed ) );
Buy = Cross( r, 30 );
Sell = Cross( 70, r );
PlotShapes( shapeUpArrow * Buy + shapeDownArrow * Sell,
       IIf( Buy, colorGreen, colorRed ) );
```

ParamColor - Add user user-definable color parameter

Syntax:
ParamColor("name", defaultcolor)

Returns:
NUMBER

Function: Adds a new user-definable parameter, which will be accessible via Parameters dialog :

Right-click over chart pane and select "Parameters" or press Ctrl+R to change chart parameters - changes are reflected immediately.

"name" - defines parameter name that will be displayed in the parameters dialog

defaultcolor - defines default color value of the parameter

colorCycle - accepted only by ParamColor function as default value, causes default color to cycle through red, blue, green, turquoise, gold, violet, bright green, dark yellow

Example: Plot(RSI(), "RSI", ParamColor("RSI Color", colorRed));

ParamDate - Add user user-definable date parameter

Syntax:
ParamDate("Name", "Default date", format = 0);

Returns:
NUMBER
STRING

Function: Adds a new user-definable date parameter, which will be accessible via Parameters dialog :

right click over chart pane and select "Parameters" or press Ctrl+R to change chart parameters - changes are reflected immediately.

"name" - defines parameter name that will be displayed in the parameters dialog

"default date" - is a string holding date in any any format: YYYY-MM-DD, MM/DD/YY, DD-MM-YY, etc.

format - defines return value format, allowable values are:

0 - return value is a NUMBER and holds DateNum. ie: 990503 for May 3, 1999,

1 - return value is a STRING formatted holding date according to your windows regional settings

Default parameter has to be a constant, because these values are cached and are not re-read during subsequent formula evaluations.

Example:

```
start = ParamDate( "Start Date", "2003-05-03" );
```

ParamField - Creates price field parameter

Syntax:
ParamField("name", field = 3)

Returns:
ARRAY

Function: Allows picking the Price field for the indicator (field which is used to calculate values of the indicator). Function returns the array defined by field parameter. Default value = 3 returns Close array. The possible values of field parameter are:

-1 - ParamField returns the values of the indicator that was inserted as a first one into the pane, or Close if no indicator was present

0 - returns Open array

1 - returns High array

2 - returns Low array

3 - returns Close array (default)

4 - returns Average array = (H+L+C)/3

5 - returns Volume array

6 - returns Open Interest array

7,8,9,.... - return values of indicators inserted into the pane.

Example:

```
p = ParamField("p");
Plot (p,"P", colorRed,styleLine);
```

ParamList - Creates the parameter that consist of the list of choices

Syntax:
ParamList("Name", "Values", defaultval = 0)

Returns:
STRING

Function: Creates the parameter that consist of the list of choices (specified in "values" parameter - | or comma separated). defaultval parameter defines ordinal position of the default string value specified in "values" parameter. Returned value is a STRING representing choosen item.

Example: OrderType = ParamList("Order Type", "MKT|LMT|STP");

ParamStr - Add user user-definable string parameter

Syntax:
ParamStr("name", "default")

Returns:
STRING

Function: Adds a new user-definable parameter, which will be accessible via Parameters dialog :

right-click over chart pane and select "Parameters" or press Ctrl+R to change chart parameters - changes are reflected immediately.

"name" - defines parameter name that will be displayed in the parameters dialog

"default" - defines default value of the parameter

Example: ticker = ParamStr("Ticker", "MSFT");

ParamStyle - Select styles applied to the plot

Syntax:

ParamStyle("name", defaultstyle = styleLine, mask = maskDefault)

Returns:

NUMBER

Function: Allows selection of the styles applied to plot.

Parameters:

name - parameter name

defaultstyle - default value of style. Takes a combination of style constants

mask - binary mask that defines which styles should be visible in the drop down list

maskDefault - show thick, dashed, hidden, own scale styles (this is the default mask for ParamStyle)

maskAll - show all style flags

maskPrice - show thick, hidden, own scale, candle, bar

maskHistogram - show histogram, thick, hidden, own scale, area

Example:

```
P = ParamField("Price field",-1);
Periods = Param("Periods", 15, 2, 200, 1, 10 );
Plot( EMA( P, Periods ), _DEFAULT_NAME(),
       ParamColor( "Color", colorCycle ),
       ParamStyle("Style") );
```

ParamTime - Add user user-definable time parameter

Syntax:
ParamTime("Name", "Default time", format = 0);

Returns:
NUMBER
STRING

Function: Adds a new user-definable time parameter, which will be accessible via Parameters dialog :

right click over chart pane and select "Parameters" or press Ctrl+R to change chart parameters - changes are reflected immediately.

"name" - defines parameter name that will be displayed in the parameters dialog

"default time" - is a string holding time in any format: HH:MM:SS, HH:MM, etc.

format - defines return value format, allowable values are:

0 - return value is a NUMBER and holds TimeNum. Ie: 133515 for 13:35:15

1 - return value is a STRING formatted holding time according to your windows regional settings

Default parameter must be a constant. This is because these values are cached and are not re-read during subsequent formula evaluations.

Example:

```
start = ParamTime( "Start Time", "09:30" );
```

ParamToggle - create Yes/No parameter

Syntax:
ParamToggle("name","values",defaultval=0)

Returns:
NUMBER

Function: Allows use of boolean (Yes/No) parameters.

"name" - the name of the parameter

"values" - parameter values (separated with | character, e.g. "No|Yes" - first string represents false value and second string represents true value)

defaultval - default value of the parameter

Example:

```
PlotTheGrids = ParamToggle("Plot grids","No|Yes",0);
if (PlotTheGrids ==1)
{
PlotGrid(0);
PlotGrid(-100);
PlotGrid(100);
PlotGrid(-200);
PlotGrid(200);
}
```

ParamTrigger - Creates a trigger (button) in the parameter dialog

Syntax:

ParamTrigger("Name", "Button text")

Returns:

NUMBER

Function: Creates trigger (button) in the Parameter dialog.

If you place ParamTrigger in the indicator code it will create a "button" in Parameter dialog that can be pressed. Normally ParamTrigger will return zero (0), but when the button in the param window is pressed, it will refresh the chart and ParamTrigger will return 1 (one) for this single execution (further refreshes will return zero, until the button is pressed again)

Example:

```
trigger = ParamTrigger("Place Order",
            "Click here to place order");
if( trigger )
{
// your one-shot code here
}
```

Plot - Plot indicator graph

Syntax:

Plot(array, name, color/barcolor, style = styleLine,
minvalue = {empty}, maxvalue = {empty}, XShift = 0)

Returns:

NUMBER

Function: Plots the graph using array data. Parameters:

array - data array to be plotted

name - defines graph name used for displaying values in a title bar.

color - defines plot color that could be static (if third argument is a number) or dynamic (when third argument is an array). Color indexes are related to the current palette (see Preferences/Color)

style is a combination of one or more of following values:

- styleLine = 1 - normal (line) chart (default)
- styleHistogram = 2 - histogram chart
- styleThick =4 - fat (thick)
- styleDots = 8 - include dots
- styleNoLine = 16 - no line
- styleDashed = 32 - dashed line style
- styleCandle = 64 - candlestick chart
- styleBar = 128 - traditional bar chart
- styleNoDraw = 256 - no draw (perform axis scaling only)
- styleStaircase = 512 - staircase (square) chart
- styleSwingDots = 1024 - middle dots for staircase chart
- styleNoRescale = 2048 - no rescale
- styleNoLabel = 4096 - no value label
- stylePointAndFigure = 8192 - point and figure
- styleArea = 16384 - area chart (extra wide histogram)
- styleOwnScale = 32768 - plot is using independent scaling
- styleLeftAxisScale = 65536 - plot is using left axis scale (independent from right axis)
- styleNoTitle - do not display values of this plot in the chart title

- styleCloud - cloud style (area between high and low arrays) - to be used with PlotOHLC function
- styleClipMinMax - clip (do not paint) area between min and max levels - note this style is incompatible with printers and WMF (metafiles).

minvalue and maxvalue - (used by styleOwnScale plots ONLY) define plot minimum and maximum values (lower and upper boundary for Y axis)

XShift - allows to visually shift the chart past the last bar.

Example:

```
// Example 20-bar Moving average shifted 10 bars
// into the future past the last bar:
Plot(Close,"Close",colorBlack,styleCandle);
Plot(MA(Close,20), "Shifted MA",
       colorRed, styleLine, Null, Null, 10 );
// Note that shift occurs during plotting
// and does not affect the source array
```

PlotGrid - Plot horizontal grid line

Syntax:

PlotGrid(level, color = colorDefault)

Returns:

NOTHING

Function: Plots horizontal grid line using built-in dotted style at given level and color.

Example: PlotGrid(25, colorRed);

Instead of number you can also use expression but it must be a numeric expression, not an array.

Use LastValue to convert:

```
your_expression = ...
PlotGrid( LastValue( your_expression ) );
```

PlotOHLC - Plot custom OHLC chart

Syntax:

```
PlotOHLC( open, high, low, close, name, color/barcolor,
          style = styleCandle | styleOwnScale,
          minvalue = {empty}, maxvalue = {empty}, XShift = 0 )
```

Returns:
NUMBER

Function: Plots the price chart using custom open, high, low, close arrays supplied as parameters. Fifth argument name defines graph name used for displaying values in a title bar. Graph color could be static (if sixth argument is a number) or dynamic (when sixth argument is an array). Color indexes are related to the current palette (see Preferences/Color)

style defines chart plot style (see Plot() function for possible values)

minvalue and maxvalue - (used by styleOwnScale plots only) define plot minimum and maximum values (lower and upper boundary for Y axis)

XShift - Visually shifts the chart into future (blank) bars.

Example:

```
PlotOHLC( 1.1*Open, 1.1* High, 1.1* Low, 1.1* Close,
          "Price chart shifted 10% up", colorRed, styleCandle );
```

PlotShapes - Plots arrows and other shapes

Syntax:

```
PlotShapes( shape, color, layer = 0, yposition = graph0, offset = -12 );
```

Returns:
NOTHING

Function: Plots arrows and other shapes on any chart pane.

- shape defines type of the symbol. When shape is 0 (zero) nothing is plotted. Values other than zero cause plotting various pre-defined shapes. Odd values plot the shape below the indicator, even values plot the shape above the indicator.
- color defines color of shape

- layer defines layer number on which shapes are plotted
- yposition defines Y-position where shapes are plotted (by default they are plotted 'around' graph0 (first indicator) line)
- offset - (or distance) parameter (by default -12), Offset is expressed in screen pixels. Negative offsets shift symbols down, positive offsets shift symbols up. To place the shape exactly at yposition, specify 0 as offset
- Constants for shapes:

  shapeNone, shapeUpArrow, shapeDownArrow, shapeHollowUpArrow, shapeHollowDownArrow, shapeSmallUpTriangle, shapeSmallDownTriangle, shapeHollowSmallUpTriangle, shapeHollowSmallDownTriangle, shapeUpTriangle, shapeDownTriangle, shapeHollowUpTriangle, shapeHollowDownTriangle, shapeSmallSquare, shapeHollowSmallSquare, shapeSquare, shapeHollowSquare, shapeSmallCircle, shapeHollowSmallCircle, shapeCircle, shapeHollowCircle, shapeStar, shapeHollowStar, shapeDigit0, shapeDigit1, shapeDigit2, shapeDigit3, shapeDigit4, shapeDigit5, shapeDigit6, shapeDigit7, shapeDigit8, shapeDigit9, shapePositionAbove

Example 1:

```
PlotShapes( IIF( buy, shapeDigit9 + shapePositionAbove,
       shapeNone ), colorGreen );
```

Example 2:

```
Graph0=MACD();
Graph1=Signal();
Buy=Cross(Graph0, Graph1);
Sell=Cross(Graph1, Graph0);
PlotShapes( ( Buy OR Sell ) * ( 1 + Cum( Buy OR Sell ) % 52 ),
       IIf( Buy, colorGreen, colorRed ), 5 );
GraphXSpace = 5;
```

PlotVAPOverlay - Plot Volume-At-Price overlay chart

Syntax:
PlotVAPOverlay(lines = 300, width = 5, color = colorGreen, vapstyle = 0);

Returns:
NOTHING

Function: Plots Volume-At-Price (VAP) overlay chart. There must be at least one regular Plot function in your formula for this to work, and there can be only one PlotVAPOverlay in one indicator

- vapstyle = 0 - left side, area fill, on top of all plots
- vapstyle = 1 - right side, area fill, on top of all plots
- vapstyle = 2 - left side, lines only, on top of all plots
- vapstyle = 3 - right side, lines only, on top of all plots
- vapstyle = 4 - left side, area fill, behind all plots
- vapstyle = 5 - right side, area fill, behind all plots
- vapstyle = 6 - left side, lines only, behind all plots
- vapstyle = 7 - right side, lines only, behind all plots

Example:
```
Plot( Close, "Price", colorWhite, styleCandle );
PlotVAPOverlay( Param("lines",300,10,1000,1),
        Param("width",10,1,99,1),
        ParamColor("color", colorDarkBlue),
        Param("style",0,0,7,1) );
```

SelectedValue - Retrieves value of the array at currently selected date/time point

Syntax:
SelectedValue(ARRAY)

Returns:
NUMBER

Function: Retrieves array value at currently selected bar. The main purpose is for commentary and interpretation code.

Example: SelectedValue(close)

SelectedValue(array) is a function that retrieves the 'selected element' of the array.

Since the 'selection line' is available only for charts, SelectedValue gives the value of array at the bar that is currently selected in chart by vertical line.

This is how it works in indicators, interpretation, and chart commentary, because they are relative to the selected bar.

In AA window 'selected element' means the last bar of the currently selected analysis range. It is the last available bar for "all quotes" and "last n quotes" range. It is the the bar corresponding to "End Date" when using "From-To" range.

If you choose range: "all quotes" in AA, SelectedValue function is equivalent to array[BarCount - 1]

SetChartOptions - Set/clear/overwrite defaults for chart pane options

Syntax:

```
SetChartOptions( Mode = 0, Flags = 0,
        gridFlags = chartGridMiddle, ymin = 0, ymax = 0 )
```

Returns:

NOTHING

Function: Allows set/clear/overwrite/set defaults for chart pane options

Mode - specifies how options are set:

- 0 - set only the default values for new chart. Defaults are applied only once when chart is inserted in a new pane, so later you can modify any option using Indicator Builder
- 1 - overwrite - the values specified in 2nd and 3rd argument overwrite any previously set values
- 2 - set flag - flags specified in 2nd and 3rd parameter are binary-ORed with the current values, so effectively these options are set while those remaining are unchanged
- 3 - reset flag - flags specified in 2nd and 3rd parameter are cleared while the others remain unchanged.

Flags - allowable flags are:

chartShowDates, chartLogarithmic, chartShowArrows, chartWrapTitle, chartHideQuoteMarker.
chartHideQuoteMarker - hides the quote selector line on per-pane basis, the same as Parameter dialog > Axes & Grid > Vert. quote marker: Show/Hide

gridFlags - (for internal AmiBroker use - do not use it in your own coding as this parameter will eventually be removed) allowable values are:

chartGridDiv100, chartGridPercent, chartGridDiv1000, chartGridMargins chartGridMiddle, chartGrid0, chartGrid30, chartGrid70, chartGrid10, chartGrid90, chartGrid50,chartGrid100,chartGrid20,chartGrid80,chartGrid1

ymin, ymax - these parameters specify Y-axis minimum and maximum values for custom scaling. If you specify any values that meet the condition ymin < ymax, AmiBroker will turn OFF automatic scaling and use specified min/max values for Y scale. The Mode argument controls when these settings are applied (0 - only when new chart is created, 1 - always), when modes 2 and 3 are used - scaling is not changed.

Example 1:

```
//to mark "Show arrows" by default in a new chart use
SetChartOptions( 0, chartShowArrows );
```

Example 2:

```
SetChartOptions(2, chartWrapTitle );
Title="this is a test of automatic wrapping of title text
that is too long to fit in single line, for that reason this
sample formula uses very long text. I hope you are enjoying the
sample";
```

SetSortColumns - Sets the columns which will be used for sorting in AA window

Syntax:
SetSortColumns(col1, col2, ...)

Returns:
NOTHING

Function: Sets the columns which will be used for sorting. col1, col2, ... col10. Column numbers are one-based. Positive number means sort ascending, negative number means sort descending. Upto 10 columns can be specified for multiple-column sort. Each subsequent call to SetSortColumns overwrites previous one.

Examples:
```
// sort by 5th column in ascending order
SetSortColumns( 5 )

// sort by 3rd column in descending order
SetSortColumns( -3 )

// sort by 1st column in ascending order
// and then by Second column in descending order
// (multiple-column sort).
SetSortColumns( 1, -2 );
```

WriteIf - Commentary conditional text output

Syntax:
WriteIf(EXPRESSION, "TRUE TEXT", "FALSE TEXT")

Returns:
STRING

Function: If EXPRESSION evaluates to "true", then the TRUE TEXT string is displayed within the commentary. If EXPRESSION evaluates to "false", then the FALSE TEXT string is displayed.

WriteIf in fact does not "write" anything. The name is misleading but it is left for easy translation of MS formulas to AmiBroker.

WriteIf issimilar to "TextIIF". It returns string value depending on condition.

Example: WriteIf(C>MA(C,200),
"The close is above the 200-period moving average.",
"The close is below the 200-period moving average.") ;

WriteVal - Write number or value of the array

Syntax:

WriteVal(NUMBER, format = 1.3, separator=True)
WriteVal(ARRAY, format = 1.3, separator=True)

Returns:

STRING

Function: It is used to display the numeric value of NUMBER or ARRAY. The second parameter - format - allows you to control output formatting (decimal places and leading spaces). The integer part of the number controls minimum number of characters used to display the number (if you specify high number the output will be space-padded). The fractional part defines how many decimal places to display, for example 1.0 - will give you a number without fractional part at all, and 1.2 - will display two digits past the decimal point

There is also a special format constant formatDateTime that allows to print date/time returned by DateTime() function formatted according to Windows regional settings. Third parameter separator (true by default) controls if thousand separator is added or not.

Thousands separator is definable in Tools > Preferences > Misc.

WriteVal always returns *one* value of the array (not an array of values). In almost all cases this is LastValue of the array but in indicators it is "selected value" - the one that is selected by the vertical line.

NumToStr is a synonym for WriteVal function and NumToStr is preferred in new coding.

Examples:

```
// Simple use (no custom format)
WriteVal( StochK(39) - StochK(12) );

// Display rate of change with 2 decimal digits
// and % appended to the end
WriteVal( ROC( Close, 20 ), 1.2 ) + "%";

// Display date/time according to regional settings
WriteVal( DateTime(), formatDateTime );
```

_DEFAULT_NAME - Retrieve default name of the plot

Syntax:
_DEFAULT_NAME()

Returns:
STRING

Function: This function returns the default name of plot in the drag-drop section. The default name consists of section name and comma separated list of values of numeric parameters defined in given section.

Example:

```
_SECTION_BEGIN("MA1");
P = ParamField("Price field");
Periods = Param("Periods", 15, 2, 200, 1, 10 );
Plot( MA( P, Periods ), _DEFAULT_NAME(),
       ParamColor( "Color", colorCycle ),
       ParamStyle("Style") );
_SECTION_END();
```

_DEFAULT_NAME will evaluate to "MA1(Close,15)" string.

_N - No text output

Syntax:
_N(string)

Returns:
NOTHING

Function: Inhibits printing string to the commentary output window

Example:

```
_N( ticker = name() );
// thanks to _N function ticker symbol is not printed
```

_PARAM_VALUES - Retrieve param values string

Syntax:
_PARAM_VALUES()

Returns:
STRING

Function: _PARAM_VALUES retrieves the values of the parameters defined in current drag-drop section. It works the same as _DEFAULT_NAME except that no section name is included (so only the list of parameter values is returned).

Example:
```
_SECTION_BEGIN("MACD");
r1 = Param( "Fast avg", 12, 2, 200, 1 );
r2 = Param( "Slow avg", 26, 2, 200, 1 );
r3 = Param( "Signal avg", 9, 2, 200, 1 );
Plot( ml = MACD(r1, r2),
    StrFormat(_SECTION_NAME()+"(%g,%g)", r1, r2),
    ParamColor("MACD color", colorRed ),
    ParamStyle("MACD style") );
Plot( sl = Signal(r1,r2,r3), "Signal" + _PARAM_VALUES(),
    ParamColor("Signal color", colorBlue ),
    ParamStyle("Signal style") );
Plot( ml-sl, "MACD Histogram",
    ParamColor("Histogram color", colorBlack ),
    styleNoTitle | ParamStyle("Histogram style",
    styleHistogram | styleNoLabel,
    maskHistogram ) );
_SECTION_END();
```

_SECTION_BEGIN - Section begin marker

Syntax:
_SECTION_BEGIN("section name")

Returns:
NOTHING

Function: Marks beginning of the drag-drop section.

"section name" must be a constant, literal string, enclosed in double quotation marks. You must not use a variable here.

Example:

See _PARAM_VALUES() entry.

_SECTION_END - Section end marker

Syntax:
_SECTION_END()

Returns:
NOTHING

Function: Marks end of drag-drop section

Example:

See _PARAM_VALUES() entry.

_SECTION_NAME - Retrieve current section name

Syntax:
_SECTION_NAME()

Returns:
STRING

Function: The function that gives the name of the drag-drop section (given in previous _SECTION_BEGIN call).

Example:

See _PARAM_VALUES() entry.

Date/Time

BarIndex - Get zero-based bar number

Syntax:
BarIndex()

Returns:
ARRAY

Function: Returns a zero-based bar number - the same as Cum(1)-1 but it is much faster than Cum(1) when used in Indicators

When QuickAFL is ON, the BarIndex() may not be equal to array item index.

Actual array item corresponding to bar index can be found this way:

```
bi = BarIndex();
arrayitem = SelectedValue( bi ) - bi[ 0 ];
"Close at selected bar:" + Close[ arrayitem ];
```

Example: ThisIsLastBar = BarIndex() == LastValue(BarIndex());

This statement compares each element of an array, BarIndex(), to a number, LastValue(BarIndex()), and produces array as a result. The array, ThisIsLastBar, will have 0 in every element except the one where BarIndex() does equal LastValue(BarIndex()), which will have a value of 1.

BeginValue - Value of the array at the beginning of the range

Syntax:
BeginValue(ARRAY)

Returns:
NUMBER

Function: This function gives the single value (number) of the ARRAY at the beginning of the selected range. If no range is marked then the value at the first bar is returned.

To select the range you have to double click in the chart at the beginning of the range and then double click in the chart at the end of the range. Then > < markers will appear above date axis.

Examples:

```
// Simple commentary:
WriteVal( BeginValue( DateTime() ), formatDateTime );
WriteVal( EndValue( DateTime() ), formatDateTime );
"Percentage change of close is " +
WriteVal( 100 * (EndValue( Close ) - BeginValue( Close ))
       /BeginValue( Close ) ) + "%";


// Get the number of bars in the range and
// calculate some stats for that range:

Period = EndValue( BarIndex() ) - BeginValue( BarIndex() );
StandardDeviationInTheRange =
       EndValue( StDev( Close, Period ) );
```

Date - Date

Syntax:

Date()

Returns:

STRING

Function: It is used to display the selected date in commentary / interpretation window

Example: Title =Date()+" "+Name()+" Close"+WriteVal(C);

DateNum - Date number

Syntax:
DateNum()

Returns:
ARRAY

Function: Returns the array with numbers that represent quotation dates coded as follows:

10000 * (year - 1900) + 100 * month + day, so 2001-12-31 becomes 1011231 and 1995-12-31 becomes 951231

Example:

```
DateOfInterest = (DateNum()==1080820); // August 20, 2008
Plot(DateOfInterest,"DI",colorRed,styleLine);
```

DateTime - Retrieves encoded date time

Syntax:
DateTime()

Returns:
ARRAY

Function: Returns array of encoded date/time values suitable for using with AddColumn and formatDateTime constant to produce date time formatted according to your system settings.

Examples:

```
// Simple date/time column
AddColumn( DateTime(), "Date / Time", formatDateTime );

// Produces signal file accepted by various other programs
Buy=Cross(MACD(),Signal());
Sell=Cross(Signal(), MACD());
Filter=Buy OR Sell;
SetOption("NoDefaultColumns", True );
AddColumn( DateTime(), "Date", formatDateTime );
AddColumn( IIf( Buy, 66, 83 ), "Signal", formatChar );
```

DateTimeConvert - Date/time format conversion

Syntax:
DateTimeConvert(format, date, time = Null)

Returns:
NUMBER
ARRAY

Function: The function allows conversion from DateTime format to DateNum and TimeNum and vice versa.

format parameter controls the direction of conversion:

- format = 0 - converts DateTime format to DateNum format. Example: mydatenum = DateTimeConvert(0, DateTime()); // - this returns DateNum
- format = 1 - converts DateTime format to TimeNum format. Example: mytimenum = DateTimeConvert(1, DateTime()); // - returns timenum
- format = 2 - converts from DateNum and optionally TimeNum to DateTime format. Example: mydatetime = DateTimeConvert(2, DateNum(), TimeNum());
- format = 3 - converts DateTime format to Seconds (00..59). Example: myseconds = DateTimeConvert(3, DateTime());
- format = 4 - converts DateTime format to Minutes(00..59). Example: myminute = DateTimeConvert(4, DateTime());
- format = 5 - converts DateTime format to Hours (00..23). Example: myhour = DateTimeConvert(5, DateTime());

Example:

```
mydatenum = DateTimeConvert( 0, DateTime() );//returns DateNum
mytimenum = DateTimeConvert( 1, DateTime() );// returns timenum
mydatetime = DateTimeConvert( 2, DateNum(), TimeNum() );
mydatetime = DateTimeConvert( 2, DateNum() );
```

Day - day of month

Syntax::
    Day()

Returns:
    ARRAY

Function: Returns the array with days (1-31)

Example:
```
writeif( day() < 3,
    "Beginning of the month",
    "The rest of the month" );
```

DayOfWeek - Day of week

Syntax:
    DayOfWeek()

Returns:
    ARRAY

Function: Returns the array with day of week (0-6):

0 - Sunday

1 - Monday

...

5 - Friday

6- Saturday

Example:

```
buy = dayofweek() == 1; // buy on Monday
sell = dayofweek() == 5; // sell on Friday
```

DayOfYear - Get ordinal number of day in a year

Syntax:
DayOfYear()

Returns:
ARRAY

Function: Returns the calendar day number counting from beginning of the year January 1st is 1. Maximum number returned is 366

Example:

```
Filter=1;
AddColumn(DayOfYear(),"Day of Year");
```

EndValue - Value of the array at the end of the selected range

Syntax:
EndValue(ARRAY)

Returns:
NUMBER

Function: This function gives the single value (number) of the ARRAY at the end of the selected range. If no range is marked then the value at the last bar is returned.

To select the range you have to double click in the chart at the beginning of the range and then double click in the chart at the end of the range. Then >< markers will appear above date axis.

Examples:

```
// Simple commentary:
WriteVal( BeginValue( DateTime() ), formatDateTime );
WriteVal( EndValue( DateTime() ), formatDateTime );
"Precentage change of close is " +
WriteVal( 100 * (EndValue( Close ) - BeginValue( Close ))/Beg-
inValue( Close ) ) + "%";

// Get the number of bars in the range and
// calculate some stats for that range:
Period = EndValue( BarIndex() ) - BeginValue( BarIndex() );
StandardDeviationInTheRange =
       EndValue( StDev( Close, Period ) );
```

GetPlaybackDateTime - Get bar replay position date/time

Syntax:
GetPlaybackDateTime()

Returns:
NUMBER

Function: The function returns bar replay playback position in date-time format, or zero if bar replay is not active

Example:

```
// new function to retrieve playback position date/time
//returns zero if bar replay is NOT active
pt = GetPlaybackDateTime();
if( pt )
{
  Title = "Playback time: " + DateTimeToStr( pt );
}
else
{
  Title = "Bar Replay not active";
}
```

Hour - Get current bar's hour

Syntax:
Hour()

Returns:
ARRAY

Function: Retrieves the current bar's hour

Example: Hour()*10000 + Minute() * 100 + Second()

Interval - Get bar interval (in seconds)

Syntax:
 Interval(format = 0)

Returns:
 NUMBER

Function: Interval() function returns the bar interval.

Possible formats: format = 0 - returns bar interval in seconds format = 1 - as above plus TICK bar intervals are returned with negative sign so Interval() function applied to 10 tick chart will return -10 format = 2 - returns STRING with name of interval such as "weekly/monthly/daily/hourly/15-minute/5-tick"

Time intervals in seconds:

- tick bars = 0
- 5 sec bars = 5
- 1 min bars = 60 (inMinute constant)
- hourly bars = 3600
- daily bars = 86400 (inDaily constant)
- weekly bars = 432001 (inWeekly constant)
- monthly bars = 2160001 (inMonthly constant)

Example: "Interval in seconds " + WriteVal(Interval());

Minute - Get current bar's minute

Syntax:
 Minute()

Returns:
 ARRAY

Function: Retrieves the current bar's minute

Example: Hour()*10000 + Minute() * 100 + Second()

Month - month

Syntax:
Month()

Returns:
ARRAY

Function: Returns the current bar's month

Example: buy = (month() == 1) and day < 3; // buy in January

Now - Gets current system date/time

Syntax:
Now(format = 0)

Returns:
STRING
NUMBER

Function: Returns the current date / time in numerous formats:

- format = 0 - returns string containing current date/time formatted according to system settings
- format = 1 - returns string containing current date only formatted according to system settings
- format = 2 - returns string containing current time only formatted according to system settings
- format = 3 - returns DATENUM number with current date
- format = 4 - returns TIMENUM number with current time
- format = 5 - returns DATETIME number with current date/time
- format = 6 - returns current DAY (1..31)
- format = 7 - returns current MONTH (1..12)
- format = 8 - returns current YEAR (four digit)
- format = 9 - returns current DAY OF WEEK (1..7, where 1=Sunday, 2=Monday, and so on)
- format = 10 - returns current DAY OF YEAR (1..366)

Example: AddTextColumn(Now(), "Current time");

Second - Get current bar's second

Syntax:
Second()

Returns:
ARRAY

Function: Retrieves the current bar's second

Example: Hour()*10000 + Minute() * 100 + Second()

TimeNum - Get current bar time

Syntax:
TimeNum()

Returns:
ARRAY

Function: Returns the current bar's time coded as follows:

10000 * hour + 100 * minute + second, so 12:37:15 becomes 123715

Example: TimeNum()

Year - Year

Syntax:
Year()

Returns:
ARRAY

Function: Returns the current bar's years (full four digits 1900-....)

Example: WriteVal(year());

Time Frame functions

TimeFrameCompress - Compress single array to given time frame

Syntax:

TimeFrameCompress(array, interval, mode = compressLast)

Returns:

ARRAY

Function: The TimeFrameCompress function compresses single array to given interval using given compression mode available modes:

- compressLast - last (close) value of the array within interval
- compressOpen - open value of the array within interval
- compressHigh - highest value of the array within interval
- compressLow - lowest value of the array within interval
- compressVolume - sum of values of the array within interval

To expand the compressed array you should use the TimeFrameExpand function.

The TimeFrameCompress function is provided for completeness and it can be used when you want to compress single array without affecting built-in OHLCV arrays. If you call TimeFrameCompress it does not affect results of other functions (opposite to TimeFrameSet).

Example:

```
wc = TimeFrameCompress( Close, inWeekly );
/* now the time frame is still unchanged
(say daily) and our MA will operate on daily data */
dailyma = MA( C, 14 );
/* but if we call MA on compressed array,
it will give MA from other time frame */
weeklyma = MA( wc, 14 );
// note that argument is time-compressed array
Plot( dailyma, "DailyMA", colorRed );
weeklyma = TimeFrameExpand( weeklyma, inWeekly );
// expand for display
Plot( weeklyma, "WeeklyMA", colorBlue );
```

TimeFrameExpand - Expand time frame compressed array

Syntax:
TimeFrameExpand(array, interval, mode = expandLast)

Returns:
ARRAY

Function: The TimeFrameExpand function expands time-compressed array from interval time frame to base time frame (interval parameter must match the value used in TimeFrameCompress or TimeFrameSet)

The TimeFrameExpand is used to decompress array variables that were created in different time frame. Decompressing is required to properly display the array created in different time frame. For example if you want to display weekly moving average it must be 'expanded' so the data of one weekly bar covers five daily bars (Monday-Friday) of corresponding week.

Available modes:

- expandLast - the compressed value is expanded starting from last bar within given period (so for example weekly close/high/low is available on Friday's bar)
- expandFirst - the compressed value is expanded starting from first bar within given period (so for example weekly open is available from Monday's bar)
- expandPoint - the resulting array gets not empty values only for the last bar within given period (all remaining bars are Null (empty)).

Caveat: expandFirst used on price different than open may look into the future. For example if you create a weekly high series, expanding it to daily interval using expandFirst will enable you to know on Monday what will be the high for entire week.

Example:

```
wc = TimeFrameCompress( Close, inWeekly );

/* now the time frame is still unchanged (say daily) and our MA
will operate on daily data */
dailyma = MA( C, 14 );

/* but if we call MA on compressed array, it will give MA from
other time frame */
weeklyma = MA( wc, 14 ); // note that argument is time-com-
pressed array

Plot( dailyma, "DailyMA", colorRed );

weeklyma = TimeFrameExpand( weeklyma, inWeekly ); // expand for
display

Plot( weeklyma, "WeeklyMA", colorBlue );
```

TimeFrameGetPrice - Retrieve O, H, L, C, V values from other time frame

Syntax:

TimeFrameGetPrice(pricefield, interval, shift = 0, mode = expandFirst)

Returns:

ARRAY

Function: The TimeFrameGetPrice - retrieves OHLCV fields from other time frames. This works immediately without need to call TimeFrameSet at all.

- pricefield - is one of the following: "O", "H", "L", "C", "V", "I" (open interest).
- interval is bar interval in seconds. You can use pre-defined interval constants: in1Minute, in5Minute, in15Minute, inHourly, inDaily, inWeekly, inMonthly. Or integer multiples like (3*in1Minute) for 3 minute bars
- shift allows to reference past (negative values) and future (positive values) data in higher time frame. For example -1 gives previous bar's data (like in Ref function but this works in higher time frame).

mode - one of available modes:

- expandLast - the compressed value is expanded starting from last bar within given period (so for example weekly close/high/low is available on Friday's bar)
- expandFirst - the compressed value is expanded starting from first bar within given period (so for example weekly open is available from Monday's bar)
- expandPoint - the resulting array gets not empty values only for the last bar within given period (all remaining bars are Null (empty)).

Note these functions work like these 3 nested functions:

> TimeFrameExpand(Ref(TimeFrameCompress(array, interval, compress(depending on field used)), shift), interval, expandFirst)

Therefore, if shift = 0 compressed data may look into the future (weekly high can be known on Monday). If you want to write a trading system using this function please make sure to reference PAST data by using negative shift value.

The only difference is that TimeFrameGetPrice is 2x faster than nested Expand/Compress.

Example:

```
// Example 1. get previous week Open price
TimeFrameGetPrice( "O", inWeekly, -1 )

// Example 2. get weekly Close price 3 weeks ago
TimeFrameGetPrice( "C", inWeekly, -3 )

// Example 3. get weekly High price 2 weeks ago
TimeFrameGetPrice( "H", inWeekly, -2 )

// Example 4. get this week Open price.
TimeFrameGetPrice( "O", inWeekly, 0 )

// Example 5. get previous Day High
// when working on intraday data
TimeFrameGetPrice( "H", inDaily, -1 )
```

TimeFrameMode - Switch time frame compression mode

Syntax:
TimeFrameMode(mode)

Returns:
NOTHING

Function: Switches time frame functions to different operating modes. Where mode is one of 0, 1, or 2.

- TimeFrameMode(0);
  - switches time frame functions to time-based operation (the default)
- TimeFrameMode(1);
  - switches time frame functions to N-tick operation (positive values passed to TimeFrameSet are treated now as N-tick)
- TimeFrameMode(2);
  - switches time frame functions to N-volume bar operation (positive values passed to TimeFrameSet are treated now as N-volume bars)
- TimeFrameMode(3);
  - switches time frame functions to N-Range bar operation (positive values passed to TimeFrameSet are treated now as N-range bars)

Note: N-volume bars are very different from time-based bars (compression of data to N-volume bar may actually deliver more output bars - for example if one tick is 1000 shares and you have specified 100V bars then single tick will be expanded to ten 100V bars - ten times original size)

TimeFrame functions are protected against array overrun and will not decompress beyond original array size (you will get an "Error 47. N-volume bar compressed data longer than base time frame"). Also switching main time frame to some weird N-volume bar value will result in limiting the output to maximum twice original data size(without error message).

You should keep that in mind and avoid using too small N-volume bar intervals that could lead to such condition. Also due to the nature of N-volume bars only the TimeFrameSet() function will yield correct N-volume bar values, TimeFrameGetPrice() may give slightly distorted results.

It is also possible to use n-volume bars in TimeFrame functions without calling TimeFrameMode() - it is then necessary to specify n-volume bars as a negative number offset by -1000000 (minus one million):

TimeFrameSet(-1000000 - 2000);

Example:

```
TimeFrameMode( 2 );
TimeFrameSet( 50000 ); // 50'000 share bars..
//...do something ...
TimeFrameRestore();
```

TimeFrameRestore - Restores price arrays to original time frame

Syntax:
TimeFrameRestore()

Returns:
NOTHING

Function: The TimeFrameRestore function restores price arrays replaced by TimeFrameSet.

Note that only OHLC, V, OI and Avg built-in variables are restored to original time frame when you call TimeFrameRestore().

All other variables created when being in the different time frame remain compressed.

To de-compress them to original interval you have to use TimeFrameExpand.

Example:

```
TimeFrameSet( in5Minute ); // switch to 5 minute frame
/* MA now operates on 5 minute data,
ma5_13 holds time-compressed 13 bar MA of 5min bars */
ma5_13 = MA( C, 13 );
TimeFrameRestore(); // restore time frame to original
TimeFrameSet( inHourly ); // switch now to hourly
mah_9 = EMA( C, 9 ); // 9 bar moving average from hourly data
TimeFrameRestore(); // restore time frame to original
Plot( Close, "Price", colorWhite, styleCandle );
// plot expanded average
Plot( TimeFrameExpand( ma5_13, in5Minute),
        "13 bar moving average from 5 min bars", colorRed );
Plot( TimeFrameExpand( mah_9, inHourly),
        "9 bar moving average from hourly bars", colorRed );
```

TimeFrameSet - switch price arrays to a different time frame

Syntax:

TimeFrameSet(interval)

Returns:

NOTHING

Function: The TimeFrameSet function replaces the current price/volume arrays, open, high, low, close, volume, openint, and avg, with time-compressed bars of the specified interval. Once you switch to a different time frame, all calculations and built-in indicators operate on newly selected time frame. To get back to the original interval, call the TimeFrameRestore() function. Before calling TimeFrameSet again in the same formula with a different interval, you have to restore the original time frame first using TimeFrameRestore.

interval defines time frame interval in seconds. So 60 means 1-minute. For the convenience the following interval constants are pre-defined:

- in1Minute = 60
- in5Minute = 5 * 60
- in15Minute = 15 * 60
- inHourly = 3600
- inDaily = 24 * 3600
- inWeekly = 5 * 24 * 3600 + 1 = 432001
- inMonthly = 25 * 24 * 3600 + 1 = 2160001

To get other intervals you can use a multiple of pre-defined intervals, for example: (3 * in1Minute) gives 3 minute bars. Or you can use 3 * inDaily for 3-day bars.

You can also use negative values for N-tick charts: -5 gives a 5-tick chart. Note that N-tick compression works correct only if you have 1-tick base time interval selected in database settings.

You can also use TimeFrameSet to create N-volume bars as well as Range bars. See TimeFrameMode() function for more details.

Very Important:

- inWeekly constant is now 432001 (5*inDaily + 1) - in previous version it was 432000
- inMonthly constant is now 2160001 (25*inDaily + 1) - in previous version it was 2160000
- It is changed because now N-day custom intervals are supported and they will interfere with weekly/monthly.

Note that 5*inDaily is now different than inWeekly. 5*inDaily creates 5-day bars that do not necessarily cover Monday-Friday while inWeekly always creates bars that begin on Monday and end on Friday. Also 25*inDaily creates 25-day bars that do not represent a full month, while inMonthly always begins with first day of the month and ends at the last day of the month

Once you switch the time frame using TimeFrameSet , all AFL functions operate on this time frame until you switch back the time frame to original interval using TimeFrameRestore or set to different interval again using TimeFrameSet. It is a good idea to always call TimeFrameRestore when you are done processing in other time frames.

When the time frame is switched to other than the original interval the results of all functions called since TimeFrameSet are time-compressed too. If you want to display them in the original time frame you need to 'expand' them as described later. Variables created and assigned before call to TimeFrameSet() remain in the time frame they were created. This behavior allows mixing unlimited different time frames in a single formula.

Please note that you can only compress data from shorter interval to longer interval. So when working with 1-minute data you can compress to 2, 3, 4, 5, 6, ...N-minute data. But when working with 15 minute data you can not get 1-minute data bars. In a similar way if you have only EOD data you can not access intraday time frames.

Example:

```
TimeFrameSet( in5Minute ); // switch to 5 minute frame
/* MA now operates on 5 minute data,
ma5_13 holds time-compressed 13 bar MA of 5min bars */
ma5_13 = MA( C, 13 );
TimeFrameRestore(); // restore time frame to original
TimeFrameSet( inHourly ); // switch now to hourly
mah_9 = EMA( C, 9 ); // 9 bar moving average from hourly data
TimeFrameRestore(); // restore time frame to original
Plot( Close, "Price", colorWhite, styleCandle );
// plot expanded average
Plot( TimeFrameExpand( ma5_13, in5Minute),
       "13 bar moving average from 5 min bars", colorRed );
Plot( TimeFrameExpand( mah_9, inHourly),
       "9 bar moving average from hourly bars", colorRed );
```

INFORMATION / CATEGORIES

CategoryAddSymbol - Adds a symbol to a category

Syntax:
CategoryAddSymbol(symbol, category, number)

Returns:
NOTHING

Function: The CategoryAddSymbol function adds the symbol to the given category. Note that for markets, groups, industries 'adding' means moving from one category to another, since the symbol is assigned always to one and only one market, group, industry and sector. This limitation does not apply to watchlists, favorites, and index categories. When symbol string is empty ("") then current symbol is used.

category is one of the following:

- categoryMarket
- categoryGroup
- categorySector
- categoryIndustry
- categoryWatchlist
- categoryFavorite
- categoryIndex

number is a market/group/industry/sector/watchlist number:

- 0..255 for categoryMarket, categoryGroup, categoryIndustry
- 0..63 for categorySector
- no limit for categoryWatchlist.
- ignored for categoryFavorite, categoryIndex

Example:

```
// the code adds symbols with last day volume > 100000
// to the watchlist number 1
if( LastValue( V ) > 100000 )
{
   CategoryAddSymbol( “”, categoryWatchlist, 1 );
}
```

CategoryFind - Search for category by name

Syntax:
CategoryFind("name", category)

Returns:
NUMBER

Function: Allows a search for category by name. It takes category name and kind as parameters and returns INDEX (ordinal number).

For example it allows finding the index of a watchlist by searching for its name. The index (wlnumber in the example below) can be used later in functions that need the index (like CategoryGetSymbols).

Example:

```
wlnumber = CategoryFind("MyWatchList 1", categoryWatchlist );
mysymbols = CategoryGetSymbols(categoryWatchlist, wlnumber );
```

CategoryGetName - Get the name of a category

Syntax:
CategoryGetName(category, number)

Returns:
STRING

Function: The CategoryGetName function retrieves the name of category.

category is one of the following:

- categoryMarket
- categoryGroup
- categorySector
- categoryIndustry
- categoryWatchlist
- categoryFavorite
- categoryIndex

number is a market/group/industry/sector/watchlist number:

- 0..255 for categoryMarket, categoryGroup, categoryIndustry
- 0..63 for categorySector
- no limit for categoryWatchlist.
- ignored for categoryFavorite, categoryIndex

Example: CategoryGetName(categoryWatchlist, 1);

CategoryGetSymbols - Retrieves comma-separated list of symbols belonging to given category

Syntax:
CategoryGetSymbols(category, index)

Returns:
STRING

Function: Retrieves comma-separated list of symbols belonging to given category Supported categories:

- categoryMarket
- categoryGroup
- categorySector
- categoryIndustry
- categoryWatchlist
- categoryFavorite
- categoryIndex

index is a market/group/industry/sector/watchlist number:

- 0..255 for categoryMarket, categoryGroup, categoryIndustry
- 0..63 for categorySector
- no limit for categoryWatchlist.
- ignored for categoryFavorite, categoryIndex

Use StrExtract function to extract individual symbols from the list.

Example:

```
/* note: if given watchlist contains lots of symbols
** performance may be poor
** AVOID SUCH CODES IN REAL-TIME MODE !
*/
function CreateAverageForWatchList( listnum )
{
   // retrive comma-separated list of symbols in watchlist
   list = CategoryGetSymbols( categoryWatchlist, listnum );

   Average = 0; // just in case there are no watchlist members

   for( i = 0; ( sym = StrExtract( list, i ) ) != “”; i++ )
   {
      f = Foreign( sym, “C” );
      if( i == 0 ) Average = f;
      else Average = Average + f;
   }
   return Average / i; // divide by number of components
}

Plot( CreateAverageForWatchList( 1 ), “Avg of WL 1”, colorGreen
);
```

CategoryRemoveSymbol - Remove a symbol from a category

Syntax:

CategoryRemoveSymbol(symbol, category, number)

Returns:

NOTHING

Function: Removes the symbol from given category.

Note that for markets, groups, industries ‘removing’ means moving from the given category to a category with number zero, since the symbol is always assigned to one and only one market, group, industry, and sector. This limitation does not apply to watchlists, favorites, and index categories. When symbol string is empty (“”) then current symbol is used.

category is one of the following:

- categoryMarket
- categoryGroup
- categorySector
- categoryIndustry

- categoryWatchlist
- categoryFavorite
- categoryIndex

number is a market/group/industry/sector/watchlist number:

- 0..255 for categoryMarket, categoryGroup, categoryIndustry
- 0..63 for categorySector
- no limit for categoryWatchlist.
- ignored for categoryFavorite, categoryIndex

Example:

```
// the code removes the symbols with last day volume < 1000
// from the watchlist number 1
if( LastValue( V ) < 1000 )
{
   CategoryRemoveSymbol( "", categoryWatchlist, 1 );
}
```

FullName - Full name of the symbol

Syntax:
FullName()

Returns:
STRING

Function: The function returns the symbol's full name, which is definable by the user in Symbol > Information window.

Example: printf(FullName());

GetCategorySymbols - Retrieves a comma-separated list of symbols belonging to a given category

Syntax:
GetCategorySymbols(category, index)

Returns:
STRING

Function: This function is obsolete. The same process is available under the new name CategoryGetSymbols. The old name is left only for backward compatibility.

Please use the new name in all new codes.

GetDatabaseName - Retrieves folder name of current database

Syntax:
GetDatabaseName()

Returns:
STRING

Function: Retrieves the name of the database - the last part (folder) of the database path

Example: dbname = GetDataBaseName();

GetFnData - Get fundamental data

Syntax:
GetFnData("field")

Returns:
NUMBER

Function: GetFnData allows accessing fundamental data from Information window (View > Information).

"field" parameter can be one of the following:

- "EPS"
- "EPSEstCurrentYear"

- "EPSEstNextYear"
- "EPSEstNextQuarter"
- "PEGRatio"
- "SharesFloat"
- "SharesOut"
- "DividendPayDate"
- "ExDividendDate"
- "BookValuePerShare"
- "DividendPerShare"
- "ProfitMargin"
- "OperatingMargin"
- "OneYearTargetPrice"
- "ReturnOnAssets"
- "ReturnOnEquity"
- "QtrlyRevenueGrowth"
- "GrossProfitPerShare"
- "SalesPerShare"
- "EBITDAPerShare"
- "QtrlyEarningsGrowth"
- "InsiderHoldPercent"
- "InstitutionHoldPercent"
- "SharesShort"
- "SharesShortPrevMonth"
- "ForwardDividendPerShare"
- "ForwardEPS"
- "OperatingCashFlow"
- "LeveredFreeCashFlow"
- "Beta"
- "LastSplitRatio"
- "LastSplitDate"

Example:

```
AddColumn( Close / GetFnData( "EPS" ) , "Current P/E ratio" );
AddColumn( Close / GetFnData( "EPSEstNextYear" ) ,
        "Est. Next Year P/E ratio" );
Filter = Status("lastbarinrange");
```

GroupID - Get group ID/name

Syntax:
groupid(mode = 0)

Returns:
NUMBER
STRING

Function: Retrieves the current stock group ID/name.

- When mode = 0 (the default value) this function returns numerical group ID (consecutive group number)
- When mode = 1 this function returns name of the group.

Example:

```
Filter = GroupID() == 7 OR GroupID() == 9;
AddTextColumn( GroupID( 1 ), "Group name" );
```

IndustryID - Get industry ID / name

Syntax:
IndustryID(mode = 0)

Returns:
NUMBER
STRING

Function: Retrieves the current stock industry ID/name.

- When mode = 0 (the default value) this function returns the numerical industry ID (consecutive industry number)
- When mode = 1 this function returns the name of the industry.

Example:

```
Filter = IndustryID() == 7 OR IndustryID() == 9;
AddTextColumn( IndustryID( 1 ), "Industry name" );
```

InWatchList - Watchlist membership test (by ordinal number)

Syntax:
InWatchList(listno)

Returns:
NUMBER

Function: Checks if the stock belongs to a watchlist number listno. If yes - the function returns 1 otherwise 0.

Example: Filter= InWatchList(3) OR InWatchList(5);

InWatchListName - Watchlist membership test (by name)

Syntax:
InWatchList("name")

Returns:
NUMBER

Function: Checks if the stock belongs to a watchlist number "listname". If yes - the function returns 1 otherwise 0.

Example: Filter= InWatchListName("My Hotlist") OR
InWatchList("My Second Hotlist");

IsContinuous - Checks 'continuous quotations' flag state

Syntax:
IsContinuous()

Returns:
NUMBER

Function: Returns 1 if current symbol has 'continuous quotations' flag turned on in Symbol > Information window. Returns zero otherwise.

Example: ic = IsContinuous();

IsFavorite - Check if current symbol belongs to favorites

Syntax:
IsFavorite()

Returns:
NUMBER

Function: The IsFavorite function returns True (1) if current symbol belongs to favorites, returns False (0) otherwise.

Example:

```
if( IsFavorite() )
{
  printf( Name() + " belongs to favorites " );
}
```

IsIndex - check if current symbol is an index

Syntax:
IsIndex()

Returns:
NUMBER

Function: The IsIndex function returns True (1) if current symbol is an index, returns False (0) otherwise.

Example:

```
if( IsIndex() )
{
  printf( Name() + " is an index" );
}
```

MarketID - Market ID / name

Syntax:
MarketID(mode = 0)

Returns:
NUMBER
STRING

Function: Retrieves current stock market ID/name.

- When mode = 0 (the default value) this function returns numerical marketID (consecutive market number)
- When mode = 1 this function returns name of the market.

Example:

```
Filter = MarketID() == 7 OR MarketID() == 9;
AddTextColumn( MarketID( 1 ), "Market name" );
```

Name - Ticker symbol

Syntax:
Name()

Returns:
STRING

Function: It is used to display the stock short name (ticker)

Example: Name()

SectorID - Get sector ID / name

Syntax:
SectorID(mode = 0)

Returns:
NUMBER
STRING

Function: Retrieves current stock sector ID/name.

- When mode = 0 (the default value) this function returns numerical sector ID (consecutive sector number)
- When mode = 1 this function returns name of the sector.

Example:

```
Filter = SectorID() == 7 OR SectorID() == 9;
AddTextColumn( SectorID( 1 ), "Sector name" );
```

Referencing Other Symbol Data

Foreign - Access foreign security data

Syntax:
Foreign(TICKER, DATAFIELD, fixup = 1)

Returns:
ARRAY

Function: Allows reference to other (than the current) tickers in the AFL formulas. TICKER is a string that holds the symbol of the stock. DATAFIELD defines which array is referenced. Allowable data fields: "open", "close", "high", "low", "volume", "interest".

The last parameter - fixup - accepts following values

0 - the holes are not fixed

1 - default value - missing data bar OHLC fields are all filled using previous bar Close and volume is set to zero.

Note: you can use Foreign/RelStrength without specifying last parameter:

Foreign("ticker", "field"), RelStrength("ticker") - then the holes will be fixed.

2 - causes filling the holes in the data with previous O, H, L, C, V values

Unless you know what you are doing you should use the default value of fixup parameter (Fixup=1). If you do not use fixup=1, data holes will have the value of Null that you would need to handle by yourself.

Foreign function synchronizes the data file you are referencing with the currently selected symbol.

Synchronization makes sure that each bar of foreign data matches exactly with each bar of currently selected symbol.

So if DateNum() function returns 990503 for given bar then Close array represents the close of currently selected symbol at May

3, 1999 and Foreign("SYMBOL", "C") represents close of foreign symbol at May 3, 1999 too.

This is absolutely necessary because otherwise you won't be able to do any meaningful operations involving both selected symbol and foreign symbol.

This is also needed for the display so when you mark the quote with a vertical line it will always match the date displayed regardless if you use Foreign or not.

Please note that if you have data holes in the currently selected symbol, then in order to synchronize bars, the Foreign function will remove bars that exist in Foreign symbol but do not exist in currently selected symbol.

Examples:

```
// Plotting spread between currently
// selected symbol and another one
Graph0 = Close - Foreign( "MSFT", "Close" ) ;

// EXAMPLE 2:
// Built-in relative performance chart
_N( TickerList = ParamStr("Tickers", "^DJI,MSFT,GE") );
NumBars = 20;
fvb = Status("firstvisiblebar");
Plot( 100 * ( C - C[ fvb ] ) / C[ fvb ], Name(), colorBlue );
for( i = 0; ( symbol = StrExtract( TickerList, i ) ) != ""; i++
)
{
  fc = Foreign( symbol, "C" );

  if( ! IsNull( fc[ 0 ] ) )
  {
     Plot( 100 * ( fc - fc[ fvb ] )/ fc[ fvb ],
          symbol,
          colorLightOrange + ( (2*i) % 15 ),
          styleLine );
  }
}
PlotGrid( 0, colorYellow );
_N( Title = "{{NAME}} - Relative Performance [%]. {{VALUES}}"
);
```

GetBaseIndex - Retrieves symbol of relative strength base index

Syntax:
GetBaseIndex( )

Returns:
STRING

Function: Retrieves the base relative-strength index for given security as defined in Symbol > Categories.

Example: AddTextColumn(GetBaseIndex(), "Base index");

PlotForeign - Plot foreign security data

Syntax:
PlotForeign(tickersymbol, name, color/barcolor,
style = styleCandle | styleOwnScale, minvalue = {empty},
maxvalue = {empty}, XShift = 0)

Returns:
NUMBER

Function: Plots the foreign-symbol price chart (symbol is defined by tickersymbol parameter). Second argument name defines graph name used for displaying values in a title bar. Graph color could be static (if third argument is a number) or dynamic (when third argument is an array). Color indexes are related to the current palette (see Preferences/Color)

style defines chart plot style (see Plot() function for possible values)

minvalue and maxvalue - (used by styleOwnScale plots ONLY) define plot minimum and maximum values (lower and upper boundary for Y axis)

XShift - allows visually shifting the chart into future (blank) bars.

Example: PlotForeign("^DJI", "Dow Jones", colorRed);

RelStrength - Comparative relative strength

Syntax:
RelStrength("tickername", fixup = 1)

Returns:
ARRAY

Function: Calculates relative strength of currently selected security compared to "tickername" security. When you give an empty string as the argument, a standard relative strength base security taken from Stock > Categories will be used.

The last parameter - fixup - with the default value of 1 - causes filling the holes in the data with previous values. If fixup is 0 - the holes are not fixed.

Note: you can still use Foreign/RelStrength in the old way:
Foreign("ticker", "field"), RelStrength("ticker")
then the holes will be fixed.

Example: RelStrength("^DJI")

RestorePriceArrays - Restore price arrays to original symbol

Syntax:
RestorePriceArrays(tradeprices = False)

Returns:
NOTHING

Function: The RestorePriceArrays restores original price and volume arrays after the call to SetForeign.

tradeprices parameter has to match the one used in SetForeign() function.

When tradeprices argument is set to TRUE, then not only OHLC, V, OI, Avg arrays are restored, but BuyPrice, SellPrice, ShortPrice, CoverPrice, PointValue, TickSize, RoundLotSize, MarginDeposit variables are too.

Example:

```
// Example 1: Plot the indicator using foreign security data
SetForeign("MSFT");
Plot( Ultimate(), "Ultimate from MSFT", colorRed );
RestorePriceArrays();
// Example 2: Use SetForeign with Equity function
SetForeign("MSFT", True, True );
Buy = Cross( MACD(), Signal());
Sell = Cross( Signal(), MACD());
e = Equity(); // backtest on MSFT
RestorePriceArrays( True ); // <- should match parameter used
in SetForeign
```

SetForeign - Replace current price arrays with those of foreign security

Syntax:
SetForeign(ticker, fixup = True, tradeprices = False)

Returns:
NUMBER

Function: The SetForeign function replaces current price/volume arrays with those of foreign security, returns True (1) if ticker exists, False (0) otherwise.

If ticker does not exist (and function returns false) price arrays are not changed at all.

fixup parameter controls whether data holes are filled with previous bar data or not. If fixup is False then data holes are filled with Null value. For detailed discussion on fixup parameter please check Foreign function.

tradeprices parameter controls whether trade price arrays should be replaced too. If it is set to TRUE, then not only OHLC, V, OI, Avg arrays are set to foreign symbol values, but also BuyPrice, SellPrice, ShortPrice, CoverPrice, PointValue, TickSize, RoundLotSize, MarginDeposit variables are set to correspond to foreign security. This allows Equity() to work well with SetForeign.

The single SetForeign(“ticker”) call is equivalent to the following sequence:

C = Foreign(“ticker”, “C”);

O = Foreign(“ticker”, “O”);

H = Foreign(“ticker”, “H”);

L = Foreign(“ticker”, “L”);

V = Foreign(“ticker”, “V”);

OI = Foreign(“ticker”, “I”);

Avg = (C + H + L)/3;

but 6x faster. (SetForeign takes about the same time as single foreign). To restore original prices call RestorePriceArrays()

Examples:

```
// Example 1: Plot the indicator using foreign security data
SetForeign(“MSFT”);
Plot( Ultimate(), “Ultimate from MSFT”, colorRed );
RestorePriceArrays();

// Example 2: Use SetForeign with Equity function
SetForeign(“MSFT”, True, True );
Buy = Cross( MACD(), Signal());
Sell = Cross( Signal(), MACD());
e = Equity(); // backtest on MSFT
RestorePriceArrays( True );
// <- should match parameter used in SetForeign
```

File Input/Output functions

fclose - Close a file

Syntax:
fclose(filehandle)

Returns:
NOTHING

Function: Closes a file.

The filehandle (NUMBER) should be the handle returned by fopen function.

Example:

```
fh = fopen( "myfile.txt", "w");
if( fh )
{
   fputs( "Testing", fh );
   fclose( fh );
}
```

fdelete - Deletes a file

Syntax:
fdelete("filename")

Returns:
NUMBER

Function: This function deletes a file.

"filename" is a path to the file name (relative or full path). If just file name without path is specified then AmiBroker directory is used, returns TRUE if file successfully deleted, FALSE otherwise

Example: fdelete("test.csv")

feof - Test for end-of-file

Syntax
feof(filehandle)

Returns:
NUMBER

Function: The feof function returns a nonzero value after the first read operation that attempts to read past the end of the file. It returns 0 if the current position is not end of file. There is no error return value.

filehandle is a file handle returned by fopen function.

Example:

```
// The following code (commentary) reads
// all lines from the external file and
// displays it in commentary window

fh = fopen( “quotes.csv”, “r”);
if( fh )
{
   while( ! feof( fh ) )
   {
      printf( fgets( fh ) );
   }
}
else
{
   printf(“ERROR: file can not be found (does not exist)”);
}
```

fgets - get a string from a file

Syntax:
fgets(filehandle)

Returns:
STRING

Function: The fgets function reads a string from the input file (defined by filehandle argument) and returns the string as a result.

fgets reads characters from the current file position to and including the first newline character, or to the end of the file whichever comes first. The newline character, if read, is included in the returned string.

The filehandle argument is a number returned by fopen function. The file has to be opened with "r" flag (for reading).

Example:

```
// The following code (commentary) reads
// all lines from the external file and
// displays it in commentary window

fh = fopen( "quotes.csv", "r");
if( fh )
{
   while( ! feof( fh ) )
   {
      printf( fgets( fh ) );
   }
}
else
{
   printf("ERROR: file can not be found (does not exist)");
}
```

fgetstatus - Retrieves file status/properties

Syntax:
fgetstatus(filename, what, format = 0)

Returns:
NUMBER
STRING

Function: The function that retrieves file properties/status.

Returns NUMBER or STRING depending on format parameter. If file does not exist it returns Null.

Parameters:

- filename - the name of the file (with or without full path) to query
- what - specifies what file property to retrieve, allowable values

  0 - the date/time the file was created

  1 - the date/time the file was last modified

  2 - the date/time the file was last accessed for reading

  3 - the file size in bytes

  4 - attribute byte of the file
- format - specifies return format of date/time values (format specifications are the same as in Now() function): allowed values:

  0 - returns string containing date/time formatted according to system settings

  1 - returns string containing date only formatted according to system settings

  2 - returns string containing time only formatted according to system settings

  3 - returns DATENUM number with date

  4 - returns TIMENUM number with time

  5 - returns DATETIME number with date/time

6 - returns date DAY (1..31)

7 - returns date MONTH (1..12)

8 - returns date YEAR (four digit)

9 - returns date DAY OF WEEK (1..7, where 1=Sunday, 2=Monday, and so on)

10 - returns date DAY OF YEAR (1..366)

Note that Windows supports only 2 second resolution of file date/time stamps.

Example:

```
// get modification date string of portfolio.afl file
fgetstatus("formulas\\Equity\\portfolio.afl",1,0);
```

fmkdir - Creates (makes) a directory

Syntax:
fmkdir("dirname")

Returns:
NUMBER

Function: Creates (makes) a directory.

"dirname" specifies the path of the directory to be created. This function creates only one directory at a time. If you want to create a nested directory tree, you have to call it multiple times. For example to create C:\MyDirectory\MySubDirectory folder you have to call it twice:

```
fmkdir( "C:\\MyDirectory" );
fmkdir( "C:\\MyDirectory\\MySubDirectory" );
```

It is safe to call fmkdir even if directory already exists - there will be no change to file system.

Returns TRUE if directory successfully created, FALSE otherwise

Example: fmkdir("C:\\TestResults");

fopen - Open a file

Syntax:
fopen(filename, mode)

Returns:
NUMBER

Function: Opens file, returns filehandle (NUMBER).

File handle is non-zero if the file opened successfully, zero on failure.

Parameters:

- filename - STRING - contains the path to the file name. Note that single backslash "\" in path must be written in AFL as a double backslash "\\".
- mode - STRING - access mode can be "r" - for reading, "w" for writing, "a" for appending (and all other regular C-runtime library modes)

Example:

```
fh = fopen( "myfile.txt", "w");
if( fh )
{
   fputs( "Testing", fh );
}
else
{
   printf("Error opening file");
}
```

fputs - Write a string to a file

Syntax:

fputs(string, filehandle)

Returns:

NOTHING

Function: Writes (puts) the string to the file.

The filehandle must be a number returned by fopen function used to open the file. The file has to be open for writing or appending ("w" or "a") for this fputs to work.

Example:

```
// The following code exports quotes
// of current stock to quotes.csv
// comma separated file
//

fh = fopen( "quotes.csv", "w");
if( fh )
{
   fputs( "Date,Open,High,Low,Close,Volume\n", fh );

   y = Year();
   m = Month();
   d = Day();

   for( i = 0; i < BarCount; i++ )
   {
      ds = StrFormat("%02.0f-%02.0f-%02.0f,",
                     y[ i ], m[ i ], d[ i ] );
      fputs( ds, fh );

      qs = StrFormat("%.4f, %.4f, %.4f, %.4f, %.0f\n",
                     O[ i ], H[ i ], L[ i ], C[ i ], V[ i ] );
      fputs( qs, fh );
   }

   fclose( fh );
}
```

frmdir - Removes a directory

Syntax:
frmdir("dirname")

Returns:
NUMBER

Function: This function removes a directory

"dirname" specifies the path of the directory to be removed. This function removes only one directory at a time. So if you want to remove a nested directory tree you have to call it multiple times, for example:

```
frmdir( "C:\\MyDirectory\\MySubDirectory" ); // delete nested
subdir first
frmdir( "C:\\MyDirectory" );
```

The directory must be empty before removing it otherwise it will not be possible to remove it.

Returns TRUE if directory successfully removed, FALSE otherwise

Example: frmdir ("C:\\OldTest");

String manipulation

Asc - Get ASCII code of character

Syntax:

Asc(string, pos = 0)

Returns:

NUMBER

Function: Returns the ANSI character code corresponding to the first letter in a string (if position is not specified) or code of character at specified position. If you don't specify position (pos argument) then first character is used. Negative values of pos reference characters counting from the end of string.

Useful for creation of exploration that displays single letters for signals instead of numbers.

Example:

```
Buy = Cross(MACD(),Signal());
Sell = Cross(Signal(),MACD());
Filter = Buy OR Sell;
AddColumn( IIf( Buy, Asc("B"), Asc("S")), "Signal", formatChar
);
```

DateTimeToStr - Convert datetime to string

Syntax:

DateTimeToStr(NUMBER)

Returns:

STRING

Function: Converts number representing date/time value (for example obtained using GetCursorXPosition(), Now(), DateTime() functions) to the corresponding STRING (text).

Example:

```
ToolTip="X="+DateTimeToStr(GetCursorXPosition())
+"nY="+GetCursorYPosition();
```

NumToStr - Convert number to string

Syntax:

NumToStr(NUMBER, format = 1.3, separator=True)
NumToStr(ARRAY, format = 1.3, separator=True)

Returns:

STRING

Function: It is used to convert numeric value of NUMBER or ARRAY to string.

The second parameter - format - allows you to control the output formatting (decimal places and leading spaces). The integer part of the number controls the minimum number of characters used to display the number (if you specify high number the output will be space-padded). The fractional part defines how many decimal places to display, for example 1.0 - will give you a number without fractional part at all, and 1.2 - will give two digits past the decimal point.

There is also a special format constant formatDateTime that allow conversion of date/time returned by DateTime() function formatted according to Windows regional settings.

Third parameter - separator (true by default) - controls whether the thousand separator is added or not.

Thousands separator is definable in Tools > Preferences > Misc.

Note: NumToStr is a synonym for WriteVal function, and is the preferred function.

Examples:

```
// Simple use (no custom format)
NumToStr( StochK(39) - StochK(12) );

// Display rate of change with 2 decimal digits
// and % appended to the end
NumToStr( ROC( Close, 20 ), 1.2 ) + "%";

// Display date/time according to regional settings
NumToStr( DateTime(), formatDateTime );
```

printf - Print formatted output to the output window

Syntax:
printf(formatstr, ...)

Returns:
NOTHING

Function: The printf function formats and prints a series of characters and values to the output window, which can be either the commentary or the interpretation window.

If arguments follow the format string, the format string must contain specifications that determine the output format for the arguments.

printf and StrFormat behave identically except that printf writes output to the window, while StrFormat does not write anything to output window but returns resulting string instead.

For numbers always use %f, %e, or %g formatting; %d or %x will not work because there are no integers in AFL.

As of now only numbers and arrays can be printed. For arrays, 'selected value' is printed.

Read more about various % format specifiers on Microsoft site: *http://msdn2.microsoft.com/en-us/library/56e442dc(VS.80).aspx*

Example:

```
for( i = 0; i < 10; i++ )
{
   printf( "Hello world, line %gn", i );
}
```

StrExtract - Extracts given item (substring) from comma-separated string

Syntax:
StrExtract(list, item)

Returns:
STRING

Function: Extracts given item (substring) from comma-separated list of items. item is a zero-based index of the item in the list.

If no substring at given index is found then an empty string is returned ("").

Useful to retrieve symbols from the list obtained via GetCategorySymbols function.

Example:

```
StrExtract( "MSFT,AAPL,AMD,INTC", 2 ) will return AMD

StrExtract( "MSFT,AAPL,AMD,INTC", 0 ) will return MSFT

StrExtract( "MSFT,AAPL,AMD,INTC", 200 ) will return empty
string ""
```

StrFind - Find substring in a string

Syntax:
StrFind(string, substring)

Returns:
NUMBER

Function: The StrFind function finds the first occurrence of substring in string.

Returns 0 if not found, otherwise returns character index (one-based) of first occurrence.

Example:

```
if( StrFind( Name(), ".L" ) )
{
   printf( "The " + Name() + " has .L suffix ");
}
else
{
   printf( "The " + Name() + " does not have .L suffix ");
}
```

StrFormat - Write formatted output to the string

Syntax:
StrFormat(formatstr, ...)

Returns:
STRING

Function: The StrFormat function formats and returns a series of characters and values in the result string.

If arguments follow the format string, the format string must contain specifications that determine the output format for the arguments.

StrFormat and printf behave identically except that printf writes output to the window, while StrFormat does not write anything to output window but returns resulting string instead.

StrFormat function is useful in conjunction with fputs function that allows writing a string to a file.

For numbers always use %f, %e, or %g formatting; %d or %x will not work because there are no integers in AFL.

As of now only numbers and arrays can be used. For arrays, 'selected value' is used.

Example:

```
fh = fopen("Test.csv", "w" );
for( i = 0; fh && i < 10; i++ )
{
    text = StrFormat( "Hello world, line %g\n", i );
   fputs( text, fh );
}

fclose( fh );
```

StrLeft - Extracts the leftmost part

Syntax:
StrLeft(STRING, count)

Returns:
STRING

Function: Extracts the first (that is, leftmost) count characters from STRING and returns a copy of the extracted substring. If count exceeds the string length, then the entire string is extracted.

Example: newstring = StrLeft(string, 4);

StrLen - string length

Syntax:
StrLen(STRING)

Returns:
NUMBER

Function: Calculates the length of the string

Example: This function could be used for (for example) filtering out only 3 letter stock codes: Buy = something AND StrLen(name()) == 3;

StrMid - Extracts part of the string

Syntax:
StrMid(STRING, start, count)

Returns:
STRING

Function: Extracts a substring of length count characters from STRING, starting at position start (zero-based). The function returns a copy of the extracted substring.

Example: newstring = StrMid(string, 1, 2);

StrReplace - String replace

Syntax:
StrReplace(srcstring, oldsubstring, newsubstring)

Returns:
STRING

Function: Given an original string srcstring, replace all occurrences of oldsubstring with newsubstring. The string may grow or shrink as a result of the replacement, that is oldsubstring and newsubstring do not have to be equal in length. The function performs case-sensitive matches.

Example:

```
// the expression below will
// result in string in which 'red' is replaced with 'brown'
StrReplace("This fox is red", "red", "brown" );
```

StrRight - Extracts the rightmost part of the string

Syntax:
StrRight(STRING, count)

Returns:
STRING

Function: Extracts the last (that is, rightmost) count characters from STRING and returns a copy of the extracted substring. If count exceeds the string length, then the entire string is extracted.

Example: newstring = StrRight(string, 4);

StrToDateTime - Convert string to datetime

Syntax:
StrToDateTime("string")

Returns:
NUMBER

Function: Converts a string representing date/time value to the corresponding DateTime number. The resulting string can later be compared to output of DateTime() function, for example.

Example: Buy = DateTime() == StrToDateTime("2005-Mar-05");

StrToLower - Convert to lowercase

Syntax:
StrToLower("string")

Returns:
STRING

Function: This function converts input string to all lower case.

Example: Title = StrToLower("MiXeD CaSe");

StrToNum - Convert string to number

Syntax:
StrToNum(string)

Returns:
NUMBER

Function: Converts string to number.

Example:

```
List = "123,456,789";
for( i = 0; ( Item = StrExtract( List, i ) ) != ""; i++ )
{
   printf( "%gn", StrToNum( Item ) );
}
```

StrToUpper - Convert to uppercase

Syntax:
StrToUpper("string")

Returns:
STRING

Function: This function converts input string to all upper case.

Example: Title = StrToUpper("MiXeD CaSe");

Trading System Toolbox

AlertIf - Trigger alerts

Syntax:

```
AlertIf( BOOLEAN_EXPRESSION, command, text, type = 0,
         flags = 1+2+4+8, lookback = 1 );
```

Returns:

NOTHING

Function: Triggers alert action if BOOLEAN_EXPRESSION is true.

BOOLEAN_EXPRESSION is the expression that if it evaluates to True (non zero value) triggers the alert. If it evaluates to False (zero value) no alert is triggered. Only lookback most recent bars are considered.

The command string defines the action taken when alert is triggered. If it is empty, the alert text is simply displayed in the Alert output window (View > Alert Output). Other supported values of command string are:

SOUND the-path-to-the-WAV-file. Plays the WAV file once.

EMAIL command sends the e-mail to the account defined in the settings (Tools > Preferences > E-mail). The format of the e-mail is as follows: Subject: Alert type_name (type) Ticker on Date/Time

Body: text

EXEC the-path-to-the-file-or-URL. Launches an external application or file or URL specified after EXEC command are attached after file name and text is attached at the end

EXEC command uses ShellExecute function and allows not only EXE files but URLs too.

Text defines the text that will be printed in the output window or sent via e-mail or added as argument to the application specified by EXEC command

Type defines type of the alert. Pre-defined types are 0 - default, 1 - buy, 2 - sell, 3 - short, 4- cover. You may specify higher values and they will get the name "other"

Flags control behavior of AlertIF function. This field is a combination (sum) of the following values:

> (1 - display text in the output window, 2 - make a beep (via computer speaker), 4 - don't display repeated alerts having the same type, 8 - don't display repeated alerts having the same date/time) By default all these options are turned ON.

lookback parameter controls how many recent bars are checked

Example:

```
Buy = Cross( MACD(), Signal() );
Sell = Cross( Signal(), MACD() );
Short = Sell;
Cover = Buy;
AlertIF( Buy, "EMAIL", "A sample alert on "+FullName(), 1 );
AlertIF( Sell, "SOUND C:\\Windows\\Media\\Ding.wav", "Audio
alert", 2 );
AlertIF( Short, "EXEC Calc.exe", "Launching external applica-
tion", 3 );
AlertIF( Cover, "", "Simple text alert", 4 );
```

ApplyStop - Apply built-in stop

Syntax:

ApplyStop(type, mode, amount, exitatstop, volatile = False, ReEntryDelay = 0)

Returns:

NOTHING

Function: Controls the built-in stops from the formula level. This allows optimization of stops.

Parameters:

type:

0 = stopTypeLoss - maximum loss stop,

1 = stopTypeProfit - profit target stop,

2 = stopTypeTrailing - trailing stop,

3 = stopTypeNBar - N-bar stop

mode:

0 - disable stop (stopModeDisable),

1 - amount in percent (stopModePercent), or number of bars for N-bar stop (stopModeBars),

2 - amount in points (stopModePoint);

3 - amount in percent of profit (risk)

amount:

percent/point loss/profit trigger/risk amount.

This could be a number (static stop level) or an array (dynamic stop level)

ExitAtStop:

ExitAtStop = 0 - means check stops using only trade price and exit at regular trade price

(if you are trading on the close it means that only the close price will be checked for exits and exit will be done at the close price)

ExitAtStop = 1 - check High-Low prices and exit intraday on price equal to stop level on the same bar when stop was triggered

ExitAtStop = 2 - check High-Low prices but exit next bar on regular trade price.

volatile:

decides if amount (or distance) (3rd parameter) is sampled at the trade entry and remains fixed during the trade (Volatile = FALSE - old behavior) or if it can vary during the trade (Volatile = TRUE) (allows single line Chandelier exit implementation)

ReEntryDelay:

how many bars to wait until entering the same stock is allowed.

Note on using stops:

Scenario 1:

You trade on next bar Open and want to exit intraday on stop price

Correct settings:

ActivateStopsImmediately turned ON

ExitAtStop = 1

Trade delays set to one

Trade price set to Open

Scenario 2:

You trade on today's Close and want to exit intraday on stop price

Correct settings:

ActivateStopsImmediately turned OFF

ExitAtStop = 1

Trade delays set to zero

Trade price set to Close

Scenario 3:

You trade on next day Open and want to exit by stop on Open price when previous day's H-L range hits stop

Correct settings:

ExitAtStop = 2

Trade delays set to one

Trade price set to Open

a) (if you want to have stops executed after regular signals, so cash from stopped out positions is not available to enter trades the same day)

ActivateStopsImmediately turned ON

b) (if you want to have stops executed before regular signals, so cash from stopped out positions is available to enter new trades the same day)

ActivateStopsImmediately turned OFF

Scenario 4:

You trade on today's Close and want to exit only when today's Close price hits the stop level

Correct settings:

ActivateStopsImmediately turned OFF

ExitAtStop = 0

Trade delays set to zero

Trade price set to Close

Notes:

1. If you are trading at the Close with zero delays be sure to unmark "Activate Stops Immediately" in Settings.

2. For visual conformation of ApplyStop function, add the following lines below your ApplyStop formula in Indicator Builder:

```
Equity(1); // THIS EVALUATES STOPS

Plot(Sell==4,"ApplyStop Sell",colorRed,1|styleOwnScale);
Plot(Cover==4,"ApplyStop Cover",colorGreen,1|styleOwnScale);
```

3. If two or more different stops are triggered on the same bar then they are evaluated in this fixed order:

   Fixed Ruin stop (losing 99.96% of the starting capital)

   Max. loss stop

   Profit target stop

   Trailing stop

   N-bar stop

4. Depending on kind of the stop various values are written back to sell/cover array to enable you to distinguish if given signal was generated by regular rule or by stop.

   1 - regular exit

   2 - max. loss

   3 - profit target

   4 - trailing

   5 - n-bar stop

   6 - ruin stop

5. ExitAtStop has a new meaning for N-BAR stop type.

   If ExitAtStop = 0 then N-bar stop has the lowest priority (so if for example profit target stop is hit on the same bar then the profit target is evaluated first)

   If ExitAtStop = 1 then N-bar stop has highest priority and it is evaluated before all other stops.

   The same effect is obtained by checking the "Has priority" box in AA Settings window.

6. ApplyStop function is designed to be used to simulate stop orders placed at the exchange or simulated by the brokerage.

   These explain how stops operate for Interactive Brokers:

   http://www.interactivebrokers.com/en/trading/orders/stop.php?ib_entity=uk

   http://www.interactivebrokers.com/en/trading/orders/trailingStops.php?ib_entity=uk

Example:

```
/* max loss stop optimization */
ApplyStop(stopTypeLoss,
        stopModePercent,
        Optimize( "max. loss stop level", 10, 2, 30, 1 ),
        True );

/* single-line implementation of Chandelier exit */
ApplyStop(stopTypeTrailing, stopModePoint, 3*ATR(14), True,
True );

/* N-bar stop */
ApplyStop( stopTypeNBar, stopModeBars, 5 );
```

BarsSince - Bars since

Syntax:
BarsSince(ARRAY)

Returns:
ARRAY

Function: Calculates the number of bars (time periods) that have passed since ARRAY was true (or 1)

Example: BarsSince(MACD() < 0)

Cross - Crossover check

Syntax:
Cross(ARRAY1, ARRAY2)

Returns:
ARRAY

Function: Gives a "1" or true on the day that ARRAY1 crosses above ARRAY2. Otherwise the result is "0".

To find out when ARRAY1 crosses below ARRAY2, use the formula Cross(ARRAY2, ARRAY1)

Example: Cross(Close, EMA(Close,9))

EnableRotationalTrading - Turns on rotational-trading mode of the backtester

This function is now marked as obsolete.
Use SetBacktestMode(backtestRotational) in new formulas.
But the information is still relevant.

Unless you specifically want to implement fund-switching/rotational trading system you should not use this mode. Rotational trading is a limited subset of AmiBroker's general portfolio testing.

Syntax:
EnableRotationalTrading()

Returns:
NOTHING

Function: When placed on the top of system formula it turns on the rotational-trading (aka. fund-switching) mode of the backtester.

Rotational trading is a popular method for trading mutual funds. It is also known as fund-switching or scoring&ranking. Its basic premise is to rotate among symbols all the time so only the top N issues ranked according to some user-definable score are held. The number of positions open depend on "Max. open positions" setting and available funds and position size. Once a position is entered, it remains in place until the security's rank drops below WorstRankHeld (can be set via SetOption("WorstRankHeld", 5)). Regular buy/sell/short/cover signals are not used at all.

The rotational trading mode uses "buy price" and "buy delay" from the Settings | Trade page as trade price and delay for both entries and exits (long and short).

To enter this mode you have to call EnableRotationalTrading() function at the very beginning of your formula. Use of buy/sell/short/cover variables is not allowed. Only PositionScore variable will be used to rank securities and trade top N securities..

A simple rotational trading formula (stocks with high RSI are best candidates for shorting while stocks with low RSI are best candidates for long positions):

```
EnableRotationalTrading();
SetOption("WorstRankHeld",5);

PositionSize = -25; // invest 25% of equity in single security
PositionScore = 50 - RSI();
```

The score (PositionScore) for all securities is calculated first. Then all scores are sorted according to absolute value of PositionScore. Then top N are chosen to be traded. N depends on available funds and "max. open positions" setting. Backtester successively enters the trades starting from highest ranked security until the number of positions open reaches "max. open positions" or there are no more funds available. The score has the following meaning:

higher positive score means better candidate for entering long trade

lower negative score means better candidate for entering short trade

the score of zero means no trade (exit the trade if there is already an open position on a given symbol)

the score equal to scoreNoRotate constant means that already open trades should be kept and no new trades entered

the score equal to scoreExitAll constant causes the rotational mode backtester to exit all positions regardless of HoldMinBars. Note that this is a global flag and it is enough to set it for just any single symbol to exit all currently open positions, no matter on which symbol you use scoreExitAll (it may be even on symbol that is not currently held). By setting PositionScore to scoreExitAll you exit all positions immediately regardless of HoldMinBars setting

Exits are generated automatically when security's rank drops below "worst rank held". There is no real control over when exits happen except for setting low score to force exits. You can also set the score on any (at least one) security to the value of scoreNoRotate to prevent rotation (so already open positions are kept). But this is global and does not give you individual control.

Equity - Calculate single-symbol equity line

This function is left here for backward compatibility.

Equity() function uses so called "old" single-security backtester that offers only a subset of features of new backtester. To retrieve the value of portfolio-level equity generated by the new backtester use Foreign("~~~EQUITY", "C").

Syntax:

Equity(Flags = 0, RangeType = -1, From = 0, To = 0)

Returns:

ARRAY

Function: Returns single-security Equity line based on buy/sell/short/cover rules, buy/sell/short/coverprice arrays, all apply stops, and all other backtester settings. Flags - defines the behavior of Equity function

Flags:

0 : (default) Just calculates the equity array.

1 : works as 0, but additionally updates buy/sell/short/cover arrays so all redundant signals are removed exactly as it is done internally by the backtester plus all exits by stops are applied so it is now possible to visualize ApplyStop() stops.

2 : (advanced) works as 1 but updated signals are not moved back to their original positions if buy/sell/short/cover delays set in preferences are non-zero. Note: this value of flag is documented but in 99% of cases should not be used in your formula. Other values are reserved for the future.

RangeType - defines quotations range being used:

-1 : (default) use range set in the Automatic analysis window

0 : all quotes

1 : n last quotes (n defined by 'From' parameter)

2 : n last days (n defined by 'From' parameter)

3 : From/To dates

From : defines start date (datenum) (when RangeType == 3) or "n" parameter (when RangeType == 1 or 2)

To: defines end date (datenum) (when RangeType == 3) otherwise ignored

datenum defines date the same way as DateNum() function as YYYMMDD

where YYY is (year - 1900), MM is month, DD is day

December 31st, 1999 has a datenum of 991231. May 21st, 2001 has a datenum of 1010521

All these parameters are evaluated at the time of the call of Equity function. Complete equity array is generated at once. Changes to buy/sell/short/cover rules made after the call have no effect. Equity function can be called multiple times in single formula.

Example:

```
Buy = Cross (C, MA(C,5)); // Your buy rule
Sell = Cross (MA(C,5),C); // Your Sell rule;
e = Equity();
Plot (C,  "C", colorBlack, styleCandle);
Plot (e, "Equity", colorGreen, styleLine | styleOwnScale);
```

ExRem - Remove excess signals

Syntax:
ExRem(ARRAY1, ARRAY2)

Returns:
ARRAY

Function: Removes excess signals

returns 1 on the first occurrence of "true" signal in Array1

then returns 0 until Array2 is true even if there are "true" signals in Array1

Example:

```
Buy = ExRem( Buy, Sell );
Sell = ExRem( Sell, Buy );
```

ExRemSpan - Remove excess signals spanning given number of bars

Syntax:
ExRemSpan(ARRAY1, numbars)

Returns:
ARRAY

Function: Removes excess signals that span numbars bars since initial signal.

(In other words first non-zero bar passes through, then all subsequent non-zero bars are ignored (zero is returned) until numbars bars have passed since initial signal. From then on a new signal may pass through)

This function makes easy writing exits after a fixed number of bars, for example if you want to always sell 5 bars after the buy you should now use a combination of ExRemSpan and Ref(). It will work even if initial buy array has lots of redundant signals.

Example:

```
Buy = 1;
Buy = ExRemSpan( Buy, 5 );
Sell = Ref( Buy, -5 );
```

Flip - Creates State signals from Impulse signals

Syntax:
Flip(ARRAY1, ARRAY2)

Returns:
ARRAY

Function: Works as a flip/flop device or "latch"

returns 1 from the first occurrence of "true" signal in Array1 until a "true" occurs in Array2 which resets the state back to zero until next "true" is detected in Array1.

Example:

```
Buy = Cross(C,MA(C,5));
Sell = Cross (MA(C,5),C);
// Comment out the next two lines
//  to see the effect of Flip.
Buy = Flip(Buy,Sell);
```

```
Sell = Flip(Sell,Buy);

Plot(Buy,"Buy",colorGreen,styleLine);
Plot(Sell, "Sell", colorRed,styleLine);
```

GetBacktesterObject - Get access to the backtester object

Syntax:
GetBacktesterObject()

Returns:
OBJECT

Function: This function is used in custom backtester procedures to get access to the backtester object. Note that GetBacktester method should only be called when Status("action") returns actionPortfolio.

For more details please read Custom Backtester documentation

Example:

```
if( Status("action")== actionPortfolio )
{
    // retrieve the interface to portfolio backtester
     bo = GetBacktesterObject();

     //...here is your custom backtest formula.
}
```

GetOption - Gets the value of option in automatic analysis settings

Syntax:
GetOption("fieldname")

Returns:
NUMBER

Function: Gets the value of various options in automatic analysis settings.

field - is a string that defines the option to read. There are following options available:

- "NoDefaultColumns" - if set to True - exploration does not have default Ticker and Date/Time columns
- "InitialEquity"
- "AllowSameBarExit"
- "ActivateStopsImmediately"
- "AllowPositionShrinking"
- "FuturesMode"
- "InterestRate"
- "MaxOpenPositions" - maximum number of simultaneously open positions (trades) in portfolio backtest/optimization
- "WorstRankHeld" - the worst rank of symbol to be held in rotational trading mode (see EnableRotationalTrading for more details)
- "MinShares" - the minimum number of shares required to open the position in the backtester/optimizer. If you don't have enough funds to purchase that many, trade will NOT be entered
- "MinPosValue" - (4.70.3 and above) the minimum dollar amount required to open the position in the backtester/optimizer. If you don't have enough funds trade will NOT be entered
- "PriceBoundChecking" - if set to False - disables checking and adjusting buyprice/sellprice/coverprice/shortprice arrays to current symbol High-Low range.

- CommissionMode -
  - 0 - use portfolio manager commission table
  - 1 - percent of trade
  - 2 - $ per trade
  - 3 - $ per share/contract
- CommissionAmount - amount of commission in modes 1..3
- AccountMargin - (in old versions it was 'MarginRequirement') - account margin requirement (as in settings), 100 = no margin
- ReverseSignalForcesExit - reverse entry signal forces exit of existing trade (default = True)
- UsePrevBarEquityForPosSizing - Affects how percent of current equity position sizing is performed.
  - False (default value) means: use current (intraday) equity to perform position sizing,
  - True means: use previous bar closing equity to perform position sizing

Example: InitialEquity = GetOption("InitialEquity");

GetTradingInterface - retrieves OLE automation object to automatic trading interface

Syntax:
GetTradingInterface()

Returns:
OBJECT

Function: Retrieves the OLE (Object Linking and Embedding) automation object to automatic trading interface. "Name" is the interface name. You have to have the trading interface installed separately to make it work, otherwise you will get the error message attempting to use this function. Trading interface for Interactive Brokers is available from download section: *http://www.amibroker.com/download.html*

Hold - Hold the alert signal

Syntax:
Hold(EXPRESSION, periods)

Returns:
ARRAY

Function: Holds a "true" result of EXPRESSION for the specified number of periods. This true result is held true over the number of periods specified even if a "false" result is generated.

Example: Hold(Cross(RSI(14),70),5)

IIf - Immediate IF function

Syntax:
IIf(EXPRESSION, TRUE_PART, FALSE_PART)

Returns:
ARRAY

Function: "Immediate-IF" - a conditional function that returns the value of the second parameter (TRUE_PART) if the conditional expression defined by the first parameter (EXPRESSION) is true; otherwise, the value of third parameter is returned (FALSE_PART).

IIF is a function - so the result of evaluation is returned by that function and should be assigned to some variable. IIf always evaluates both TRUE_PART and FALSE_PART, even though it returns only one of them. Because of this, you should watch for undesirable side effects.

A common error assumes that IIf is a flow control statement. It is not. IIf is a function.

This is the correct way to use IIf:

```
result = IIf( condition, 7, 9 );
```

And this is a common, but incorrect way:

```
IIf( condition, result = 7, result = 9 );
```

Example: The formula result = IIf(MACD()<Signal(), Volume, -Volume) will assign positive volume values to the result variable on days when macd was below its signal line, and negative volume values on the other days.

LastValue - Last value of the array

Syntax:

LastValue(ARRAY, lastmode = True)

Returns:

NUMBER

Function: Returns the last calculated value of the specified ARRAY. The result of this function can be used in place of a constant (NUMBER) in any function argument.

If ARRAY is undefined (e.g., only 100-days loaded and you request the last value of a 200-day moving average) then the lastvalue function returns zero.

Warning: since this function fills an entire data array with the last value of another array, it allows a formula to look into the future.

lastmode parameter (affects only commentary/interpretation):

True - the last value is always returned

False - then in commentary the 'selected' value is returned

Optimize - Define optimization variable

Syntax:

Optimize("description", default, min , max, step)

Returns:

NUMBER

Function: Defines the optimization process parameters.

With normal backtesting, scanning, exploration, and commentary modes the optimize function returns default value, so the above function call returns default.

In optimization mode the optimize function returns successive values from min to max (inclusively) with step stepping. "description" is a string that is used to identify the optimization variable and is displayed as a column name in the optimization result list. default is a default value that the optimize function returns in exploration, indicator, commentary, scan, and normal back test modes. min is a minimum value of the variable being optimized; max is a maximum value of the variable being optimized; step is an interval used for increasing the value from min to max.

Example: variable = Optimize("my optimization var", 9, 2, 20, 1);

Notes:

1. You can refresh your Equity chart after each Optimization step and observe (like a slide show) how the linearity of your Equity curve is affected by adding these two lines to the very end of your code:

   ```
   AB = CreateObject("Broker.Application");
   AB.RefreshAll();
   ```

   Important note: Do not use in commentary, interpretation, or indicator builder because it will cause a loop.

2. Here it is a function that combines Param() and Optimize():

   ```
   function ParamOptimize( pname, defaultval, minv, maxv, step )
   {
       return Optimize( pname,
           Param( pname, defaultval, minv, maxv, step ),
           minv, maxv, step );
   }
   ```

Ref - Reference past/future values of the array

Syntax:
Ref(ARRAY, period)

Returns:
ARRAY

Function: References a previous or subsequent element in an ARRAY. A positive period references "n" periods in the future; a negative period references "n" periods ago.

Example: The formula "ref(CLOSE, -14)" returns the closing price 14 periods ago. Thus, you could write the 14-day price rate-of-change (expressed in points) as "C - ref(C, -14)." The formula "ref(C, 12)" returns the closing price 12 periods ahead (this means looking up the future)

SetBacktestMode - Sets working mode of the backtester

Syntax:
SetBacktestMode(mode)

Returns:
NOTHING

Function: Sets the working mode of the backtester. A 'mode' parameter is one of the following backtest modes:

Supported backtest modes:

- backtestRegular - regular, signal-based backtest, redundant signals are removed.
- backtestRegularRaw - signal-based backtest, redundant (raw) signals are not removed, only one position per symbol allowed
- backtestRegularRawMulti - signal-based backtest, redundant (raw) signals are not removed, multiple positions per symbol will be open if BUY/SHORT signal is "true" for more than one bar and there are free funds. Sell/Cover exits all open positions on a given symbol, Scale-In/Out works on all open positions of given a symbol at once.
- backtestRotational - rotational trading system.

Examples:

```
SetBacktestMode( backtestRegular );
SetBacktestMode( backtestRegularRaw );
SetBacktestMode( backtestRegularRawMulti );

// rotational trading mode.
// The equivalent of EnableRotationalTrading()
SetBacktestMode( backtestRotational );
```

SetCustomBacktestProc - Define custom backtest procedure formula file

Syntax:
SetCustomBacktestProc(filename, enable = True)

Returns:
NOTHING

Function: This function allows changing custom backtest procedure file from AFL formula level.

To learn more about the custom backtester please read:

- Portfolio Backtester Interface Reference Guide in the AmiBroker User's Guide.
- An excellent article in the AmiBroker User's Knowledge Base: *http://www.amibroker.org/userkb/2008/03/16/amibroker-custom-backtester-interface-2/*

This description of the custom backtester comes from Wayne, GP, author of the article in User's Knowledge Base.

From version 4.67.0, AmiBroker provides a custom backtester interface to allow customizing the operation of the backtester's second phase which processes the trading signals. This allows a range of special situations to be achieved that aren't natively supported by the backtester. AmiBroker tends to refer to this as the Advanced Portfolio Backtester Interface, but it is widely referred to as the Custom Backtester Interface.

Due to the object model used by the backtester interface, a higher level of programming knowledge is required than for simple AFL or looping. This document starts by discussing that model, so is aimed at AFL programmers who are already proficient and comfortable with basic AFL use, array indexing, and looping.

Parameters

filename parameter instructs backtester to use external formula file as custom backtest procedure, if empty - it means use current formula

enable = True (default) - enables custom backtesting procedure (the same as SetOption("UseCustomBacktestProc", True);
enable = False - disables custom proc

Example: SetCustomBacktestProc("Formulas\MyCustomBacktest.afl", True);

SetFormulaName - Set the name of the formula

Syntax:
SetFormulaName(string)

Retruns:
NOTHING

Function: Sets the name of the formula that is displayed in the backtest result explorer.

Example: SetFormulaName("My Holy Grail System");

SetOption - Sets options in automatic analysis settings

Syntax:
SetOption(field, value)

Returns:
NOTHING

Function: Sets various options in automatic analysis settings. Also affects Equity() function results.

field - is a string that defines which option to change. There are the following options available:

- "NoDefaultColumns" - if set to True - exploration does not have default Ticker and Date/Time columns
- "InitialEquity"
- "AllowSameBarExit"
- "ActivateStopsImmediately"
- "AllowPositionShrinking"
- "FuturesMode"
- "InterestRate"
- "MaxOpenPositions" - maximum number of simultaneously open positions (trades) in portfolio backtest/optimization
- "WorstRankHeld" - the worst rank of symbol to be held in rotational trading mode (see EnableRotationalTrading for more details)
- "MinShares" - the minimum number of shares required to open the position in the backtester/optimizer. If you don't have enough funds to purchase that many, trade will not be entered
- "MinPosValue" - the minimum dollar amount required to open the position in the backtester/optimizer. If you don't have enough funds trade will not be entered
- "PriceBoundChecking" - if set to False - disables checking and adjusting buyprice/sellprice/coverprice/shortprice arrays to current symbol High-Low range.
- CommissionMode -
  - 0 - use portfolio manager commission table
  - 1 - percent of trade
  - 2 - $ per trade
  - 3 - $ per share/contract

- CommissionAmount - amount of commission in modes 1..3
- AccountMargin (in old versios it was 'MarginRequirement') - account margin requirement (as in settings), 100 = no margin
- ReverseSignalForcesExit - reverse entry signal forces exit of existing trade (default = True)
- UsePrevBarEquityForPosSizing - Affects how percent of current equity position sizing is performed.
    - False (default value) means: use current (intraday) equity to perform position sizing,
    - True means: use previous bar closing equity to perform position sizing
- PortfolioReportMode - sets backtester report mode:
    - 0 - trade list
    - 1 - detailed log
    - 2 - summary
    - 3 - no output (custom only)
- UseCustomBacktestProc - True/False - allows turning on/off custom backtest procedure
- EveryBarNullCheck - allows turning on checking for Nulls in arithmetic operations on every bar in the array (by default it is off - i.e. AmiBroker checks for nulls that appear in the beginning of the array and in the end of the array and once non-null value is detected it assumes no further holes (nulls) in the middle). Turning "EveryBarNullCheck" to True allows extending these checks to each and every bar.
  Note however that turning it on gives huge performance penalty (arithmetic operations are performed even 4x slower when this option is on, so don't use it unless you really have to).
- HoldMinBars - Number - if set to value > 0 - it disables exit during user-specified number of bars even if signals/stops are generated during that period
- EarlyExitBars - Number if set to value > 0 - causes that special early exit (redemption) fee is charged if trade is exited during this period
- EarlyExitFee - defines the % (percent) value of early exit fee
- HoldMinDays - Number - if set to value > 0 - it disables exit during user-specified number of calendar days (not bars) even if signals/stops are generated during that period

- EarlyExitDays - Number if set to value > 0 - causes that special early exit (redemption) fee to be charged if trade is exited during the period specified in calendar days (not bars).
- DisableRuinStop - if set to TRUE, built-in ruin stop is disabled.
- Generate report - allows to suppress/force generation of backtest report. Allowable values: 0, 1, or 2.
  By default backtest reports are generated only for portfolio backtests and for individual backtests if individual reporting is turned on in the settings. Reports are disabled for optimization.
  Now with the SetOption() function you can either suppress report generation for backtests or enable report generation during certain optimization steps, all from code level.
  - SetOption("GenerateReport", 0); // suppress generation of report
  - SetOption("GenerateReport", 1); // force generation of full report
  - SetOption("GenerateReport", 2); // only one-line report is generated (in results.rlst file) viewable as single line in Report Explorer

Warning: If you change the option on *per-symbol* basis the composite results (%profit for example) will be distorted since calculations assume that the options are constant for all symbols in one backtest run. 'HoldMinBars', 'EarlyExit..." options are an exception from this rule (i.e. can be safely set on per-symbol basis)

Examples:

```
SetOption("InitialEquity", 5000 );
SetOption("AllowPositionShrinking", True );
SetOption("MaxOpenPositions", 5 );
PositionSize = -100/5;
SetPositionSize - set trade size
```

SetPositionSize - Set trade size

Syntax:
SetPositionSize(size, method)

Returns:
ARRAY

Function: This function allows control of trade (position) size in four different ways, depending on 'method' parameter.

- size (ARRAY) defines desired trade size
- method (ARRAY) defines how 'size' is interpreted
  - spsValue (=1) - dollar value of size
  - spsPercentOfEquity (=2) - size expressed as percent of portfolio-level equity (size must be from ..100 (for regular accounts) or .1000 for margin accounts)
  - spsShares (=4) - size expressed in shares/contracts (size must be > 0)
  - spsPercentOfPosition (=3) - size expressed as percent of currently open position (for scaling in and scaling out only)
  - spsNoChange (=0) - don't change previously set size for given bar

Examples:

```
// To liquidate 50% of position
SetPositionSize( 50, spsPercentOfPosition * ( Buy == sigScale-
Out ) );
```

Special value spsNoChange (=0) means don't change previously set size for given bar. This allows writing constructs like:

```
SetPositionSize( 100, spsShares ); // 100 shares by default
// for scale-out use 50% of current position size
SetPositionSize( 50,
   IIf(Buy==sigScaleOut, spsPercentOfPosition, spsNoChange));
```

SetTradeDelays - Control trade delays applied by the backtester

Syntax:

SetTradeDelays(buydelay, selldelay, shortdelay, coverdelay)

Returns:

NOTHING

Function: Sets trade delays applied by the backtester. This function allows you to override trade delays from the "Settings" page.

Example: SetTradeDelays(1, 1, 1, 1)

ValueWhen - Get value of the array when some condition was met

Syntax:
ValueWhen (EXPRESSION, ARRAY, n = 1)

Returns:
ARRAY

Function: Returns the value of the ARRAY when the EXPRESSION was true on the n -th most recent occurrence. Note: this function also allows 0 and negative values for n, which enables referencing the future

Example:

```
dd = ValueWhen( Cross( Close, MA(Close,5)),MACD(),1 );
printf("dd = " + NumToStr(dd));
```

Low-level Graphics

These functions control low-level graphics. To learn more about low-level graphic functions please read the tutorial, "Using low-level graphics" in the AmiBroker User's Guide. This introduction to low-level graphics is taken from that tutorial.

> Completely new low-level graphic AFL interface allows complete flexibility in creating any kind of user-defined display.
>
> The interface closely mimics Windows GDI API, with the same names for most functions for easier use for GDI-experienced programmers. The only differences are:
>
> 1. compared to Windows GDI all functions are prefixed with 'Gfx'
>
> 2. pen/brush/font creation/selection is simplified to make it easier to use and you don't need to care about deletion of GDI objects
>
> 3. three overlay modes are available so you can mix low-level graphics with regular Plot() statements
>
> (mode = 0 (default) - overlay low-level graphic on top of charts, mode = 1 - overlay charts on top of low-level graphic, mode =2 - draw only low-level graphic (no regular charts/grid/titles/etc))
>
> All functions use pixels as co-ordinates (when used on screen). For printouts and metafiles pixels are mapped to logical units to match the higher resolution of printers. Use Status("pxwidth") and Status("pxheight") to find pixel dimensions of the drawing surface.
>
> The available low-level gfx functions are described on the pages that follow.

GfxArc - Draw an arc

Syntax:

GfxArc(x1, y1, x2, y2, x3, y3, x4, y4)

Returns:

NOTHING

Function: Draws an elliptical arc. The arc drawn by using the function is a segment of the ellipse defined by the specified bounding rectangle.

The actual starting point of the arc is the point at which a ray drawn from the center of the bounding rectangle through the specified starting point intersects the ellipse. The actual ending point of the arc is the point at which a ray drawn from the center of the bounding rectangle through the specified ending point intersects the ellipse. The arc is drawn in a counterclockwise direction.

Parameters

- x1 - x-coordinate of the upper left corner of the bounding rectangle
- y1 - y-coordinate of the upper left corner of the bounding rectangle
- x2 - x-coordinate of the lower right corner of the bounding rectangle
- y2 - y-coordinate of the lower right corner of the bounding rectangle
- x3 - x-coordinate of the arc's starting point.
- y3 - y-coordinate of the arc's starting point.
- x4 - x-coordinate of the arc's ending point.
- y4 - y-coordinate of the arc's ending point.

Example:

```
GfxSelectPen( colorRed );
GfxArc(100,0,200,100,150,0,200,50);
```

GfxChord - Draw a chord

Syntax:
GfxChord(x1, y1, x2, y2, x3, y3, x4, y4)

Returns:
NOTHING

Function: Draws a chord (a closed figure bounded by the intersection of an ellipse and a line segment). The (x1, y1) and (x2, y2) parameters specify the upper-left and lower-right corners, respectively, of a rectangle bounding the ellipse that is part of the chord. The (x3, y3) and (x4, y4) parameters specify the endpoints of a line that intersects the ellipse. The chord is drawn by using the selected pen and filled by using the selected brush.

Parameters

- x1 - x-coordinate of the upper left corner of the bounding rectangle
- y1 - y-coordinate of the upper left corner of the bounding rectangle
- x2 - x-coordinate of the lower right corner of the bounding rectangle
- y2 - y-coordinate of the lower right corner of the bounding rectangle
- x3 - x-coordinate of the chord's starting point.
- y3 - y-coordinate of the chord's starting point.
- x4 - x-coordinate of the chord's ending point.
- y4 - y-coordinate of the chord's ending point.

Example:

```
GfxSelectPen( colorRed );
GfxSelectSolidBrush( colorBlue );
GfxChord(100,0,200,100,150,0,200,50);
```

GfxCircle - Draw a circle

Syntax:

GfxCircle(x, y, radius)

Returns:

NOTHING

Function: Draws a circle. The center of the circle is given by x and y parameters. The circle is drawn with the current pen, and its interior is filled with the current brush.

Parameters

- x - x-coordinate of the center of the circle
- y - y-coordinate of the the center of the circle
- radius - radius of the circle

This function is essentially the same as GfxEllipse(x - radius, y - radius, x + radius, y + radius);

Example:

```
GfxCircle( 100, 100, 50 );
```

GfxDrawText - Draw a text (clipped to rectangle)

Syntax:

GfxDrawText("text", left, top, right, bottom, format = 0)

Returns:

NOTHING

Function: Formats and draws text in the given rectangle. It formats text by expanding tabs into appropriate spaces, aligning text to the left, right, or center of the given rectangle, and breaking text into lines that fit within the given rectangle. The type of formatting is specified by format argument. When format is not specified the text is aligned to the top/left corner.

Parameters:

- "text" - string to be drawn
- left - x-coordinate of upper left corner of the clipping rectangle
- top - y-coordinate of upper left corner of the clipping rectangle
- right - x-coordinate of lower right corner of the clipping rectangle

- bottom - y-coordinate of lower right corner of the clipping rectangle
- format - specifies the method of formatting the text. It can be any combination of the following values (combine using the bitwise OR operator):
    - DT_BOTTOM = 8 - Specifies bottom-justified text. This value must be combined with DT_SINGLELINE.
    - DT_CENTER = 1 - Centers text horizontally.
    - DT_END_ELLIPSIS = 32768 or DT_PATH_ELLIPSIS = 16384 - Replaces part of the given string with ellipses, if necessary, so that the result fits in the specified rectangle. You can specify DT_END_ELLIPSIS to replace characters at the end of the string, or DT_PATH_ELLIPSIS to replace characters in the middle of the string. If the string contains backslash (\) characters, DT_PATH_ELLIPSIS preserves as much as possible of the text after the last backslash.
    - DT_EXPANDTABS = 64 - Expands tab characters. The default number of characters per tab is eight.
    - DT_LEFT = 0 - Aligns text flush-left.
    - DT_NOCLIP = 256 - Draws without clipping. DrawText is somewhat faster when DT_NOCLIP is used.
    - DT_NOPREFIX = 2048 - Turns off processing of prefix characters. Normally, DrawText interprets the ampersand (&) mnemonic-prefix character as a directive to underscore the character that follows, and the two-ampersand (&&) mnemonic-prefix characters as a directive to print a single ampersand. By specifying DT_NOPREFIX, this processing is turned off.
    - DT_RIGHT = 2 - Aligns text flush-right.
    - DT_SINGLELINE = 32 - Specifies single line only. Carriage returns and linefeeds do not break the line.
    - DT_TOP = 0 - Specifies top-justified text (single line only).
    - DT_VCENTER = 4 - Specifies vertically centered text (single line only).
    - DT_WORDBREAK = 16 - Specifies word-breaking. Lines are automatically broken between words if a word would extend past the edge of the rectangle specified by lpRect. A carriage return–linefeed sequence will also break the line.

Note: DT_ constants come from Windows API and are provided here for reference only. They are not defined in AmiBroker therefore you should use numerical values instead.

EXAMPLE

```
// formatted text output sample via low-level gfx functions

CellHeight = 20;
CellWidth = 100;
GfxSelectFont( "Tahoma", CellHeight/2 );

function PrintInCell( string, row, Col )
{
    GfxDrawText( string, Col * CellWidth, row * CellHeight,
        (Col + 1 ) * CellWidth, (row + 1 ) * CellHeight, 0 );
}

PrintInCell( "Open", 0, 0 );
PrintInCell( "High", 0, 1 );
PrintInCell( "Low", 0, 2 );
PrintInCell( "Close", 0, 3 );
PrintInCell( "Volume", 0, 4 );

GfxSelectPen( colorBlue );
for( i = 1; i < 10 && i < BarCount; i++ )
{
PrintInCell( StrFormat("%g", O[ i ] ), i, 0 );
PrintInCell( StrFormat("%g", H[ i ] ), i, 1 );
PrintInCell( StrFormat("%g", L[ i ] ), i, 2 );
PrintInCell( StrFormat("%g", C[ i ] ), i, 3 );
PrintInCell( StrFormat("%g", V[ i ] ), i, 4 );
GfxMoveTo( 0, i * CellHeight );
GfxLineTo( 5 * CellWidth, i * CellHeight );
}
GfxMoveTo( 0, i * CellHeight );
GfxLineTo( 5 * CellWidth, i * CellHeight );

for( Col = 1; Col < 6; Col++ )
{
GfxMoveTo( Col * CellWidth, 0);
GfxLineTo( Col * CellWidth, 10 * CellHeight );
}
```

GfxEllipse - Draw an ellipse

Syntax:
GfxEllipse(x1, y1, x2, y2)

Returns:
NOTHING

Function: Draws an ellipse. The center of the ellipse is the center of the bounding rectangle specified by x1, y1, x2, and y2. The ellipse is drawn with the current pen, and its interior is filled with the current brush.

Parameters

- x1 - x-coordinate of the upper left corner of the bounding rectangle
- y1 - y-coordinate of the upper left corner of the bounding rectangle
- x2 - x-coordinate of the lower right corner of the bounding rectangle
- y2 - y-coordinate of the lower right corner of the bounding rectangle

Example: GfxEllipse(10, 10, 200, 100);

GfxGradientRect - Draw a rectangle with gradient fill

Syntax:
GfxGradientRect(x1, y1, x2, y2, fromcolor, tocolor)

Returns:
NOTHING

Function: Draws a rectangle. The interior of the rectangle is filled using gradient color.

Parameters

- x1 - x-coordinate of the upper left corner of the rectangle
- y1 - y-coordinate of the upper left corner of the rectangle
- x2 - x-coordinate of the lower right corner of the rectangle
- y2 - y-coordinate of the lower right corner of the rectangle
- fromcolor - the 'upper' color of the gradient fill
- tocolor - the 'lower' color of the gradient fill

The rectangle extends up to, but does not include, the right and bottom coordinates. This means that the height of the rectangle is y2 - y1 and the width of the rectangle is x2 - x1. Both the width and the height of a rectangle must be greater than 2 and less than 32767.

Example: GfxGradientRect(10, 10, 100, 100, colorWhite, colorGrey50);

GfxLineTo - Draw a line to a specified point

Syntax:
GfxLineTo(x, y)

Returns:
NOTHING

Function: Draws a line from the current position up to, but not including, the point specified by x and y. The line is drawn with the selected pen. The current position is set to x,y.

Parameters

- x - Specifies the x-coordinate of the end point of the line.
- y - Specifies the y-coordinate of the end point of the line.

Example:

```
GfxMoveTo( 0, 0 );
GfxLineTo( 100, 100 );
```

GfxMoveTo - Move graphic cursor to new position

Syntax:
GfxMoveTo(x, y)

Returns:
NOTHING

Function: Moves the current position to the point specified by x and y.

Parameters

- x - Specifies the x-coordinate of the new position.
- y - Specifies the y-coordinate of the new position.

Example: GfxMoveTo(10, 20);

GfxPie - Draw a pie

Syntax:
GfxPie(x1, y1, x2, y2, x3, y3, x4, y4)

Returns:
NOTHING

Function: Draws a pie-shaped wedge by drawing an elliptical arc whose center and two endpoints are joined by lines. The center of the arc is the center of the bounding rectangle specified by x1, y1, x2, and y2. The starting and ending points of the arc are specified by x3, y3, x4, and y4.

The arc is drawn with the selected pen, moving in a counterclockwise direction. Two additional lines are drawn from each endpoint to the arc's center. The pie-shaped area is filled with the current brush. If x3 equals x4 and y3 equals y4, the result is an ellipse with a single line from the center of the ellipse to the point (x3, y3) or (x4, y4).

Parameters

- x1 - x-coordinate of the upper left corner of the bounding rectangle
- y1 - y-coordinate of the upper left corner of the bounding rectangle
- x2 - x-coordinate of the lower right corner of the bounding rectangle
- y2 - y-coordinate of the lower right corner of the bounding rectangle
- x3 - x-coordinate of the arc's starting point. This point does not have to lie exactly on the arc.
- y3 - y-coordinate of the arc's starting point. This point does not have to lie exactly on the arc.
- x4 - x-coordinate of the arc's ending point. This point does not have to lie exactly on the arc.
- y4 - y-coordinate of the arc's ending point. This point does not have to lie exactly on the arc.

Example:

```
GfxSelectPen( colorRed );
GfxSelectSolidBrush( colorBlue );
GfxPie(100,0,200,100,150,0,200,50);
```

GfxPolygon - Draw a polygon

Syntax:

GfxPolygon(x1, y1, x2, y2, ...)

Returns:

NOTHING

Function: Draws a polygon consisting of two or more points (vertices) connected by lines, using the current pen. The system closes the polygon automatically, if necessary, by drawing a line from the last vertex to the first.

This function takes a variable number of arguments and accepts up to 12 points (24 arguments = 12 co-ordinate pairs). The number of arguments must be even as each pair represents (x,y) co-ordinates of the vertex.

The polygon is filled with the current brush and the outline is painted with the current pen.

Parameters:

- x1 - x co-ordinate of first point
- y1 - y co-ordinate of first point
- x2 - x co-ordinate of second point
- y2 - y co-ordinate of second point
- ...
- x12 - x co-ordinate of 12th point
- y12 - y co-ordinate of 12th point

Example:

```
GfxSelectPen( colorGreen, 2 );
GfxSelectSolidBrush( colorYellow );
GfxPolygon(250,200,200,200,250,0,200,50);
```

GfxPolyline - Draw a polyline

Syntax:

GfxPolyline(x1, y1, x2, y2, ...)

Returns:

NOTHING

Function: Draws a set of line segments connecting the points specified by arguments (x1,y1), (x2,y2), ... The lines are drawn from the first point through subsequent points using the current pen. Unlike the GfxLineTo function, the GfxPolyline function neither uses nor updates the current position.

This function takes a variable number of arguments and accepts up to 12 points (24 arguments = 12 co-ordinate pairs). The number of arguments must be even as each pair represents (x,y) co-ordinates of the point.

Parameters:

- x1 - x co-ordinate of first point
- y1 - y co-ordinate of first point
- x2 - x co-ordinate of second point
- y2 - y co-ordinate of second point
- ...
- x12 - x co-ordinate of 12th point
- y12 - y co-ordinate of 12th point

Example:

```
GfxSelectPen( colorGreen, 2 );
GfxPolyline(250,200,200,200,250,0,200,50);
```

GfxRectangle - Draw a rectangle

Syntax:
GfxRectangle(x1, y1, x2, y2)

Returns:
NOTHING

Function: Draws a rectangle using the current pen. The interior of the rectangle is filled using the current brush.

Parameters

- x1 - x-coordinate of the upper left corner of the rectangle
- y1 - y-coordinate of the upper left corner of the rectangle
- x2 - x-coordinate of the lower right corner of the rectangle
- y2 - y-coordinate of the lower right corner of the rectangle

The rectangle extends up to, but does not include, the right and bottom coordinates. This means that the height of the rectangle is y2 - y1 and the width of the rectangle is x2 - x1. Both the width and the height of a rectangle must be greater than 2 and less than 32767.

Example: GfxRectangle(10, 10, 30, 30)

GfxRoundRect - Draw a rectangle with rounded corners

Syntax:
GfxRoundRect(x1, y1, x2, y2, x3, y3)

Returns:
NOTHING

Function: Draws a rectangle with rounded corners using the current pen. The interior of the rectangle is filled using the current brush.

Parameters

- x1 - x-coordinate of the upper left corner of the rectangle
- y1 - y-coordinate of the upper left corner of the rectangle
- x2 - x-coordinate of the lower right corner of the rectangle
- y2 - y-coordinate of the lower right corner of the rectangle
- x3 - the width of the ellipse used to draw the rounded corners
- y3 - the height of the ellipse used to draw the rounded corners

The rectangle extends up to, but does not include, the right and bottom coordinates. This means that the height of the rectangle is y2 - y1 and the width of the rectangle is x2 - x1. Both the width and the height of a rectangle must be greater than 2 and less than 32767.

Example: GfxRoundRect(10, 10, 100, 100, 15, 15);

GfxSelectFont - Create / select graphic font

Syntax:

GfxSelectFont("facename", pointsize, weight = fontNormal, italic = False, underline = False, orientation = 0)

Returns:

NOTHING

Function: Initializes a font with the specified characteristics. Then selects that font as current for subsequent drawing operations.

Parameters:

- "facename" - specifies the typeface name of the font
- pointsize - specifies point size of the font (fractional numbers are allowed), for example 11.5 gives 11.5 point font.
- weight - specifies the font weight (in inked pixels per 1000). Typical values are: 300 - light, 400 - normal, 700 - bold, 800 - ultrabold
- italic - specifies whether the font is italic
- underline - specifies whether the font is underlined
- orientation - specifies the angle (in 0.1-degree units) between the baseline of a character and the x-axis. The angle is measured counterclockwise from the x-axis.

Example:

```
GfxSelectFont("Tahoma", 20, 700 );
GfxSetBkMode(1);
GfxSetTextColor(colorBrown);
GfxTextOut("Testing graphic capabilites", 20, 28 );
```

GfxSelectPen - Create / select graphic pen

Syntax:
GfxSelectPen(color, width = 1, penstyle = penSolid)

Returns:
NOTHING

Function: GfxSelectPen initializes (if not already initialized) a pen with the specified style, width, and color. Then selects the pen as current for subsequent drawing operations.

Parameters:

- color - specifies color for the pen
- penstyle - specifies the style for the pen. Solid=0, Dash=1, Dot=2, Null=5 (invisible pen). Lines of width > 1 can only use solid style. For a list of other possible values, see the Microsoft docs on CreatePen Windows API function.
- width - specifies the width of the pen. If this value is 0, the width in device units is always 1 pixel, regardless of the mapping mode (this is useful for drawing hairline lines on printer outputs).

More info on pens in Windows GDI: *http://msdn2.microsoft.com/en-us/library/ms535467*

Example:

```
GfxSelectPen( colorGreen, 2 );
GfxSelectSolidBrush( colorYellow );
GfxPolygon(250,200,200,200,250,0,200,50);
```

GfxSelectSolidBrush - Create / select graphic brush

Syntax:
GfxSelectSolidBrush(color)

Returns:
NOTHING

Function: GfxSelectSolidBrush initializes a brush with a specified solid color. Then selects the brush as current for subsequent drawing operations.

Parameters:

- color - specifies color for the brush

Example:

```
GfxSelectPen( colorGreen, 2 );
GfxSelectSolidBrush( colorYellow );
GfxPolygon(250,200,200,200,250,0,200,50);
```

GfxSetBkColor - Set graphic background color

Syntax:
GfxSetBkColor(color)

Returns:
NOTHING

Function: Sets the current background color to the specified color. If the background mode is OPAQUE (see GfxSetBkMode), the system uses the background color to fill the gaps in styled lines, the gaps between hatched lines in brushes, and the background in character cells.

Parameters:

- color - specifies the new background color

Example: GfxSetBkColor(ColorRGB(10, 20, 30));

GfxSetBkMode - Set graphic background mode

Syntax:
GfxSetBkMode(bkmode)

Returns:
NOTHING

Function: Sets the background mode. The background mode defines whether the system removes existing background colors on the drawing surface before drawing text, hatched brushes, or any pen style that is not a solid line.

Parameters:

- bkmode - Specifies the mode to be set. This parameter can be either of the following values:

  OPAQUE = 2 - Background is filled with the current background color before the text, hatched brush, or pen is drawn. This is the default background mode.

  TRANSPARENT = 1 - Background is not changed before drawing

Example: GfxSetBkMode(1); // set transparent mode

GfxSetOverlayMode - Set low-level graphic overlay mode

Syntax:
GfxSetOverlayMode(mode = 0)

Returns:
NOTHING

Function: Sets overlay mode for low-level graphics.

Parameters:

- mode - desired overlay mode. Possible values are:

  0 - (default) low-level graphic is overlaid on top of charts

  1 - charts are overlaid on top of low-level graphics

  2 - only low-level graphics are displayed (no charts, no grids, etc)

Example: GfxSetOverlayMode(2); // don't display charts nor grids

GfxSetPixel - Set pixel at specified position to specified color

Syntax:
GfxSetPixel(x, y, color)

Returns:
NOTHING

Function: Sets the pixel at the specified x, y coordinates to the specified color. The point must be in the visible part drawing surface (otherwise it won't be painted). Parameters

- x - Specifies the x-coordinate of the point.
- y - Specifies the y-coordinate of the point.
- color - specifies the color to be used to paint the point

Example: GfxSetPixel(20, 20);

GfxSetTextAlign - Set text alignment

Syntax:

GfxSetTextAlign(align)

Returns:

NOTHING

Function: Sets the text-alignment flags.

The GfxTextOut function uses these flags when positioning a string of text on a display or device. The flags specify the relationship between a specific point and a rectangle that bounds the text. The coordinates of this point are passed as parameters to the TextOut member function. The rectangle that bounds the text is formed by the adjacent character cells in the text string.

Parameters:

- align - combination (binary-OR) of one or more the following flags:
  - X-direction alignment:
    TA_CENTER = 6 - Aligns the point with the horizontal center of the bounding rectangle.
    TA_LEFT = 0 - Aligns the point with the left side of the bounding rectangle. This is the default setting.
    TA_RIGHT = 2 - Aligns the point with the right side of the bounding rectangle.
  - Y-direction alignment
    TA_BASELINE = 24 - Aligns the point with the base line of the chosen font.
    TA_BOTTOM = 8 - Aligns the point with the bottom of the bounding rectangle.
    TA_TOP = 0 - Aligns the point with the top of the bounding rectangle. This is the default setting.
  - flags that determine whether the current position is updated when text is written:
    TA_NOUPDATECP = 0 - Does not update the current position after each call to a text-output function. This is the default setting.
    TA_UPDATECP = 1 - Updates the current x-position after each call to a text-output function. The new position is at the right side of the bounding rectangle for the text. When

this flag is set, the coordinates specified in calls to the Gfx-TextOut member function are ignored

Note: TA_ constants come from Windows API, they are given for reference only. They are not predefined in AmiBroker, so you need to use numerical values.

Example: GfxSetTextAlign(6 | 24); // center and baseline alignment

GfxSetTextColor - Set graphic text color

Syntax:
GfxSetTextColor(color)

Returns:
NOTHING

Function: Sets the text color to the specified color. AmiBroker will use this text color when writing text to this window using GfxTextOut or GfxDrawText.

The background color for a character is specified by the GfxSetBkColor and GfxSetBkMode member functions.

Parameters:

- color - Specifies the color of the text

Example:

```
GfxSetTextColor( colorRed );
GfxSetTextColor( ColorRGB( 100, 200, 100 ) );
```

GfxTextOut - Writes text at the specified location

Syntax:

GfxTextOut("text", x, y)

Returns:

NOTHING

Function: Writes a character string at the specified location using the currently selected font.

Parameters:

- "text" - Specifies the character string to be drawn
- x - Specifies the x-coordinate of the starting point of the text
- y - Specifies the y-coordinate of the starting point of the text

Character origins are at the upper-left corner of the character cell. By default, the current position is not used or updated by the function.

The font used can be set using GfxSelectFont() function. Text color can be set using GfxSetTextColor() function.

If a formula needs to update the current position when it calls GfxTextOut, the formula can call the GfxSetTextAlign function with flags set to 1 (TA_UPDATECP Windows flag). When this flag is set, GfxTextOut function ignores the x and y parameters on subsequent calls to GfxTextOut, using the current position instead.

The output of this function is not clipped. If you want clip text to user-defined rectangle, use GfxDrawText() function instead.

Example:

```
GfxSelectFont("Times New Roman", 16, 700, True );
GfxTextOut("Percent of shares held by:", 10 , 10 );
```

Miscellaneous Functions

#include - Preprocessor include command

Syntax:
 #include

Returns:
 NOTHING

Function: Includes external AFL files into your formula.

Notes:

- include statement needs a single backslashes in the path (this is different than normal AFL string parsing).
- Using #include command may slow down formula execution even considering the fact that AmiBroker tries to include only once and cache pre-processed text.
- No error message is given if #include fails and this code is experimental.
- Nesting #include commands is supported.
- By default, files #included are cached by AmiBroker. To turn off caching use #pragma nocache before any #include statements.
- include accepts alternative way of specifying file names to include:

  #include <filename.afl>

  (note < > braces instead of " ") if you specify the file name this way AmiBroker will look for the file in "standard include path" that is definable using new prefs setting in Tools > Preferences > AFL. It is much shorter to write includes and you can move include folder now without changing all AFL codes using #includes.

For example, if you have set the standard include path to "C:\AFL\MyIncludes" and write in your formula:

#include <common.afl>

then AmiBroker will look for the C:\AFL\MyIncludes\common.afl file.

- include reports file(s) not found in regular error message box.

Example: #include "C:\Program Files\AmiBroker\AFL\common.afl"

#include_once - Preprocessor include (once) command

Syntax:
 #include "formula file path"

Returns:
 NOTHING

Function: Includes external AFL files into your formula. Similar to #include but #include_once performs inclusion only once per formula. So if a single formula has multiple #include_once commands for the same file (for example because of drag-and-drop overlay) it prevents syntax errors that could occur due to repeated definitions of functions in included file. More information can be found in #include command docs.

Example: #include_once "myfile.afl"

#pragma - Sets AFL pre-processor option

Syntax:
 #pragma optionname

Returns:
 NOTHING

Function: Sets various AFL pre-processor options. Pre-processor is a part of AFL engine that processes formulas before they are executed. Currently the only task of the pre-processor is to include external files via #include command.

Currently the only option available via #pragma is nocache.

#pragma nocache causes #included files to not be cached, so they are re-read with every execution.

#pragma nocache must be placed before any #include commands.

Note: between '#pragma' and 'nocache' there must be exactly one single space.

Disabling caching may slow down execution of the formula, especially in indicators.

Example:

```
#pragma nocache
#include "myfile.afl"
```

ClipboardGet - Retrieves current contents of Windows clipboard

Syntax:
ClipboardGet()

Returns:
STRING

Function: Retrieves the current contents of Windows clipboard

Example: "Contents of the Windows clipboard" + ClipboardGet();

ClipboardSet - Copies the text to the Windows clipboard

Syntax:
ClipboardSet("Text");

Returns:
NUMBER

Function: Copies the "text" to the Windows clipboard.

Returns True (1) on success and 0 on failure

Example:

```
// this can be used to put dynamically-constructed texts into
// clipboard
ClipboardSet( "The price of " + FullName() + " is " + Close );
```

ColorHSB - Specify color using Hue-Saturation-Brightness

Syntax:
ColorHSB(hue, saturation, brightness)

Returns:
NUMBER

Function: The function allows specification of color out of 16 million color (24 bit) palette using Hue, Saturation and Brightness parameters.

The return value is a number that can be used in Plot, PlotOHLC, PlotForeign, AddColumn, AddTextColumn functions to specify chart or column color.

Parameters:

- hue - represents gradation of color within the optical spectrum (as in rainbow)
- saturation represents "vibrancy" of the color
- brightness represents brightness.

Each parameter ranges from 0 to 255, where 0 represents 0% saturation/brightness or 0 degree hue in HSV color wheel, and 255 represents 100% saturation/brightness or 360 degrees hue in HSV color wheel.

When you modify hue from 0 to 255 you will see consecutive rainbow colors starting from red, through yellow and green to blue and violet.

For more information about HSB color space please read: *http://en.wikipedia.org/wiki/HSB_color_space*

Examples:

```
// 3-d multicolor multiple moving average cloud chart
side = 1;
increment = Param("Increment",2, 1, 10, 1 );
for( i = 10; i < 80; i = i + increment )
{
     up = MA( C, i );
     down = MA( C, i + increment );

   if( ParamToggle("3D effect?", "No|Yes" ) )
     side = IIf(up<=down AND Ref( up<=down, 1 ), 1, 0.6 );

   PlotOHLC( up,up,down,down, "MA"+i, ColorHSB( 3*(i - 10),
   Param("Saturation", 128, 0, 255 ),
     side * Param("Brightness", 255, 0, 255 ) ), styleCloud |
styleNoLabel );
}


//Color-parade exploration
Filter=1;
for( i = 0; i < 256; i = i + 16 )
  AddColumn( C, "C", 1.2, colorDefault,
    ColorHSB( ( BarIndex() + i ) % 256, 255-i, 255 ) );
```

ColorRGB - specify color using Red-Green-Blue components

Syntax:
ColorRGB(red, green, blue)

Returns:
NUMBER

Function: The function specifies color out of 16 million color (24 bit) palette using Red, Green, Blue components.

The return value is a number that can be used in Plot, PlotOHLC, PlotForeign, AddColumn, AddTextColumn functions to specify chart or column color.

Parameters:

red, green, blue - represent color component values in range 0..255 each

For more information about RGB color model please read: *http://en.wikipedia.org/wiki/RGB_color_model*

Example:

```
Plot( MA(C,10), "Light Red", ColorRGB( 255, 128, 128 ) );
Plot( MA(C,20), "Light Green", ColorRGB( 128, 255, 128 ) );
Plot( MA(C,30), "Light Blue", ColorRGB( 128, 128, 255 ) );
```

CreateObject - create COM object

Syntax:
CreateObject()

Returns:
OBJECT

Function: Creates the instance of "Server.Class" COM object. The return value should be assigned to a variable that is used latter for calling the methods of the object.

Note: this function creates the instance of the object every time the formula is executed (the object is released automatically at the end of the formula - no explicit freeing is necessary)

Example:

```
myobj = CreateObject("MyOwnActiveX.Class1");
myobj.Method( 1, 2, Close ); // call the method of myobj COM
object
```

CreateStaticObject - create static COM object

Syntax:
CreateStaticObject()

Returns:
OBJECT

Function: Creates the single static instance (one per AmiBroker session) of "Server.Class" COM object. The return value should be assigned to a variable that is used later for calling the methods of the object. This function is useful for "heavyweight" COM object like QuotesPlus ActiveX for example.

Note: this function creates the instance of the object only once when the formula is executed for the first time. Then the object is cached internally for all consecutive calls. It is also shared if multiple formulas use the same object using CreateStaticObject call. The object is automatically released when AmiBroker is closed.

Example:

```
myobj = CreateStaticObject("MyOwnActiveX.Class1");
myobj.Method( 1, 2, Close ); // call the method of myobj COM
object
```

EnableScript - Enable scripting engine

Syntax:
EnableScript("enginename")

Returns:
NOTHING

Function: Enables AFL scripting host. enginename specifies which scripting language will be used. Allowable values: "jscript", "vbscript".

Example:

```
EnableScript( "jscript" );
EnableScript("vbscript");
```

EnableTextOutput - Enables/disables text output in the Chart Commentary window

Syntax:
EnableTextOutput(enable)

Returns:
NOTHING

Function: Enable or disable text output in the guru chart commentary window

Example:

```
EnableTextOutput(False);
variable = "text"; // this won't be written to commentary win-
dow
EnableTextOutput(True);
```

GetExtraData - Get extra data from external data source

Syntax:

GetExtraData()

Returns:

NUMBER

ARRAY

STRING

Function: Retrieves data-source specific data.

Currently only Quotes Plus and TC2000 plug-isn support this function.

The list of fields available via QP2 plug-in:

- "AnnDividend"
- "Shares"
- "SharesFloat"
- "IssueType" (string)
- "SharesOut"
- "SharesShort"
- "TTMsales"
- "Beta"
- "TTMEps"
- "HiPERange"
- "LoPERange"
- "PEG"
- "InstHolds"
- "LTDebtToEq"
- "CashFlowPerShare"
- "ROE"
- "TTMSales"
- "Yr1EPSGrowth"

- "Yr5EPSGrowth"
- "Yr1ProjEPSGrowth"
- "Yr2ProjEPSGrowth"
- "Yr3to5ProjEPSGrowth"
- "BookValuePerShare"
- "Briefing" (string)
- "QRS" (array)
- "HasOptions"
- "EPSRank" (array)
- "Sales" (array)
- "EPS" (array)
- "LastMainDate" - (number) date of last update of given symbol in YYYYMMDD format
- "Exchange" - (string) - exchange code
- "ExchangeSub" - (string) exchange sub-code
- "Flags" - (string)
- "MarginFlag" - (string)
- "CUSIP" - (string)
- "SIC" - (string)
- "IssueStatus" - (string) - with default settings all symbols should have issue status = 0 other possible values: 0 = actively trading; 1, P = trading on a when issued basis, 5, 6, 7, A, B, C, D, E, M = not trading 4, N = new symbol, G, K, X, R, Z = changes to symbol, cusip, name, etc.

The list of fields available via TC2000 plug-in:

- "BOP" - balance of power indicator
- "MoneyStream" - money stream indicator

Example:

```
GetExtraData("briefing"); /* gives briefing text (STRING) */
graph0 = GetExtraData("QRS");
/*gives Quotes Plus relative strength (ARRAY) */
```

GetPerformanceCounter - Retrieves the current value of the high-resolution performance counter

Syntax:
GetPerformanceCounter(bReset = False)

Returns:
NUMBER

Function: GetPerformanceCounter retrieves the current value of the high-resolution performance counter. Returned value is in milliseconds. Resolution is up to 0.001 ms (1 microsecond). The value of high-resolution counter represents number of milliseconds from either system start (boot) or from the last counter reset. To reset the counter you need to call GetPerformanceCounter function with bReset parameter set to True.

Note that resetting counters inside one formula does not affect counters in other formulas. Since returned values are very large (time in milliseconds since system start is usually quite large), for precise measurements of a single function or small function block execution times it is strongly recommended to reset counter at the beginning of the block so floating point resolution (7 digits) does not affect the precision of measurement.

GetPerformanceCounter function can also be used in trading system automation to measure time in milliseconds between various events . Subtract values returned by GetPerformanceCounter() during two different events.

Caveat: this function relies on Windows API QueryPerformanceCounter function and CPU RTDSC instruction and it may yield inaccurate results if you have a multiple-core processor and AMD's "Cool and Quiet" enabled in BIOS or other CPU clock stepping technologies enabled. If this applies to you, you may check Microsoft hotfix to this problem at: *http://support.microsoft.com/?id=896256*

Examples:

```
// EXAMPLE 1
// The code shows that 1000 iterations of sin() calculation
// takes about 1.7 milliseconds.
// Note that call to the GetPerformanceCounter()
// has overhead of about 0.015 ms (15 microseconds)
GetPerformanceCounter(True); // reset counter to zero
for( i = 0; i < 1000; i++ )
{
   k = sin( i );
}
elapsed=GetPerformanceCounter();
"Time [ms] = "+elapsed;


// EXAMPLE 2
// GetPerformanceCounter function
// may also be used to report time since system start.
elapsed=GetPerformanceCounter();
StrFormat("Time since system start %.0f days, %.0f hours,
    %.0f minutes, %.0f seconds, %.0f milliseconds ",
    floor(elapsed/(24*60*60*1000)),
    floor( elapsed/(60*60*1000) ) % 24,
    floor( elapsed/(60*1000) ) % 60,
    floor( elapsed/1000 ) % 60,
    elapsed % 1000 );
```

GetRTData - Retrieves the real-time data fields

Syntax:
GetRTData("fieldname")

Returns:
NUMBER

Function: Retrieves the last (the most recent) value of the following fields reported by streaming real-time data source:

- "Ask" - current best ask price
- "AskSize " - current ask size
- "Bid" - current best bid price
- "BidSize " - current bid size
- "52WeekHigh" - 52 week high value
- "52WeekHighDate" - 52 week high date (in datenum format)
- "52WeekLow" - 52 week low value
- "52WeekLowDate" - 52 week low date (in datenum format)
- "Change" - change since yesterdays close
- "Dividend" - last dividend value
- "DivYield" - dividend yield
- "EPS" - earnings per share
- "High" - current day's high price
- "Low" - current day's low price
- "Open" - current day's open price
- "Last" - last trade price
- "OpenInt" - current open interest
- "Prev" - previous day close
- "TotalVolume" - total today's volume
- "TradeVolume" - last trade volume
- "ChangeDate" - datenum (YYYMMDD) of last data change
- "ChangeTime" - timenum (HHMMSS) of last data change
- "UpdateDate" - datenum (YYYMMDD) of last data update
- "UpdateTime" - timenum (HHMMSS) of last data update
- "Shares" - total number of shares

Notes:

1. This function is available only in the Professional edition. Calling it using the Standard edition will give you NULL values for all fields.
2. Works only if data source uses real-time data source (plugin).
3. Availability of data depends on underlying data source - check the real-time quote window to see if the given field is available.
4. Function result represents the current value at the time of the call or formula execution. They will be refreshed depending on chart or commentary refresh interval (which can be set in preferences). Built-in real-time quote window is refreshed much more often (at least 10 times per second).

Example:

```
"Bid = "+GetRTData("Bid");
"Ask = "+GetRTData("Ask");
"Last = "+GetRTData("Last");
"Vol = "+GetRTData("TradeVolume");

"EPS = "+GetRTData("EPS");
"52week high = "+GetRTData("52weekhigh");
```

GetRTDataForeign - Retrieves the real-time data fields (for specified symbol)

Syntax:
GetRTDataForeign("fieldname" , "symbol")

Returns:
NUMBER

Function: This function is similar to GetRTData but allows specification of symbol other than currently selected. And it is much faster than SetForeign / GetRTData combo.

The function retrieves the last (the most recent) value of the following fields reported by streaming real-time data source for the specified symbol:

- "Ask" - current best ask price
- "AskSize " - current ask size
- "Bid" - current best bid price
- "BidSize " - current bid size
- "52WeekHigh" - 52 week high value
- "52WeekHighDate" - 52 week high date (in datenum format)
- "52WeekLow" - 52 week low value
- "52WeekLowDate" - 52 week low date (in datenum format)
- "Change" - change since yesterdays close
- "Dividend" - last dividend value
- "DivYield" - dividend yield
- "EPS" - earnings per share
- "High" - current day's high price
- "Low" - current day's low price
- "Open" - current day's open price
- "Last" - last trade price
- "OpenInt" - current open interest
- "Prev" - previous day close
- "TotalVolume" - total today's volume
- "TradeVolume" - last trade volume
- "ChangeDate" - datenum (YYYMMDD) of last data change

- "ChangeTime" - timenum (HHMMSS) of last data change
- "UpdateDate" - datenum (YYYMMDD) of last data update
- "UpdateTime" - timenum (HHMMSS) of last data update
- "Shares" - total number of shares

Notes:

1. This function is available only in the Professional edition. Calling it using Standard edition will give you NULL values for all fields.
2. Works only if data source uses real-time data source (plugin).
3. Availability of data depends on the underlying data source - check the real-time quote window to see if the given field is available .
4. Function result represents the current value at the time of the call or formula execution. And they will be refreshed depending on chart or commentary refresh interval (settable in preferences). Built-in real-time quote window is refreshed much more often (at least 10 times per second)

Example:

```
"Bid = "+GetRTDataForeign("Bid");
"Ask = "+GetRTData("Ask");
"Last = "+GetRTData("Last");
"Vol = "+GetRTData("TradeVolume");
"EPS = "+GetRTDataForeign("EPS", "AAPL");
"52week high = "+GetRTDataForeign("52weekhigh", "MSFT");
```

GetScriptObject - Get access to script COM object

Syntax:

GetScriptObject( )

Returns:

OBJECT

Function: Retrieves AFL host's script object. This allows calling of functions defined in JScript/VBScript directly from AFL.

Example:

```
EnableScript("jscript")
<%
function MyAdd(x, y)
{
return x+y;
}
%>
script = GetScriptObject();
// call the function defined in JScript
WriteVal( script.MyAdd( 7, 9 ) );
```

IsEmpty - Empty value check

Syntax:

IsEmpty(ARRAY)

Returns:

ARRAY

Function: Returns 1 (or 'true') when given point in array is {empty}

Note: {empty} value is used internally by AFL to mark bars when the value is not available - for example for the first 20 bars the value of 20-day simple moving average is not available ({empty})

IsNull is a synonym for IsEmpty. It is preferable to use IsNull in new formulas, because of naming consistency with Null constant.

Example:

```
movagv = MA( Close, 30 );
WriteIF( IsEmpty( movavg ), "Moving average not available yet",
    WriteVal( movavg ) );
```

IsFinite - Check if value is finite

Syntax:
IsFinite(x)

Returns:
NUMBER
ARRAY

Function: Returns 1 (TRUE) if its argument x is finite, that is, if –INF < x < +INF. It returns 0 (FALSE) if the argument is infinite or a NaN.

x can be a number or an array

Example: IsFinite(1/0);

IsNan - Checks for NaN (not a number)

Syntax:
IsNan(x)

Returns:
NUMBER
ARRAY

Function: Returns {empty} if the argument x is a NaN; if the argument is a number, it returns 0 (FALSE). A NaN is generated when the result of a floating-point operation cannot be represented in Institute of Electrical and Electronics Engineers (IEEE) format.

Example: IsNan(0/0);

IsNull - Check for Null (empty) value

Syntax:
IsNull(x)

Returns:
NUMBER
ARRAY

Function: This function is a synonym of IsEmpty(). Gives True if value is equal to Null (empty) value.

Example:

```
MAvg = MA( Close, 30 );
for (i=25; i<=35; i++)
{
    //printf(NumToStr(MAvg[i]));
    printf(WriteIf( IsNull( MAvg[i] ),
        "Moving average NOT avail able yet",
        WriteVal( MAvg[i]) ) + "\n");
}
```

IsTrue - True value (non-empty and non-zero) check

Syntax:
IsTrue(ARRAY)

Returns:
ARRAY

Function: Returns 1 (TRUE) when the given point is not {empty} and not zero.

Example:

```
dd = IsTrue( 4 > 2);
printf ( NumToStr(dd) );
```

NoteGet - Retrieves the text of the note

Syntax:
NoteGet("Symbol")

Returns:
STRING

Function: Retrieves note linked to "symbol". If symbol is "" (empty string) then current symbol is used.

Example: "You have entered the following text in the notepad" + NoteGet("");

NoteSet - sets text of the note

Syntax:
NoteSet("Symbol", "Text..");

Returns:
NUMBER

Function: Sets text of the note linked to "symbol".

If symbol is "" (empty string) then current symbol is used.

If you overwrite note from AFL level that is opened at the same time in Notepad editor, the editor will ask you (when you switch the focus to it) if it should reload new text or be allowed to save your manually entered text.

Returns True (1) on success, 0 on failure.

Example: NoteSet("AMD", "Jun 15, 2004: AMD will deliver its first multi-core processors next year");

NZ - Null (Null/Nan/Infinity) to zero

Syntax:
Nz(x, valueifnull = 0)

Returns:
NUMBER
ARRAY

Function: Converts Null/Nan/Infinity values to zero (or user defined value)

x can be a number or an array.

You can use the Nz function to return zero, or another specified value, when argument x is Null or Nan or Infinite.

For example, you can use this function to convert a Null (empty) value to another value and prevent it from propagating through an expression. If the optional valueifnull argument is included, then the Nz function will return the value specified by that argument if the x argument is Null (or Nan or Infinity).

Example: You can use the Nz function as an alternative to the IIf function.

Instead of:

```
varTemp = IIf( IsFinite( (H-L)/(C-L) ), (H-L)/(C-L), 0 );
```

You can write:

```
varTemp = Nz( (H-L)/(C-L) );
```

PopupWindow - display pop-up window

Syntax:

PopupWindow(bodytext, captiontext, timeout = 5, left = -1, top = -1);

Returns:

NOTHING

Function: The function creates and displays pop-up window with specified bodytext, captiontext.

Parameters:

- bodytext - the string containing the text of the window body
- caption - the string containing the text of the window caption
- timeout - auto-close time in seconds (default 5 seconds)
- left - top-left corner X co-ordinate (default = -1 -means auto-center)
- top - top-left corner Y co-ordinate (default = -1 - means auto-center)

Example:

```
if( ParamTrigger("Display Popup Window", "Press here" ) )
{
    PopupWindow("Current time is: " + Now(),"Alert", 2,
       640*mtRandom(), 480*mtRandom());
}
```

Prefs - Retrieve preferences settings

Syntax:
    Prefs(index)

Returns:
    NUMBER
    STRING

Function: Retrieves preferences setting. Allowed index values are:

- 0: FatLineChart;
- 1: MarkQuotations;
- 2: ChartVolumeType;
- 3: ShortTimeMA;
- 4: STMARange;
- 5: MidTimeMA;
- 6: MTMARange;
- 7: BollingerBands;
- 8: Pref.BBFactor;
- 9: ROC;
- 10: RSI;
- 11, 12, 13: MACD;
- 14: StochSlow;
- 15, 16, 17: Ultimate;
- 18: VolumeType;
- 19-22: /* reserved amiga only */
- 23: AutoArrange;
- 24: LogChartScale;
- 25: MaxChartQuot;
- 26: TRIX;
- 27: LongTimeMA;
- 28: LTMARange;
- 29: VolMARange;
- 30: RelativeStrengthBase (string);
- 31: LimitSave;
- 32: LimitSaveRange;
- 33: CCI;

- 34: CCIAvg;
- 35: Tooltips;
- 36: MFI;
- 37, 38: Chaikin;
- 39: DataPath (string)
- 40: DataTooltips;
- 41: LoadAllWhenSelect;
- 42: PartialLoad;
- 43: PartialLoadQty;
- 44, 45: TRIN;
- 46: STMAType;
- 47: MTMAType;
- 48: LTMAType;
- 49: ADX;
- 50, 51: ParabolicSAR;
- 52: EnableMainChartSAR;
- 53: DefaultPriceStyle;
- 54: StockTreeMode;
- 55: TickerListMode;

Example:

```
dd =  MACD( Prefs( 11 ), Prefs( 12 ) );
printf ( NumToStr(Prefs(11)) + NumToStr(Prefs(12))
       + NumToStr(dd) );
```

Say - Speaks provided text

Syntax
Say("text")

RETURNS:
NOTHING

Function: Say() function speaks user-specified text (you may need to install Microsoft Speech API. The voice settings are in Windows Control Panel)

Example:

```
// simple example
Say("Testing text to speech engine");

// helpful helper functions

function SayOnce( text )
{
   if( StaticVarGetText("lastsaidtext") != text )
   {
      Say( text );
      StaticVarSetText("lastsaidtext", text );
   }
}

function SayNotTooOften( text, Minperiod )
{
   elapsed=GetPerformanceCounter()/1000;
   Lastelapsed = Nz( StaticVarGet("lastsaytime") );

  if( elapsed - Lastelapsed > Minperiod )
   {
     StaticVarSet("lastsaytime", elapsed );

     Say( text );
   }
}

SayOnce("Testing "+Name() );
SayNotTooOften( "Say not more often than every 60 seconds",
       60 );
```

SetBarsRequired - Set number of previous and future bars needed for script/DLL to properly execute

Syntax:
SetBarsRequired(backwardref = -1, forwardref = -1)

Returns:
NOTHING

Function: Set the number of previous and future bars needed for script/DLL to properly execute. If your formula is pure AFL you don't need to use this function at all, as AmiBroker automatically calculates the number of bars required for all its built-in functions. But if you are using script or a DLL you may need to use this function to make sure that your indicators are properly calculated in QuickAFL mode. Specifying -1 means no change. For example if you are using the script that calculates 100 bar moving average you may need to call SetBarsRequired(100, 0); at the very beginning of your formula. Please note that in most cases it is not necessary (even if you are using script or DLL) because AmiBroker always provides at least 30 past data bars more than needed.

Example: SetBarsRequired(100000, 100000)
// require all past and all future bars

StaticVarGet - Gets the value of static variable

Syntax:
StaticVarGet("varname")

Returns:
NUMBER
STRING

Function: Gets the value of static variable.

Static variable - the variable has static duration (it is allocated when the program begins and deallocated when the program ends) and initializes it to Null unless another value is specified. Static variables allow sharing values between various formulas. Only NUMBER and STRING static variables are supported now (not ARRAYS).

StaticVarGetText - Gets the value of static variable as a string

Syntax:
StaticVarGetText("varname")

Returns:
STRING

Function: Gets the value of static variable as a string.

The only difference between StaticVarGet is that this function always returns a string. So if a given static variable does not exist it returns an empty string "" instead of Null. Numbers are also converted to string.

Static variable - the variable has static duration (it is allocated when the program begins and deallocated when the program ends) and initializes it to Null unless another value is specified. Static variables allow sharing values between various formulas. Only NUMBER and STRING static variables are supported now (not ARRAYS).

Example:

```
myvar = StaticVarGetText("MyVariable");

if( myvar  == "" )
{
  printf("Not Set");
}
else
{
  printf("Variable Set: " + myvar);
}
```

StaticVarRemove - remove static variable

Syntax:
StaticVarRemove("variablename")

Returns:
NOTHING

Function: This function removes static variable and releases associated memory.

StaticVarSet - sets the value of static variable

Syntax:
StaticVarSet("varname", value)

Returns:
NUMBER

Function: Sets the value of static variable. Returns 1 on success, 0 on failure.

Static variable - the variable has static duration (it is allocated when the program begins and deallocated when the program ends) and initializes it to Null unless another value is specified. Static variables allow sharing values between various formulas. Only NUMBER and STRING static variables are supported now (not ARRAYS).

StaticVarSetText - Sets the value of static string variable.

Syntax:
StaticVarSetText("varname", "value")

Returns:
NUMBER

Function: Sets the value of static string variable.
Returns 1 on success, 0 on failure.

Static variable - the variable has static duration (it is allocated when the program begins and deallocated when the program ends) and initializes it to Null unless another value is specified. Static variables allow sharing values between various formulas. Only NUMBER and STRING static variables are supported now (not ARRAYS).

Example:

```
dd =  StaticVarSetText( "varname","value" );
printf (  NumToStr(dd) );
```

Status - Get run-time AFL status information

Syntax:
    Status("statuscode")

Returns:
    ARRAY

Function: Returns run-time status of the analysis engine.
    Supported status codes:

- "stocknum" - gives you the ordinal number of currently analysed symbol
- "action" - gives information in what context given formula is run: 1 - Indicator, 2 - Commentary, 3 - Scan, 4 - Exploration, 5 - Backtest / Optimize
- "rangefromdate", "rangetodate" - return current auto-analysis From-To range as DateNums
- "rangefromtime", "rangetotime" - return current auto-analysis From-To range as DateNums
- "barinrange" - returns 1 when current bar is within current auto-analysis From-To range
- "barvisible" - (custom indicators only) returns 1 when current bar is visible in current view
- "firstbarinrange" and "lastbarinrange". They return 1 (or True) on the first/last bar of analysis range.
- "buydelay", "selldelay", "shortdelay", "coverdelay" - return delays set in the Settings window
- "firstbarintest" and "lastbarintest" - similar to "firstbarinrange" and "lastbarinrange" but they return the settings of last Backtest / Optimization and intermediate scans/ explorations do not affect them
- "firstvisiblebar", "lastvisiblebar", "firstvisiblebarindex", "lastvisiblebarindex" - return bar number or bar index of first/ last visible bar. Available in indicator mode only.
- "redrawaction" - returns 0 (zero) for regular refreshes, and 1 for refreshes triggered via RequestTimedRefresh().
- "pxwidth" - returns pixel width of chart window pane (indicators only, low-level gfx)

- "pxheight" - returns pixel height of chart window pane (indicators only, low-level gfx) (AmiBroker 4.94 or higher)
- "axisminy" - retrieves the minimum (bottom) value of Y axis (indicators only, low-level gfx)
- "axismaxy" - retrieves the maximum (top) value of Y axis (indicators only, low-level gfx)
- "pxchartleft" - returns x-coordinate of top-left corner of chart area
- "pxcharttop" - returns y-coordinate of top-left corner of chart area
- "pxchartright" - returns x-coordinate of bottom-right corner of chart area
- "pxchartbottom" - returns y-coordinate of bottom-right corner of chart area
- "pxchartwidth" - returns width chart area (right-left)
- "pxchartheight" - returns width chart area (bottom-top)

Examples:

```
// Example 1:
if( Status("redrawaction") ==1 )
{
_TRACE("nTIMED REFRESH"+Now());
}
RequestTimedRefresh(1);


// Example 2 (low-level graphic overlay + pixel co-ordinate
conversion):
_SECTION_BEGIN("GfxOverlaySampleNew");
function GetVisibleBarCount()
{
 lvb = Status("lastvisiblebar");
 fvb = Status("firstvisiblebar");
 return Min( Lvb - fvb, BarCount - fvb );
}

function GfxConvertBarToPixelX( bar )
{
 lvb = Status("lastvisiblebar");
 fvb = Status("firstvisiblebar");
 pxchartleft = Status("pxchartleft");
 pxchartwidth = Status("pxchartwidth");

 return pxchartleft + bar  * pxchartwidth / ( Lvb - fvb + 1 );
}
```

```
function GfxConvertValueToPixelY( Value )
{
 local Miny, Maxy, pxchartbottom, pxchartheight;

 Miny = Status("axisminy");
 Maxy = Status("axismaxy");

 pxchartbottom = Status("pxchartbottom");
 pxchartheight = Status("pxchartheight");

 return pxchartbottom - floor( 0.5 +
        ( Value - Miny ) * pxchartheight/ ( Maxy - Miny ) );
}

Plot(C, "Price", colorBlack, styleHistogram );

GfxSetOverlayMode(0);
GfxSelectSolidBrush( colorRed );
GfxSelectPen( colorRed );

AllVisibleBars = GetVisibleBarCount();
fvb = Status("firstvisiblebar");

for( i = 0; i < AllVisibleBars ; i++ )
{
   x = GfxConvertBarToPixelX( i );
   y = GfxConvertValueToPixelY( C[ i + fvb ] );

  GfxRectangle( x-1, y-1, x + 2, y+1 );
}

//SetChartBkGradientFill( ColorRGB(200,200,200),
       ColorRGB( 255,255,255) );
_SECTION_END();
```

Study - Reference hand-drawn study

Syntax:

Study(STUDYID, CHARTID = 1)

Returns:

ARRAY

Function: Generates an array equivalent to a trendline study drawn by the user - allows detecting trendline breakouts from AFL.

STUDYID is a two-character identifier of the study. Identifiers are: "UP" - uptrend, "DN" - downtrend, "SU" - support, "RE" - resistance, "ST" - stop loss, however you can use any identifiers (there are no limitations except that AmiBroker accepts only 2 letter codes).

CHARTID - identifies the chart pane where the study was drawn - you can find out what the chart ID is for a given chart by looking in Parameters dialog, Axes & Grid, Miscellaneous: Chart ID or using GetChartID() AFL function.

More information about this function is included in the Tutorial: Using Studies in AFL formulas

Example:

```
// this example plots filled area between
// support (SU) and resistance (RE) lines

Plot(C, "Price", colorBlack, styleCandle );
su = Study("SU", GetChartID() );
re = Study("RE", GetChartID() );
PlotOHLC( re,  re,  su, su, "", colorYellow,styleCloud );
```

VarGet - Gets the value of dynamic variable

Syntax:
VarGet("varname")

Returns:
ARRAY
NUMBER

Function: Gets the value of dynamic variable.

Returns the NUMBER or ARRAY depending on the type of underlying variable.

Dynamic variables are variables that are named dynamically, typically by creating a variable name from a static part and a variable part. The following example dynamically constructs the variable name from a variable prefix and a static suffix.

Example:

```
//  First run the example at VarSet
//
for( i = 1; i < 10; i++ )
{
Plot( VarGet( "C"+i ), "C"+i, colorRed );
}
```

VarGetText - gets the text value of dynamic variable

Syntax:
VarGetText("varname")

Returns:
STRING

Function: Gets the text (string) value of dynamic variable.

Similar to VarGet but always returns string values (if the underlying variable has different type it is converted to string) Allows, for example, appending text variable no matter if it is defined earlier or not as shown in the example below.

Dynamic variables are variables that are named dynamically, typically by creating a variable name from a static part and a variable part. The following example dynamically constructs the variable name from a variable prefix and a static suffix.

Example:

```
Title = VarGetText("Title") + "something";
// above will work correctly regardless of whenever
//  title was defined earlier or not
```

VarSet - sets the value of dynamic variable

Syntax:
VarSet("varname", value)

Returns:
NUMBER

Function: Sets the value of dynamic variable. Returns 1 on success, 0 on failure.

Dynamic variables are variables that are named dynamically, typically by creating a variable name from a static part and a variable part. The following example dynamically constructs the variable name from a variable prefix and a static suffix.

Example:

```
for( i = 1; i < 10; i++ )
{
VarSet( "C"+i, Ref( C, -i ) );
}
```

```
// creates variables C1, C2, C3, C4, ...., C10
// equal to Ref( C, -1 ), Ref( C, -2 ),   ...,
// Ref( C, -10 ) respectively
```

VarSetText - sets dynamic variable of string type

Syntax:
VarSetText("varname", "valuetext")

Returns:
STRING

Function: Sets the text (string) value of dynamic variable.

Similar to VarSet but allows assigning a string (text) instead of a number or an array.

Dynamic variables are variables that are named dynamically, typically by creating a variable name from a static part and a variable part.

Version - Get version info

Syntax:
Version(minrequired = 0)

Returns:
NUMBER

Function: Returns the AmiBroker version number as a float (3.90 for example). Additionally when you specify Version(4.0) AmiBroker will issue an error message when running the formula on AB earlier than 4.0 :)

Example: Version(3.90);

_TRACE - Print text to system debug viewer

Syntax:
_TRACE("string")

Returns:
NOTHING

Function: Write debug messages from AFL code to system debug viewer. (it calls internally OutputDebugString Win API function).

To view debug messages you have to run DebugView freeware program from *http://www.sysinternals.com/Utilities/DebugView.html*

Example:

```
_TRACE("This is a test");
_TRACE("This is selected value of close: " + Close );
_TRACE("This is first element of close array: " + Close[ 0 ] );
```

Chapter 9

Analysis

The Analysis pull-down menu gives access to the major tools for writing, testing, and validating trading systems; and for monitoring them for trading signals.

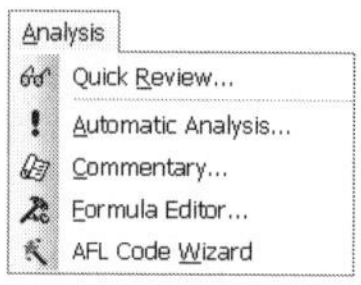

QUICK REVIEW

The Quick Review gives quick access to lists of daily price quotations and period-over-period price changes.

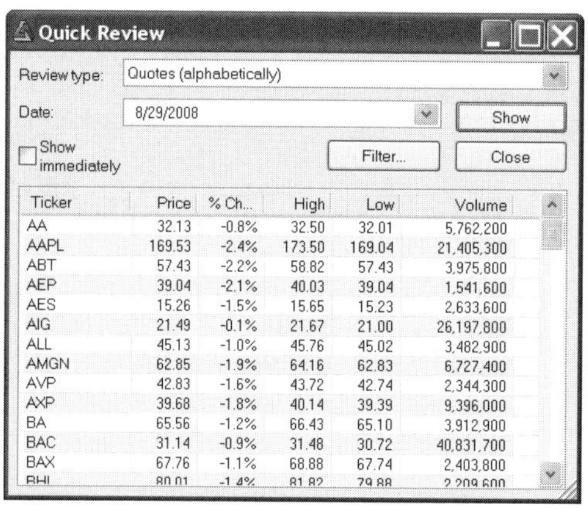

The **Date** menu opens a calendar tool that lets you select the report date - the date you want as the base date of the report.

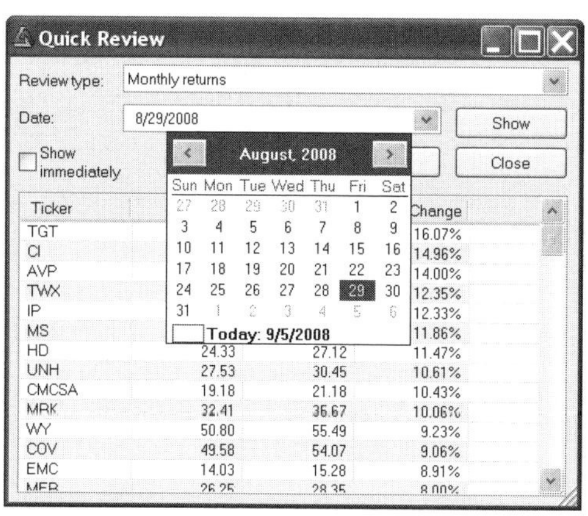

Clicking the **Filter** button opens the Filter settings dialog. This allows you to specify the group of symbols that will be processed. There are two tabs, **Include** and **Exclude**, and they have the same controls. Using the pull-down menus for any of the categories, you can include whatever you want the report to show, then exclude whatever portion of those included that you do not want. This example shows including the watchlist containing the members of the S&P 100 index.

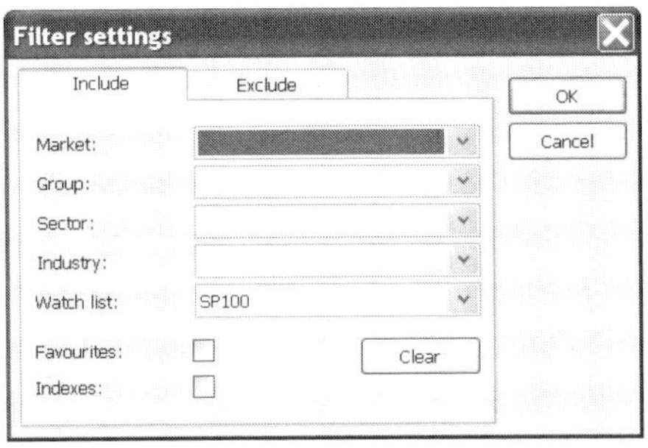

The **Review type** menu lets you select what type of report it will calculate.

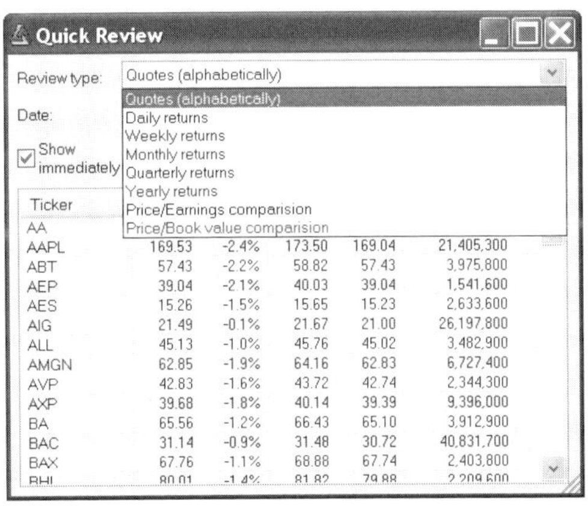

Quotes (Alphabetically) lists the closing price, day-over-day price change, high, low, and volume. The first image in this section, page 252, shows the Quotes report for stocks in the S&P 100.

The next options are:

- Daily returns
- Weekly returns
- Monthly returns

- Quarterly returns
- Yearly returns

These are all calculations of price change from one period ago to the report date. The report shows the price at the period earlier, the current price, and the percentage change. It is sorted into descending order by percentage change, but you can sort on any column by clicking the column header. Here is an example of a monthly report:

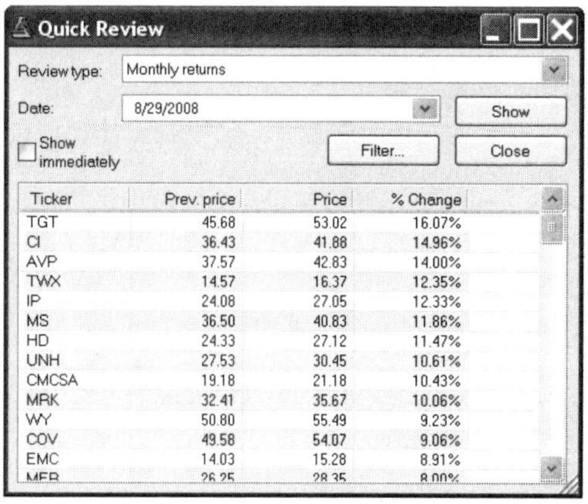

Clicking the **Show** button starts the calculations that produce the report. Checking the **Show Immediately** box lets the results display as soon as they are calculated, rather than waiting until the entire report is complete before displaying results.

Getting results for the final two report type options:

- Price/Earnings comparison
- Price/Book value comparison

requires that your database has entries for earnings and book value.

Automatic Analysis

As you worked through the Examples in Chapter 3, you saw some of the features and tools of Automatic Analysis. This chapter adds more detail.

Main Window

When you select Automatic Analysis from the Analysis menu, this window opens.

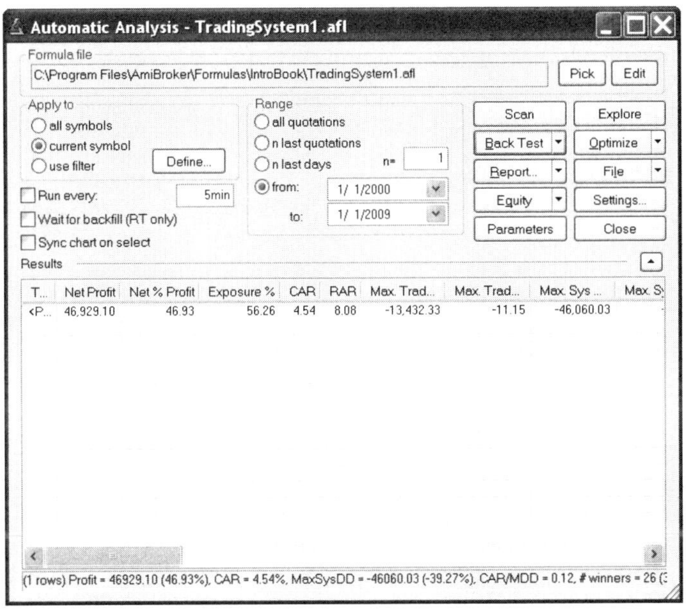

Begin by examining some of the controls on this window, then go into detail behind the buttons.

Formula file

Left to right in the Formula file area, there are three items:

- a display of the path of the file that is currently selected or active.
- a Pick button that lets you navigate to and select a file to become the active file.
- an Edit button that opens the Formula Editor so that you can modify the selected file.

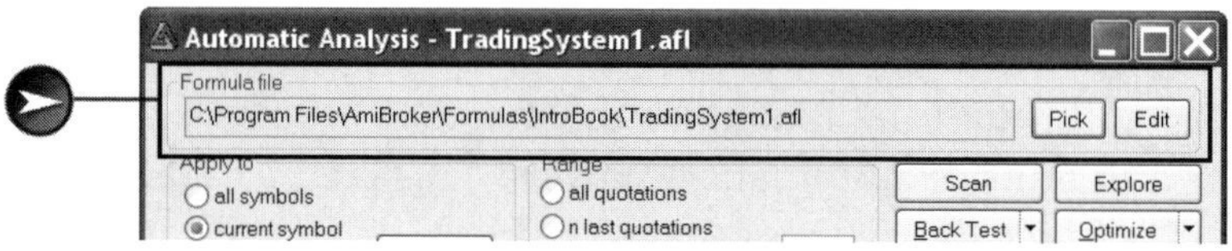

Apply To

The Apply To area gives you three choices of what the analysis will be applied to:

- all symbols - use all the symbols in the database.
- current symbol - use only the single symbol that is active or selected.
- use filter - clicking the Define button opens the Filter settings dialog and lets you select a group of symbols based on their membership in categories. See the image of the Filter settings dialog on page 479.

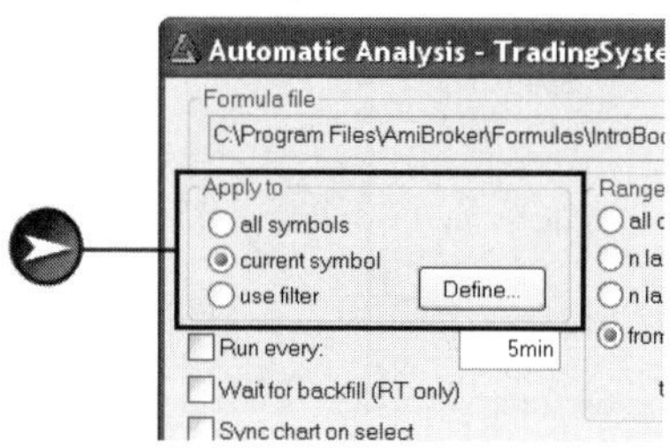

Range

The Range area gives you four choices for the date range that the analysis will be applied to:

- all quotations - uses all the data in the database.
- n last quotations - enter the number of quotations you want to use in the n= field.
- n last days - enter the number of days you want to use in the n= field.
- from / to - you can either type the date directly, or use the menu to open a calendar. Select the starting date and ending date.

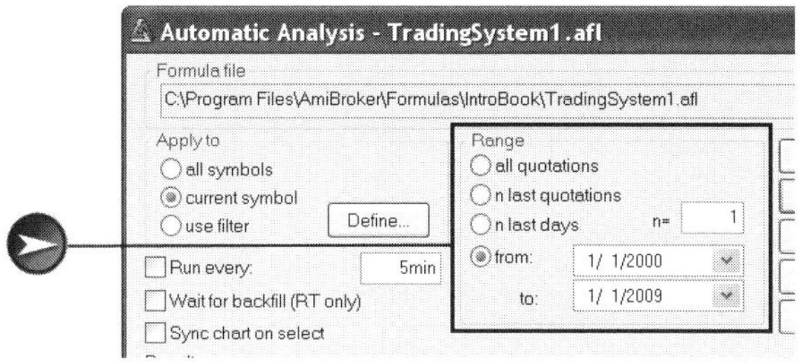

Miscellaneous

Checking the **Run every** box, and filling in the number of minutes, requests that the analysis be repeated periodically on the schedule you want. This is useful if you are receiving real-time data or intra-day snapshots and want the results of the analysis refreshed.

Checking the **Wait for backfill** box, which is only meaningful if you are receiving real-time data, requests that the analysis not begin until the data is up-to-date and data for any historical period you have defined has been received.

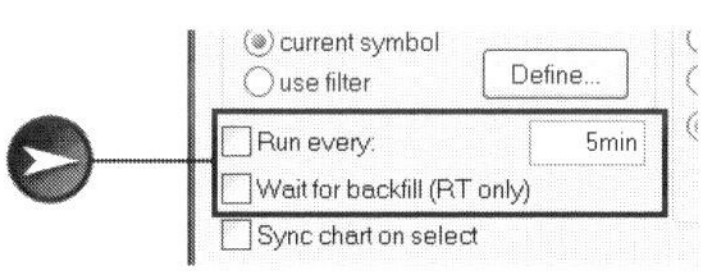

Checking the **Sync chart on select** box is meaningful only after having run an analysis on multiple issues. Click on any of the rows in the Results window and the symbol in that row will be loaded and become the selected issue. All the charts will be redrawn using the newly loaded symbol.

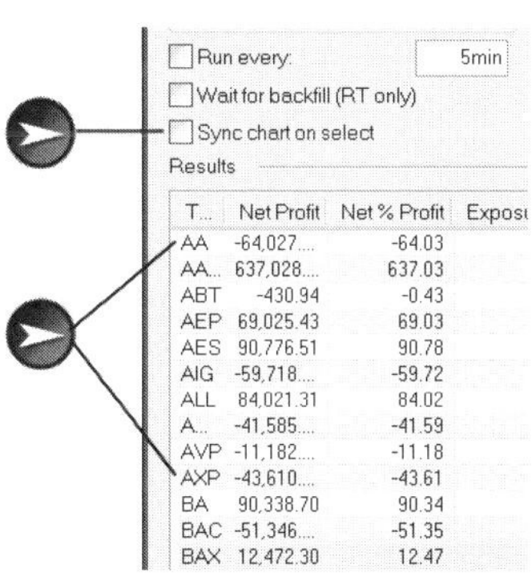

Settings Button

Clicking the **Settings** button on the main AA window opens the Backtester settings dialog. It has six tabs. Each will be discussed.

General tab

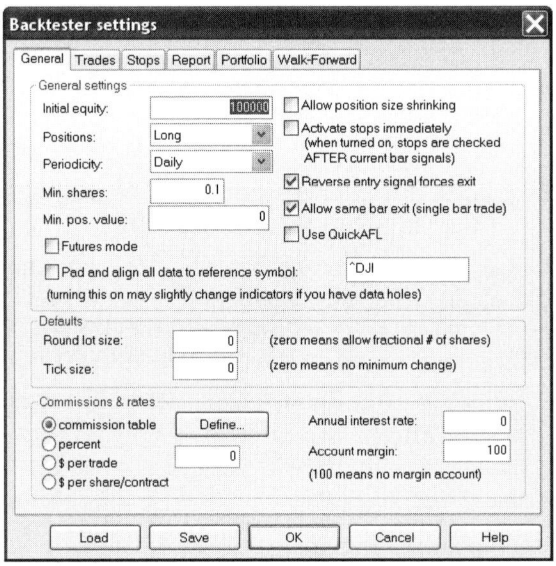

Initial equity - Enter the starting balance for the trading account.

Positions - The menu gives three choices. Select whichever is meaningful for your trading system.

- Long
- Short
- Long and Short

Periodicity - The menu gives choices consistent with your database. If you have an end-of-day database, you will only see choices of daily and longer. If you have an intraday database, you will see shorter time periods.

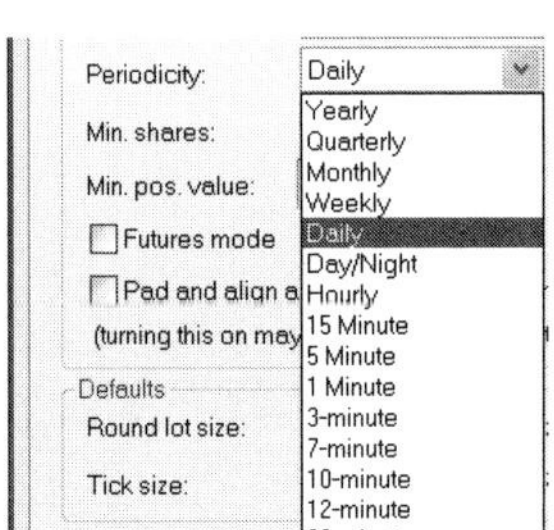

Min Shares - The minimum number of shares required to open a position. If your account does not have enough cash to purchase this many shares, it will pass on the trade.

Min pos value - The minimum dollar amount required to open a position. If your account does not at least this much cash, it will pass on the trade.

Futures mode - Check this box to have the trade accounting done using margin deposit and point value.

Pad and align all data to reference symbol - This is off by default. When checked, it will be turned on. When on, the quotes of all symbols are padded and aligned to the reference symbol. Padding and aligning insures that there will be data for exactly the same dates and times in both series. The symbol being tested will have data removed for periods when the reference symbol has no data, and will have data added (previous value copied) for periods when it has no data but the reference symbol does. Enter the ticker for the reference symbol in the box.

Allow position size shrinking - When checked, allows position size to shrink so that a partial position can be taken if cash is insufficient for a full position.

Activate stops immediately - When you trade on open and want to have built-in stops activated on the same bar, check this box. When you trade on close and want built-in stops to be activated from the next bar, uncheck this box.

Reverse entry signal forces exit - Check this box to turn on, uncheck to turn off. When on, a signal to entry a short position forces an exit to a long position being held, and vice versa. When off, an entry to a short position does not force the exit of a long position - the long position waits for its own exit signal.

Allow same bar exit - Check this box to turn on, uncheck to turn off. When on, the exit from a trade can occur on the same bar as the entry. When off, the earliest exit is the next bar.

Use QuickAFL - When checked, use QuickAFL. QuickAFL examines the visible charts and recomputes indicators using only as much data as necessary to redraw the visible portion or recompute the selected range.

Round lot size - The minimum number of shares, or contracts, that can be purchased. For mutual funds, where it is possible to purchase fractional shares, enter 0.

Tick size - The smallest change in the price that can be recorded. A setting made on this screen is a global setting and will apply to all symbols. You can enter a value for each symbol, which will override the global setting, using Symbol > Information.

Commissions & rates - Can be set from a table, or you can enter a number to be used as a percentage, a cost per trade, or a cost per share.

Annual interest rate - The rate you earn on funds that are in cash and not invested in a position.

Account margin - This setting is for your entire account. It is not related to margin for futures. It is the percentage of the funds in your trading account that comes from your cash. 100 means all of your account comes from your own money. 50 means that 50 percent of your account comes from your own money and you are borrowing the other 50 percent.

Trades tab

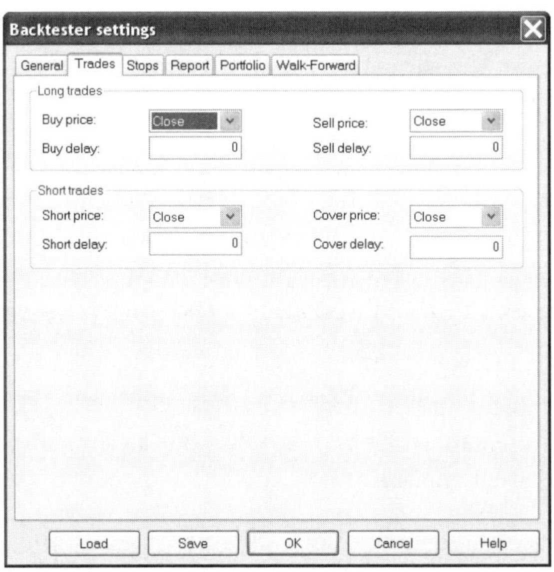

Buy Price - The menu gives you a choice of Close, Open, High, Low, or Average. This price will be used if your trading system issues a market order. That is, if it only signals Buy or Sell without specifying the

BuyPrice or SellPrice. You can use an AFL statement (BuyPrice = xxx) to override settings made on this screen. Sell Price, Short Price, and Cover Price are the same.

Buy Delay - The number of bars between the generation of the signal and the execution of the trade. If you are using daily bars, computing signals in the evening, and trading the next day, use a value of 1. If you are watching the market intra-day, get a signal near the close, and make the trade on that same bar, use a value of 0. You can use an AFL statement (SetTradeDelays) to override settings made on this screen.

Stops tab

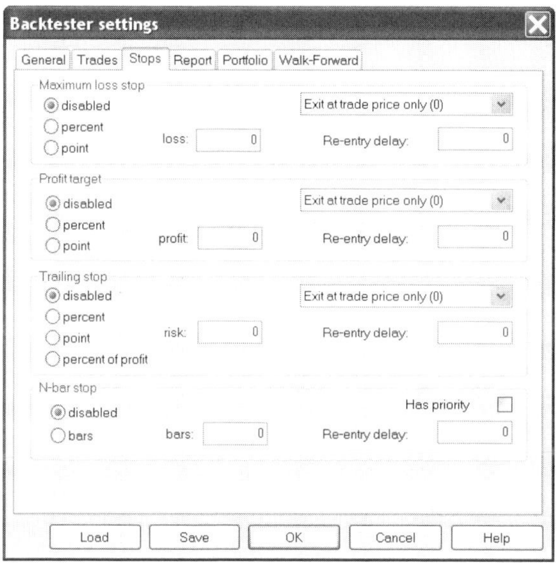

Maximum Loss Stop - You have a choice of:

- Disabled - No maximum loss stop is active.
- Percent - Enter a maximum loss stop as a percentage of the entry price. Enter the percentage number in the field.
- Point - Enter a maximum loss stop as a fixed number of points. Enter the number of points in the field.

The **Exit at** menu gives you three choices.

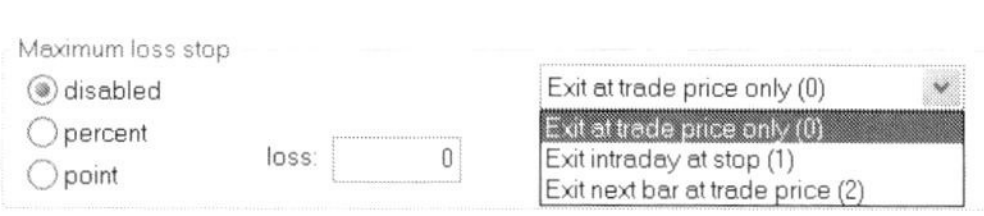

- Exit at trade price only - Use the price set on the Trades tab. If you have set your sell to be at the close, the stop will be executed at the close, at the closing price.
- Exit intraday at stop - Use the price computed by the AFL code.
- Exit next bar at trade price - Use the price set on the Trades tab, and exit on the next bar.

Re-entry delay - Number of bars to wait before taking a new position in this same issue.

Profit target and **Trailing stop** are controlled in the same way.

N-bar stop - You have a choice of:

- Disabled - No N-bar stop in place.
- bars - Enter the number of bars in the field. An exit will be made after this number of bars.

Has priority - When checked, the N-bar stop has priority over other exits that are signalled for the same bar. When unchecked, other stops are considered first, such as a profit target hit on the same bar as the N-bar exit stop.

Report tab

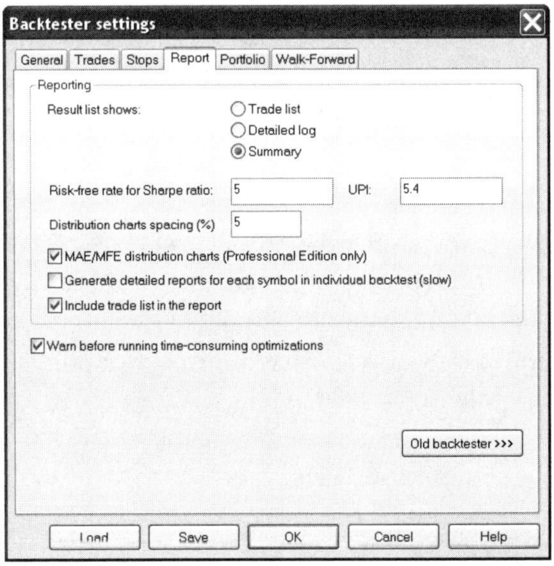

Result list shows - give you a choice of:

- Trade list - Report a listing with a row for every trade made.
- Detailed log - Report a listing with a row for every bar, including information about scores and positions.
- Summary - Report a listing with one entry per backtest.

Risk free rates - Interest rates used when computing Sharpe ratio and Ulcer Performance Index.

Distribution charts spacing - Controls the spacing between bars on some of the charts.

MAE/MFE distribution charts - Only available with Professional Edition of AmiBroker. When checked, produce the Maximum Adverse Excursion and Maximum Favorable Excursion distribution charts.

Generate detailed reports for each symbol in individual backtest - When checked, generate a full report for each symbol. This will increase the time of the run and increase the disk space used.

Include trade list in the report - Check to turn on, which is the default. When turned on, generates a trade list with every backtest.

Warn before time consuming operations - Check to turn on, which is the default. When turned on, pop-up a dialog box asking for confirmation to continue when a long run has been requested.

Old Backtester - Provides access to a previous version of the backtester. At the introductory level, you probably do not need the old backtester.

Portfolio tab

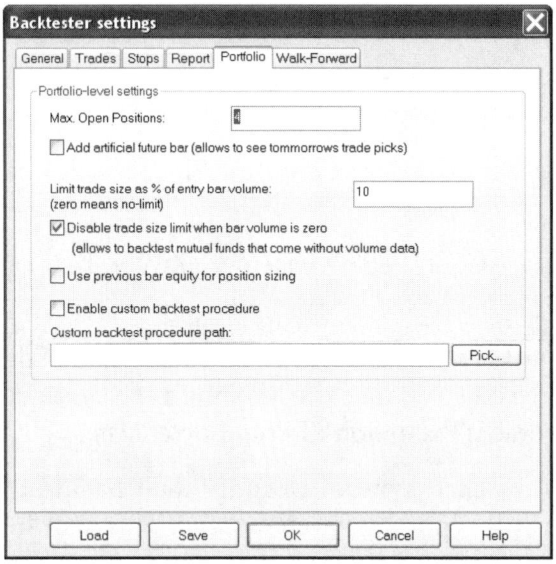

Max open positions - Maximum simultaneous open positions. This can also be set by AFL code (SetOption("MaxOpenPositions", number)), which overrides the value entered on the Portfolio tab.

Add artificial future bars - Add empty bars onto which you can plot indicators. Useful for plotting the value of stops and profit targets to be used the next day.

Limit trade size as percentage of entry bar volume - Set a limit so that your trade does not dominate the trading or try to take impossible positions.

Disable trade size limit when bar size is zero - Useful when trading mutual funds and indices that have no volume information.

Use previous bar equity for position sizing - When unchecked, which is the default, all funds are immediately available, so use intra-day equity when taking new positions.

Enable custom backtest procedure - Allows you to specify a procedure to use as the fitness function. This topic is beyond the introductory level, and is thoroughly described in *Quantitative Trading Systems*.

Walk-Forward tab

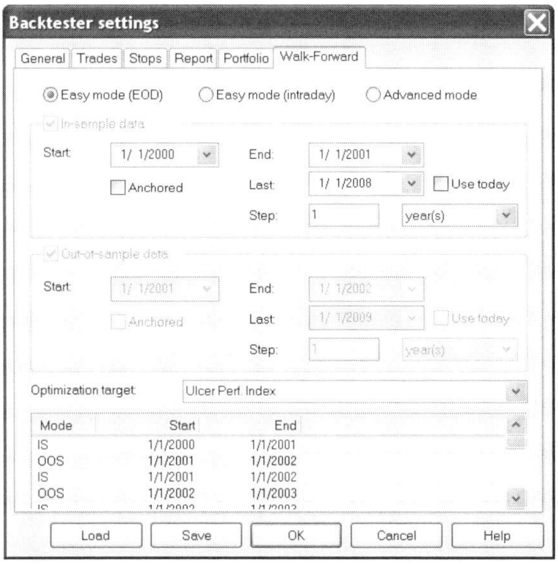

You have a choice of:

- **Easy mode (EOD)** - End-of-Day easy mode - AmiBroker handling the coordination of dates so in-sample and out-of-sample periods align properly.
- **Easy Mode (Intraday)** - Intraday easy mode - AmiBroker handling the coordination of dates so in-sample and out-of-sample periods align properly.
- **Advanced Mode** - You have complete control over the length of the in-sample period, the length of the out-of-sample period, and the alignment of the two.

This description is for the Easy mode EOD.

Start - The first date for the first in-sample period.

End - The last date for the first in-sample period.

Last - The last date for the last full in-sample period.

Step - The length of the out-of-sample period.

Anchored - When checked, the beginning of every in-sample period is the date of the first day of the first in-sample period. With each successive step, the length of the in-sample period grows longer. When unchecked, the in-sample periods are all the same number of days long, and the starting dates move forward in time by the length given for Step.

Use today - When checked, do not accept a date for Last. Instead, continue the in-sample and out-of-sample periods using all the data available.

Optimization target - The menu gives a list of the built-in metrics that can be used as fitness functions. Developers who want to reward equity growth while penalizing drawdown might want to try one of the metrics that have that characteristic:

- RAR/MDD
- CAR/MDD
- RRR (Risk-Reward Ratio)
- Ulcer Performance Index
- K-Ratio

Advanced developers can:

- Use advanced mode to completely control the walk forward stepping.
- Write their own fitness function and instruct the backtester to use it.

Explore Button

The previous sections - Main Window and Settings Button - explained how to set up for Automatic Analysis (AA) runs. When you click the Explore Button on the main AA window, you start an AA run.

The exploration runs an AFL program that searches for conditions that you specify, then produces a report.

Every program that will be run as an exploration has a Filter statement in it. In order for a result to appear in the report, that result must pass the filter. For example, you might want a report showing which members of the S&P 100 have both today's price and today's volume greater than their 10 day averages.

Follow these steps:

1. Use the Formula Editor to write the AFL code and save it in a file named ExploreRisingPriceAndVolume.afl.

```
// ExploreRisingPriceAndVolume.afl
//
// An AFL program to run as an Exploration.
// Use with a category such as a watchlist.
//
// Produce a report listing every member of the
// group that has both today's price and today's
// volume above the 10 day averages.
//
PriceRising = C > MA( C, 10 );
VolumeRising = V > MA( V, 10 );

Filter = PriceRising AND VolumeRising;

AddColumn( C, "C", 1.2 );
AddColumn( MA( C, 10 ), "MA(C,10)", 1.2 );
AddColumn( V, "V", 1.0 );
AddColumn( MA( V, 10 ), "MA(V,10)", 1.0 );
```

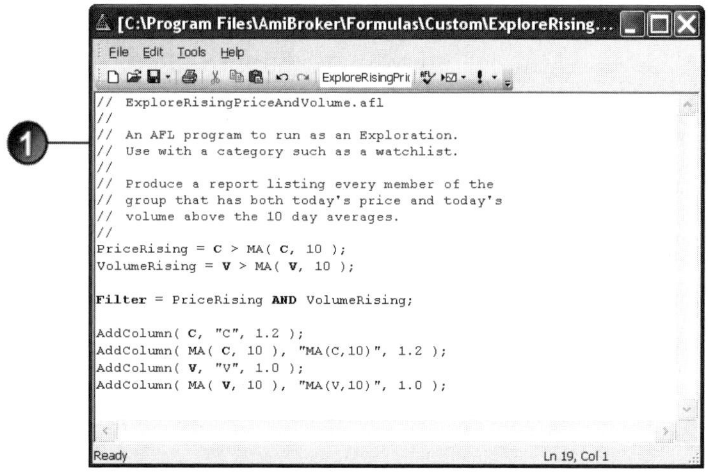

2. In **Automatic Analysis**, click **Pick**, navigate to the file you just created, and select it.

3. Click **Use filter**, click **Define**, select the category you want to use.

4. Click **n last days**, set n to **1**.

5. Click **Explore**.

The list of issues in your category meeting the criteria in your AFL appear in the results window.

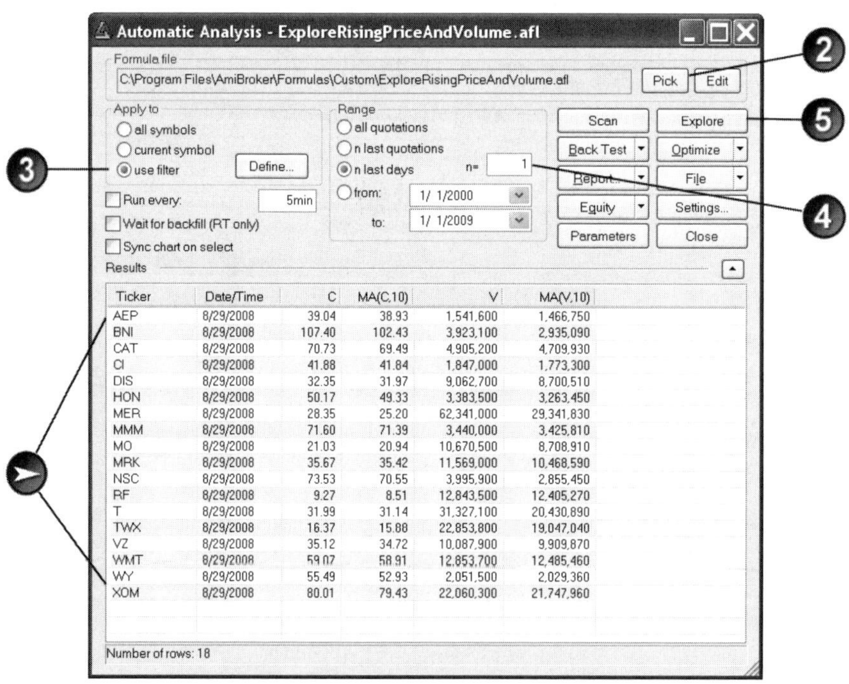

The elements of AFL code that are unique to explorations are:

- The Filter statement.
- The AddColumn statements.

The Filter statement has the form:

```
Filter = any expression that evaluates to True or False;
```

If you want an entry in the report for every symbol in the watchlist, use this:

```
Filter = 1;
```

The AddColumn statement has the form:

```
AddColumn (Array, "Name", format);
```

Where Array is the value to be reported, "Name" is the heading for the column, and format is the format of the output.

Format is a pair of digits with a decimal point between them, such as 1.4.

The first digit is the number of spaces to use. 6.4 guarantees 6 spaces for the number, even if it only requires 2.

The second digit is the number of decimal places to display. 6.4 displays the result to 4 decimal places.

Backtest Button

The Backtest Button begins execution of a backtest. That is, a test of the profitability of the buy and sell rules defined in an AFL program as it is applied to historical data. The AFL code that buys and sells is a trading system.

The backtest button has a pull-down menu that gives three choices:

- Portfolio Backtest - Apply the backtest program to a group of issues, all of which are candidates to be held. The backtester calculates the buy and sell signals for each individual issue in the group. Then it goes through the signals in order by time. Whenever there is a buy signal and there is cash available to take the trade, a position is taken. If there is not enough cash, the trade is passed. Whenever there is a sell signal, the position is sold and the cash made available for another purchase. The equity curve (running account balance) and report are produced for the portfolio as a whole.
- Individual Backtest - As above, apply the backtest to a group of issues, all of which are candidates to be held. The backtester calculates the buy and sell signals for each individual in the group. Then, differing from the portfolio method, it assumes each of the issues is the only candidate to be held, and calculates a report for each of the issues individually.
- Old Backtester - Runs an earlier version of the backtester. For more information, see the AmiBroker User's Guide, Old Backtester Report.

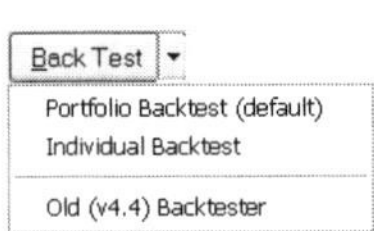

The same AFL code can be run as a portfolio backtest and an individual backtest.

In order to run a backtest on a portfolio, you must click **use filter** and define a group. Then click **Backtest** (portfolio backtest is the default) or use the menu and choose **portfolio backtest**.

In order to run a backtest on a single issue, click **current symbol** and click **backtest**. The result will be titled <portfolio>. If you want the result to list the ticker symbol, use the menu and choose **individual backtest**.

In order to run a backtest on several issues in one pass, treating them as individuals rather than as a portfolio, click **use filter**, use the menu and choose **individual backtest**. There will be a result for every symbol in the group, but no portfolio result.

In processing the AFL file, the backtester performs the calculations and assignment statements. The key component is the set of buy and sell (and, perhaps, short and cover) signals.

The format of a buy statement is:

```
Buy = whatever condition you want to signal taking
       a new position;
```

And of a sell statement:

```
Sell = whatever condition you want to signal exiting
       that position;
```

When the calculations that make up the condition to buy evaluate to True, or 1, that constitutes a buy signal.

When the calculations that make up the condition to sell evaluate to True, or 1, that constitutes a sell signal.

A very simple trading system, often used as an example because of its simplicity, not because of its profitability, is a moving average crossover.

Look at the code from Example 6B, Chapter 3.

```
//  Example6B.afl
//  A trading system based on the
//  crossover of two moving averages.
//  Buy when the faster moving average
//  crosses up through the slower moving
//  average.
//  Sell when the faster moving average
//  crosses down through the slower
//  moving average.

FastMALength = 5;      //Guess that 5 is a good value
SlowMALength = 20;     //Guess that 20 is a good value

FastMA = MA( C, FastMALength );
SlowMA = MA( C, SlowMALength );

Buy = Cross( FastMA, SlowMA );
Sell = Cross( SlowMA, FastMA );
```

When ever the right-hand side of the Buy = statement evaluates to be True, that is a buy signal. The Cross function returns a value of true on every bar where the first argument is higher than the second argument on this bar, but the first argument was lower than the second argument on the previous bar. That is - where the first argument crossed up through the second argument.

Example 6, Chapter 3, demonstrates a trading system based on a moving average crossover. Review that example now.

In order to test the profitability of a trading system when it is applied to a portfolio, the system must have some way of controlling the number of positions held at any one time. It must also be able to allocate funds to each new position. There are AFL statements that do that.

The statement:

```
SetOption ("MaxOpenPositions", 3);
```

tells the backtester that there can be a maximum of 3 open positions. If 3 positions are being held and a buy signal comes from a symbol not being held, it is ignored and that trade is passed. If fewer than 3 positions are being held and there are sufficient funds to take a new position, a position will be taken in the symbol that generated that buy signal.

Having the possibility of holding 3 positions implies that there is funding for 3 "tracks". The statement:

```
PositionSize = -100 / 3;
```

tells the backtester that each new position is funded by one third of the account equity. As the equity grows, more money is available for purchases in each of the three tracks - they share the funds equally.

You might want a way to test the effect of allowing a differing number of maximum positions. These statements are equivalent to the ones above, but give the flexibility of changing the maximum number easily.

```
PosQty = 3; // There can be 3 open positions
SetOption("MaxOpenPositions", PosQty );
PositionSize = -100/PosQty; // invest 100% of portfolio
                // equity divided by PosQty
```

Put these statements at the beginning of the code from Example 6B, and save it under a new file name, say BacktestExample.afl.

```
// BacktestExample.afl
// A trading system based on the
// crossover of two moving averages.
// Buy when the faster moving average
// crosses up through the slower moving
// average.
// Sell when the faster moving average
// crosses down through the slower
// moving average.

PosQty = 3; // There can be 3 open positions
SetOption( "MaxOpenPositions", PosQty );
PositionSize = -100 / PosQty; // invest 100% of
// portfolio equity divided by PosQty

FastMA = MA( C, 5 );
SlowMA = MA( C, 20 );

Buy = Cross( FastMA, SlowMA );
Sell = Cross( SlowMA, FastMA );

Plot( C, "C", colorBlack, styleCandle );
e = Equity();
Plot( e, "equity", colorGreen, styleLine | styleOwnScale );
```

When you have the program changed and are in the Formula Editor, click the **Analysis** icon (the "!" in the toolbar). This causes the file being edited to becomes the active or selected file and Automatic Analysis opens.

Click **use filter**, then **Define**, and select a watchlist with 5 or more symbols in it. The 9 S&P sector exchange traded funds make a good watchlist for testing. The 9 symbols are: XLB, XLE, XLF, XLI, XLK, XLP, XLU, XLV, XLY.

Set the range to 1/1/2000 to 1/1/2007.

Click **Backtest**.

The Results area will show the results of running the system as a portfolio.

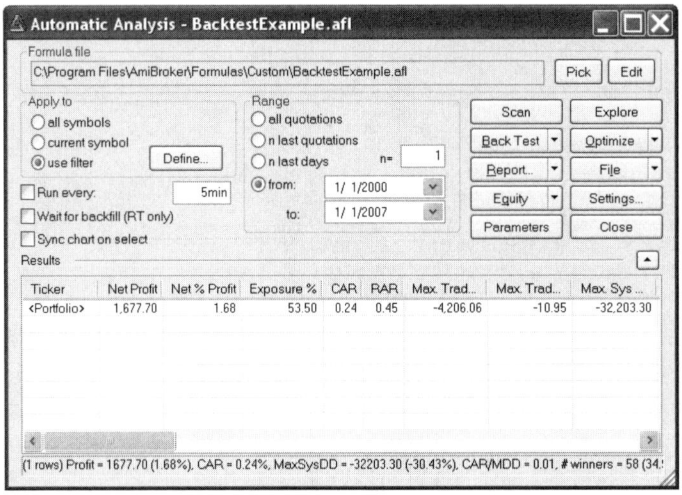

The results are poor, but perhaps they can be improved later.

Click the **Report** button. The Report will open. Expand it and look at the statistics on the first tab. Look at the trades on the Trades tab. Note that there are several positions held at a given time - between 0 and 3.

Click the **Equity** button and scroll back and forth. Blue areas are positions, green are cash. You can see when there were 0, 1, 2, and 3 positions held.

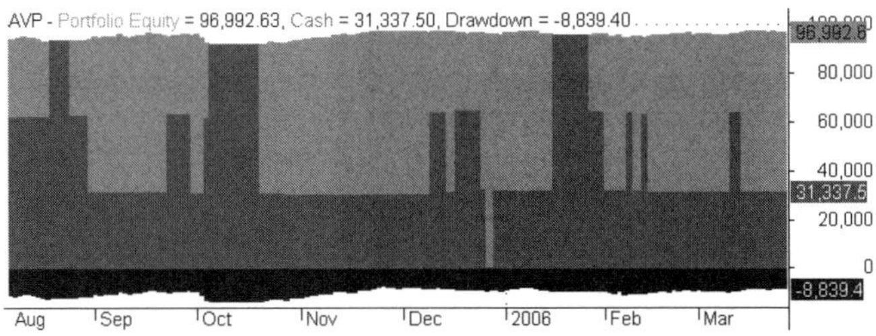

Use the pull-down menu at the right side of the Backtest button and select **Individual Backtest**. The Results area will show the results - one line for each of the members of the watchlist.

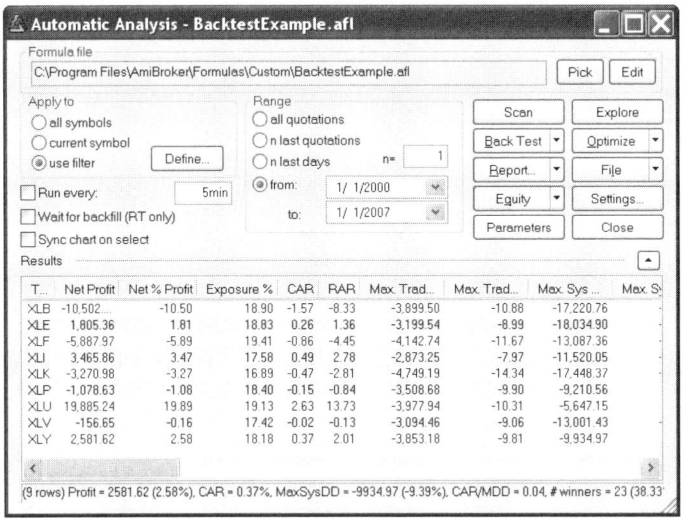

T...	Net Profit	Net % Profit	Exposure %	CAR	RAR	Max. Trad...	Max. Trad...	Max. Sys ...	Max. S
XLB	-10,502....	-10.50	18.90	-1.57	-8.33	-3,899.50	-10.88	-17,220.76	
XLE	1,805.36	1.81	18.83	0.26	1.36	-3,199.54	-8.99	-18,034.90	
XLF	-5,887.97	-5.89	19.41	-0.86	-4.45	-4,142.74	-11.67	-13,087.36	
XLI	3,465.86	3.47	17.58	0.49	2.78	-2,873.25	-7.97	-11,520.05	
XLK	-3,270.98	-3.27	16.89	-0.47	-2.81	-4,749.19	-14.34	-17,448.37	
XLP	-1,078.63	-1.08	18.40	-0.15	-0.84	-3,508.68	-9.90	-9,210.56	
XLU	19,885.24	19.89	19.13	2.63	13.73	-3,977.94	-10.31	-5,647.15	
XLV	-156.65	-0.16	17.42	-0.02	-0.13	-3,094.46	-9.06	-13,001.43	
XLY	2,581.62	2.58	18.18	0.37	2.01	-3,853.18	-9.81	-9,934.97	

If you click the **Equity** button (portfolio equity is the default), the portfolio equity chart shows that there is either one position or none. This is because the last backtest was not a portfolio test, so there is no portfolio result to display. Instead, the equity for one of the individual issues is displayed using the portfolio equity format of blue and green columns.

Use the pull-down menu to the right of the Equity button and select **Individual Equity**. A new pane will open and plot the equity of the symbol in the row that has been selected, this time in individual equity format. Click another row and get the equity curve for that symbol. The solid red part is the equity from the trading system; the blue line is the equity from buy-and-hold.

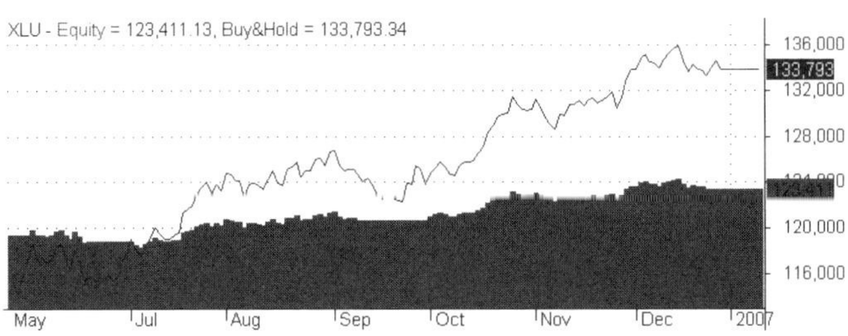

Context Menu

After an Automatic Analysis run where there are results in the results window, right-click anywhere in the window to bring up the AA Context menu. There are two rather different types of processing on the context menu:

1. Show arrows resulting from trades taken on a single security - the top three.
2. Send symbols resulting from runs taken over a group of securities to watchlists - the next four.

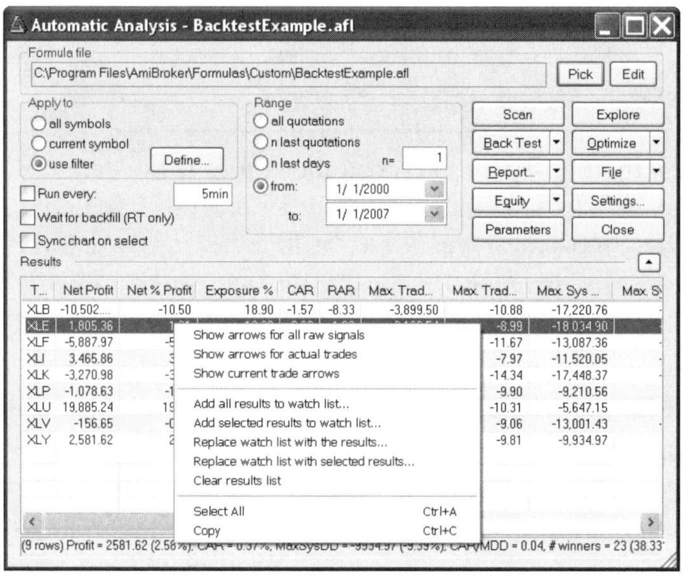

We'll demonstrate in two examples.

First example. Running a trading system on a single security will get us to the first set of three options. To get things set up, follow these steps:

1. From the **Analysis** menu, select Automatic Analysis. Click **Pick** and select **Example6B** again.
2. Click **Edit**, which will open the Formula Editor and display the AFL code of the system. Add these three lines to the bottom of the program:

```
Plot( C, "C", colorBlack, styleCandle );
Plot( FastMA, "FastMA", colorRed, styleLine );
Plot( SlowMA, "SlowMA", colorBlue, styleLine );
```

Save the program as Example6X.afl.

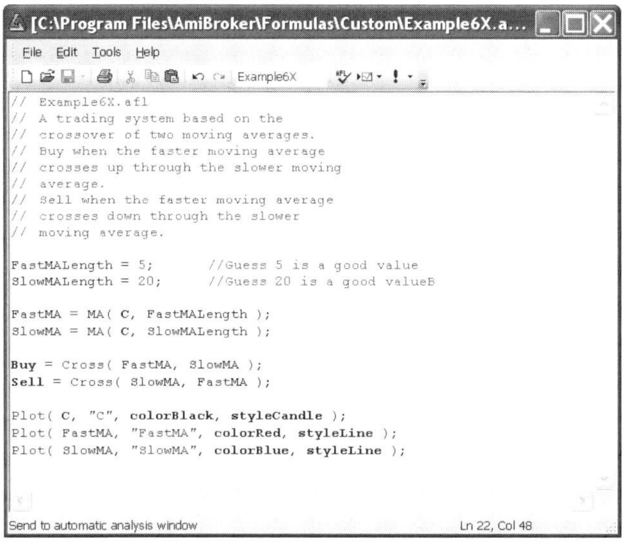


```
// Example6X.afl
// A trading system based on the
// crossover of two moving averages.
// Buy when the faster moving average
// crosses up through the slower moving
// average.
// Sell when the faster moving average
// crosses down through the slower
// moving average.

FastMALength = 5;       //Guess 5 is a good value
SlowMALength = 20;      //Guess 20 is a good valueB

FastMA = MA( C, FastMALength );
SlowMA = MA( C, SlowMALength );

Buy = Cross( FastMA, SlowMA );
Sell = Cross( SlowMA, FastMA );

Plot( C, "C", colorBlack, styleCandle );
Plot( FastMA, "FastMA", colorRed, styleLine );
Plot( SlowMA, "SlowMA", colorBlue, styleLine );
```

3. Click the **Verify Syntax** icon to test for typing errors.
4. Using the **Apply** icon, drop down its menu and use the **Insert** option. A new pane will open with the price in a candlestick chart, a 20 period simple moving average, and a 5 period simple moving average.
5. Right-click the pane with the new chart, bringing up the Chart Pane Context menu. Set the options to show the date axis and to show trading arrows. Click OK to leave the context menu. (Review Chart Pane Context Menu if necessary.)

6. Set some parameters for Automatic Analysis.
   - Use just the current symbol.
   - Set the date range for a year or two.
   - Positions to Long.
   - Periodicity to Daily.
   - Buy and Sell on the Close with Delay 0.
   - Reporting show a Trade List.

7. Click **Backtest**. The Results window will show results.

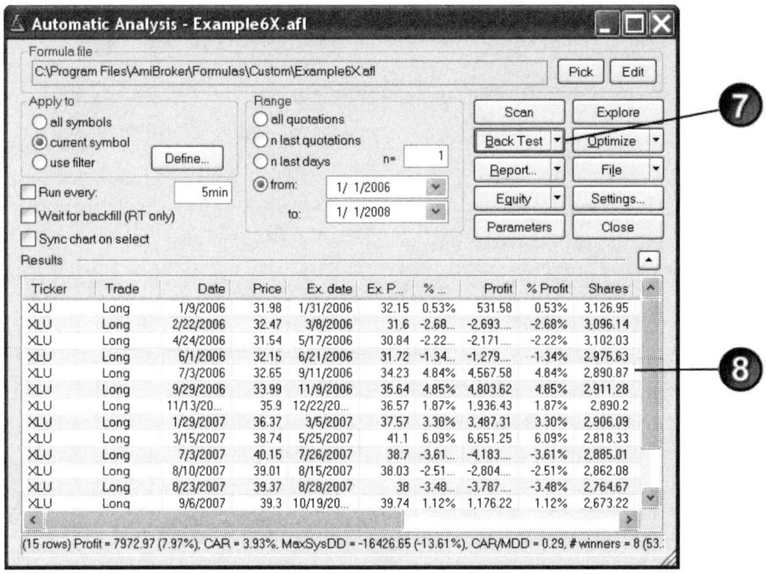

8. Right-click the Results window to bring up the context menu.

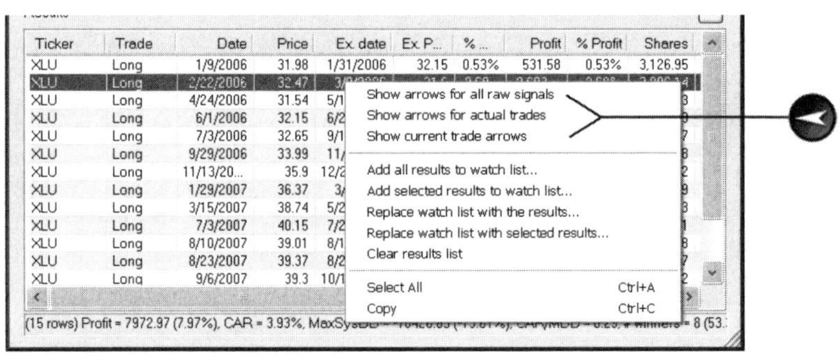

9. Since this run was made on a single symbol, the top three options are meaningful.

   - Show arrows for all raw signals - Sometimes there are signals that do not result in trades. This option shows all signals.
   - Show arrows for actual trades - Shows those signals that became trades.
   - Show current trade arrows - Each row of the results represents one trade. Select one trade. This option scrolls the chart and shows the arrows for that one trade.

This chart shows arrows for actual trades. (The arrows drawn for the first option result in the same chart, because there are no extraneous signals.)

Second example. Options four through seven come after running the system using a group of stocks. Follow these steps (1 through 5 are the same as the previous example):

1. From the Analysis menu, select **Automatic Analysis**. Click **Pick** and select **Example6X**.
2. Click **Edit**, which will open the Formula Editor and display the AFL code of the system.
3. Click the **Verify Syntax** icon to test for typing errors.
4. Using the Apply icon, drop down its menu and use the **Insert** option. A new pane will open with the price in a candlestick chart, a 25 period simple moving average, and a 5 period simple moving average.
5. Right-click the pane with the new chart, bringing up the Chart Pane Context menu. Set the options to show the date axis and to show trading arrows. Click OK to leave the context menu. (Review Chart Pane Context Menu if necessary.)
6. Set some parameters for Automatic Analysis.

    Use filter and select a watchlist of your choosing.
    Set the date range for a year or two.
    Positions to Long.
    Periodicity to Daily.
    Buy and Sell on the Close with Delay 0.
    Reporting show Summary.

7. On BackTest's drop-down menu, select **individual backtest**. You will see a progress bar as the system is applied to each symbol in the watchlist.

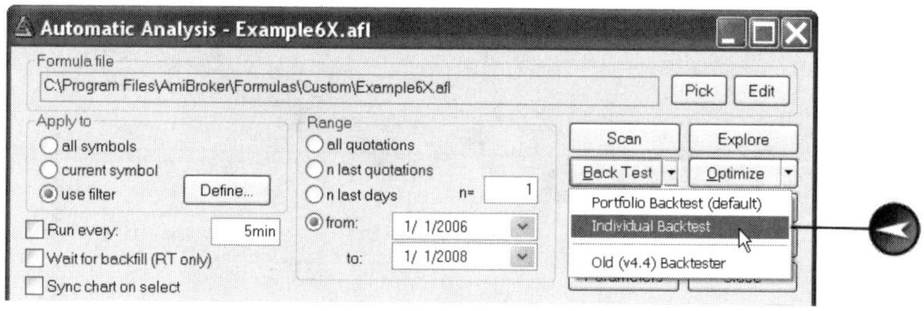

The Results window will show results. Sort the results as you wish by clicking a column header.

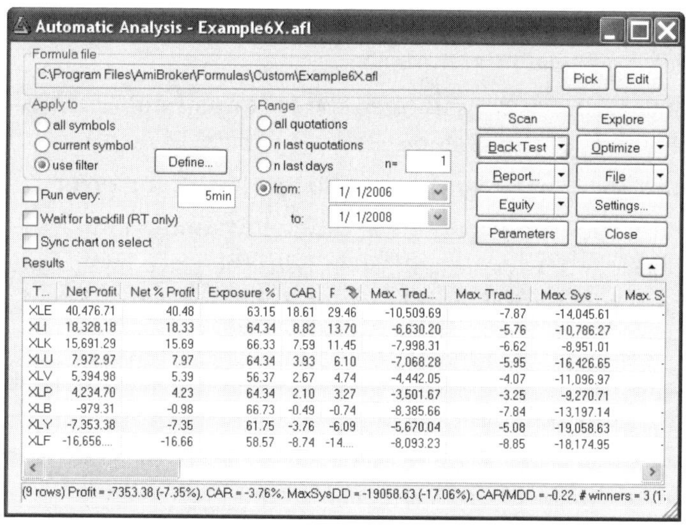

8. Each row represents the result of running this system on an individual symbol. Select several rows by holding the CONTROL key while left-clicking the rows you want. Right-click the Results window to bring up the context menu.

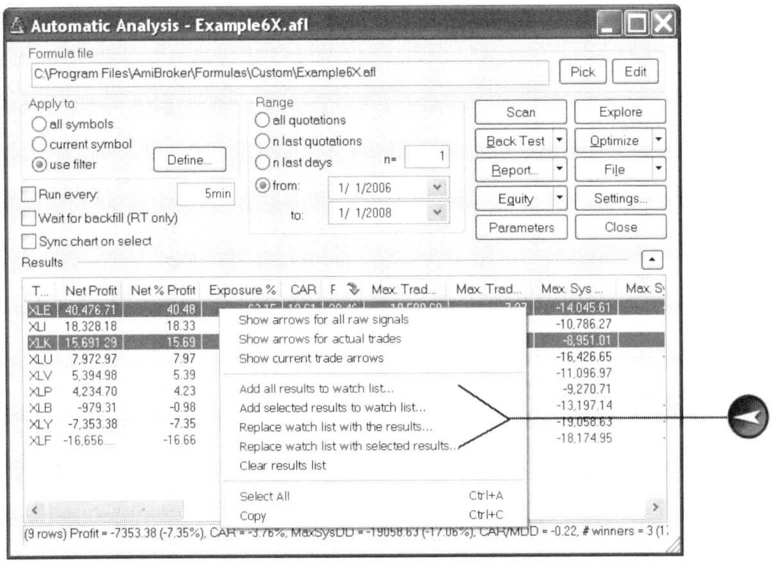

9. The four options marked are applicable:

- Add all results to watchlist - Adds all the symbols in the results list to the watchlist. Duplicates will be removed.
- Add selected results to watchlist - Adds the symbols in the rows you have selected to the watchlist.
- Replace watchlist with the results - Makes the watchlist empty, then adds all the symbols in the results list.
- Replace watchlist with selected results - Makes the watchlist empty, then adds the symbols in the rows you have selected to the watchlist.

File Button

The file button has a pull-down menu that gives two choices.

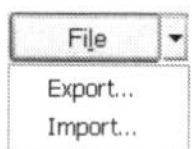

- Export - Export the contents of the Results window to a file in a directory of your choice. The format of the saved file can be either .csv, which can be opened in a spreadsheet for further analysis, or .html, which can be printed, e-mailed, or imported back into the results window.
- Import - Import a file in .html format that was previously exported. The import works best if the file being imported was created by AmiBroker using the Export command.

If the File button is clicked without pulling down the menu, the default operation is Export.

Equity Button

The equity button has a pull-down menu that gives two choices.

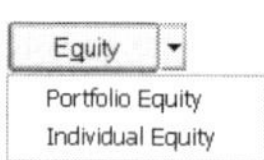

- Portfolio Equity - Opens a new pane and displays the equity for the most recent run using the portfolio format.

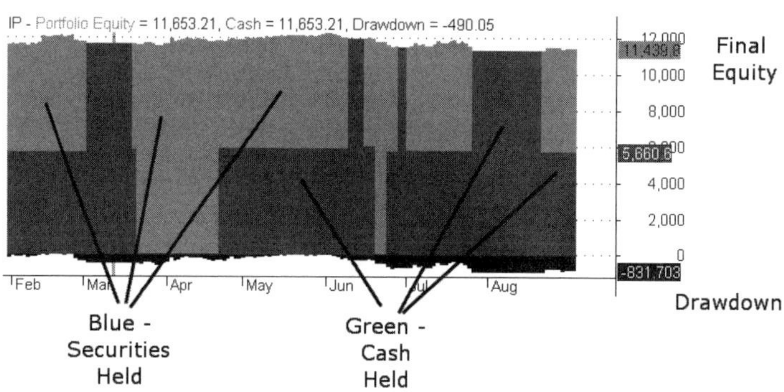

- Individual Equity - Opens a new pane and displays the equity for the most recent run using the current symbol as the price series tested. Changing the current symbol, either by clicking a row in the results window or by selecting a new symbol, changes the equity plot to reflect testing that symbol.

[The plot style in the image shown has been changed so that the trading system equity is a line for better printing. On the default plot it is a solid area.]

Report Button

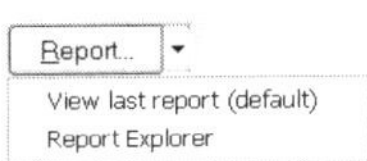

The report button has a pull-down menu that gives two choices.

- View last report - Opens the report for the most recent backtest. The report is in .html format, with one html page per tab of the report. Reports are saved in the directory C:\Program Files\AmiBroker\Reports. They stay there until you remove them.

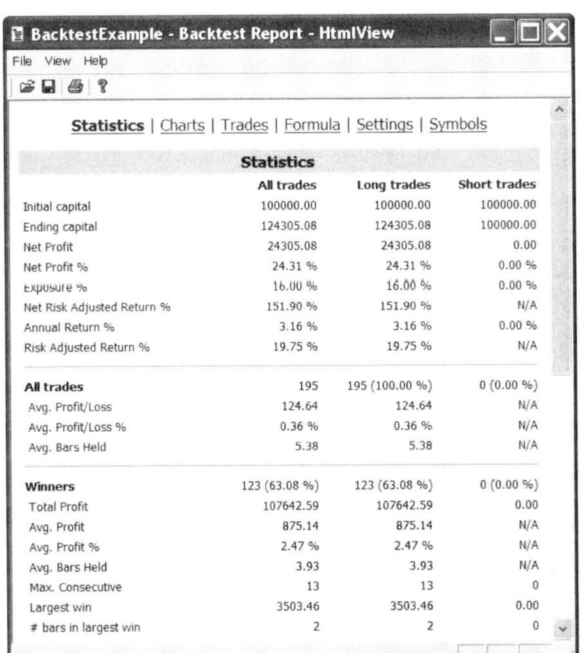
BacktestExample - Backtest Report - HtmlView

File View Help

Statistics | Charts | Trades | Formula | Settings | Symbols

Statistics

	All trades	Long trades	Short trades
Initial capital	100000.00	100000.00	100000.00
Ending capital	124305.08	124305.08	100000.00
Net Profit	24305.08	24305.08	0.00
Net Profit %	24.31 %	24.31 %	0.00 %
Exposure %	16.00 %	16.00 %	0.00 %
Net Risk Adjusted Return %	151.90 %	151.90 %	N/A
Annual Return %	3.16 %	3.16 %	0.00 %
Risk Adjusted Return %	19.75 %	19.75 %	N/A
All trades	195	195 (100.00 %)	0 (0.00 %)
Avg. Profit/Loss	124.64	124.64	N/A
Avg. Profit/Loss %	0.36 %	0.36 %	N/A
Avg. Bars Held	5.38	5.38	N/A
Winners	123 (63.08 %)	123 (63.08 %)	0 (0.00 %)
Total Profit	107642.59	107642.59	0.00
Avg. Profit	875.14	875.14	N/A
Avg. Profit %	2.47 %	2.47 %	N/A
Avg. Bars Held	3.93	3.93	N/A
Max. Consecutive	13	13	0
Largest win	3503.46	3503.46	0.00
# bars in largest win	2	2	0

- Report Explorer - Opens the Report Explorer (which runs as a separate program), and loads a summary line for each report in the Reports directory. You can sort the list by clicking on the header of any column.

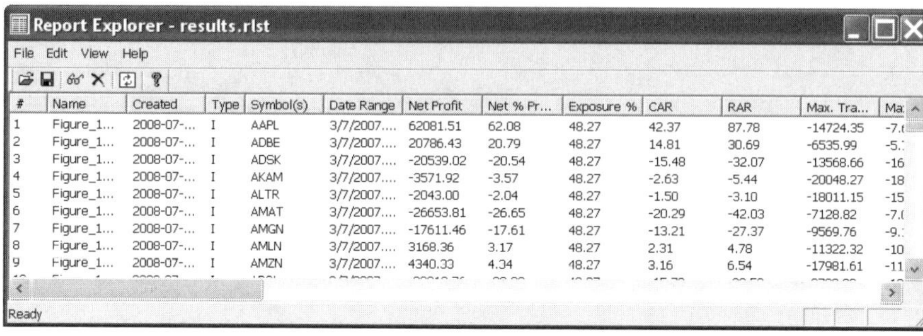

If you have previously turned on the feature that generates detailed reports (on Automatic Analysis > Settings > Report, click Generate detailed reports for each symbol in individual backtest), clicking one of the rows in the report listing will open the detailed report.

The menus for the Report Explorer give a method for selecting and deleting unneeded reports. Use the Edit menu. Either select and delete individual rows. Or select all and then delete.

Optimize Button

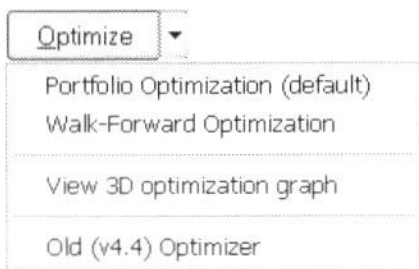

To optimize is to make an organized search for the set of values for the parameters of a trading system that maximize the objective function you are using to compare alternative systems.

There is one statement that must be added to a trading system to allow it to be optimized.

```
var  =  Optimize ( “name” , def , min , max , step );
```

`var` is a variable in your AFL program.

`name` is a string literal that will be used as a label when reporting.

`def` is the default value given to var whenever the program is evaluated in a mode other than optimize.

`min` is the minimum value of the range you wish to search.

`max` is the maximum value of the range you wish to search.

`step` is the increment by which the value is increased for each optimization.

For example,

```
MALength = Optimize ( “MALength”, 5, 1, 21, 2 );
```

The variable named MALength will be given values of 1, 3, 5, ... 21 in successive optimization passes.

Example 8, Chapter 3, ran an optimization. Review that example now.

Portfolio Optimization

If you click the Optimize button without pulling down the menu to make other choices, you are asking for a portfolio optimization. Review the section on the backtest button and note that it, too, defaults to a portfolio test.

If you have checked **use filter,** clicked **define,** and selected a watchlist or some other list of symbols, the backtest and the optimization are carried out on that group as a portfolio.

If the watchlist you have selected contains a single symbol, or if you checked **use current**, then your portfolio is a single issue, and the backtest or optimization is carried out on the single issue.

Optimization Basics

An optimization is simply a series of backtest runs, each run made with a different set of values for the parameters. If you were patient enough, you could type each variable in your program individually and make the same series of backtests. The advantage of having the optimization done by AmiBroker is that the details are handled by the program, and the results are displayed in the Results window for your evaluation.

After the alternative runs have been made (whether you used the optimizer or hand-entered the values), you must decide which set of values to use; and that is a decision you must make for yourself. Your level of comfort with the system that emerges from your design and testing will reflect the method you used to choose the best alternative.

The period of time, and the data associated with that period, that is processed as each of the backtest or optimization runs is made is called the in-sample data. When searching for the best set of values for the parameters, the in-sample data is being searched. The in-sample results will be good — they are always good — we do not stop working with the system until they are good. The real test is see whether those results are due to a good model that correctly identified the signal portion of the data, the patterns, rather than the noise. To make that test, change the dates to a period that follows the in-sample data and that has not been used to select the parameter values. That new data and time period is called the out-of-sample data. If the results obtained by running the system on the out-of-sample data are good, then there is a possibility that the system can, indeed, identify patterns that precede profitable trading opportunities.

But please be careful. It is too easy to run an optimization (on in-sample data), pick the best values, run the system on the out-of-sample data, notice that an adjustment to the system would make the out-of-sample results much better, change the code for the system, and rerun the system. Every time that is done, the data that was previously out-of-sample has become increasingly in-sample. Eventually the results from both the in-sample and out-of-sample runs will be good; but that success is partially due to expanding the in-sample data set. A new, fresh, out-of-sample set of data is now required.

Objective Functions

AmiBroker has 20-some built-in metrics that are automatically computed and reported for each run. If the ranking produced by one of these metrics agrees with your own ranking, then you can use that metric as your objective function (also called a fitness function). If you want a custom function, you can write the AFL that describes it, tell AmiBroker to compute a score using that function for each run, and rank the results by that function. There are examples of doing that in the AmiBroker User's Guide and in *Quantitative Trading Systems*

Most trading system development platforms do not provide the power and flexibility in creation and use of custom objective functions that AmiBroker does.

In fact, most have a default objective function of net profit, and most have no way to specify any other. Unfortunately, net profit is a poor choice for an objective function.

Net profit is one of the metrics that tends to perform well in-sample, but poorly out-of-sample. That is, most trading systems can be adjusted until they produce high net profit results on the in-sample data, but profit for the out-of-sample data is often poor.

Better choices of metrics are those that reward equity growth while penalizing drawdown. AmiBroker has several of those as built-in metrics. They include:

- RAR/MDD - Risk adjusted Annual Return / Maximum DrawDown.
- CAR/MDD - Compound Annual Return / Maximum DrawDown.
- K-ratio - a metric developed by Lars Kestner.
- RRR - Risk - Reward Ratio.
- Ulcer Performance Index.

Exhaustive versus Non-Exhaustive Optimizing

If you do nothing special, when you code your optimize functions and then click the optimize button, AmiBroker will use every combination of parameter values you have given - an exhaustive search. If one variable goes from 2 to 100 in steps of 2, that is 50 values; if another goes from 1 to 20 in steps of 1, that is 20 values. An exhaustive optimization would run a backtest for each of the 1000 (20 times 50) alternatives. After the 1000 runs, AmiBroker will sort them into descending order according to the metric you chose and display the results. Since every possible combination has been evaluated, the best one is at the top of the list.

AmiBroker has two alternative methods of carrying out the search that will probably find the best alternative, and will do it in much less time because it does not search the entire space. The search space, as the universe of all possible combinations of parameter values is called, will have some regions where the objective function values are high, and other regions where they are low. There are some optimization methods that focus their search efforts on those areas that are more promising and skip lightly over the less promising areas. These are called non-exhaustive search methods. The two implemented in AmiBroker are:

- CMAE (Covariance Matrix Adaptation Evolutionary Strategy)
- "Tribes" - an adaptive, parameter-less version of PSO (Particle Swarm Optimization) non-exhaustive optimizer.

Appendix C, Resources, has URLs to references for both these methods.

The absolute best score of all the alternatives, and the set of values for the parameters that are associated with it, is called the global maximum. It is the best solution. An exhaustive search will find the global maximum. Other regions will have scores higher than the surrounding areas, but will not be the absolute highest. They are called local maximums. Non-exhaustive search methods sometimes find local maximums, but not the global maximum; although usually they do find the global maximum.

There are advantages to using the non-exhaustive methods.

- One is that they are quicker to converge — quicker to find the region that contains the maximum. If your optimization has only a few thousand alternatives to consider, you may not notice the difference. If it has 100,000 or more, a run that would take hours or days to complete, you will definitely notice the difference.

- Another is that the algorithm used to evaluate the objective function can be clever and can take into account the surrounding points. One of the goals is to pick a set of values that score well, but that also are stable and robust. A robust area of a search space has good scores not only at the maximum, but also in the surrounding area.

To use either of these non-exhaustive methods, place a statement at the start of your program:

```
OptimizerSetEngine("cmae");

OptimizerSetEngine("trib")
```

According to the literature, the cmae technique is superior.

3D Visualization

If your program has exactly two variables being optimized, you can see what the response surface looks like. The response surface is the plot of the objective function in the vertical direction versus the two variables in the two horizontal directions. After running an optimization (either exhaustive or non-exhaustive), pull down the menu at the right of the optimize button and click **view 3D optimization graph**. The controls allow you to rotate and tilt the graph, and to raise and lower the water level.

For all trading systems, the model (the AFL code) is the static representation of the underlying market it is modeling. When the model and the market are in synchronization, as they always are for the in-sample period, the objective score for the best parameter values will be high. When the underlying market shifts, as it will in the out-of-sample period, the optimal point will shift as well. A slight shift in the market has the same effect as moving the optimal peak slightly. If the new position has a lower objective score, the system will be less profitable, or unprofitable. So the best solution to the optimization is to find a region of the parameter space that not only scores well, but is robust — in the 3D view, an area that has a high score and is the top of a broad, flat, plateau.

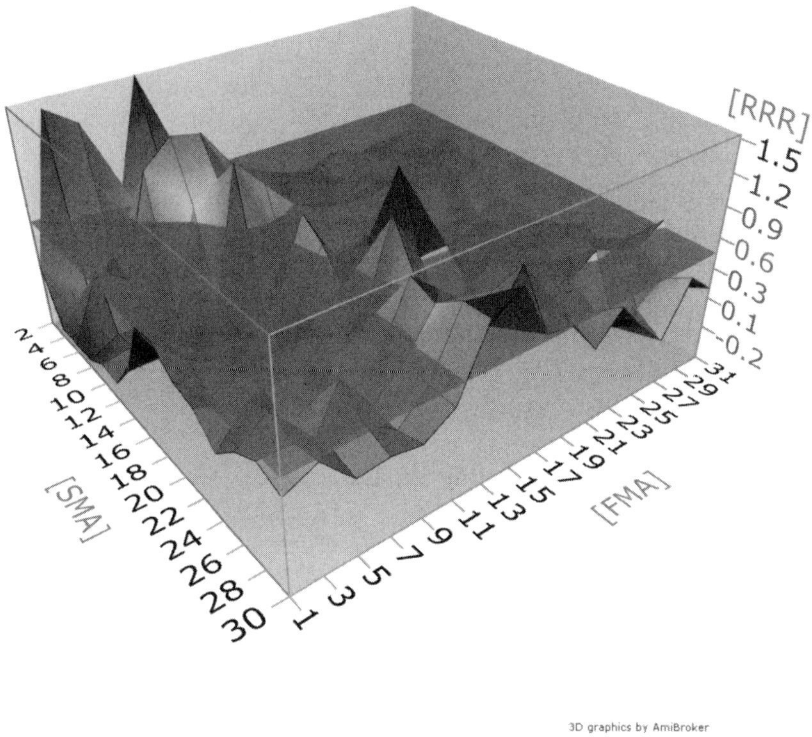

If you look at the 3D visualization and find that the best region is at one of the borders, expand the range being searched and run again — the best region may get even better in the area not tested in the first runs.

Some Optimizing Tricks

- Thanks to Herman van den Bergen for contributing this technique to the AmiBroker library.

  You can Optimize parameters with custom number series by using the numbers generated by the Optimize() function as an index to access numbers in a custom array. Here is an example using a custom array FB[] of Fibonacci numbers:

  ```
  FB[0] = 0.0; FB[1] = 23.6; FB[2] = 38.2; FB[3] = 50.0; FB[4]
  = 61.8; FB[5] = 100; FB[6] = 161.8; FB[7] = 261.8; FB[8] =
  423.6;

  FBindex = Optimize("FBindex",0,0,8,1);

  FibNum = FB[FBindex];

  ... place your Code using FibNum here ...
  ```

- Thanks to Tomasz Janeczko for this one.

  You can refresh your equity chart after each optimization step, and observe how the linearity of your equity curve is affected, by adding these two lines to the very end of your code:

  ```
  AB = CreateObject("Broker.Application");
  AB.RefreshAll();
  ```

  Important note: Do not use in commentary, interpretation, or indicator builder because it will cause loop.

- And thanks to Tomasz again for this.

  Some asked for a function that combines Param() and Optimize(). Here it is:

  ```
  function ParamOptimize( pname, defaultval, minv, maxv,
  step )
  {
  return Optimize( pname,
  Param( pname, defaultval, minv, maxv, step ),
  minv, maxv, step );
  }
  ```

Walk Forward

To start a walk forward run, pull down the menu next to the Optimize button and select Walk-Forward Optimization.

Example 9, Chapter 3, ran a walk forward. Review that example now.

Background and Justification

While there is nothing special about the optimization process - it is just an organized way to look at a lot of alternatives - there is something very special about the walk forward process. The walk forward process is the best tool available to you for trading system validation. While you are developing your trading system, you have access to all the data. Using your best efforts, you try to develop your system using in-sample data and test it using out-of-sample data. But what will happen when you start actually trading the system? The walk forward process can give you an idea of what might happen.

In the development phase, you used the in-sample data and ran optimizations to search for patterns, then tested on out-of-sample data. The walk forward process automates this for you and provides several important things:

- It automates the process of optimizing over a set of in-sample data.
- It automates selection of the best set of values.
- It automates testing over the out-of-sample data.
- For each walk forward step, it gives you a look at what happens when your system goes from in-sample to out-of-sample.
- It gives you an idea of how long your system remains in synchronization with the market it is modeling.
- It provides a set of out-of-sample results that you can use as a baseline to compare the actual results of your own trading.

The walk forward process is the culmination of the steps of:

- Choose your own objective function.
- Optimize in-sample.
- Test out-of-sample.

Note that in the walk forward process, the best set of values for the parameters is chosen, and the out-of-sample results are calculated using those values. At this point, you do not choose which set to use; you have already incorporated the criteria that are important to you into your objective function. For a deeper discussion of objective functions, see *Quantitative Trading Systems*.

Mechanics of Walk Forward

By the time you get to the walk forward stage, you have a trading system you like and you know what tradables it models well. You are looking for three things:

- How long is the in-sample period?
- How long is the out-of-sample period?
- What is the out-of-sample performance?

The underlying market is changing as the fundamentals upon which it is based change. These could be interest rates, the strength of the currency, the phase of the economic cycle, the profitability of the sector and of the specific company, and so forth. Your model is able to identify the important characteristics and identify profitable trading opportunities, but the model and the market drift from being in synchronization to out. The length of the in-sample period must be shorter than the period of synchronization. Your system sets its parameter values in the in-sample period and trades in the out-of-sample period. So, your system must sync-up during the in-sample period, then trade for as long as the synchronization remains strong.

Open **Automatic Analysis**, click the **Settings** button, and the **Walk-Forward** tab.

1. Click **Easy mode (EOD)**.

Decide when to begin your walk forward. Of course, you must have data from the starting date to the present. But you may decide not to use all of your historical data. By using your judgement, or by running some tests, decide whether the oldest data you have has the same characteristics as the more recent data. For example, the characteristics of the entire equities market changed after October 1987, so you may not want to use data earlier than 1988. If your preferred markets ran up sharply in the late 1990s and fell off dramatically in the early 2000s, you may want to include that data, or you may want to exclude it.

2. Set your starting date in the **Start** box.
3. Leave **Anchored** unchecked.

Each model and market combination has a unique relationship. There is no way to tell in advance what the optimum length of the in-sample period is. You must run tests to determine it. By the time you are running the walk forward tests, you should have a very good idea of what length in-sample period to use.

4. Set that length as your in-sample length on the walk forward tab. That is, set the **End** date so that the length of time between Start and End is the length of your in-sample period.

5. Decide what date you want as the last day of the last in-sample period. (You may want to withhold some data from the walk-forward process, just as you withheld some data from the backtesting runs you made earlier.) Enter that date in the **Last** field. Alternatively, check **Use today**.

Your system will remain profitable as long as the model and the market remain in sync during the out-of-sample period. The length you set as the step sets both the re-optimization period and the out-of-sample length. By running tests, you can determine how long, typically, the system remains profitable in the out-of-sample period. That is the longest you can wait between re-optimizations.

6. Set the length you want to use for your out-of-sample and re-optimization in the **Step** field, and use the pull-down menu to select the time increment.

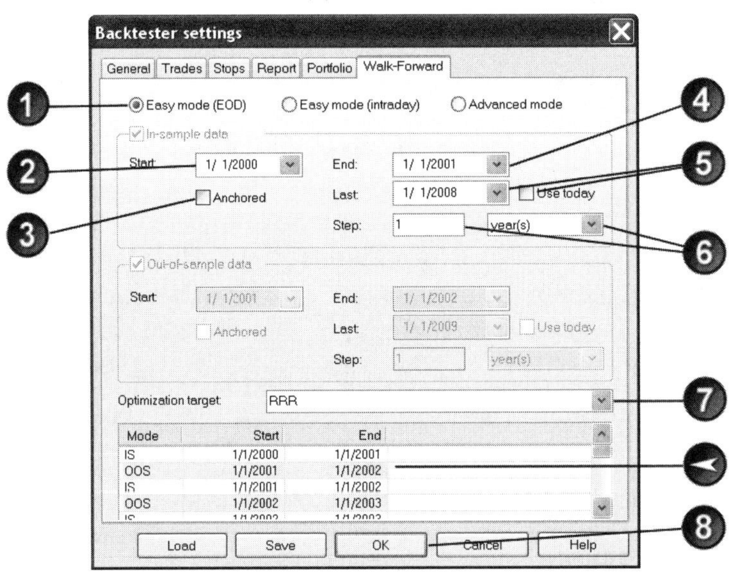

The dates that will be used for each in-sample run and each out-of sample run will be computed and entered into the table. Scroll up and down and review these dates. Be certain they reflect what you want.

7. Select your optimization target from the pull-down list. You should already have selected an objective function and been using it all along during your system development and backtesting. RRR is a good choice.

8. Click **OK**. This exits the Walk Forward setup dialog.

Each of the walk forward runs is evaluated as it takes place. After an in-sample optimization, the best set of parameter values is chosen and a single test run is made using those values and that specific in-sample period. The equity curve for that in-sample run is calculated. Next, a single test run is made, using those same values, for the out-of-sample period that immediately follows. The equity curve for that out-of-sample run is calculated.

There are two reports you can watch as the walk forward runs take place.

The first is the set of in-sample and out-of-sample summaries. These are produced automatically and displayed on a separate tab in the main chart window.

Mode	Begin	End	No.	Net Profit	Net % Profit	Exposure %	CAR	RAR	Max. Trade
IS	1/1/2000	1/1/2001	168	29717.14	29.72	71.10	30.09	42.32	
OOS	1/1/2001	1/1/2002	1	-3414.31	-3.41	64.19	-3.43	-5.35	
IS	1/1/2001	1/1/2002	24	36514.88	36.51	51.61	36.75	71.21	
OOS	1/1/2002	1/1/2003	1	-5164.02	-5.16	68.65	-5.19	-7.56	
IS	1/1/2002	1/1/2003	21	10505.40	10.51	64.00	10.57	16.51	
OOS	1/1/2003	1/1/2004	1	4774.69	4.77	61.45	4.80	7.81	

The second is the concatenation of the in-sample equity curves and out-of-sample equity curves. These are displayed in a pane of the main chart window. But you must first insert the indicator that will display them. Using the charts tabbed menu, expand the equity category, right-click **IS and OOS Equity**, then left-click **Insert**.

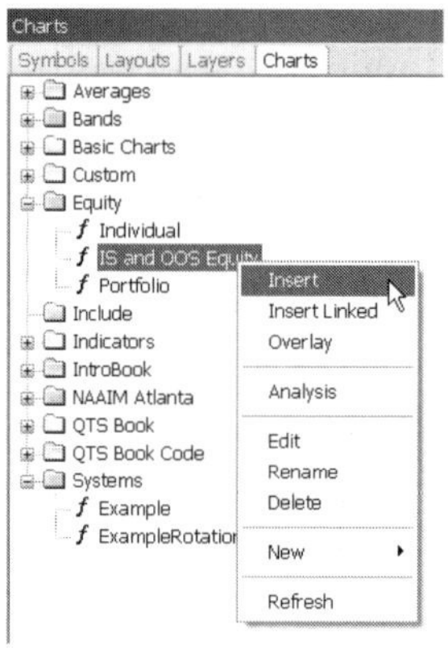

As the walk forward progresses, you can click on the main chart tab and watch the equity curves develop. This example illustrates a classic example of a system that does well in-sample, but poorly out-of-sample. It has learned the noise, but not the signal.

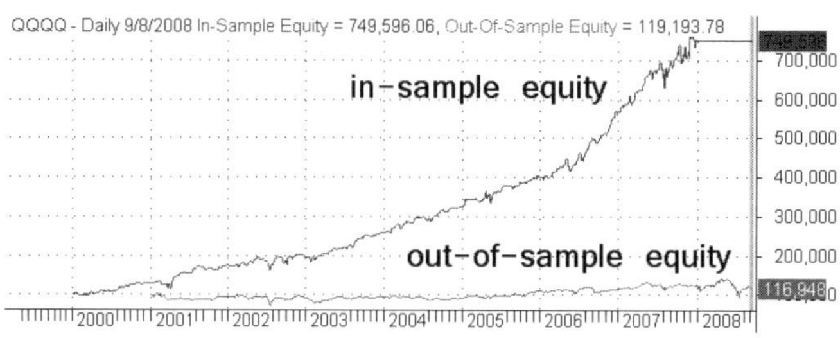

The in-sample results are (almost) always better than the out-of-sample results. Good trading systems have out-of-sample results that rise steadily in all the out-of-sample periods, like the one shown here.

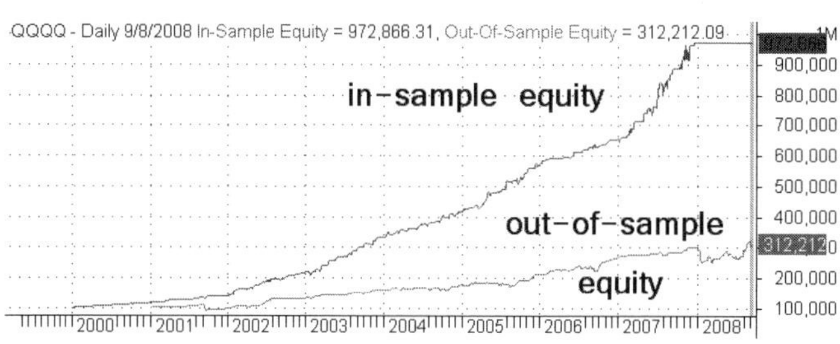

Back on the Automatic Analysis screen:

1. Select your trading system.
2. Define your watchlist.
3. Pull down the menu next to the Optimize button, click Walk-Forward Optimization.

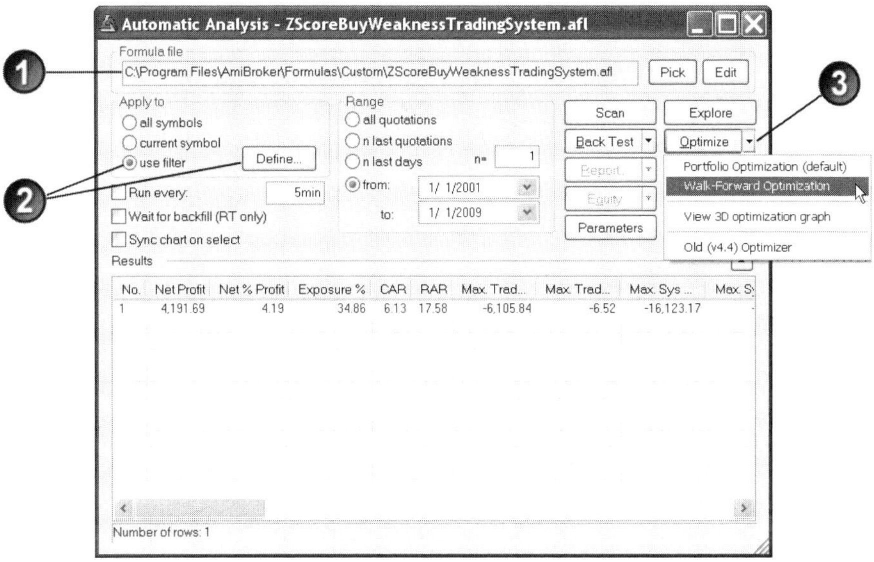

Look at the equity curves and the in-sample and out-of-sample summaries. If they look good, your system is ready for trading.

Commentary and Interpretation

You can write commentary that will appear in the Commentary window or the Interpretation window. The commentary is specific to the active symbol, the active pane, and the selected bar. The explanation for Commentary is first, then Interpretation.

Commentary

Using the **Analysis** menu, select **Commentary**. The commentary window has two tabs - Commentary and Formula. Use the Formula tab to enter the AFL code you want to use, and the Commentary tab to display the output.

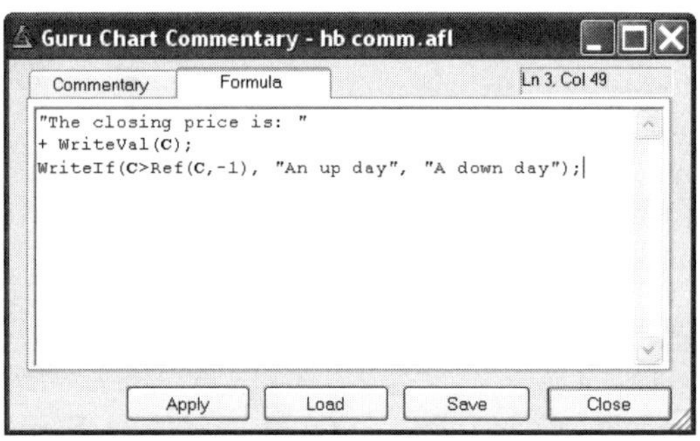

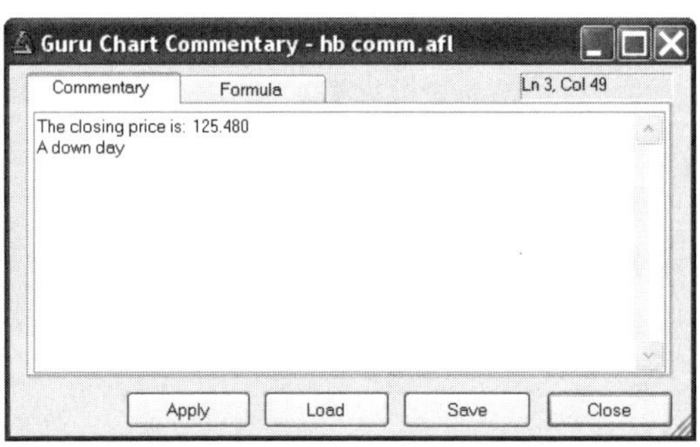

A commentary formula consists of two elements: static text and dynamic content.

Static Text

Static text elements are enclosed in quotes and terminated with a semicolon. The text is displayed in the commentary window exactly as it is written. Each statement will be placed on a new line. Including the two characters "\n" will force a line break in the output whenever that is necessary (and it will be necessary in Interpretation). A simple example of static text is:

```
"The closing price is: ";
```

Dynamic Content

Two AFL functions are useful for creating dynamic content: WriteVal() (or its equivalent function, NumToStr), and WriteIf().

WriteVal

Syntax:

WriteVal(NUMBER);

WriteVal(ARRAY);

Returns:

STRING

Description:

WriteVal does not really write anything; it converts either a number or an array to a string and returns the string value. WriteVal can only be used within a commentary.

Any expression that evaluates to a number or numeric array can be uses as an argument to WriteVal. For example:

```
WriteVal(Close - Ref(Close,-1));
```

WriteVal always returns *one* value of the array (not an array of values). In almost all cases this is LastValue of the array but in indicators it is "selected value" - the one that is selected by the vertical line.

WriteIf - Conditional Output

Syntax

WriteIf(Expression, "True Text", "False Text");

Returns

STRING

Description

The WriteIf function is very similar to the IIf function. An expression is evaluated. If the result is True, then whatever is in the True Text string is returned. If the result is False, then whetever is in the False Text string is returned. For example:

```
WriteIf(C>Ref(C,-1), "An up day", "A down day");
```

Concatenation means join together by appending one to the other. The concatenation operator is "+". To join two strings together, put the "+" between them. Any expression that evaluates to a string can be concatenated into the output by using the "+" operator. For example:

```
"The closing price is: " + WriteVal(Close);
```

The calculation and nesting can be as complex as you wish. For example:

```
Indicator1 = ...;
Indicator2 = ...;
Indicator3 = ...;
"The indicator status today is " +
WriteIf(Indicator1>3, "Very Bullish",
WriteIf(Indicator2>12, "Bullish",
WriteIf(Indicator3<0, "Bearish", "Neutral" )));
```

Use

Commentary code is written by typing it into the Formula tab of the Commentary window; no editor is needed. The **Save** button opens a Save As dialog and you can save the commentary just as you would save any other AFL program.

If you have already written a commentary, clicking the **Load** button opens a dialog box so you can locate and load the program you want to use.

Click the **Apply** button to run the code. Click the **Results** tab to see the commentary that applies to the bar that is selected.

Interpretation

To convert the code you have written for the commentary window so that it appears in the interpretation window, enclose every string that is being written so that it becomes an argument to a Printf function.

Syntax

```
printf(formatstr);
```

Returns

Nothing

Description

Printf sends the string portion of formatstr, formatted according to the format portion of formatstr, to the output.

In this case, the output is the interpretation window. The code must be appended to the AFL code of the system or function that is displayed in a pane. In order to see the output, make the pane active. The commentary output will appear in the interpretation window. As bars are selected, the output will be interpreted for each bar.

In the image that follows:

A. Add the commentary code to the AFL for a trading system that has a plot statement.
B. Use the Apply Indicator icon to open a new pane and plot the indicator.
C. Click in the pane that has the commentary code attached to it.
D. Read the commentary in the Interpretation window.

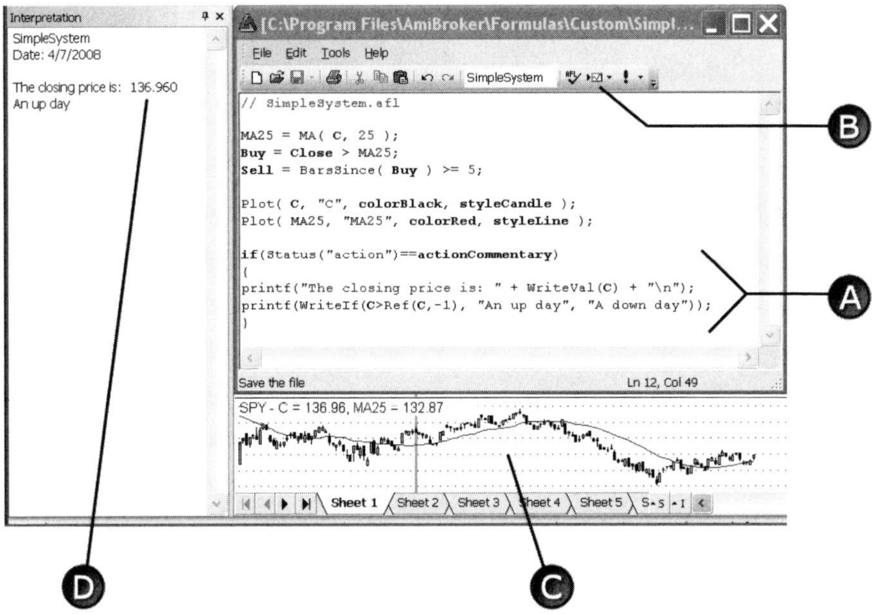

If you click a bar, you will see the interpretation for that bar. If you click a different pane, you will see the commentary associated with that pane.

Performance Tip

To get the best performance, enclose the commands that compute the values used only by the commentary, and the statements that produce the output, in a set of braces and precede them by a conditional test. For example:

```
If(Status("action")==actionCommentary)
{
// computations needed only for the commentary

// WriteVal, WriteIf, and PrintIf statements

}
```

This section of code will only be executed if the commentary will be visible if produced, thus saving execution time.

Chapter 10

Write It Yourself

The previous chapters have shown examples of functions, indicators, and trading systems. This chapter explains in more detail how you go about writing your own. The examples in this chapter all assume that the data is end-of-day and comes from the exchange. Forex and after-hours trading are not considered. The data bars are daily bars and have at least a closing price, perhaps open, high, and low. It can be stocks, mutual funds, exchange traded funds, or commodities - the techniques apply to all and we will not distinguish.

Before you start coding

A few questions need answers before you start.

When will you be collecting the data, running your trading system, and issuing your signals? When will you place your orders? When will the orders be executed?

The answers will help you specify the BuyPrice and Trade Delay.

Trading Next Day Open (NDO)

Assume you have a day job and you are doing your data collection in the evening, running your trading systems in the evening, generating signals from the values of the most recent bar, placing orders in the evening, and anticipating execution at the opening price the next trading day.

You must specify Trade Delay of 1. Your signals come today, your trades happen tomorrow - one day later.

If you plan to issue Market On Open orders, you must specify your BuyPrice as Open.

Note: If you are trading mutual funds and the only price point and trading opportunity tomorrow is the close, then you must specify you BuyPrice as Close.

There are two methods of telling AmiBroker about those choices.

The first is using Analysis > Automatic Analysis > Settings > Trades, and filling in the BuyPrice and BuyDelay. Entering your preferences there sets them as defaults. See page 486.

The second is in your AFL code.

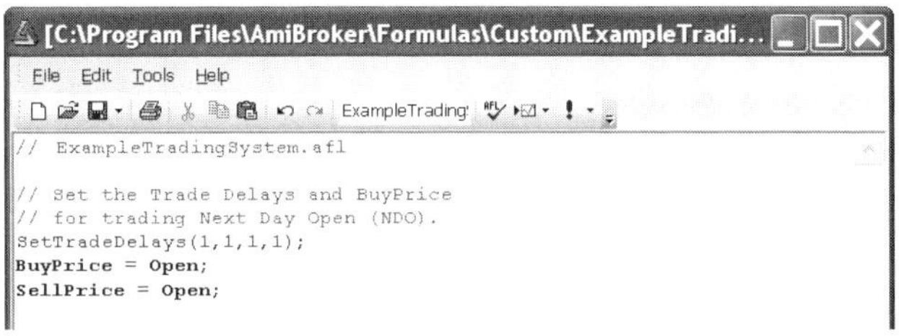

These lines go at the top of your code.

The SetTradeDelays procedure has four numbers. They represent the trade delay for the Buy, Sell, Short, and Cover, respectively.

The BuyPrice = Open; line tells AmiBroker that you want market orders executed at the open. In AmiBroker, a market order is any order that does not explicitly state a price and a condition. Buy = Cross(C,MA(C,5)); issues a market order, since no price or other condition is specified.

Trading Same Day Close

If you have an accurate and profitable short term trading system - one that holds only a few days - you will probably find that the price change between the close of the bar that generates your signal and the open on the next bar is in the same direction as your signal. That overnight move is often the most profitable portion of the holding period. In order to capture it, you must be able to anticipate the price that will give you a signal before the close of trading, then execute your trade and take your position on the close.

Your TradeDelay is 0, and your BuyPrice is Close.

There are several ways to anticipate the signal.

- Use real-time quotes, either snapshot or streaming, to estimate the closing price just before the closing time.
- Use the formula for the code that generates your signal to precalculate what price would trigger your signal. Either enter that as a Limit On Close order, or be ready to place the order

yourself.

- Use a root-finding algorithm to precalculate the price necessary for any condition, whether you have the formula or not. For example, you can precalculate the price at which a moving average will cross through a 2 ATR band, and have your order ready when that condition happens. This procedure is explained in detail in *Quantitative Trading Systems.*

Whatever your trading delays and buy price are, if you use AFL statements to set them, the values given in the AFL override the values set in Settings.

Portfolio Considerations

You may be planning a system that trades only one thing - perhaps a broad market index. In that case, the number of positions you hold will always be either zero or one. And you need to make no special arrangements for portfolio management.

You may also be planning to write several trading systems, each for a single tradable, and manage the position allocation outside AmiBroker. Again, you need no special portfolio code.

You may be planing a trading system that keeps track of a universe of potential holdings - say the Fidelity Select Funds, or the S&P Sector ETFs. Your system monitors each of them every day. Whenever there is a buy signal, you want AmiBroker to take a position, but only if there is room in your holdings. In this case you do need special arrangements to handle the portfolio.

There are no settings that let you manage a portfolio - this can only be done in AFL code. Expanding on the previous example, add these lines at the top of your code.

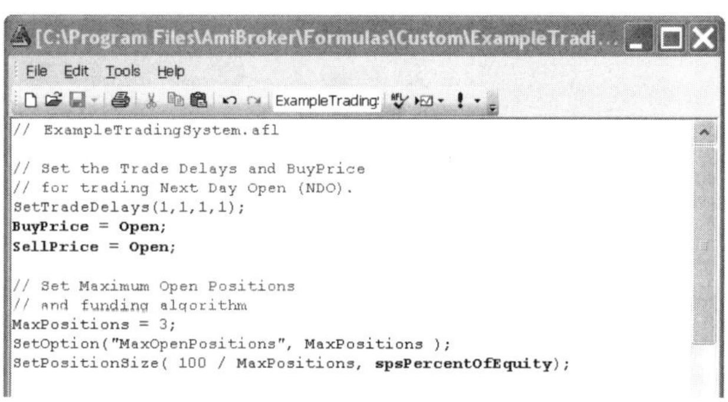

```
MaxPositions = 3;
```

MaxPositions is not a reserved variable. It is one of your variables, and it is used so that you can easily change its value, or optimize it.

```
SetOption("MaxOpenPositions", MaxPositions );
```

SetOption, using the "MaxOpenPositions" option and MaxPositions identifier, tells AmiBroker than the maximum number of open positions is found in the variable MaxPositions.

```
SetPositionSize( 100 / MaxPositions, spsPercentOfEquity);
```

[The older method producing the same result is:
`PositionSize = -100 / MaxPositions;`]

SetPositionSize tells AmiBroker how to allocate funds. If the second argument is spsPercentOfEquity, treat whatever number the first argument is as a percentage. Allocate that percentage of the equity to each new position taken. With MaxPositions having a value of 3, each new position gets 33.33% of the equity.

If the second argument is spsValue, then that number of dollars will be used.

If there is not enough in cash to make the full purchase, AmiBroker checks the Setting to see whether **Allow Position Size Shrinking** has been checked. If it has been checked, then all the remaining cash will be used to take the new position.

As you progress, there are additional statements you will want to use to be certain that AmiBroker manages the system as you want it to. For now, let's move on.

Enter a Long Position - Buy

The AFL statement that tells AmiBroker to issue a Buy signal is:

```
Buy = something;
```

Buy is a reserved variable. It is an array and it has values for every day. Those days when your system does not generate a Buy signal, the value for that day is False, or 0. Those days when your system does generate a Buy signal, the value for that day is True, or 1. Whether the value is a 0 or a 1, False or True, depends on the result of evaluating the right hand side - the something.

Whenever there is a Buy Signal and no position is held, there will be a purchase. If there is already a position, the signal will be ignored.

Recall that every statement of this type has an expression on the right hand side and a variable on the left hand side separated by the "=" sign. The "=" sign is the assignment operator.

Processing the statement requires two steps: evaluating the right hand side so that it returns a unique result of the same type as the variable on the left hand side; then assigning that value to (or storing that value in) the variable.

Since Buy needs to be assigned the value of True, or 1, whenever the system generates a Buy signal, the right hand side is usually an expression that is either True or False, 1 or 0.

Some simple examples:

- ```
  Buy = DayOfWeek() == 2;
  ```

  DayOfWeek is a built-in function that evaluates what day of the week the current bar is. It returns a value of 0 for Sunday, 1 for Monday, 2 for Tuesday, and so forth. The "==" is a comparison operator that checks what is on its left and what is on its right and returned a value of either True, the two are the same, or False, the two are different. If the bar being evaluated is Tuesday, DayOfWeek() returns 2, and the "==" operator returns True - the two are the same. So the value of True, or 1, for the right hand side is assigned to, or stored in, Buy. AmiBroker sees that Buy is True and issues a Buy signal. If you are running a backtest, a new position is taken. If you are running a scan, the report tells you that there is a new Buy signal at the close of today's bar.

- ```
  Buy = Cross ( C, MA(C,5) );
  ```

  Cross is a built-in function that returns a value of True when the first argument, C, has a greater value after this bar than the second variable, MA(C,5); and the first variable had a lower value than the second variable after the previous bar. Said differently, Cross returns True when the first variable crosses up through the second variable. The two being compared do not need to be variables; constants and expressions are also acceptable.

The first variable is the current bar's close. The second variable is the current bar's 5 day simple moving average. If the close was below the 5 day moving average yesterday and is above it today, then Cross returns a True. The evaluation of the right hand side is complete and the True is assigned to Buy. A Buy Signal is generated.

This is called an impulse signal. It is True for one bar, then False. After a few bars it may be True again, but only for one bar.

- ```
  SetUp = C > MA(C,5);
  StochSignal = Cross(StochD(),30);
  Buy = SetUp AND StochSignal;
  ```

  This represents a setup and a trigger. The first line is the setup. The right hand side evaluates to True on every bar where the close is above its 5 day simple moving average. That will be one day or several days in a row. This type of signal is called a state signal. The second line evaluates to True on those bars when the StochD indicator crosses up though the 30 line. The Buy Signal is generated when both are True - the And operator evaluates to True when both its right hand side and its left hand side are true.

Exit a Long Position - Sell

Sell works the same as Buy.

```
Sell = whatever;
```

Whenever the right hand side evaluates to True, a Sell signal is generated. If there is a position, it will be sold. If there is no position, the signal will be ignored.

Some simple examples:

- ```
  Sell = DayOfWeek() == 5;
  ```

  Sell on Friday.

- `Sell = Cross ( MA(C,5),C );`

  Cross is True when the first argument, MA(C,5), has a greater value after this bar than the second variable, C,; and the first variable had a lower value after the previous bar. That is, when MA(C,5) rose through C — or when C fell through MA(C,5).

Exit a Long Position via Stop

There are several ways to exit a long position:

- A Sell signal, as was just described.
- A timed exit, or n-bar stop.
- A profit target, or profit stop.
- A trailing stop.
- A maximum loss stop.

AmiBroker has built-in stops. Review the sections of this book and the AmiBroker User's Guide for descriptions of stops.

A Timed Exit

For trading systems that hold only a short period - perhaps a few days - the timed exit may be valuable. This stop exits after 5 days.

```
ApplyStop( stopTypeNBar, stopModeBars, 5 );
```

A Profit Target

Also for systems that hold only a short period, exit when the trade has a profit. This stop exits when it can book a 5 percent profit.

```
ApplyStop( stopTypeProfit, stopModePercent, 5 );
```

A Trailing Stop

Trailing stops work well for positions that are held a longer time. They follow along behind a rising price - rising when the price goes up, but never declining. If the price declines enough to cross through the stop price, the position is sold. This stop, called a chandelier stop, trails at 3 times the Average True Range below the price.

```
ApplyStop(stopTypeTrailing, stopModePoint, 3*ATR(14), True,
True );
```

A Maximum Loss Stop

The maximum loss stop is the last resort. Well designed systems seldom have positions exited because the price hit a maximum loss stop. This is a 15 percent maximum loss stop.

```
ApplyStop( stopTypeLoss, stopModePercent, 15 );
```

Write Looping Code

Often, you can do everything you want to with the functions built-in to AmiBroker. Occasionally, you need to examine the data bar-by-bar. A very simple example will be used to illustrate looping — the calculation of a 5 day simple moving average of the closing price for every bar of data.

The AmiBroker code is easy:

```
MABuiltIn = MA(C,5);
```

To explain the looping code, a diagram will help. You will see a small box for every day of data. There is an arrow pointing to an arbitrary index position labeled i. Index i is the day having its average computed. i starts at 0, the first bar, and goes up through BarCount-1, the last bar. There is also an arrow pointing to a group of 5 bars that will be used to compute the 5 day moving average. A separate index, j, will be used to move through these 5 bars.

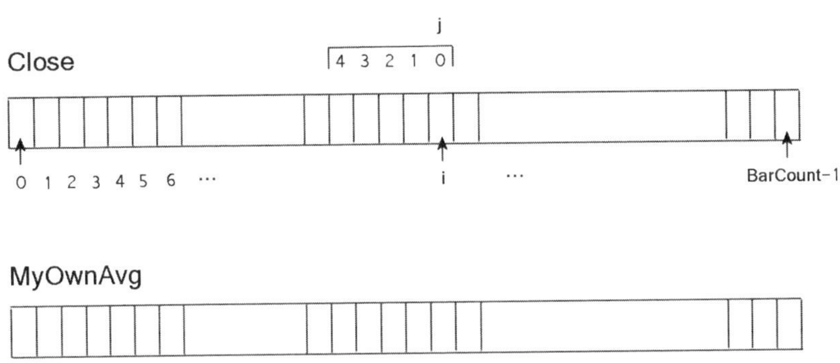

The AFL code to compute a 5-day simple moving average of the Close, and store that average in MyOwnAvg, is:

```
for ( i = 0; i < 4; i++ )
{
    MyOwnAvg[i] = C[i];
}

for ( i = 4; i < BarCount; i++ )
{
    Summer = 0;

    for ( j = 0; j <= 4; j++ )
    {
        Summer = Summer + C[i-j];
    }

    MyOwnAvg[i] = Summer / 5;
}
```

The first for loop handles the first part of the series where there is not enough data to compute a 5 day average. MyOwnAvg is set to the same value as Close for those 4 cells.

The second for loop starts at the 5th cell, the one whose index is 4 (array index numbers start at 0). And it goes up to and includes BarCount-1, the end of the series. The variable i is the index of the cell being worked on at any given time.

To compute the 5 day simple moving average, the values of the current cell and the previous 4 cells are added together, then that sum is divided by 5. The third for loop does that. Note that the j variable used to add up the 5 values counts backwards; that makes the coding easier.

Good programming practices strongly discourage use of specific numbers, such as 4 and 5, in programs. And it would be impractical to have to write a new program for every different moving average length. Here is the same code written using a variable for the length of the moving average:

```
MALen = 5;

for ( i = 0; i < MALen; i++ )
{
    MyOwnAvg2[i] = C[i];
}
```

```
for ( i = MALen - 1; i < BarCount; i++ )
{
    Summer = 0;

    for ( j = 0; j < MALen; j++ )
    {
        Summer = Summer + C[i-j];
    }

    MyOwnAvg2[i] = Summer / MALen;
}
```

Write a Custom Function

AmiBroker has hundreds of built-in functions. But eventually you will come across an indicator or a function that you want to use that is not built-in. The code that follows implements the simple moving average again, this time as a function.

```
// MyOwnAvgFunction.afl
//

function MACustom ( Price, Length )
{

    for ( i = 0; i < Length; i++ )
    {
        Result[i] = Price[i];
    }

    for ( i = Length - 1; i < BarCount; i++ )
    {
        Summer = 0;

        for ( j = 0; j < Length; j++ )
        {
            Summer = Summer + Price[i-j];
        }

        Result[i] = Summer / Length;
    }

    return Result;
}

BuiltInAvg = MA( C, 5 );
MyOwnAvg = MACustom( C, 5 );

Plot( C, "C", colorBlack, styleCandle );

Plot( MyOwnAvg, "MyOwnAvg", colorRed, styleLine );
Plot( BuiltInAvg, "BuiltInAvg", colorBlue, styleLine );
```

Variable Length Parameter

The MyOwnAvgFunction has two parameters - Price and Length. Price is an array, perhaps of closing prices, perhaps of some other indicator. It is expected that there will be variation among the values in that array. Length is constant throughout the calculation of the average. The next example illustrates that the length can be an array, and its elements variable.

There must be some way of determining what values to put in the array. The ADX indicator is sometimes used to indicate the strength of a trend. High values of ADX correspond with long cycle periods, low values of ADX with short periods. This example uses the value of the ADX indicator as the length of the moving average. Readers will want to experiment with using other indicators of period or cycle length.

```
// MyOwnAvgVariableFunction.afl
//
function MACustomVariable ( Price, Length )
{
    Ignore = int( LastValue( Highest( Length ) ) );

    for ( i = 0; i < Ignore; i++ )
    {
        Result[i] = Price[i];
    }

    for ( i = Ignore; i < BarCount; i++ )
    {
        ThisLength = int( 0.5 * Length[i] );
        Summer = 0;

        for ( j = 0; j < ThisLength; j++ )
        {
            Summer = Summer + Price[i-j];
        }

        Result[i] = Summer / ThisLength;
    }
    return Result;
}

ADXVal = ADX( 14 );
//Plot(ADXVal,"ADXVal",colorBlue,styleLine|styleOwnScale);

BuiltInAvg = MA( C, 10 );
MyOwnAvg = MACustomVariable( C, ADXVal );

Plot( C, "C", colorBlack, styleCandle );

Plot( MyOwnAvg, "MyOwnAvg", colorRed, styleLine );
Plot( BuiltInAvg, "BuiltInAvg", colorBlue, styleLine );
```

This line computes how many elements at the beginning of the series should be ignored. There are more sophisticated ways to compute that, but the point is that it must be considered.

```
Ignore = int( LastValue( Highest( Length ) ) );
```

Instead of Length being constant throughout, it varies. The value needed is in the cell with the same index number as the series being averaged.

This line extracts the value of the variable length and makes it an integer, so it can be used as an index into the arrays. The 0.5 factor is a fudge factor. Since there is so much delay in the ADX indicator, its value is cut in half to make it more responsive.

```
ThisLength = int( 0.5 * Length[i] );
```

Note how the built-in average stays about the same distance from the closing prices, but the custom average with the variable lengths tightens up when the direction is changing, and lags behind when there is a trend.

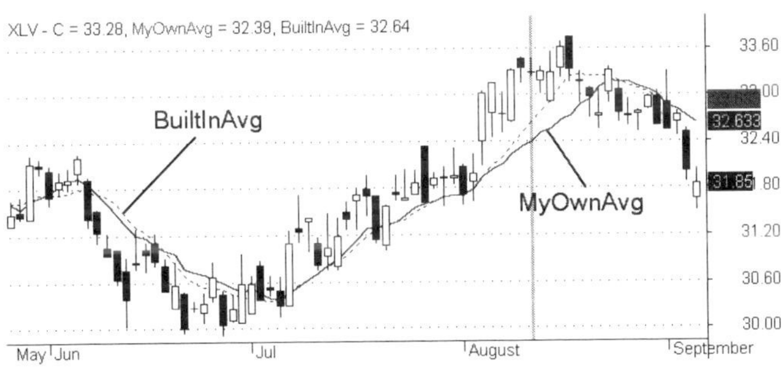

A Trend Following Trading System

```
// TrendFollowing.afl
//
// Using end of day data,
// generating signals in the evening,
// placing trades for execution
// the next day on the open.
//
// Takes only long positions.
//
// Holds up to 3 positions.
//
// Moving average crossover to enter,
// moving average crossover to exit,
// chandelier trailing stop.
//
// Variables are set up for optimization
// and walk forward testing.
//
// Try this using a watchlist of the nine
// S&P sector exchange traded funds.
//
// This is just an example.
// Do Not trade this system.
// Do you own research.
//

OptimizerSetEngine( “cmae” );

SetTradeDelays( 1, 1, 1, 1 );
BuyPrice = Open;
SellPrice = Open;

PosQty = Optimize( “PosQty”, 2, 1, 3, 1 );
SetOption ( “maxopenpositions”, PosQty );
SetPositionSize( 100 / PosQty, spsPercentOfEquity );

MAL1 = Optimize( “MAL1”, 50, 1, 51, 2 );
MAL2 = Optimize( “MAL2”, 30, 2, 52, 2 );

MA1 = MA( C, MAL1 );
MA2 = MA( C, MAL2 );

Buy = Cross( MA1, MA2 );
Sell = Cross ( MA2, MA1 );

ATRMult = Optimize( “ATRMult”, 3.75, 1, 5, 0.25 );

ApplyStop( stopTypeTrailing, stopModePoint,
           ATRMult * ATR( 14 ), True, True );
```

A Mean Reversion Trading System

```
// MeanReversion.afl
//
// Using end of day data,
// generating signals just before the close,
// placing trades for execution
// the same day at the close.
//
// Takes only long positions.
//
// Holds up to 3 positions.
//
// Moving average crossover to enter,
// moving average crossover to exit,
// chandelier trailing stop.
//
// Variables are set up for optimization
// and walk forward testing.
//
// Try this using a watchlist of the nine
// S&P sector exchange traded funds.
//
// This is just an example.
// Do Not trade this system.
// Do you own research.
//

function zscore( price, Lookback )
{
    zs = ( price - MA( price, Lookback ) ) / StDev( price,
Lookback );
    return zs;
}

OptimizerSetEngine( "cmae" );

SetTradeDelays( 0, 0, 0, 0 );
BuyPrice = Close;
SellPrice = Close;

PosQty = Optimize( "PosQty", 1, 1, 3, 1 );
SetOption ( "maxopenpositions", PosQty );
SetPositionSize( 100 / PosQty, spsPercentOfEquity );

ZSLength = Optimize( "ZSLength", 34, 4, 50 , 1 );
zs = zscore( C, ZSLength );

BuyLevel = Optimize( "BuyLevel", -2.0, -4.0, 0.0, 0.25 );

Buy = Cross( BuyLevel, zs );
Sell = Cross( zs, 0 );

HoldDays = Optimize( "HoldDays", 9, 1, 10, 1 );
ApplyStop( stopTypeNBar, stopModeBars, HoldDays );

ProfitPercent = Optimize( "ProfitPercent", 3, 0.5, 5, 0.25 );
ApplyStop ( stopTypeProfit, stopModePercent, ProfitPercent );
```

Feedback

We hope this book has been useful to you.

We will appreciate your feedback regarding it.

If you feel that:

- There are topics that have been particularly helpful.
- Topics that seem to be confusing.
- Topics that are missing or inadequately covered.

Or you just want to make a comment about something related to the book, please send an e-mail to us at:

comments@introductiontoamibroker.com

We cannot guarantee a personal response, but your comments will help make the next edition of this book, and our other books, better.

Thank you.

Appendix A

Glossary

accumulation Buying is dominant over selling.

active An element of a graphical display that has the focus, or has been selected, usually by clicking on it.

alpha The rate of return of an asset, relative to the market. The intercept of the regression line describing the relative rates of return of the asset and the market.

argument In computer science terms, a procedure has formal parameters that describe the process being programmed, and actual arguments that are used to evaluate the procedure for a specific case. Most people are rather informal about the distinction between parameters and arguments. When the distinction is unimportant, either term may be used.

array In computer science, an array is a data structure consisting of a group of elements that are accessed by indexing. In most programming languages each element has the same data type and the array occupies a contiguous area of storage. Some programming languages, including AmiBroker's AFL, support array programming which generalizes operations and functions to work transparently over arrays as they do with scalars, instead of requiring looping over array members.

asset A resource having economic value. A resource that is bought or sold.

atr - average true range A measure of volatility. Computed by taking the difference between the true high (the maximum of yesterday's close and today's high) and the true low (the minimum of yesterday's close and today's low). These daily figures are averaged over some period, say 14 days.

bad tick An erroneous tick that does not represent a trade.

backtest Testing the profitability of a trading strategy on prior periods of time.

bar A consolidation of all ticks received over a given period of time into a single graphic element with values for the open, high, low, and closing values during that period.

beta The volatility of an asset, relative to the market. The slope of the regression line describing the relative rates of return of the asset and the market.

breakout A trade at a price higher than the highest high over a given period, or lower than the lowest low over a given period.

capital asset pricing model In finance, the Capital Asset Pricing Model (CAPM) is used to determine a theoretically appropriate required rate of return of an asset given that asset's non-diversifiable (systemic or market) risk.

close The price of the final tick or transaction in a bar.

commodity A basic economic good that is traded as a futures contract.

constant expiration A method of computing the prices of a synthetic futures contract based on an average of all active contracts.

continuous contract A synthetic futures contract constructed by splicing together individual contracts as they roll over.

contract A single unit of a commodity or future, such as 42000 gallons of crude oil, traded on one of the futures exchanges.

correlation A statistical measurement of the similarity of two data series, measured over a selected period of time.

curve-fit The term applied to a model that fits the data points too well, probably modeling the noise rather than the signal, and unlikely to represent the general patterns in the data.

database In AmiBroker, a directory holding the historical price data for the symbols in that database, and information about the charts associated with it. A layout defines how the database is used.

data mining Searching data series for patterns. Sometimes a derisive term implying a search for correlated data without regard for probable underlying association.

data plug-in A utility program that coordinates external database with AmiBroker. Each data vendor's data plug-in is unique to that vendor's database.

day trading Buying and selling within a single trading day based on signals taken from analysis of intraday data.

degrees of freedom A statistical measurement based on the relationship between the number of independent observations in a data series and the number of parameters that are estimated using that data. The number of data points minus the number of estimates is called the residual degrees of freedom. The lower the residual degrees of freedom, the less likely that the model has learned a general pattern.

delayed real-time Real-time data that has been delayed, usually by about 20 minutes, before being broadcast.

diffusion index An index formed by comparing the number or total amount of increases with the number or total amount of decreases over a group of tradable issues.

displacement A term describing the shifting of an indicator or a graph either forward or backward in time, often to reduce the effect of the lag of the indicator.

distribution Selling is dominant over buying.

Donchian A trading system method that buys on a breakout to new highs and sells on a breakout to new lows. Based on work done by Richard Donchian in the 1970s and 80s.

Drag and Drop A Windows technique for moving or copying from one location to another. Left-click the material to be copied (say, an indicator) and hold the left mouse button down, drag to the location (say, a pane of a chart window), drop the material (release the left mouse button).

drawdown The peak to trough decline in the value of a position or an account, usually measured as a percentage.

efficient The central point of several theories of market prices and movements. Proponents of the strong form of efficiency believe that all information, whether public or private, is represented in the price of the asset at all times, and that there is no profit to be made by analyzing prices, earnings, estimates, or anything else. Quantitative analysis and technical analysis are based on the belief that the markets are sufficiently inefficient that analysis of price patterns will lead to profitable trades.

end-of-day Data reported after the market has closed, and representing one day's activity. End-of-day data for stocks and futures is usually reported as a set of four data points, the opening trade, the high, the low, and the closing trade. Mutual fund data is usually only the closing price.

equity curve The value of the trading account over time, often presented as a graph.

evolutionary operation A search technique that fixes the values of all variables except one, and searches for the best model by varying that one. Then repeats for all other variables, and continues to cycle through until an optimum solution has been found. This method works well in industrial processes, but not for financial data.

exchange The organization responsible for regulating the trading of stocks, futures, or options.

exhaustive search A search technique that examines every possible data point.

expectancy The average amount or percentage won or lost on an average trade by a trading system. The expectancy must be positive for a system to be profitable.

expiration The time at which an individual futures contract or option ceases to exist.

exploration The AmiBroker term for the analysis of a group of issues, resulting in a report listing information about each item. The report can contain anything that AmiBroker has access to or can compute, including indicators and buy and sell signals.

exposure The percentage of time a given trading system is in a position. Whenever it is not exposed, the system has no position and is flat.

external database A database maintained by a data vendor, such as Quotes Plus or Norgate Premium Data. Cannot be modified by Quote Editor.

fast market Market conditions characterized by heavy trading, market imbalances, and high volatility.

first notice The date when holders of futures contracts are notified that the specific contract they hold will be expiring shortly, and they need to either exit their position or prepare for delivery of the commodity that contract represents.

fitness function Objective function.

focus An element of a graphical display that is active, or has been selected, usually by clicking on it.

fold A method used to develop out-of-sample periods from a set of data. The data is divided into several periods, each in turn reserved as out-of-sample data while the remaining data is in-sample. This method is not appropriate for modeling financial trading systems.

forex Short for Foreign Exchange. Trading of currencies, usually as pairs with a transaction being the purchase of one currency and the simultaneous sale of the other.

friction The costs of trading – primarily slippage and commission.

front month The futures contract that is most active and closest to expiration.

function In AmiBroker, a method of encapsulating a calculation into a single segment of code that can be called using its name. An example is the square root function.

future A tradable asset that represents the future delivery of some physical commodity or financial asset.

future leak A future leak occurs when a trading system looks ahead to data that will not be available in real-time to make its buy and sell decisions.

global When used with respect to layout — means a layout that can be used with more than one database. When used with respect to variables and functions — means variables that are defined outside the function and can be referenced inside the function. See local.

high The highest price traded for the period defined.

historical data The data series comprised of the historical records of all the individual reports for trades for an asset.

holding period The amount of time a position is held from buy to sell.

impulse signal A signal that fires (is set to True) once when an event occurs. For example Cross(C,MA(C,5)) is True (1) on the bar where the C is higher than its moving average but was not higher the previous bar; False (0), all other times. Compare with state signal.

indicator A representation of some characteristic of a tradable issue. Indicators are often mathematical in nature, such as a moving average, and are displayed graphically. The states or values of indicators are key components of trading systems.

in-sample During the model development process, data is divided into two sections. The in-sample data is used to develop the model, the out-of-sample data is used to verify that the model has detected patterns in the data that are predictable and profitable.

intraday When referring to data bars, data that is shorter than a full day. When referring to trading, trades that are made during the trading day rather than at the open or close of trading.

jackknife Same as fold.

K-ratio A metric used to measure the goodness or fitness of a trading system developed by Lars Kestner. K-ratio is essentially the slope of the equity line divided by the standard error of the equity line.

lag The amount of time or number of bars that an indicator is behind the series it has been applied to. For example, a 21 day simple moving average has a lag of 11 days - half the moving average period.

layout The top level of the AmiBroker structure. Layouts are associated with databases. Layouts contain windows, which contain sheets, which contain panes, which contain charts and formulas.

leverage The relationship between the value of the asset being traded and the amount of money the trader has put up for that trade. Unless margin is used, stock trades are unleveraged. Futures trades are usually leveraged.

limit-if-touched order An order placed with a broker that becomes a limit order when a trade occurs at the price specified.

limit-on-close order An order placed with a broker that becomes a market-on-close order if the closing price is within the limit specified.

limit-on-open order An order placed with a broker that becomes a market-on-open order if the opening price is within the limit specified.

limit order An order that is placed with a broker to buy at a price below the lowest offer, or to sell at a price above the highest bid.

linear scale Equal distances on the graph represent equal increments. Compare with logarithmic.

local When used with respect to layout, means a layout that can be used with only one database. When used with respect to variables and functions, means variables that are defined inside the function and cannot be referenced outside the function. See global.

logarithmic equal distances on the graph represent equal percentage changes. Compare with linear.

long A long position has purchased the asset, but not yet sold it.

low The lowest price traded for the period defined.

market When referring to orders to buy or sell, a market order is executed at the current offer or bid. When referring to tradable assets in general, the market is the broad category to which the tradable belongs.

market order An order placed with a broker to buy or sell at the current offer or bid price.

market-if-touched order An order placed with a broker that becomes a market order when a trade occurs at the price specified.

market-on-close order An order placed with a broker to buy or sell at the closing price.

market-on-open order An order placed with a broker to buy or sell at the opening price.

mean The arithmetic average.

mean reversion A trading system method based on an expectation that prices return to a mean level. Mean reversion systems buy weakness and sell strength.

metric A measure. The term is often used when discussing the fitness of a trading system.

model The idea or method that becomes the computer code portion of a trading system.

Monte Carlo A technique used in system validation that makes repeated selections from random data to test the stability and sensitivity of trading systems.

native database The database that AmiBroker maintains. Can be modified by Quote Editor.

object linking and embedding (OLE) A technique in Microsoft's Component Object Model that allows one program to delegate part of a task to another program, then re-import the results.

objective function A single-valued measurement of the fitness of a trading system. Optimization techniques are guided by maximizing the value of the objective function.

one-cancels-all order A set of orders placed with a broker. When any one of the orders is executed, all of the others are canceled.

ohlc The four data points associated with a bar of data – open, high, low, and close.

open The first price traded for the period specified.

open interest For futures contracts, the number of contracts that exist.

optimal f A position sizing technique based on methods developed by Ralph Vince that computs the optimal number of contracts to hold for any given trade in order to maximize future account equity.

optimization The organized search of alternative values of variables in a trading system.

outlier A legitimate data point that is outside the normal range of data points.

out-of-sample During the model development process, data is divided into two sections. The in-sample data is used to develop the model, the out-of-sample data is used to verify that the model has detected patterns in the data that are predictable and profitable.

parameter In computer science terms, a procedure has formal parameters that describe the process being programmed, and actual arguments that are used to evaluate the procedure for a specific case. Most people are rather informal about the distinction between parameters and arguments. When the distinction is unimportant, either term may be used.

pattern system A trading system based on the assumption that recognizable price patterns precede opportunities to make profitable trades.

perpetual contract The same as continuous contract.

pessimistic return ratio A metric designed by Ralph Vince that attempts to estimate the out-of-sample performance of a trading systems by adjusting statistics measured from in-sample performance.

phantom signal A phenomenon of walk-forward testing (or trading systems that have future leaks) where a signal or position changes without warning.

real-time When referring to price quotations, data that is reported and broadcast as soon after the transactions take place as is possible.

regression A modeling technique that computes the best fit of a line or curve to the data.

rollover Rollover takes place when one futures contract expires, or drops off significantly in volume, and the next in time sequence becomes the front month.

scalar A variable that takes only a single value. Compare with array.

scan In AmiBroker, running a program that checks the group of tickers for signals.

seasonality system A trading system based on the premise that prices move up or down at predictable times of the day, month, year, or other time period.

selected An element of a graphical display that has the focus, or has been made active, usually by clicking on it.

sensitivity A technique used in modeling to test the ability of the model to detect general patterns. Values of parameters are changed by small amounts to see if the fitness values remain at or near optimum.

Sharpe ratio A measure of performance based on the ratio of the return of the portfolio to the standard deviation of the return. The return is adjusted to be the excess return minus a risk-free rate, such as short term treasury bills.

short A short position has sold the asset, and will need to purchase it back later to close out the trade.

signals A trading system analyzes the data according to its rules and issues buy and sell signals.

snapshot data Snapshot data is real-time, or delayed real-time, data that is checked periodically intraday, but does not contribute toward building a real-time intraday database.

Sortino ratio A measure of market risk similar to the Sharpe ratio, but using only the downside volatility in the denominator rather than the standard deviation.

standard deviation A statistical measure of the variability or volatility of a set of data. The square root of the variance.

standard error A statistical measure of variability somewhat similar to the standard deviation, but based on repeated measurements. The standard error can be thought of as the standard deviation of the means of repeated samples.

state signal A signal that remains set to True as long as the condition tested remains True. For example: C>MA(C,5) will be True (1) on every bar where the close is above its moving average. Compare with impulse signal.

stationary The statistical concept that the characteristics of the data being modeling change very little over time. Financial time series are notoriously non-stationary.

stop and reverse A trading method where the exit from a long trade signals the entry to a short trade, and the exit from a short trade signals the entry to a long trade. The system is always in a position.

stop order An order placed with a broker to buy or sell at the market when a trade occurs at the price specified.

stop limit order An order placed with a broker to trade, but only at a limit price, when the market trades at the price specified.

survivor bias Optimistic bias introduced into tests of historical data due to the fact that failed organizations drop out of existence and are no longer in the database.

symbol space Just as the range of values for any variable being optimized can be thought of as a numeric space, the range of tickers available for testing can be thought of as the ticker space or symbol space.

synchronization Agreement between a profitable trading model, written in AFL, and the data the model processes. When the two are in sync, the system remains profitable.

system A trading system, in the context of this book, is a combination of a model and one or more data streams.

tick The report of a single transaction. Also, the minimum upward or downward movement in the price of a security.

toolbar A narrow panel in a graphical user interface where buttons and icons can be placed.

tooltip A window that pops up displaying information about the data at the cursor's location.

tradable Any asset that can be bought and sold, and modeled as a component of a trading system.

trading frequency The number of times per day, month, or year that a trading system issues buy or sell signals.

trading range Every market can be characterized as being in either trending mode, where prices predominantly move in one direction, or a trading range mode, where prices return to the recent average.

trailing stop For a long position, the trailing stop rises as the price and the trade's profit rises, but never drops back when the price falls.

If the price drops to the level of the trailing stop, a market order to exit the position is issued.

trend Every market can be characterized as being in either a trending mode, where prices predominantly move in one direction, or a trading range mode, where prices return to the recent average.

trend following A trading system method that recognizes that the market is in a trending mode and takes a position in the direction of that trend. Trend following systems buy strength and sell weakness.

Treynor ratio A risk adjusted measure of return for a trading system similar to the Sharpe ratio, but using beta as the measure of volatility instead of standard deviation.

true high The maximum of today's high and yesterday's close.

true low The minimum of today's low and yesterday's close.

true range True high minus true low.

ulcer index A metric that uses the depth and length of drawdowns as a measure of the performance of a trading system.

validation Validation is the process of applying statistical tests to data from the out-of-sample trading to estimate the likelihood that a trading system will be profitable in the future.

VAMI Value Added Monthly Index – a measure of portfolio performance based on monthly changes in the portfolio equity.

variance A statistical measure of variability or volatility of a set of data. The sum of the squared deviations of the individual data points from their mean.

volume The number of shares or contracts traded over a given period.

walk forward The technique of repeatedly optimizing over an in-sample period, testing over an out-of-sample period, and moving both periods forward in time. The concatenated results from the out-of-sample periods are used to estimate the likelihood of future profitability.

watchlist A list of symbols that you create and store in one of the watchlists in the symbols tree. Use the watchlist to restrict the group of symbols that are processed in automatic analysis.

Appendix B

Industries and Sectors

Industry	Industry Code	Sector	Sector Code
Advertising	0	Services	8
Aerospace & Defense	1	Capital Goods	1
Air Courier	2	Transportation	10
Airline	3	Transportation	10
Apparel/Accessories	4	Consumer Cyclical	3
Appliance & Tool	5	Consumer Cyclical	3
Audio & Video Equipment	6	Consumer Cyclical	3
Auto & Truck Manufacturers	7	Consumer Cyclical	3
Auto & Truck Parts	8	Consumer Cyclical	3
Beverages (Alcoholic)	9	Consumer/Non-Cyclical	4
Beverages (Non-Alcoholic)	10	Consumer/Non-Cyclical	4
Biotechnology & Drugs	11	Healthcare	7
Broadcasting & Cable TV	12	Services	8
Business Services	13	Services	8
Casinos & Gaming	14	Services	8
Chemical Manufacturing	15	Basic Materials	0
Chemicals - Plastics & Rubber	16	Basic Materials	0
Coal	17	Energy	5
Communications Equipment	18	Technology	9
Communications Services	19	Services	8
Computer Hardware	20	Technology	9
Computer Networks	21	Technology	9
Computer Peripherals	22	Technology	9
Computer Services	23	Technology	9
Computer Storage Devices	24	Technology	9
Conglomerates	25	Conglomerates	2
Constr. - Supplies & Fixtures	26	Capital Goods	1
Constr. & Agric. Machinery	27	Capital Goods	1
Construction - Raw Materials	28	Capital Goods	1
Construction Services	29	Capital Goods	1
Consumer Financial Services	30	Financial	6
Containers & Packaging	31	Basic Materials	0
Crops	32	Consumer/Non-Cyclical	4
Electric Utilities	33	Utilities	11
Electronic Instruments & Controls	34	Technology	9
Fabricated Plastic & Rubber	35	Basic Materials	0
Fish/Livestock	36	Consumer/Non-Cyclical	4

Food Processing	37	Consumer/Non-Cyclical	4
Footwear	38	Consumer Cyclical	3
Forestry & Wood Products	39	Basic Materials	0
Furniture & Fixtures	40	Consumer Cyclical	3
Gold & Silver	41	Basic Materials	0
Healthcare Facilities	42	Healthcare	7
Hotels & Motels	43	Services	8
Insurance (Accident & Health)	44	Financial	6
Insurance (Life)	45	Financial	6
Insurance (Miscellaneous)	46	Financial	6
Insurance (Prop. & Casualty)	47	Financial	6
Investment Services	48	Financial	6
Iron & Steel	49	Basic Materials	0
Jewelry & Silverware	50	Consumer Cyclical	3
Major Drugs	51	Healthcare	7
Medical Equipment & Supplies	52	Healthcare	7
Metal Mining	53	Basic Materials	0
Misc. Capital Goods	54	Capital Goods	1
Misc. Fabricated Products	55	Basic Materials	0
Misc. Financial Services	56	Financial	6
Misc. Transportation	57	Transportation	10
Mobile Homes & RVs	58	Capital Goods	1
Money Center Banks	59	Financial	6
Motion Pictures	60	Services	8
Natural Gas Utilities	61	Utilities	11
Non-Metallic Mining	62	Basic Materials	0
Office Equipment	63	Technology	9
Office Supplies	64	Consumer/Non-Cyclical	4
Oil & Gas - Integrated	65	Energy	5
Oil & Gas Operations	66	Energy	5
Oil Well Services & Equipment	67	Energy	5
Paper & Paper Products	68	Basic Materials	0
Personal & Household Prods.	69	Consumer/Non-Cyclical	4
Personal Services	70	Services	8
Photography	71	Consumer Cyclical	3
Printing & Publishing	72	Services	8
Printing Services	73	Services	8
Railroads	74	Transportation	10
Real Estate Operations	75	Services	8
Recreational Activities	76	Services	8

Recreational Products	77	Consumer Cyclical	3
Regional Banks	78	Financial	6
Rental & Leasing	79	Services	8
Restaurants	80	Services	8
Retail (Apparel)	81	Services	8
Retail (Catalog & Mail Order)	82	Services	8
Retail (Department & Discount)	83	Services	8
Retail (Drugs)	84	Services	8
Retail (Grocery)	85	Services	8
Retail (Home Improvement)	86	Services	8
Retail (Specialty)	87	Services	8
Retail (Technology)	88	Services	8
S&Ls/Savings Banks	89	Financial	6
Schools	90	Services	8
Scientific & Technical Instr.	91	Technology	9
Security Systems & Services	92	Services	8
Semiconductors	93	Technology	9
Software & Programming	94	Technology	9
Textiles - Non Apparel	95	Consumer Cyclical	3
Tires	96	Consumer Cyclical	3
Tobacco	97	Consumer/Non-Cyclical	4
Trucking	98	Transportation	10
Waste Management Services	99	Services	8
Water Transportation	100	Transportation	10
Water Utilities	101	Utilities	11

Appendix C

Resources

AmiBroker Directory Structure

```
C:\Program Files
      AmiBroker
            ADK                   // Application Dev Kit (C++)
            AmiQuote              // AmiQuote Program
            ASX-PremiumData       // Database Norgate EOD
            Data                  // Database Yahoo EOD
            DataAsDistributed     // Database Yahoo EOD
            Formats               // For ASCII Import
            Formulas              // AFL code
                  Averages        // Built-in
                  Bands           // Built-in
                  Basic Charts    // Built-in
                  Custom          // Your code
                  Drag-Drop       // Built-in
                  Equity          // Built-in
                  Include         // Built-in
                  Indicators      // Built-in
                  Intro Book      // Code for this book
                  Systems         // Built-in
            Intraday              // Database AN Intraday
            IQ Realtime           // Database DTN IQ Real-time
            Layouts               // Layout definitions
            Notes                 // Notes you write
            Plugins               // Built-in
            QP End of Day         // Database Quotes Plus EOD
            QP Realtime           // Database Quotes Plus Real-time
            Reports               // Reports from AA
            Scripts               // Scripts to run
```

Web Sites

AmiBroker Home page:
http://www.amibroker.com

AmiBroker Knowledge Base (provided by AmiBroker):
http://www.amibroker.com/kb/

AmiBroker Newsletter archives:
http://www.amibroker.com/newsletter/

AmiBroker On-line User's Guide:
http://www.amibroker.com/guide/

AmiBroker On-line Video Tutorials (one example of many):
http://www.amibroker.com/video/uicustomize.html

AmiBroker Order page:
http://www.amibroker.com/order.html

AmiBroker Support page:
http://www.amibroker.com/support.html

AmiBroker User's Knowledge Base (provided by user community)
http://www.amibroker.org/userkb/

AddToComposite document:
http://www.amibroker.org/3rdparty/IntroToAtc.pdf

AN Futures:
http://www.anfutures.com/

AStyle.dll:
http://www.amibroker.com/bin/astyle.dll

Blue Owl Press (publisher of this book):
http://www.blueowlpress.com

Custom Backtest Procedure document:
http://www.amibroker.org/userkb/2008/03/16/amibroker-custom-backtester-interface-2/

DebugView:
http://www.sysinternals.com/utilities/debugview.html

DTN IQ Feed:
http://www.iqfeed.net

Format specifiers for printf statement:
http://msdn2.microsoft.con/en-us/library/56e442dc(VS.80).aspx

Graphics pens, from Microsoft:
http://msdn2.microsoft.com/en-us/library/ms535467

HSB color space:
http://en.wikipedia.org/wiki/HSB_color_space

Interactive Broker's stop operation:
http://www.interactivebrokers.com/en/trading/orders/stop.php?ib_entity=uk
http://www.interactivebrokers.com/en/trading/orders/trailingstops.php?ib_entity=uk

Interactive Broker's Trading Interface:
http://www.amibroker.com/download.html

Introduction to AmiBroker Resource Links:
http://www.introductiontoamibroker.com/resources

Norgate Premium Data:
http://www.premiumdata.net

Norgate Premium Data - AmiBroker plug-in:
http://www.premiumdata.net/support/amibroker.php

Optimization using the Covariance Matrix Adaptation Evolutionary Strategy (CMA-ES):
http://www.bionik.tu-berlin.de/user/niko/cmaesintro.html
http://www.bionik.tu-berlin.de/user/niko/cec2005.html

Optimization using the "Tribes" method of Particle Swarm Optimization (PSO):
http://www.particleswarm.info/Tribes_2006_Cooren.pdf

Quantitative Trading Systems:
http://www.quantitativetradingsystems.com

Quotes Plus:
http://www.qp2.com/joomla/index.php

RGB color space:
http://en.wikipedia.org/wiki/RGB_color_model

Russell Investments, home of Russell 1000 and Russell 2000:
http://www.russell.com

Windows API QueryPerformanceCounter information:
http://support.microsoft.com/?id=896256

Yahoo AmiBroker Forum:
http://finance.groups.yahoo.com/group/amibroker

Yahoo Financial site:
http://finance.yahoo.com/

INDUSTRIES.JS SCRIPT PROGRAM

```
/*
** AmiBroker/Win32 scripting Example
**
** File:         Industries.js
** Created:      Tomasz Janeczko, November 26th, 2000
** Last updated: Tomasz Janeczko, December 17th, 2000
** Purpose:      Import industy assignments
** Language:      JavaScript (Windows Scripting Host)
**
** The data is stored in lines with following format
** <ticker>,<full name>,<industry number>
**
*/

WScript.Echo( "Script Started" );

/* change this line according to your data file name */
ImportStocks("r1000fullname.txt");

WScript.Echo( "Finished" );

function ImportStocks( filename )
{
    var fso, f, r;
    var ForReading = 1;
    var AmiBroker;
    var fields;
    var stock;
```

```
    /* Create AmiBroker app object */
    AmiBroker = new ActiveXObject( "Broker.Application" );

    /* ... and file system object */
    fso = new ActiveXObject( "Scripting.FileSystemObject" );

    /* open ASCII file */
    f = fso.OpenTextFile( filename, ForReading);

    i = 1;
    /* read the file line by line */
    while ( !f.AtEndOfStream )
    {
        r =  f.ReadLine();

        /* split the lines using comma as a separator */
        fields = r.split(",");

        try
        {

            /* add a ticker - this is safe operation,
               in case that ticker already exists,
               AmiBroker returns existing one */
            stock = AmiBroker.Stocks.Add( fields[ 0 ] );

            stock.FullName = fields[ 1 ];

            stock.IndustryID = parseInt( fields[ 2 ] );
        }
        catch( e )
        {
                WScript.echo( "There is a problem in line no."
                + i + ".\nThe line looks as follows:\n'" + r
                + "'\nIt will be skipped and next lines will be
                            processed as normal" );
        }

        i++;
    }

    /* refresh ticker list and windows */
    AmiBroker.RefreshAll();

}
```

Appendix D

Schematic Diagram

Thanks to Robert Grigg, a colleague from Australia, who campaigns tireless — spreading the word about the importance of using proper trading system design and testing techniques.

Robert has graciously permitted use of his AmiBroker Schematic diagram. The schematic illustrates the relationships among and between the major components of AmiBroker. Although it is labeled unofficial, Tomasz Janeczko has complemented its accuracy.

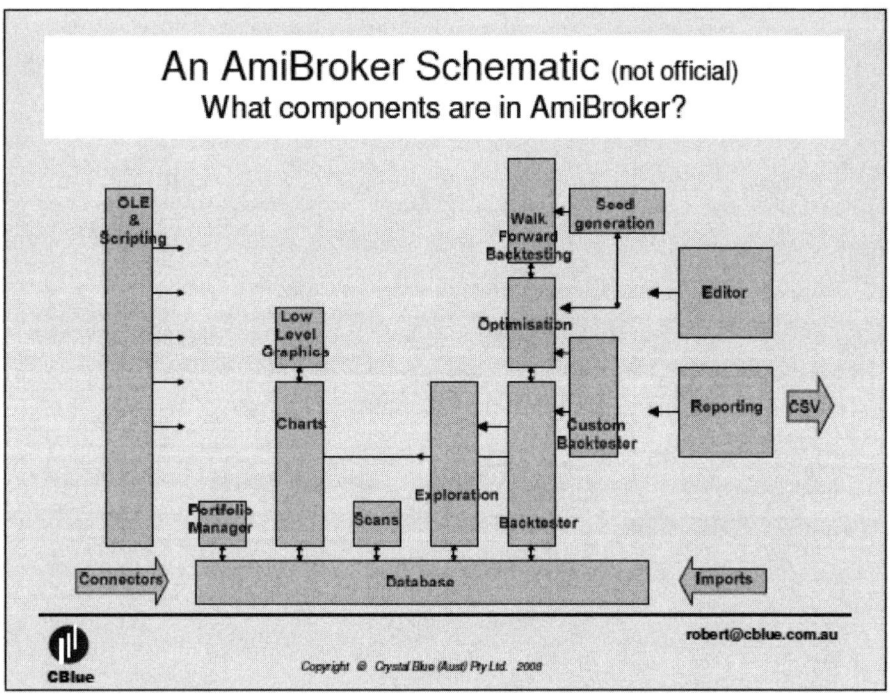

Index

m

P

q

r

If you enjoyed this book and would like to order additional copies for yourself, your friends, or your colleagues, please visit us on the web at *www.introductiontoamibroker.com* and order directly from the publisher.

You may also be interested in *Quantitative Trading Systems*, a book that discusses the design, testing, and validation of trading systems. Learn more about it at *www.quantitativetradingsystems.com* and order directly from the publisher.

Howard Bandy is the author of both books, and both are published by Blue Owl Press, *www.blueowlpress.com*.

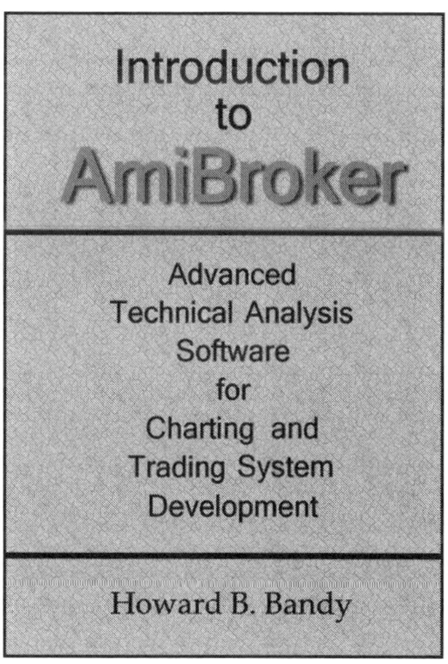

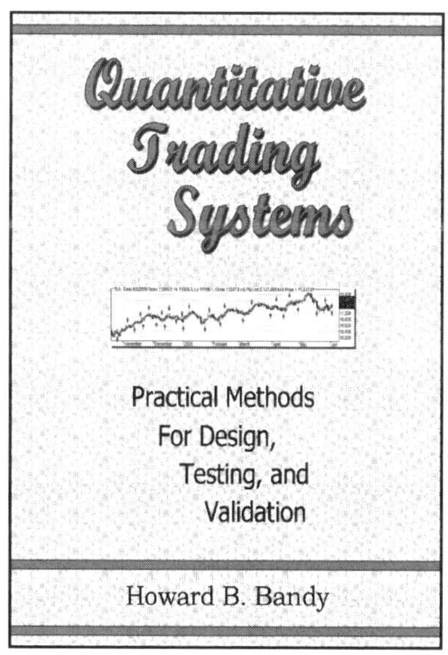

If you enjoyed this book and would like to order additional copies for yourself, your friends, or your colleagues, please visit us on the web at *www.introductiontoamibroker.com* and order directly from the publisher.

You may also be interested in *Quantitative Trading Systems*, a book that discusses the design, testing, and validation of trading systems. Learn more about it at *www.quantitativetradingsystems.com* and order directly from the publisher.

Howard Bandy is the author of both books, and both are published by Blue Owl Press, *www.blueowlpress.com*.

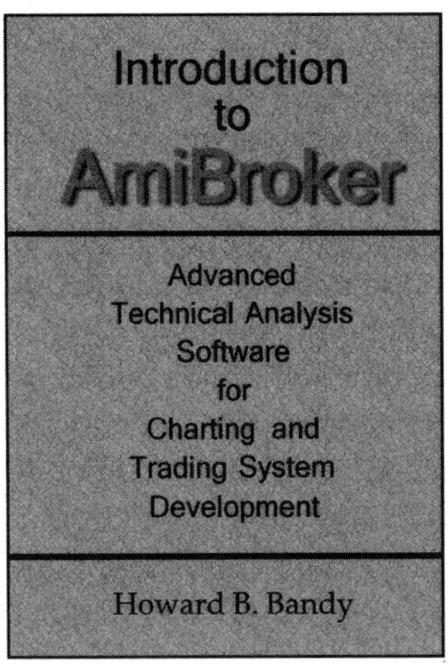

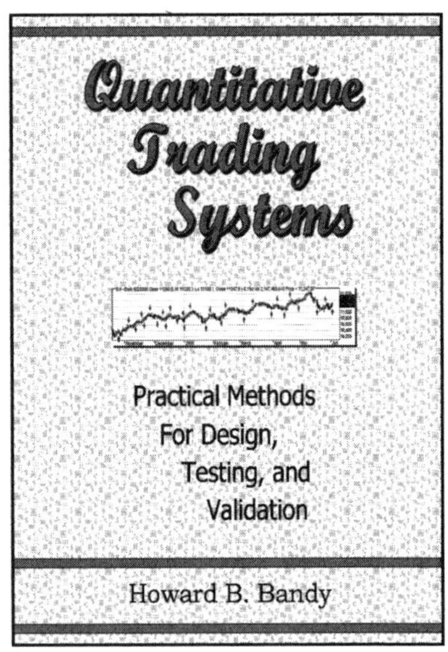